Your situation	What to do	Where to look
You know what you're looking for.	Make a search for key words.	➤ Look for topics in the Tab Guide (the reverse of this page); then go to tab sections to find detailed tables of contents. Find section numbers leading to your topic. ➤ Look for topics in the Index, and if you don't see your term, follow cross-references ("See" or "See also") to find synonymns for your topic. ➤ Look for topic markers and correction symbols at the top of each page. ➤ Look in the Brief Contents at the front of the book.
You want quick help on a specific part of a writing process.	Look for the right "How-to" box.	➤ Look at the Writing Processes chart inside the front cover to locate a "How-to" box that fits your writing situation. ➤ Read the accompanying text for more detail and examples.
You want background explanations to understand your instructor's comments.	Look for correction symbols or key words that appear in the comments.	➤ Find correction symbols identified at the back of the book, and follow references to sections indicated. ➤ Look for topic markers and correction symbols at the top of each page. ➤ Do a search for key words in the Tab Guide or Index or Brief Contents. Find section numbers leading to your topic.
You're unsure what you're looking for.	Browse.	➤ Look at the Writing Processes chart inside the front cover to locate a "How-to" box that fits your writing situation. ➤ Scan the Tab Guide (the reverse of this page); follow leads to the Brief Contents, individual tabs, and Detailed Contents for each section. ➤ Check out topic markers and correction symbols at the top of each page.

How to Find Information on a Handbook Page

Find topic markers and correction symbols at the top ⸻

"How-to" boxes give immediate help for most writing processes ⸻

Cross-references lead to Section Numbers or page numbers for related topics elsewhere in the book ⸻

Headings describe guidelines for writing, revising, or editing ⸻

Section Numbers provide a reference for each topic ⸻

Explanations give positive help, guidelines, and advice ⸻

Examples show the revisions and edits to make in this situation ⸻

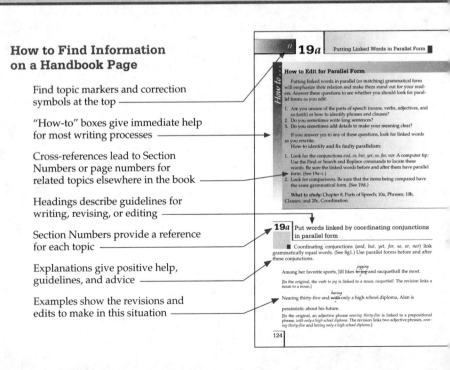

Revised Edition with
Expanded Internet Coverage

The
Ready
Reference
Handbook

Writing,
Revising,
Editing

Jack Dodds
William Rainey Harper College

Allyn and Bacon
Boston ■ London ■ Toronto ■ Sydney ■ Tokyo ■ Singapore

Editor-in-Chief, Humanities: *Joseph Opiela*
Developmental Editor: *Allen Workman*
Series Editorial Assistant: *Kate Tolini*
Marketing Manager: *Lisa Kimball*
Composition and Prepress Buyer: *Linda Cox*
Manufacturing Buyer: *Suzanne Lareau*
Cover Administrator: *Linda Knowles*
Cover Designer: *Susan Paradise*
Production Administrator: *Susan Brown*
Editorial-Production Service: *Matrix Productions*
Text Designer: *Carol Somberg for Omegatype Typography, Inc.*

Copyright © 1998, 1997 by Allyn & Bacon
A Viacom Company
Needham Heights, MA 02194
Internet: www.abacon.com

All rights reserved. No part of the material protected by this copyright
notice may be reproduced or utilized in any form or by any means,
electronic or mechanical, including photocopying, recording, or by any
information storage and retrieval system, without the written permission
of the copyright owner.

ISBN 0-205-28191-5

Printed in the United States of America
10 9 8 7 6 5 4 3 2   01 00 99 98 97

Credits appear on page xi, which constitutes a continuation of the copyright page.

A Brief Contents and Browsing Guide

Editing Grammar & Usage

part III Crafting Sentences, Choosing Words

Crafting Sentences

Choosing Words

part IV ESL Editing

ESL Editing Guide

part V Punctuation & Mechanics

Punctuating

Mechanics, Spelling, & Formatting

part VI Research–MLA Citations

The Research Project

MLA Documentation

part VII   APA & Other Documentation Styles

APA Documentation

Other Styles

part VIII   Other Writing Projects

Argument and Persuasion

Writing about Literature

Essay Examinations

Business Writing

Preface

Titles are promises to be kept. *The Ready Reference Handbook: Writing, Revising, Editing* makes three. The opening words promise a book that is *easy and quick* for writers to use. The last three words promise *practical guidance throughout the writing process*, and the term *reference handbook* promises *comprehensive information* about frequently assigned writing projects, with solutions to common writing problems.

Easy and Quick

- The ring binding allows the book to lie flat at every page.

- The insides of the front and back cover give writers an overview and access to key features: the "How-to" boxes; the tabs leading to each section; the book's reference features; common correction symbols.

- Eight tabbed dividers organize *The Ready Reference Handbook* into easy-access units. Each unit has its own detailed table of contents.

- A simple, uncluttered page layout makes information easy to find and use. Section numbers provide rapid references to headings and sub-headings that summarize practical writing guidelines.

Practical Advice for Writing

- *The Ready Reference Handbook* not only emphasizes the writing process, but also gives writers active suggestions on how to perform each stage of the process.

- The user-friendly tone, numerous examples of effective writing, and positive advice encourage writers to practice and experiment until they discover what to say and the best way of saying it.

- Advice on the writing process covers aspects of composition that often challenge college writers: assessing a writing situation; reading and thinking critically; focusing writing; imagining an audience; organizing and unifying; creating a voice right for the occasion.

- "How-to" boxes (see inside cover) give quick, focused help to writers seeking positive guidance in all phases of writing.

Comprehensive Coverage

- *The Ready Reference Handbook* provides separate advice for writing and revising essays, research projects and reports, persuasive writing, literary essays, essay examinations, and business documents.

- Critical thinking is stimulated through discussion of research strategies, the effective and responsible use of source materials, Toulmin-based argument, and the critical reading of literature.

- The unit on research methods provides a basic introduction to electronic research, including the use of electronic catalogs, Boolean searches, CD-Rom sources, and the Internet.

- Documentation units detail MLA in-text citations, APA methods, and *Chicago Manual of Style* endnote and footnote formats.

- Computerized writing suggestions are provided throughout for the processes of inventing, organizing, drafting, and editing.

- Problems of grammar are treated not only as errors, but also as unsuccessful strategies in specific rhetorical situations. The best solutions are shown as process-oriented responses to these situations.

- An ESL editing unit and brief notes throughout the handbook offer detailed advice for writers whose first language is not English.

- Annotated full-length student writing samples illustrate an informative essay, an MLA-style research project, a formal report (APA), a persuasive essay, literary essay, business letter, résumé, and memo.

Supplements

A separately published *Exercise Book* keyed to this handbook offers students extra practice in paragraphing, grammar, usage, and research documentation. Also published separately is an electronic *Online Ready Reference Handbook* available in Windows formats.

Acknowledgments

Teachers who write textbooks know first hand the benefits of collaboration. *The Ready Reference Handbook* would never have come to be without the enterprise, expertise, care, and critical eyes of all those who assisted me. To them I owe a large debt of gratitude, especially to my friends and colleagues at Harper College who have read and responded to this book in progress: Peter Sherer, Joseph Sternberg, Barbara Hickey, Corrine Johnson, XiLao Li, and Valerie Benitez. I am also thankful for solid guidance received from insightful reviews by instructors: Joe Alvarez, Central Piedmont Community College; Thomas A. Copeland, Youngstown State University; Charles Davis, Kansas State University; Joseph F. Dunne, St. Louis Community College at Meramec; Tabitha Fulkerson, Tarrant County Junior College, Northwest; Matthew Hearn, Valdosta State University; Paul Heilker, Virginia Polytechnic Institute and State University; Joyce Kinkead, Utah State University; James C. MacDonald, University of

Southwestern Louisiana; Lisa J. McClure, Southern Illinois University; Carol Pemberton, Normandale Community College; Mary Sue Ply, Southeastern Louisiana University; Audrey Roth, Miami Dade Junior College; Joyce Smoot, Virginia Polytechnic Institute and State University; Jerome Weiser, Purdue University; and Richard Zbaracki, Iowa State University.

Special thanks to all at Allyn and Bacon who have encouraged and guided this project from its inception: Joe Opiela, Vice President for Humanities, who encouraged me to write and enthusiastically guided me along the way; Kate Tolini, his assistant, who helped with reviewing; and especially Allen K. Workman, a tireless, tenacious, imaginative—and patient—editor.

Lastly, this revised edition would not have been possible without the advice and suggestions of the faculty at Metropolitan State College of Denver. I am grateful to them for helping me make the book even more useful.

And to my wife Judy, as always, I owe everything.

J.D.

Credits

Adler, Mortimer, "How to Mark a Book." *Saturday Review* 6 July 1940. Reprinted by permission of The Saturday Review © 1940, S.R. Publications, Ltd.

Ambrose, Stephen, *Crazy Horse and Custer: The Parallel Lives of Two American Warriors*. New York: Doubleday, 1986. Reprinted with permission from Doubleday, a division of Bantam Doubleday Dell Publishing Group, Inc.

American Heritage Dictionary. © 1992 by Houghton Mifflin Company. Reprinted by permission from *The American Heritage Dictionary of the English Language*, Third Edition.

Bettelheim, Bruno, *Johnny Wants to Read.* Copyright © 1982 by Bruno Bettelheim. New York: Alfred A. Knopf Inc., 1982.

Britt, Suzanne, "Neat People vs. Sloppy People" from *Show and Tell.* Copyright © 1982 by Suzanne Britt. Reprinted by permission of the author.

Burwell, Rex. "A 'Nation of Poets' at War with the United States." Reprinted by permission of the author.

Carson, Rachel, "A Fable for Tomorrow" from *Silent Spring.* Copyright © 1962 by Rachel L. Carson, renewed 1990 by Roger Christie. Reprinted by permission of Houghton Mifflin Co. All rights reserved.

Cole, K. C., "Entropy." *The New York Times,* 18 Mar. 1982. © 1982 by The New York Times Company. Reprinted by permission.

Cousins, Norman, "Who Killed Benny Paret?" *Saturday Review,* 1962. Reprinted by permission of *The Saturday Review* © 1962, S. R. Publications Ltd.

Curtin, Sharon, *Nobody Ever Died of Old Age.* Boston: Little, Brown and Company, 1972.

Daly, Christopher B., adapted from "How the Lawyers Stole Winter." *The Atlantic,* March 1995. Reprinted by permission of the author.

Dillard, Annie, excerpt from "In the Jungle" from *Teaching a Stone To Talk* by Annie Dillard. Copyright © 1982 by Annie Dillard. Reprinted by permission of HarperCollins Publishers, Inc.

Durning, Alan Thein, "The Consumer Society," from *How Much Is Enough? The Consumer Society and the Future of the Earth.* Copyright © 1992 by Worldwatch Institute. Reprinted by permission of W. W. Norton & Company, Inc.

Ehrlich, Gretel, "Rules of the Game: Rodeo," from *The Solace of Open Spaces* by Gretel Ehrlich. Copyright © 1985 by Gretel Ehrlich. Used by permission of Viking Penguin, a division of Penguin Books USA Inc.

Eiseley Loren, "The Cosmic Prison." Reprinted with the permission of Scribner, an imprint of Simon & Schuster, Inc. from "The Cosmic Prison" in *The Invisible Pyramid* by Loren Eiseley. Copyright © 1970 Loren Eiseley.

Haines, John, "The Snow." Copyright 1989 by John Haines. Reprinted from *The Stars, The Snow, The Fire* with the permission of Graywolf Press, Saint Paul, Minnesota

Hayakawa, S. I., "How Dictionaries Are Made." Excerpt from *Language in Thought and Action*, Fourth Edition by S. I. Hayakawa, copyright © 1978 by Harcourt Brace & Company, reprinted by permission of the publisher.

Hubbell, Sue, "Summer," *A Country Year*. Copyright © 1983, 1984, 1985, 1986 by Sue Hubbell. Reprinted by permission of Random House, Inc.

Leopold, Aldo, *A Sand Country Almanac: And Sketches Here and There*. New York: Oxford University Press, Inc., 1987.

Maruis, Richard, adapted from "Writing Drafts." *A Writer's Companion*. 2nd ed. New York: McGraw-Hill, 1991. Reprinted with permission of The McGraw-Hill Companies.

Maslow, Abraham H., data based on hierarchy of needs from *Motivation and Personality*, 3rd ed. by Abraham H. Maslow. Revised by Robert Frager, James Fadiman, Cynthia McReynolds, and Ruth Cox. Copyright 1954 © 1987 by Harper & Row, Publishers, Inc. Copyright © 1970 by Abraham H. Maslow. Reprinted by permission of HaperCollins Publishers, Inc.

Miller, R. Keith, "The Idea of Children." *Newsweek* 27 August 1979.

Murray, Donald, "Tricks of the Nonfiction Trade." Reprinted by permission of Roberta Pryor, Inc. p. 12.

Orwell, George, excerpt from "Shooting an Elephant" in *Shooting an Elephant and Other Essays* by George Orwell. Copyright 1950 by Sonia Brownell Orwell and renewed 1978 by Sonia Pitt-Rivers, reprinted by permission of Harcourt Brace & Company.

Petrunkevitch, Alexander, "The Spider and the Wasp." *Scientific American*, August 1952.

Rodriguez, Richard, "Aira: A Memoir of a Bilingual Childhood," *The American Scholar*, Winter 1980 by Richard Rodriguez. Reprinted by permission of Georges Borchardt, Inc. for the author.

Sanders, Scott Russell, excerpt from "The Men We Carry in Our Minds." Copyright © 1984 by Scott Russell Sanders; reprinted by permission of the author and Virginia Kidd, Literary Agent.

Stafford, William, "Traveling Through the Dark." Copyright © 1977 by William Stafford. This poem originally appeared in *Stories That Could By True* (New York: Harper & Row, 1977), and is used by permission.

Teale, Edwin Way, *Wandering Through Winter*. Copyright © 1990 by Edwin Way Teale, St. Martin's Press, Inc., New York, NY

Thomas, Lewis, "Social Talk." Copyright © 1972 by The Massachusetts Medical Society, from *The Lives of a Cell* by Lewis Thomas. Used by permission of Viking Penguin, a division of Penguin Books USA Inc.

Thomas, Lewis, "Notes on Punctuation." Copyright © 1979 by Lewis Thomas, from *The Medusa and the Snail* by Lewis Thomas. Used by permission of Viking Penguin, a division of Penguin Books USA Inc.

Webster's Collegiate Thesaurus. By permission. From Merriam-Webster's Collegiate Thesaurus © 1988 by Merriam-Webster Inc.

part I

The
Writing
Process

I. The Writing Process

Composing

Paragraphing

Composing

The Ready Reference Handbook is designed not only for college writers but also for anyone who wants practical suggestions for writing effectively. What follows is based on the experience of writers of all kinds. At the outset, you should have some basic understanding about writers and the writing they do.

Writers write. Some people assume that writers are different from everyone else. They are inspired, they have a touch of the poet, at least they have the gift of gab. But the truth is that writers are simply people who write. If they're inspired, they have worked hard for that flash of insight. If they sound poetic, they've probably had writer William Zinsser's experience of "endlessly rewriting what I had endlessly rewritten." When you write, you, too, are a writer.

Writing is a process. Writing is not a straightforward transcription of your thoughts. That would be dull work. It's a more exciting and experimental process of creating thoughts through written words. It's exciting because it involves discovery; writers don't always know what they'll say when they begin writing. It's experimental because writers play with words and ideas until they find what they want to say.

Writing is more than communication. Successful writers write first for themselves, to see what they think, and then for their readers, to communicate. Your writing will always be read by someone, of course. Even if you write only in a diary, you write for an audience of one—yourself. But before it is communication, writing is exploration, discovery, and self-expression. Successful writers almost always work in this two-step way: first finding something to say and then finding a way to communicate it.

Good writing satisfies both writers and readers. Good writing is more than good grammar or impressive-sounding words. Yes, most successful public writing is polished, well laid out, and correct. But it also carries the sound of a writer's voice speaking to readers, it contains good ideas worth writing and reading about, and it is written with power and conviction.

There are many ways to write well. Looking at a book like this, you might think that it preaches one right way to successful writing. But every successful writer has his or her own habits and techniques. Some writers are genuinely quirky, like Ernest Hemingway, who sharpened precisely eight pencils before he began each writing day, or the French writer who required the smell of apples rotting in his desk drawer to set him to work. Most successful writers, however, have more practical ways of doing their writing. This book describes many of these strategies. Consider them as options. Explore, experiment, find what works for you.

1 "Inventing" Your Writing

Writers, like inventors, create their work not all at once but in stages, through trial and error, reflection, and discovery. The following guidelines will lead you through the process of invention used by successful writers when they begin a project. Because this process differs from one writer to another and from one kind of writing to another, you'll want to practice and experiment to discover what technique is right for you and the writing you do.

1*a* | Survey the situation

When you have a project to write, make preliminary plans by looking carefully at what you need to do. Here are questions to ask yourself. You may not be able to answer them all at once, and some answers may change as your project unfolds. That's natural. But as they come, use these answers to guide your writing.

■ 1 The subject and the assignment

- Has your topic been given to you as part of an assignment? Can you adapt the topic to your interests? If you have to choose a topic, what is suitable for the assignment?

- What kind of writing does the assignment require: a letter, essay, report, review, or some other form?

- What is the scope of the assignment? Do you have to cover a broad subject? How focused must your writing be because of reader interest or length and time restrictions? How much detail will you have to use? A note on college writing: Most college writing assignments ask you to focus on a limited, specific subject and go into it in as much detail as the time allows.

- What do you know about the subject? According to the assignment, what kinds of information should be included: personal experience, facts and figures, or expert opinion? Where will you get your information: from memory, observation, reading, discussion? What experience or bias may affect your view of what you find? If you borrow others' words or ideas, what system of documentation are you required to use?

■ 2 Your purpose and role

- What purpose does the wording of the assignment set for you? Consider such phrases as "Write a personal narrative . . . ," "Write an informative essay . . . ," "Explain . . . ," "Evaluate . . . ," and "Take a position . . . ." (To learn to interpret the instructions given in writing assignments, see 60a.)

- What writer's role have your knowledge and personal experience prepared you for? Can you play the role of an autobiographer and write about yourself, a reporter informing readers, a teacher explaining ideas or procedures, a critic making an evaluation, a persuader arguing a position, or some combination of these?

■ 3 Audience

A note on college writing: Academic audiences—your instructors—may already know about the subject areas you write in, but you cannot leave details out of your writing for this reason. Your aim in most academic writing is demonstration—showing what you know. Think of academic readers as curious, intelligent, and interested in your perspective and in what you have to say. Before you begin writing, answer the following questions about all of your prospective readers:

- What key traits connect them to you and your subject? Consider your readers' ages, education, background, group membership, and how these traits relate to your writing purpose. What writing style is appropriate for addressing them, informal or formal?

- What do these readers know about your topic? What do they expect from you: personal experience, information, explanation, evaluation, proof, entertainment?

- Why are they reading your writing—from curiosity, as part of their jobs, or from personal interest in you? How much time do they have for reading your writing?

■ 4 The final draft

- Are there length specifications?

- When is it due? How much time do you have for each stage of your writing: gathering materials, planning, writing, revising, editing, typing, and proofreading?

- What is the appropriate format for your final copy? (For academic writing, see 46a; for business writing, see 61.)

1b | Explore possible topics

■   At the beginning of a project, create choices for yourself, even if you already have a topic or a list to choose from. The British novelist E. M. Forster once asked, "How can I know what I think till I see what I say?" Help yourself see what you think about possible topics by doing exploratory writing. Examine the following kinds of exploratory writing, and adapt them to your style and habits. Some may be more useful than others or only appropriate for certain kinds of writing.

■ 1   Keeping a journal or diary

These daily records of experience, reflection, and opinion can be a valuable source of personally important topics that may be transformed into public or academic writing.

■ 2   Brainstorming

To **brainstorm,** simply make free-association lists. Start with a topic or whatever first comes to mind. Follow wherever your mind leads. Don't worry if you can't think of much the first time. Lists should be easy and fast. When you finish, underline key words or phrases to explore further.

Brrr! Cold outside
Almost too cold to bike to school this morning—
Snow on the way home—
Wisconsin last spring, caught in a freak April storm
"Just look at you!" cried the woman at the quick mart where I stopped—snow mounded on my helmet, me covered with slush, soaking wet, and shaking in the cold
Drivers' strange looks when it's this cold—disbelief, mostly: "What are you doing out there?" their eyes ask.
Actually, I'm doing okay—feeling good in the crisp air. Toes don't get cold till I'm almost to school or home. Easy trip unless there's rain, snow, or headwind.
Pedal, pant, puff—endorphins flowing, a steady 17–18 mph this a.m.
In all that traffic, I'm getting where I'm going just about as fast as the cars are, backed up one after another in endless traffic jams.
Honk, inch ahead, stop, honk, inch ahead
Commuting—bicycle commuting
good for health, fitness
good for everybody's health—less pollution, one less car—

This brainstorm may make little sense to anyone but the writer, but if you look, you can see several topics that might be explored further, expanded, rearranged, and turned into the materials for a full-length writing project.

■ 3 Topic mapping (clustering and branching)

If you like to visualize what to say before you write, draw a **topic map.** Put a topic in the middle of a sheet of paper, draw a circle around it, and then draw branches that lead to related topics and subtopics. Leave room in case you think of other branches and topics to add later.

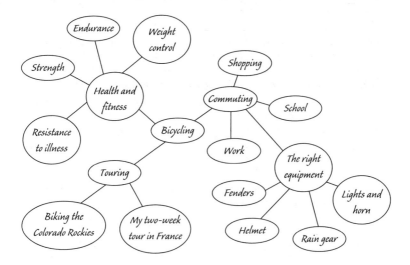

■ 4 Freewriting

Like brainstorming and mapping, **freewriting** is free association on paper. The difference is that, for most people, freewriting expresses thoughts more fully in sentence- and paragraph-length statements and may lead more deeply into a subject. Many writers find it a useful activity throughout the writing process as a way to explore new or challenging ideas. In freewriting, your aims are to loosen up your mind, go where it leads you, and record what it gives you.

■ 5 Choosing a topic

If you've surveyed the writing situation (see 1a) and explored possible topics, you'll probably see what topic is best to choose—or, if you already

How to Freewrite

You can do freewriting in two ways. In unfocused freewriting, write whatever comes to mind, whether everything connects or not. In focused freewriting, try to focus on one topic, unless you get pulled to something more interesting.

Set a time limit, usually 7 to 15 minutes. Start writing about whatever comes to mind the moment you begin. Freewrite by hand, on a typewriter, or at a computer.

Don't stop. If your mind suddenly goes blank, write "blank, blank, blank" or repeat your last word until thoughts begin flowing again.

Don't censor. Write whatever comes to mind, however strange it sounds. It may lead to something important or powerful. If you don't like what you've written when you finish, you can throw it away.

Don't change anything. If you write something one way and think of another way, put a slash (/) and write the second version.

Don't stop to correct mistakes. Don't worry about them. You're only exploring.

---

have one, you'll see more clearly what is most interesting about it. A good writing topic has these characteristics:

- It is important. A good topic is important to you and your readers.

- It is fresh. A good topic is new to you or your readers, or your approach to a familiar topic is fresh. Don't reject topics that seem quirky or strange at first. They may lead to your freshest writing.

- It's a challenge. Choose topics that challenge your thinking, curiosity, or feeling. Easy topics may lead to boredom for you and your readers.

1c | Focus your writing.

Most topics will first come to you as an inviting—sometimes perplexing—array of possibilities. They'll be open-ended, broad, general—unfocused. To **focus** a project means becoming clear about your subject, what you want to do with it, and the point you want to make about it. A reminder: You may not be able to decide everything at once. In fact, if you focus on too much too soon, you may not see important parts of your topic. But before you begin a first draft, try using the following strategies.

■ 1 Narrowing your topic

Most topics discovered in exploratory writing or listed in assignments will be too broad to cover adequately in the space and time available for the assignment. Therefore, focus on one narrow but important part of your topic and the significance of that part.

BROAD TOPICS				
				NARROW TOPICS
My life growing up on a farm	→	The benefits of a country life	→	My country education: the facts of life—and death—down on the farm
My grandmother	→	My grandmother, an old-fashioned artist	→	My grandmother's lost art: bobbin lace making
Bicycling	→	Bicycle commuting	→	How to increase bicycle commuting
America's national parks	→	Overcrowding in national parks	→	The environmental consequences of overcrowding in national parks
Charlotte Perkins Gilman's short story, "The Yellow Wall-Paper"	→	The wallpaper	→	The wallpaper as a reflection of the narrator's state of mind

■ 2 Writing a purpose statement

After surveying the requirements of the assignment and exploring your ideas, write a tentative **purpose statement.** Briefly tell yourself what you want to accomplish in your writing. This purpose may change as your project unfolds, but writing it out early will guide you.

I want to inform urban and suburban readers that, for many, bicycling is a solution to the frustrations of rush-hour commuting.

This writer's purpose is to inform; the writer's roles are to act as a reporter and a teacher.

■ 3 Asking questions

Jot down questions based on the reporter's *Who? What? When? Where? Why? How?* Ask other questions relevant to your topic. Your answers may become the materials for your project.

Who should become a bicycle commuter?

What are the problems that bicycle commuters face?

What are the benefits of bicycle commuting?

What are the best conditions for bicycle commuting?

Why do some motorists object to sharing the road with bicyclists?

How can a cyclist begin commuting by bicycle?

How can a community or business begin to encourage bicycle commuters?

1*d* Consider your voice (persona)

Everything you write has a **voice,** also called a **persona.** Whether it is personal or public, informal or formal, opinionated or objective, whether you appear in your writing (as "I") or not, your writing speaks with your voice. Readers hear it in your words and sentences, your attitude toward your subject, and your relationship with these readers. This voice is the sound of your personality in writing, and you should write and revise to express that personality. Creating a voice is one of the great pleasures of writing.

But just as you adapt your actual speaking voice to suit the occasion, so should you adapt your persona. This means adjusting its features in the same way that you adjust the volume, tone, and balance on a stereo to produce the best sound. Here are the features of a writer's personality, each of which can be adjusted toward the opposing ends of a spectrum:

Informal vocabulary	◀—•—▶	Formal vocabulary
Negative attitude	◀—•—▶	Positive attitude
Understatement	◀—•—▶	Overstatement
Irony, sarcasm, indirectness	◀—•—▶	"Straight talk"

■ **1** The persona for formal writing

In formal academic and professional writing, aim to sound fair, objective, and relatively serious. Your style should generally be direct and to the point. Use "I" to refer to yourself if necessary, but focus on your subject. Avoid slang and most contractions. Don't sound pompous or stuffy, however. Whatever you write should sound like you speaking in a voice suitable to the subject and occasion. (See also 27a1 and 2.)

■ **2** The persona for personal or informal writing

The more personal your subject, the more informal you can be. You have lots of room for variety in vocabulary, attitude, and style of expression. But keep in mind the knowledge and interests of your readers.

How to Create Your Persona

As you write, listen for your voice. It should sound like you, speaking in a way suitable to the occasion. Writing and speaking are different, of course, but good writing almost always sounds like speech. "Talk" to readers as you write.

Choose words true to your knowledge and experience. Don't worry about writing impressively. What will impress is your accuracy, honesty, and command of the facts.

As you revise, consider the formality of your words. Choose words formal or informal enough for the occasion, but also words you can imagine yourself saying. (See 27a and d.)

Consider your attitude expressed by positive, negative, or neutral words. Choose words that accurately express your feelings but that also express the amount of objectivity appropriate to the occasion.

As you revise, read aloud and listen to your sentences. If necessary, rewrite your sentences so that they emphasize your most important words but have the rhythms of speech. (See 21a–e.)

1e Write a tentative thesis

■ When you know enough about your subject and purpose, write a tentative statement of the point you want to make—your thesis. Usually a sentence but sometimes longer, a **thesis** in its final form will be the primary controlling idea holding your writing together, the basic message you want your writing to express. It may be any kind of assertion:

■ An informative thesis:

Bicycles are a safe, practical, economical solution to the problems of rush-hour commuting.

■ The theme of an autobiographical essay:

The country is a good place to grow up in. It provided me with the experiences, values, and outlook that are helping me succeed in the urban world where I now live.

Whatever its subject or purpose, a thesis is usually the most important statement of a piece of writing. At the beginning of a project, it will help you to decide what to say. In a later version based on the information you've gathered, it will act as a reference point to keep you on course as

How to Write a Tentative Thesis

Early in a writing project, use the following formula to help you write a tentative thesis:
My point is that . . .

My point is that to ease the problems of commuting, federal highway funds and state gasoline taxes should be used to create bicycle lanes on city streets and wide shoulders on secondary roads.

If you can't write a thesis early in your project because you don't yet know enough about your topic, write it later, after you've learned what you need to know.

you write a draft. Still later, as you revise your project, you'll compare your thesis to what you've actually written to see whether your point has remained the same or has changed. If it has changed, you'll rewrite it to fit your new discoveries. In this final version it will help answer the one question readers almost always ask: "So what's the point?"

■ 1 Guidelines for an effective thesis

As your knowledge grows and your thinking changes, rewrite your thesis following these guidelines:

- Write a declarative sentence, or several sentences if necessary, but not a question. If all you can write is a question, you're not ready to write a thesis. Answer your question first.

- Be sure you've written a thesis statement rather than a purpose statement. A **thesis statement** focuses on your topic and says something about it. A **purpose statement** focuses on your paper and says something about it rather than your topic. Compare the thesis in the preceding box with this purpose statement: *In my essay I plan to explain the reasons we need bicycle lanes in cities and wider shoulders on secondary roads.* See how much more the thesis says about the topic?

- Be sure your thesis is supported by the facts and other details that you've gathered.

- Replace vague words with specific words that say precisely what you mean. Avoid broad generalizations.

- Beware of writing a "So?" thesis. For example: *Much urban and suburban travel by car is unnecessary.* So? What's the point? Should something be done about this unnecessary travel? What? Make a complete assertion about your topic.

■ After you've written your essay, cut the *My point is that . . .* formula as you revise, keeping only your actual assertion. The formula has helped you make a point, but readers won't need it to get your point. With the formula removed, the sample thesis in the preceding box becomes: *To ease the problems of commuting, federal highway funds and state gasoline taxes should be used to create bicycle lanes on city streets and wide shoulders on secondary roads.*

■ 2 Unwritten thesis statements

Some kinds of writing, especially personal narratives, reports, and some kinds of arguments, may not express a thesis directly. It may be unnecessary, impossible, or unwise to come right out and state a point. Nevertheless, readers still get the message because everything supports the unwritten thesis, develops a dominant mood, or fulfills the overall purpose.

■ 3 Placement of your thesis

Thesis statements usually appear early in a writing. If they're clear and especially dramatic, they may come in the first sentence. But more often they appear at the end of an introduction, after the writer has prepared readers for the main point. Placed in the introduction, a thesis acts like a map to guide writers as they write and readers as they read.

Sometimes, especially in personal narratives or report writing, a thesis may not appear until the conclusion, revealing an important discovery or summing up what has come before. If you place a thesis at the end of a paper, your introduction will have to point the way to it, perhaps hinting at its message, describing the problem it solves, or posing the question it answers.

1f Gather the materials for your writing

■ Gather the information for your project by remembering, reflecting, observing, reading, or discussing. If the project will be brief, you can keep most of your ideas in your head or jot down a list of points to cover. But if your subject is complex or unfamiliar—the case in most college writing projects—you'll have to take notes. (see 49c and d.) Here are ways you can approach a topic. The types of information you end up using in your project will depend on your purpose and your readers' interests. (See 6b.)

■ Gather facts and figures. (See 6b4.)

■ Quote or summarize eyewitnesses, experts, or others involved with your subject. (Be sure to credit your sources when you borrow words or ideas. See 50d.)

- Describe scenes, people, features, traits, processes, and events. (See 6b3.)
- Tell stories or anecdotes. (See 6b1.)
- Give examples (6b5), compare and contrast (6b6), classify (6b9), and define (6b10).
- Explain. Depending on your topic and purpose, restate unfamiliar ideas in familiar words, give instructions, or add details to expand a subject and make it clear.
- Create metaphors and similes to dramatize feelings and ideas. (See 26c.)
- Interpret your subject. State its meaning or significance, and describe its implications—where it leads. Draw conclusions that tell what everything adds up to.

Planning
and Organizing

2*a* | Refocus your writing

Because writing is a process of discovery, your topic and what you intend to say about it will probably change as you prepare to write. New information will lead to new ideas; your original purpose may change; you may change your relations to your audience. Therefore, before you begin a first draft—or later, after completing a draft—pause, step back, and reconsider your project in light of all you've learned. Answer these questions:

- At this point in your project, what is your exact subject?
- What will your paper contain? Facts, feelings, opinions, personal experiences, or observations? Are they reliable and suitable to the occasion? For most kinds of serious informative writing, personal experience or observation may not be suitable or sufficient. Consider your audience's interests and needs.
- Do you have what you need to fulfill your purpose? If not, should you gather more information or change your purpose?
- Do you have enough to support your point (your thesis) and communicate its message? If not, what do you need? Should you rewrite your thesis to fit what you've found?

2b Plan a communications strategy

Experienced writers usually make detailed plans for communicating with readers. You'll write more effectively if you plan a communications strategy that includes the following elements.

■ 1 Organization

Arrange the contents of your essay to fulfill your purpose and satisfy readers' needs. You can organize your writing

- to tell a story (personal narrative, how-to writing, steps in a process). (See 6b1 and 2.)
- to present causes and effects. (See 6b8.)
- to describe (scenic arrangement, part-by-part analysis). (See 6b3–5.)
- to compare or contrast (point by point or the block method). (See 6b6.)
- to classify. (See 6b9.)
- to emphasize what is most important (organizing from least to most important or most to least).
- to give the pros and cons of an issue and then, perhaps, state your opinion.
- to explain a problem and pose a solution.

■ 2 Introduction

Think of an opening to attract and focus your readers' interest. (See 6c1.) It should identify your topic, suggest your purpose, and, usually, state your thesis.

■ 3 Lead

As you plan an introduction, try to think of an opening line, your lead, to start you writing and draw readers into your introduction.

■ 4 Title

Think of an original title that is informative, intriguing, or both, but don't make it a baffling mystery. Come up with a word or phrase that arouses curiosity and, if possible, suggests your topic, even your thesis.

■ 5 Conclusion

Good essays don't just stop, nor do they slowly unravel. Bring your writing to a satisfying close that ties up loose ends and leaves readers with the feeling that everything has come together. (See 6c2.)

2c | Write an outline, if necessary

For many kinds of writing, especially on difficult or unfamiliar topics, outlines are almost essential. Especially in informative, technical, and research writing, you can use outlines to organize ideas, guide your writing, and then, after you've written a draft, reveal its actual design. Depending on your project, you may write three kinds of outlines, each a version of the others: a sketch, working, and final-draft formal outline. For some papers, a sketch outline is all you'll need; for others, you'll need all three.

■ 1 Sketch outline

A **sketch outline** is just that, an outline of an outline, a list of major points in the order you want to cover them. As you begin organizing, experiment with sketch outlines until you find a good one, right for your ideas and purpose.

Bicycles are a safe, practical, economical solution to the problems of rush-hour commuting.

I. The myths and realities of bicycle commuting in America

*   A. Bicycling as a safe means of transportation*

*   B. Bicycling as a practical means of transportation*

II. Becoming a bicycle commuter

*   A. How to get started*

*   B. The benefits of bicycle commuting*

■ 2 Working outline

A **working outline** is the most detailed. Expanded from a sketch outline and divided into topics and subtopics, it should create a map to follow as you write. As a kind of rough draft of a rough draft, a good working outline has a place for almost everything:

- An introduction
- The thesis or main idea
- Major topics and subtopics, including facts, key details, illustrations, explanations, and quotations
- Major transitional statements
- A conclusion

You will, no doubt, think of other things to say while drafting, but the clearer and more detailed your plans now, the easier your first draft will be to write.

How to...

How to Organize Your Ideas and Write an Outline

Arrange your notes or other exploratory writing in a suitable order to follow as you write. Look for organizing clues in key words, the sequence of ideas in your thesis, or in the list of questions readers might ask about your topic. Use one of these strategies:

1. If your exploratory writing doesn't follow a logical sequence, number the topics in the order you'll write about them.

2. Jot down a list of topics you'll cover (a sketch outline).

3. Draw a **flow chart,** a conceptual diagram showing relations and connections. Put topics in boxes arranged in sequence, connected by lines that trace the path of your writing. Use other boxes and lines to insert advice to yourself about details to remember, quotations, facts, transitional statements, and ideas about introductions and conclusions.

4. Write a working outline that includes most of what you want to say:

   - Sort your materials to see whether everything fits under the major headings of a sketch outline. Revise your sketch outline if necessary.

   - Then arrange your materials in the order you want to follow as you write your paper. Write a detailed working outline that reflects this order.

   - Look for relationships among ideas and group them as subheadings under headings. Beware of long "shopping lists" of topics.

   - If you can't decide where to put something, put it in two or more places in your outline and trust your writing to show you where it belongs.

   - If an important idea doesn't fit, write a new outline with a place for it. If you're uncertain whether an element is necessary, write a reminder to see whether it belongs after you've written a draft.

■ 3 Final-draft formal outline

Your instructor may require a **formal outline** with the final draft of some projects. Base the outline on the organization of your finished paper, and prepare it for your readers, to give them an overview of your project. It will probably be longer than a sketch outline but shorter than a working outline, often about a page. It should include your thesis statement, list your major topics, and follow the guidelines for formal outlines listed here and illustrated below in 2c4.

- At least two subheadings under each heading. Because subheadings divide up the ideas in a heading, you must have at least two subheadings under each heading. You can't divide a topic into only one subtopic. If you have, you may have simply restated the original heading.

- Logical subheadings. Because subheadings break up or divide ideas in the headings they stand under, they must reflect the ideas and even the language of those broader headings.

- Grammatically parallel headings. If heading *I.* is a complete sentence, headings *II.* and *III.* must also be complete sentences. If *A.* under heading *II.* is a noun phrase, *B.* must also be a noun phrase, and so forth. (See 19.)

- Standard outline subdivisions.

  I.
    A.
    B.
        1.
        2.
            a.
            b.
                (1)
                (2)
                    (a)
                    (b)
  II.

■ 4   Sample formal outline

Note how the following example adheres to the guidelines for formal outlines given above in 2c3. (For a sample formal outline arranged in the format for a typed paper, see 53.)

Thesis statement
: Thesis: Bicycles are a safe, practical, economical solution to the problems of rush-hour commuting.

Logical subdivisions: Every heading has two or more subheads clearly related to the headings.
: I. The myths and realities of bicycle commuting in the United States

    A. Bicycling is a safe means of transportation.

        1. The fears motorists have about bicycling safety

        2. The facts of bicycling safety

B. Bicycling is a practical means of transportation.

    1. Motorists' objections to bicycle commuting

    2. Widespread support for bicycle commuting

       a. Numerous bicycle commuters

       b. Business support

       c. Federal, state, and local government support

II. Becoming a bicyle commuter

    A. How to begin bicycle commuting

    B. The benefits of bicycle commuting

> Parallel grammatical form: Coordinate headings are grammatically parallel. For example, I and II are noun phrases; IA and IB are complete sentences.

chapter 3   Writing, Revising, and Editing

3a | Write a first draft

■ Like experienced writers, you should expect to write more than one draft of important, complex projects. Each revision provides an opportunity for rethinking, rearranging, and rewording based on the discoveries of the preceding draft. When you write a first draft, let yourself go; you don't have to get everything right the first time. If you have the information you need and have planned your project, writing a first draft should feel almost like doing a freewriting once you get going.

3b | Revise to say what you want to say

■ Novice writers think they're nearly finished when they complete a first draft. For them, revision is correcting or touchup work. Experienced writers, however, know that a single draft rarely says all they want it to say or says it in the best way. For them, revision means "reseeing" and then rewriting based on what they've seen. How do you revise? Consider these strategies.

■ 1 Letting your writing cool off

Don't confuse the elation of ending a draft—or your frustrations—with a judgment of its quality. If you can, wait a while before you revise. Your perspective and objectivity will improve.

How to . . .

How to Write a First Draft

- Write major sections or a complete draft at one sitting. Give yourself time to get warmed up.

- Whether you write by hand, typewriter, or computer, leave lots of room to revise. Double- or triplespace; leave wide margins.

- Don't bother editing or correcting. If you're unsure of a word or phrase, write out several versions separated by slashes (/). Put a ✓ in the margin to mark passages to check later.

- If you have to stop, give yourself a thread to pick up when you return. Start writing a sentence or paragraph you know how to finish and stop in the middle.

In case of writer's block:

- Reread your plans and start writing with the first thing that comes to mind, as if you were doing a freewriting. The words and ideas will start to flow.

- If you can't begin at the beginning, start in the middle. Come back and write your opening later, after you're warmed up.

- Instead of beginning your project, write a letter to your audience. Tell them what you'd like to write about. Or write a letter to yourself about what you want to say and your frustrations.

- Try visualizing something to do with your subject. Start by writing about what you see.

- Write an advance summary of your essay. "In this essay I have . . . " Pretend you're finished. Describe what you would like to have written.

■2 Identifying the status of your draft

Ask yourself, "Is this draft a dress rehearsal, complete except for finishing touches?" "Is it exploratory, still searching for a point or something to hold it together?" "Is it experimental, trying out topics and styles?" Your answers here will help you see what to do next.

■3 Changing your focus from distance to close up

Imagine you're a camera with a telephoto lens. Look at the "big picture" first. Decide on the status of major elements such as your thesis, its support, and your overall design. Add information, cut, rearrange, condense, or substitute to make your point and fulfill your purpose. When you're satisfied with the big picture, zoom in and focus on individual paragraphs, sentences, and words. Don't waste time fixing small problems before the big ones.

■ 4 Comparing your plans and their results

- Compare the draft of your paper to the original plans you made as you first surveyed the situation. (See 1a.) Have you fulfilled the requirements of the assignment or met your readers' needs? Revise accordingly.

- Compare your original thesis with what you've written in your conclusion. Look for "Ah hah!" statements. Often, near the end of a draft, writers write something that makes them say, "Ah hah!" They think they've found a conclusion, but what they may have found is the real point of their paper—a new thesis that is different from the original. If you find such a statement, rewrite it as your new thesis, move it to the introduction of your essay, and revise to support it.

- Compare your outline to your draft. If the two are different, which makes more sense of your ideas?

■ 5 Asking for peer review

Ask others to read and respond to your paper. Use their responses to help you see your writing objectively. (Use the questions on pp. 21–22 to elicit responses.)

3c

Edit for your readers

■ 1 The aims of editing

When you revise, you're focusing primarily on your ideas and message. When you edit, you're focusing on your readers, rewriting to help them get your message. Editing is a paragraph-by-paragraph, line-by-line process. Consider the edited paragraph about bicycle commuting that follows. The student writer, John Chen, made typical editorial improvements, the kinds you'll make in your writing.

- Improving accuracy and brevity. The writer cut and added words throughout to increase precision and brevity.

- Adding important information and details. He inserted additional information and details to develop and clarify his proposal.

- Adapting the contents for the intended audience. He cut a sentence that might offend motorist readers.

- Increasing precision and vividness. He cut vague, general words and substituted descriptive details.
- Rearranging for clarity and emphasis. He moved one passage earlier in the paragraph to reorganize for emphasis.

What will end commuters' rush-hour nightmare
~The cycling solution to the problem of commuters' gridlock already

solution for all, however.
exists in sketch form. What it consists of is not a single one way for

all plan Commuting problems and needs differ from community to

community, region to region. The best solutions will be local. Each will

specific
have a number of parts, and each part will solve a local travel problem.
All that may be needed is public service announcements to encourage bicycle commuting.
In some communities, few changes are required. In other communities,

⌒*ways*   *park paths or*
converting abandoned railroad lines to green paths or improving other off-road

bikeways is the right solution. In others, parking might be restricted along

busy streets during peak travel times. The police might begin ticketing

and the courts prosecuting drivers who harass bicyclists exercising their

-s,
right to the road. In still other communities, where highways have long

repaved with widened
been crumbling, aging highways might be widened to provide wide
dangerous sewer grates might be removed, and high curbs eliminated. Larger,
shoulders, or eliminate high curbs. Clearer, more frequent signs would

well-placed
guide motorists and cyclists alike. In almost every community, bicycle
would   *commuting.*
racks and storage facilities will help encourage more bicycle commuters,

as will public service announcements to promote bicycle awareness.

■ 2 Editing symbols

As you edit, use the following copyediting symbols to make your final
draft easier to prepare.

e
insrt   new paragraph: ¶
∧
#
addspace   remove paragraph: *no* ¶
∧

3c aud/dev

delete let̸ter or ~~word~~   cAPITALIZE A LETTeR OR word

clos̑e up   L̸Øwer case a L̸etter or W̸ORD

tran�ñspose   move left: [　　　]

let it stand as written: *stet*   move right: [　　　]

■ 3 How to know when you've finished revising and editing

You may have to write several drafts before you say what you want to say in the way you want to say it. But some writers tinker and tinker, changing and changing, never sure when they've finished. When your changes aren't making your writing noticeably better, you've finished. You've written as well as you can.

How to Decide What to Revise and Edit

How to . . .

Use the answers to the following questions to help you revise and edit your writing. If possible, ask peer reviewers to read your writing and give you their responses. Tell them which questions to answer or ask them to respond to the ones they think important.

First consider the project as a whole:

1. What is its subject? Does it change from one page to the next? If so, which subject is right for this project? (See 1b5 and 1c1.)

2. Is the purpose of the writing autobiographical, informative, persuasive, or critical? Does it change? What purpose is appropriate? (See 1a2 and 1c2.)

3. Based on its contents, who is the audience for this project? Are they supposed to respond with sympathy, understanding, evaluation, agreement, or enjoyment? Will this project achieve its purpose? What changes will make it more effective? (See 1a3.)

4. Does this project have a thesis, main idea, or overall mood? Point it out or describe it. Does the writing provide enough detail to illustrate, explain, or support its point? What should be added? (See 1e and f.)

Continued

How to...

How to Decide What to Revise and Edit (continued)

5. Can you follow this project from start to finish? What reorganization would make its ideas clearer or easier to follow? (See 2b and c.)

When the project seems to say all that is necessary to fulfill its purpose, consider how effectively it will communicate with its intended audience.

6. Does the project have a distinctive writer's voice? What changes will make this voice more emphatic or appropriate? (See 1d.)

7. What does the opening do to attract readers and help them predict the project's subject, purpose, thesis, organization, or style? What changes would make the opening more interesting to its readers? (See 6c1.)

8. Consider whether each paragraph focuses on a single topic and says all that needs to be said about it. What changes would improve the paragraphs in this project or make them fit more smoothly with preceding or following paragraphs? (See Chapters 5–7.)

9. Are any sentences hard to follow? What additions, cuts, or rearrangements would make them clearer or more emphatic? (See Chapters 20–24.)

10. Are any words inaccurate, vague, abstract, or ambiguous? Are any charged with inappropriate feeling or bias? What are better alternatives? Can any words be cut without loss of meaning or feeling? (See Chapters 25–29.)

11. Does the project appear to be correct in grammar, punctuation, and spelling? Is it appropriately formatted? What changes are necessary? (See Chapters 11–19, and 33–46.)

3*d* | Prepare and proofread your final draft

As you prepare your final draft, use the appropriate manuscript format. (See 46c for the Modern Language Association format for writing in the humanities and 46d for the American Psychological Association format for writing in the social sciences.)

Proofread your final copy slowly and carefully. When many readers proofread, they miss typos because they're reading as they normally do, for the meaning, or looking for the parts they like. Follow these guidelines to systematic proofreading:

- Read your final draft aloud, slowly pronouncing each word as you've written it. Use a pencil eraser to point at each word, or lay a ruler beneath each line to guide your eyes.

- Once you've spotted and corrected an error, return to the beginning of the line to begin proofreading anew. You may have missed a second error when you saw the first out of the corner of your eye.

- If you find it hard to concentrate on your words or if you're a poor speller, read your writing backward, looking at each word. Look up any word you don't write frequently. (See 45.)

Chapter 4. Writing with a Computer, Revising with Your Peers

4a | Write with a computer or word processor

Computers and word processors are powerful tools for writers because they make exploring, drafting, revising, and editing easier. Thus, they encourage the experimentation that will improve your writing. You can add, cut, or move words, sentences, paragraphs, and pages with the click of a key or mouse. Many word-processing programs will help you prepare outlines. Some will enable you to create files to guide you as you begin a project.

Most will number your pages, include your name at the top of the page, insert headings or footnotes, arrange a bibliography, and give you many type fonts and formats for styling your documents. Style and grammar checkers will point out long or short sentences, repeated use of a word or phrase, jargon, and, of course, grammar and spelling errors. Most writers who write with computers say they write more, revise more extensively, and enjoy writing more.

■ 1 Quick References

Consult your program's quick reference to learn important word-processing commands. Many software programs are accompanied by these brief printed guides to supplement Help screens. Or you can make your own customized reference by listing the commands you use frequently.

■ 2 Templates

To help you with frequent assignments, make **templates.** These are files that you create to reuse every time you begin a new project. They may contain questions or other prompts and blank spaces that help guide you through each writing project. Consider templates for audience profiles, questions to answer about your topics, notetaking formats, outline for-

How to . . .

How to Write Successfully with Computers

Darkened screen. If you can't get started, try darkening the screen and writing out your thoughts without looking at them.

A blank line. Use a blank line _____ for easy-to-find places to fill in words or missing information after you've finished a draft.

Saving your work. Save your writing frequently. If you lose power or your program "crashes," anything not saved into permanent memory—on floppy or hard disk—will be lost. To protect against damaged disks, save files on back-up disks.

Hard copy. Revise on hard copy, another term for the printed page. Most experienced computer users move from on-screen text to printed hard copy of their writing. They find revision easier when they can lay their projects out before them, page by page, rather than scrolling back and forth through a document on screen. Revise and reprint as often as necessary.

Multiple versions. If you make significant changes to a draft and are unsure whether they're the right ones, save several versions of your draft under different file names, for example, "Essay 1a" and "Essay 1b." Compare printed versions and choose the best.

Find commands. Use Search and Replace or Find commands to locate words, punctuation, or blank lines where you want to add things.

Proofreading. Proofread on printed copy. If you proofread on screen, errors will be hard to detect.

mats, thesis or purpose statements, revision and editing checklists. Once you've created and saved an empty template file (named "Outline," for example), all you have to do is open it and begin typing at the appropriate prompt. If you want to save your work, save it under a new file name (for example, "Outline 1"). The original empty template will stay in place for your next project.

■ 3 Grammar checkers

Beware of relying too heavily on grammar or style checkers. They can identify troublesome words, phrases, and sentences, but they can't read your intentions, don't know your audience, and can't detect the feelings you want to convey. Be sure a recommended change will actually improve your writing before you accept it.

■ 4 Spell checkers

Spell checkers can't identify confused words such as *threw* for *through*, *there* for *they're* or *their*, *see* for *sea*, *so* for *sew*. If you misspell a word by typing another, correctly spelled word—*ad* instead of *and*—your spell checker can't identify that, either. Use your spell checker but proofread afterward.

■ 5 Manuscript form

For information about the manuscript form of computer-produced papers, see 46a1.

4b Ask peer reviewers to read your writing

■ Professional writers have reviewers to help them evaluate their writing. You should, too. In many college classes peer review is a frequent activity. On your own you can form readers' groups to share and improve your writing.

■ 1 Reading as a peer reviewer

When you review another's writing, your most valuable traits will be honesty, tact, sensitivity to your experiences of reading, and awareness of the writer's purpose. Your aim is not to tell the writer how to write the way you would write but to help the writer say what he or she wants to. As a reviewer, you may play three roles:

1. Respondent. Respondents give writers feedback about their experience of reading. Tell what you thought and felt as you read, what you understood or didn't, where you followed or lost the writer's thread. This role helps writers understand the impact of their writing.

2. Editor. Editors show writers how to fulfill their intentions. If asked, you may give advice about subject matter, organization, style, and grammatical matters. Be specific, detailed, and practical.

3. Critic. Critics evaluate. But the best critics are the most descriptive and factual, describing what something is or is not, what it does or doesn't do, rather than whether something is good or not. To paraphrase a famous poet, your aim is to tell the truth in the kindest words possible. Play this role only when asked by writers you know well. Tell writers what you see

as the status of their writing. Is it a dress rehearsal, nearly finished? Or does it seem exploratory or experimental? Explain your answer.

■ 2 Sharing your writing with peer reviewers

If you share your writing with readers outside class, check with your instructor for a definition of fair editorial assistance. If you know what you want, ask for specific feedback. But don't talk too much, don't explain, and don't apologize for what you've written. You'll color readers' views and prevent them from giving honest responses. As you listen, remember that this is your paper and you have the final say. If their advice makes sense, use it. If it doesn't—well, thanks, but no thanks.

■ 3 Creating discussion agendas for peer reviewers

The following list will direct you to the appropriate sets of questions that will help you read as a peer reviewer or provide your reviewers with questions to answer about your writing.

- General questions for revision and editing. See "How to decide what to revise and edit," pp. 21–22.

- Research projects. See "How to revise and edit a research project," p. 323.

- Argument and persuasion. See "How to revise and edit persuasive writing," p. 382.

- Writing about literature. See "How to revise and edit a literary essay," p. 395.

4c A sample student essay

■ The writer of the following project was instructed to "write a 3–5 page informative essay about a topic many people misunderstand." An **essay** (a frequent college assignment) is generally a brief nonfiction writing on one subject unified by a specific purpose, thesis, or mood. The writer of this essay chose to write about bicycle commuting and to explain its feasibility. For other sample essays, see the research project (53), the persuasive essay (58d), and the literary essay (59g). The writers of these essays have followed the Modern Language Association format for papers in the humanities. (See 46c.)

Chen 1

Modern
Language
Association
format
(see 46c)

John Chen

Professor Sternberg

English 101–015

September 10, 199–

Standard
heading
information

The Highway My Way

Centered
title

For most residents of America's cities and suburbs, the worst
part of any weekday is the excruciating time spent trapped in
rush hour traffic. Morning, night, and sometimes even at noon, I
watch my fellow commuters lined up, scowling, inching and
honking their way to work or school. I used to share their fender
benders, foul air, fouler tempers, frazzled nerves, clenched jaws,
high blood pressure, higher insurance premiums, the same old
tunes on the radio, the wasted time, and boredom. But no more.
Not since I parked my car and began commuting by bicycle. What
I've discovered in the process is that bicycle commuting is a safe,
practical, economical, and enjoyable alternative to short-trip car
travel. If other motorists joined me, we could bring an end to this
commuting misery.

Double
spacing
throughout

Dramatic
introductory
description
to attract
reader
interest

The writer's
informative
thesis

Many drivers, however, think of cycling, especially commuter
cycling, as anything but safe. To them, people who put their
fragile bikes and bodies on rush hour streets and highways risk
instant destruction by 4,000 pound cars and 40,000 pound trucks
and buses. How could a bicycle commuter survive even one rush
hour, they wonder.

Transition to
the first part
of the essay:
the myths
and realities
of bicycle
commuting

The truth is that cars, trucks, buses, and bicycles can
safely share most roads and streets. As reported in a recent
issue of <u>Bicycling</u> magazine, fewer than twelve percent of cycling
accidents involve cars or other motorized vehicles (Drake 18).
With increased enforcement of traffic laws, roadway redesign,
the creation of more off-road bike paths where appropriate,

A topic
sentence: the
realities of
bicycle safety

Chen 2

and improved driver and cyclist education, the incidence of
these accidents will be even lower. If millions upon millions of
bicycle commuters can pedal their way safely along the narrow,
densely crowded streets and roads of Mexico, the Netherlands,
Sweden, India, China, and many other countries, cyclists can
easily be accommodated on the United States' wider streets
and roads.

Information
that supports
the topic
sentence

Even so, many will object, what happens elsewhere is no
guide to the future of America's roads. Large-scale bicycle
commuting would be impractical. In America, the car is king.
Highway redesign and modification to accommodate cyclists
would be too complex and expensive. Another bureaucracy would
be created, they argue, and one more governmental body would
lean on us for taxes. Where would we begin?

Transition
and topic
sentence:
objections to
the practical-
ity of bicycle
commuting

The truth is that we have already begun. Already seven
percent of Americans bicycle or walk to work (Pena 38). Many
businesses now encourage bicycle commuting by providing
bicycle parking or storage and employee clean-up facilities. In all
fifty states, bicycles have for years had the same legal status as
motor vehicles, and cyclists have had the same legal rights and
responsibilities as motorists. In 1991 Congress passed the
Intermodal Surface Transportation Efficiency Act (ISTEA), which
provides 3.3 billion dollars to state and local governments to
develop more ecological modes of transportation, including
bicycles. The American Association of State Highway and
Transportation Officials has already produced a <u>Guide to the
Development of Bicycle Facilities</u>, with highway redesign
recommendations that will enable bicycles and other vehicles to
co-exist safely. The federal government and most state and local
governments already have officials to oversee the integration of

Parenthetical
in-text docu-
mentation
of borrowed
information
(see 51)

The reality of
bicycle com-
muting as a
practical
alternative

Chen 3

bicycles into transportation programs. And many municipalities--such as San Diego, Denver, Minneapolis, Chicago, and Philadelphia--have already laid out networks of bike routes to aid bicycle commuters. Some, such as Portland, Oregon, and Seattle, equip buses with bike racks to expand the possibilities for bicycle commuters.

This kind of business and government support makes it easy for other commuters to do as I did: park their cars and ride their bikes instead. Most of the trips we take by car are under ten miles. Most of the routes we drive are bicycle accessible. These are trips we could take most of the time in most weather by bicycle. Many of us already own bicycles. A call to our local government or a visit to a bike shop will give us routes and maybe even maps. What else do we need?

> Transition to the second part of the essay: becoming a bicycle commuter

-A bicycle tune-up

-A review of the rules of the road (We have to follow the same regulations motorists do.)

-A few articles of clothing and equipment (a helmet for sure, bike shorts perhaps, baskets or bags, rain gear, lights for night commuters, possibly fenders, and a horn or bell)

- Cycling companions to share the ride with us

> A list for emphasis

It takes only a little imagination to see the benefits of bicycle commuting. Those who must drive because of health, their route, or the distance will benefit from reduced traffic and commuting times. Bicyclists will benefit from increased exercise, and the money they save on gasoline and insurance can be put to better uses. Businesses will benefit. According to <u>Bicycling</u> magazine, U.S. businesses now pay $1,035 per employee per year "to compensate for lost productivity of workers stuck in traffic" (28).

> Topic sentence

> Introduction of a source of information and in-text parenthetical documentation of the page number

Chen 4

Bicycle commuters are money in the bank. Finally, all of us will benefit from the cleaner air that results from fewer cars and trucks. According to that same issue of <u>Bicycling</u>, a week of bicycle commuting by one person (a five-mile round trip) eliminates 1.5 pounds of carbon monoxide from the air (28).

Imagine a morning or afternoon when the sky is not brown with smog. Imagine broad, open streets easy and safe to travel any time of day. Imagine the scent of flowers and trees instead of gasoline and rubber. Imagine the songs of birds instead of the blare of horns, the rumble of engines, the screech of tires. Imagine feeling relaxed and exhilarated at the end of a commute, instead of frustrated, tense, angry. This is what a bicycle rush hour would be like. Instead of the worst part of the day, it just might be the best.

Descriptive conclusion that contrasts with the introduction and dramatizes the writer's thesis

Works Cited

Bicycling Mar. 1993: 28.

Drake, Geoff. <u>Bicycling</u> May 1996: 18.

Pena, Nelson. "Brothers In Arms." <u>Bicycling</u> Mar. 1993: 38.

An alphabetical list of the sources of information for this essay (see 52a)

Paragraphing

Ancient Greek writers drew a mark, called a *parágraphos,* to divide manuscripts into distinct and manageable parts. In the same way, modern **paragraphs** signal changes of subject or purpose and thus make writing and reading easier. Your paragraphs will contribute powerfully to the success of your writing when they unify ideas, develop subjects effectively, and flow coherently from one to the next.

5 Unifying Your Paragraphs

A good paragraph is like any piece of good writing. It has a purpose, focuses on a single topic, and has an overall design. In a word, a good paragraph is unified. To write unified paragraphs, do as you would in any writing.

5*a* Write topic sentences to focus your paragraphs

A **topic sentence** resembles the thesis statement of an essay. It announces a topic or makes a point. Just as everything in an essay supports its thesis, everything in a paragraph supports its topic sentence. Consider this example:

Topic sentence	Calf ropers are the whiz kids of rodeo: they're expert on the horse and on the ground, and their horses are as quick-witted.
Cowboys as expert riders	The cowboy emerges from the box with a loop in his hand, a piggin' string in his mouth, coils and reins in the other, and a network of slack line strewn so thickly over horse and rider,
Cowboys and horses working together	they look as if they'd run through a tangle of kudzu before arriving in the arena. After roping the calf and jerking the slack in the rope, he jumps off the horse, sprints down the length of nylon, which the horse keeps taut, throws the calf down, and ties three legs together with the piggin' string. It's said of Roy
A supporting example	Cooper, the defending calf-roping champion, that "even with pins and metal plates in his arm, he's known for the fastest groundwork in the business; when he springs down his rope to flank the calf, the resulting action is pure rodeo poetry." The
A concluding evaluation	six or seven separate movements he makes are so fluid they look like one continual unfolding.

(Gretel Ehrlich, "Rules of the Game: Rodeo," from *The Solace of Open Spaces*)

31

Topic sentences may appear early in a paragraph, as in the preceding example, or later, to sum up preceding information, as in the following:

Transitional phrase to link paragraphs

Details about girls' play

A topic sentence explaining girls' play

> Girls, on the other hand, play in small groups or pairs; the center of a girl's social life is a best friend. Within the group, intimacy is key: Differentiation is measured by relative closeness. In their most frequent games, such as jump rope and hopscotch, everyone gets a turn. Many of their activities (such as playing house) do not have winners or losers. Though some girls are certainly more skilled than others, girls are expected not to boast about it, or show that they think they are better than the others. Girls don't give orders; they express their preferences as suggestions, and suggestions are likely to be accepted. Whereas boys say, "Gimme that!" and "Get outta here!" girls say, "Let's do this," and "How about doing that?" Anything else is put down as "bossy." They don't grab center stage—they don't want it—so they don't challenge each other directly. And much of the time, they simply sit together and talk. Girls are not accustomed to jockeying for status in an obvious way; they are more concerned that they be liked.
>
> (Deborah Tannen, "It Begins at the Beginning," from *You Just Don't Understand*)

How to... How to Write Topic Sentences

As you organize your writing, consider items in outline headings or in lists you have made as potential topic sentences. Compose headings that you can later expand into topic sentences.

As you write a first draft and indent for new paragraphs, think of sentences to announce your topics. Where will you put them for best effect? At the beginning, to launch your paragraph? Or at the end, as a destination to aim for?

As you revise, decide whether supporting sentences support your topic sentences. If not, decide whether to cut those that don't belong, move them to another paragraph, write new topic sentences, or reorganize to create new paragraphs.

As you edit, look for topic sentences in your writing. They should appear regularly, but sometimes a topic sentence in one paragraph will announce a topic for several paragraphs. Sometimes you can imply your point rather than state it explicitly.

Reread your writing from your readers' point of view. If you suspect they might ask, "What's the point here?" add topic sentences to answer their question.

One key to successful paragraph design is the placement of the topic sentence. Organize your paragraphs to follow from the topic sentence or lead to it, as in the preceding examples. Another key is emphasis. Whenever possible, put the most important information early in your paragraph, known as **dramatic order,** or late, known as **climactic order.** In the following example, the writer opens with a topic sentence but saves her most important example for the end of her paragraph.

Topic sentence	Neat people are especially vicious with mail. They never go through their mail unless they are standing directly over a trash can. If the trash can is beside the mailbox, even better. All ads,
Clarifying description	catalogs, pleas for charitable contributions, church bulletins and money-saving coupons go straight in the trash can without being opened. All letters from home, postcards from Europe,
Supporting examples	bills and paychecks are opened, immediately responded to, then dropped in the trash can. Neat people keep their receipts only for tax purposes. That's it. No sentimental salvaging of
Most important example	birthday cards or the last letter a dying relative ever wrote. Into the trash it goes.

(Suzanne Britt, "Neat People vs. Sloppy People," from *Show and Tell*)

5*b* Adjust paragraph length to express your purpose and suit your audience

■ 1 Paragraph length, purpose, and audience

Paragraphs may be almost any length. Some are necessarily short to set them off or signal changes in topic or purpose: speeches in a dialogue, a paragraph to set off a thesis, transition statements, or emphatic paragraphs. These may be only a sentence or two—even less. Paragraphs that present and develop ideas, such as introductions, body paragraphs, or conclusions, may be much longer.

In any case, you should write paragraphs for your readers' eyes as well as their brains. Too many short paragraphs will make your writing look choppy and disconnected, even when it isn't. Too many long paragraphs may make readers think, "I can't read this; it's too difficult." Paragraphs should look readable.

■ 2 Paragraph length and contents

Paragraphs must not only look readable but must be readable, fully expressing their topic and purpose. Adjusting paragraph length involves more than combining short paragraphs and dividing up long ones. As you adjust length, be sure each paragraph connects to the preceding one, that it clearly announces its topic or purpose, and that it is complete. A paragraph may contain six kinds of sentences. Although not every paragraph contains every kind of sentence, a good paragraph has all the sentences necessary to make its point and connect it to surrounding paragraphs:

- *Transitional* sentences linking one paragraph to another

- *Introductory* sentences

- *Topic* sentences

- *Supporting* sentences that present a topic or prove a point

- *Clarifying* sentences that explain or restate

- *Concluding* sentences

As you adjust paragraph length, check to see that each paragraph has all the sentences it needs. Not every paragraph contains every kind of sentence, and individual sentences may perform more than one function. But each paragraph has to have the sentences necessary to do its job.

How to Adjust Paragraph Length

How to . . .

To divide a paragraph that seems too long, look for break points at shifts in time or place, between subtopics, or before sentences that signal logical shifts.

In double-spaced typescript, common in college writing, break for a new paragraph one to three times per page—every 100–200 words or so. Break more often to increase the pace of your writing or for special purpose paragraphs.

In single-spaced typescript, common in business letters, make your paragraphs from four or five to nine or ten lines. Break more frequently if your information is complex or if your readers may only be skimming your writing for its main ideas.

If you are writing in columns, as in technical writing and journalism, break up long paragraphs to make them look readable, usually one to three sentences in length.

If you are writing by hand, divide once or twice per page.

6 Developing Paragraphs

6a Include details to support your topic sentence

"God is in the details," said architect Louis Sullivan. As in a well-designed building, the power of a well-designed paragraph lies in its details. If you're writing to readers familiar with your topic, you may not need to say much. However, in most public writing, especially in college writing, readers want enough detail to understand fully the main idea of your topic sentence. That means writing well-developed paragraphs.

How to Write Well-developed Paragraphs

Do exploratory writing or take notes before beginning a first draft. Give yourself things to put in your paragraphs before you write them.

As you revise, ask yourself whether the points in your topic sentences are fully supported by the body of your paragraphs. Add details to prove your points or express your ideas.

A good way to see whether your paragraphs have enough detail is to read them from your readers' viewpoint. Have you said enough to answer their questions and satisfy their interest in your topic? Add details if necessary.

6b Choose appropriate methods of paragraph development to present a topic

The methods of paragraph development illustrated in this section will enable you to communicate information, experiences, feelings, ideas, and opinions. Sometimes, when an idea needs several kinds of support, you'll combine more than one method in a paragraph, as in the paragraph about calf-ropers earlier (see 5a), in which the writer combines narration, description, and example. Sometimes, when subjects are complex or your readers' need for information is great, you may extend one method of development over several paragraphs, all unified by one topic sentence. You may even use one method throughout an entire piece of writing, unified by a thesis statement.

The method you choose will depend on your purpose and your readers' needs. Though each method can serve a variety of purposes, specific methods are customarily used for specific ends, as the following examples indicate.

■ 1 Narration

Narration organizes events in chronological order to tell a story. Use it in personal experience writing and to illustrate a point in explanatory writing or argument. As in the following example, narrative paragraphs almost always include description to make actions clear and vivid.

Event 1: action and reaction

Dramatizing description

Event 2: a second shot and its effects

Event 3: a third shot and its effects

When I pulled the trigger I did not hear the bang or feel the kick—one never does when a shot goes home—but I heard the devilish roar of glee that went up from the crowd. In that instant, in too short a time, one would have thought, even for the bullet to get there, a mysterious, terrible change had come over the elephant. He neither stirred nor fell, but every line of his body had altered. He looked suddenly stricken, shrunken, immensely old, as though the frightful impact of the bullet had paralysed him without knocking him down. At last, after what seemed a long time—it might have been five seconds, I dare say—he sagged flabbily to his knees. His mouth slobbered. An enormous senility seemed to have settled upon him. One could have imagined him thousands of years old. I fired again into the same spot. At the second shot he did not collapse but climbed with desperate slowness to his feet and stood weakly upright, with legs sagging and head drooping. I fired a third time. That was the shot that did for him. You could see the agony of it jolt his whole body and knock the last remnant of strength from his legs. But in falling he seemed for a moment to rise, for as his hind legs collapsed beneath him he seemed to tower upward like a huge rock toppling, his trunk reaching skywards like a tree. He trumpeted, for the first and only time. And then down he came, his belly towards me, with a crash that seemed to shake the ground even where I lay.

(George Orwell, "Shooting an Elephant," from *Shooting an Elephant and Other Essays*)

■ 2 Process

Like narrative paragraphs, **process** paragraphs are organized in chronological order. But they emphasize the sequence of events as much as the events themselves. Process paragraphs are used frequently to explain steps or stages in informative and how-to writing.

Step 1   To define a word, then, the dictionary editor places before him
the stack of cards illustrating that word; each of the cards represents an actual use of the word by a writer of some literary or historical importance. He reads the cards carefully, discards some,
Step 2   rereads the rest, and divides up the stack according to what he
thinks are the several senses of the word. Finally, he writes his
Step 3   definitions, following the hard-and-fast rule that each definition
must be based on what the quotations in front of him reveal
about the meaning of the word. The editor cannot be influenced
by what he thinks a given word ought to mean. He must work
according to the cards or not at all.

(S. I. Hayakawa, "How Dictionaries Are Made,"
from *Language in Thought and Action*)

■ 3 Description

Description adds sensory details to personal and informative writing—whenever it is important for writers to "see" a subject. Descriptive
paragraphs are usually organized in spatial order: left to right, front to
back, top to bottom, and so forth. The following paragraph is organized
from the center to the margins of a scene.

Topic sentence   There once was a town in the heart of America where all life
seemed to live in harmony with its surroundings. The town lay
Visual details   in the midst of a checkerboard of prosperous farms, with fields of
grain and hillsides of orchards where, in spring, white clouds of
Color   bloom drifted above the green fields. In autumn, oak and maple
and birch set up a blaze of color that flamed and flickered across
a backdrop of pines. Then foxes barked in the hills and deer
Sound   silently crossed the fields, half hidden in the mists of the fall
mornings.

(Rachel Carson, "A Fable for Tomorrow," from
Silent Spring)

■ 4 Facts and figures

Factual paragraphs present **facts or statistical information** in some
clear pattern to provide information or prove a point in an argument. For
example, the following paragraph is organized according to the ways bats
are both familiar and strange to human beings.

Facts that make
bats familiar   Bats are mammals like we are. They suckle their young, and
have such wizened ancient-looking faces that they seem strangely
akin and familiar. Yet they find their way and locate food by
Facts that make   using sound that we cannot hear. They hunt by night, and in cold
bats strange to
human beings   weather some migrate and others hibernate. They are odd and
alien to us, too, so much so that we have made up fancies about
them—that they are evil and ill-omened, or at the very least will

fly into our hair. Anyone who has read *Dracula* will remember that young ladies should not moon around graveyards at night, or they will be in big trouble with bats.

(Sue Hubbell, "Summer," from *A Country Year*)

■ 5 Examples

An **example** uses individual members of a group (people, events, conditions, objects, ideas, and so forth) to explain or illustrate the whole group. Explanatory writing and argument frequently depend on examples. Occasionally, they are introduced by signal phrases: *for example, for instance,* or *such as.*

Topic sentence and the group to be explained: visible symbols of the consumer society

Examples

Signal phrase

Since its birth in the United States, the consumer society has moved far beyond its American borders, yet its most visible symbols remain American. The Disneyland near Tokyo attracts almost as many visitors each year as Mecca or the Vatican. Coca-Cola products are distributed in over 170 countries. Each day, a new McDonald's restaurant opens somewhere in the world. Singaporean youngsters can brush their teeth with the Teenage Mutant Ninja Turtle Talking Toothbrush, which says "Hey, Dudes!" in Malay. The techniques of mass marketing first perfected in the United States are now employed on every continent, teaching former East Germans, for example, to "Taste the West. Marlboro."

(Alan Thein Durning, "The Consumer Society," from *How Much Is Enough?*)

■ 6 Comparison/Contrast

Comparison/contrast presents subjects according to similarities and differences in order to explain a subject or make an evaluation. Comparison/contrast paragraphs may be organized in two ways. In **block comparison,** as in the first paragraph that follows, one subject is presented and then the other, subject A and then B. In **point-by-point comparison,** as in the second paragraph, the comparison moves back and forth, first to one point of comparison, then to a second, and so forth, $A_1 B_1$, then $A_2 B_2$, and $A_3 B_3$.

Block contrast

Custer's knowledge of his society

Crazy Horse's knowledge of his society

[George Armstrong] Custer's society was specialized. Thus, despite his range of choices, once Custer settled into an occupation, he knew relatively little about what other men in his society did for their daily bread. After becoming a soldier, Custer knew almost nothing about medicine or law or manufacturing. He never really understood how his society worked. [The Sioux warrior] Crazy Horse knew how to do everything required to make his society function. He could put up a tipi, kill buffalo, skin animals, cook, make war, treat injuries or illness, and so on. Put Crazy Horse down naked and alone on the Great Plains and within a month he would have a full set of weapons, shelter, stocks of food, and be in good shape to face the future.

Point-by-point comparison

Differences in dress

Differences in bearing

Two similarities

Beyond their bravery, Custer and Crazy Horse were individualists, each standing out from the crowd in his separate way. Custer wore outlandish uniforms, let his hair fall in long, flowing gold locks across his shoulders, surrounded himself with pet animals and admirers, and in general did all he could to draw attention to himself. Crazy Horse's individualism pushed him in an opposite direction—he wore a single feather in his hair when going into battle, rather than a war bonnet. Custer's vast energy set him apart from most of his fellows; the Sioux distinguished Crazy Horse from other warriors because of Crazy Horse's quietness and introspection. Both men lived in societies in which drugs, especially alcohol, were widely used, but neither Custer nor Crazy Horse drank. Most of all, of course, each man stood out in battle as a great risk taker.

(Stephen Ambrose, from *Crazy Horse and Custer: The Parallel Lives of Two American Warriors*)

■ 7 Analogy

As a form of comparison, **analogy** uses something simple or familiar to explain something complex or unfamiliar. To help explain what can be observed in newly fallen snow, the writer of the following paragraph compares snow to a book.

Topic sentence

The wind = pages turning

Physical details = the language of the book

To one who lives in the snow and watches it day by day, it is a book to be read. The pages turn as the wind blows; the characters shift and the images formed by their combinations change in meaning, but the language remains the same. It is a shadow language, spoken by things that have gone by and will come again. The same text has been written there for thousands of years, though I was not here, and will not be here in winters to come, to read it. These seemingly random ways, these paths, these beds, these footprints, these hard, round pellets in the snow: they all have meaning. Dark things may be written there, news of others' lives, their sorties and excursions, their terrors and deaths. The tiny feet of a shrew or a vole make a brief, erratic pattern across the snow, and here is a hole down which the animal goes. And now the track of an ermine comes this way, swift and searching, and he too goes down that white shadow of a hole.

(John Haines, "Snow," from *The Stars, the Snow, the Fire*)

■ 8 Cause/effect

Cause/effect paragraphs divide events into causes and effects in order to explain relationships within a process. They may be organized in two ways: *causes → effects* or, as in the following example, *effects → causes*. Note how the writer arranges causes into a *causal chain*, from immediate to underlying causes.

Topic sentence: an effect (literacy)	Fortunately, there are many children who manage to become literate despite the way in which they are taught reading. They do so because they are highly motivated by their home environ-
Two chief causes: home and school	ment or because of an attachment to their teacher. Studies show that nothing correlates more highly with a child's future academic success than the academic achievement of his parents. The reason for this is not just that the parents are committed to the
Underlying causes: observation and experience	merit of reading, a commitment which they pass on to their children, but also that from an early age the child can observe how important reading is to his parents and how much they enjoy it. Additionally, parents who are avid readers are more likely to read often—and with enjoyment—to their children. So the child becomes convinced that reading is important and enjoyable long before he is confronted for the first time with a primer in school. And he is then able to distance himself from the stupidity of the
Two additional effects of these causes	primers, since he knows not all books are like those. Still, many years later, that child will remember how disgusted he was with the books he had to read in early grades.

(Bruno Bettelheim, from *Johnny Wants to Read*)

■ 9 Classification

Classification divides subjects into classes according to characteristics shared by the members of each class. Classification paragraphs are often used in informative and evaluative writing to show how things differ or fit together. They may include examples or description to distinguish the members of one class from another.

Topic sentence	There are three kinds of book owners. The first has all the standard sets and best sellers—unread, untouched. (This de-
Class one	luded individual owns woodpulp and ink, not books.) The second has a great many books—a few of them read through, most
Class two	of them dipped into, but all of them as clean and shiny as the day they were bought. (This person would probably like to make books his own, but is restrained by a false respect for their physi-
Class three	cal appearance.) The third has few books or many—every one of them dog-eared and dilapidated, shaken and loosened by contin-
Descriptive details	ual use, marked and scribbled in from front to back. (This man owns books.)

(Mortimer Adler, "How to Mark a Book" in
Saturday Review, July 6, 1940.)

■ 10 Definition

In explanatory writing and argument, **definitions** explain what something is. There are several methods of definition.

- **Formal definition** puts something into a class of related items and then distinguishes it from other words in that class.

- **Functional definition** tells how something works.

- **Etymology** traces the history of a term to its origins.

- **Giving synonym**s compares words with similar or related meanings.

- **Providing examples** defines by illustrating the term.

Definition by origin, by synonym

Definition by contrast

Example and functional definition

"Niche" is a word ecologists have borrowed from church architecture. In a church, of course, a "niche" means a recess in the wall in which a figurine may be placed; it is an address, a location, a physical place. But the ecologist's "niche" is more than just a physical place: it is a place in the grand scheme of things. The niche is an animal's (or a plant's) profession. The niche of the wolf spider is everything it does to get its food and raise its babies. To be able to do these things it must relate properly to the place where it lives and to the other inhabitants of that place. Everything the species does to survive and stay "fit" in the Darwinian sense is its niche.

(Paul Colinvaux, "Every Species Has Its Niche," from *Why Big Fierce Animals Are Rare*)

6c Write introductions that attract reader interest and conclusions that create a feeling of completeness

The special purposes of introductions and conclusions require special methods of paragraph development chosen to fulfill a writer's purposes for communicating with particular readers.

■ 1 Introductions

Professional writers frequently spend a lot of time on openings. They know that a good lead will take them in the right direction as they begin a draft. They also know they have to arouse interest within the first two or three sentences or risk losing their readers. And they know that effective introductions are sometimes challenging to write because these introductions must do several things at once:

- Identify the writer's topic and, often, the purpose of the writing
- Stimulate reader interest
- Create the writer's personality and style
- State the writer's thesis or main idea
- Provide a bridge to carry readers into the body of the writing

Consider how the following introduction attracts reader interest and then focuses it on the thesis statement.

Dramatic quotation to create interest

"A name is a prison, God is free," once observed the Greek poet Nikos Kazantzakis. He meant, I think, that valuable though language is to man, it is by very necessity limiting, and creates for man an invisible prison. Language implies boundaries. A word spoken creates a dog, a rabbit, a man. It fixes their nature before our eyes; henceforth their shapes are, in a sense, our own creation. They are no longer part of the unnamed shifting architecture of the universe. They have been transfixed as if by sorcery, frozen into a concept, a word. Powerful though the spell of human language has proven itself to be, it has laid boundaries upon the cosmos.

Explanation that announces the writer's topic

Thesis statement

(Loren Eiseley, "The Cosmic Prison," from *The Invisible Pyramid*)

The best introductions usually open with something dramatic or intriguing, such as the striking quotation in the preceding example. After that, work-related writing gets down to business right away. Personal or informative writing, however, often begins more imaginatively and in more detail. Choose the introductory strategy right for the topic and the occasion.

- A quotation. Begin with a dramatic quotation, as Loren Eiseley does. Be sure to tell who is speaking and, if necessary, provide explanation to help readers understand how the quotation introduces your topic. (See 53, the sample research project.)
- Dramatic details. Open with dramatic details or description. (See 58d, the sample persuasive essay.)
- In the middle of things. Open in the middle of things at some dramatic point (also referred to as *in medias res*) and then flash back to the beginning.
- A strong statement. Write a strong statement: a warning, something that at first seems puzzling or contradictory.
- A problem. Pose a problem to solve or question to answer. (See 4c, the sample essay, and 54d, the sample report.)
- An anecdote. Tell a brief story (an anecdote) that illustrates your point.
- An analogy. Open with an analogy or comparison that describes or illustrates your topic.

■ 2 Conclusions

Conclusions are more than stopping places. For writers and readers alike, they create a sense of unity and completeness. Consider how this conclusion to an essay celebrating America's cultural diversity leads in the final sentence to a restatement of the writer's main point.

Two examples that illustrate the writer's thesis

One of our most visionary politicians said that he envisioned a time when the United States could become the brain of the world, by which he meant the repository of all of the latest advanced information systems. I thought of that remark when an enterprising poet friend of mine called to say that he had just sold a poem to a computer magazine and that the editors were delighted to get it because they didn't carry fiction or poetry. Is that the kind of world we desire? A humdrum homogeneous world of all brains but no heart, no fiction, no poetry; a world of robots with human attendants bereft of imagination, of culture? Or does North America deserve a more exciting destiny? To become a place where the cultures of the world crisscross. This is possible because the United States is unique in the world: The world is here.

Rhetorical questions that explain the examples

Answers that restate the thesis

(Ishmael Reed, "America: The Multinational Society," from *Writin' Is Fightin'*)

How to...

How to Revise Introductions and Conclusions

Introductions

Avoid repeating your title in your opening line; doing so may make your introduction sound monotonous or unimaginative.

Cut unnecessary background or warmup writing that you've used to get yourself started. Advice for movie directors is also good for writers: "Cut to the chase." Open with what will interest your readers.

Delete self-conscious purpose statements: *In this paper I will . . .* and so forth. Don't tell your readers what you'll do. Do it.

Beware of mysterious openings. It's one thing to stimulate reader curiosity, quite another to mystify readers or plunge them into the dark. Your introduction should help readers make sound predictions about your topic—even about your design and style.

Conclusions

Be sure your conclusion flows smoothly from the body of your writing. If necessary, write transitions or repeat key words.

Do more than merely reword a thesis you've already written in your introduction.

Avoid stock phrases that tell the obvious: *In conclusion . . . , In closing . . . , In summary . . . ,* and so forth.

Do not introduce new topics. Refocus attention on your original topic.

Be sure your readers will understand a closing quotation. Identify the speaker and, if necessary, explain its point.

As the preceding example illustrates, effective conclusions restate, provide food for thought, and challenge reader thinking, feeling, or action. Create a conclusion appropriate to the topic and the occasion.

- Your thesis. Conclude with your thesis or other unifying statement. Organize your writing so that it leads naturally and inevitably to your point.

- A question. Ask a rhetorical question for which the body of your paper has suggested the answer.

- A challenge. Challenge your readers to new thinking or action.

- A quotation. Conclude with an apt quotation. Introduce and explain it if necessary.

- An anecdote. Tell a brief story (an anecdote) that summarizes your thinking.

- A hook. Conclude with a **hook.** Unify your writing by returning to—hooking up with—the subject of your opening and commenting on it in light of what you've written in the body of your paper.

Creating Coherence

Effective writing is **coherent,** meaning that all of its parts fit snugly together. A more descriptive word is **fluent.** Effective writing flows from idea to idea, paragraph to paragraph, sentence to sentence, and so is easier to read than incoherent writing. Writing unified by a single topic and overall design already has the essential features of coherence.

To express that coherence while writing a draft, keep going. Write as much as possible at one sitting. If you must stop, stop in the middle of a paragraph that you'll know how to finish when you return. As you rewrite, edit for coherence. If you find a passage that seems choppy or disconnected, try the following strategies.

7a | Repeat key words and their synonyms

Some writers believe that repeated words are a sure sign of uninspired, monotonous writing. But key words that name your topics are worth repeating. Readers depend on them just as they depend on

How to Edit for Coherence

Look at your writing. Be sure you've written topic sentences and necessary transitions. If not, add them.

Mark key words. If you've written coherently, you'll see key words repeated frequently. If you have marked many *different* key words, you may have too many topics, and your writing may be disunified or incoherent. Refocus, reorganize, and rewrite to support your thesis and topic sentences.

Reread from the beginning of a paragraph. When you finish rewriting a paragraph, go back to its beginning and reread. If your rewrite fits coherently, your original and revised sentences will flow together smoothly.

Reread at your readers' pace. Writers read their writing more slowly than readers, pausing frequently to consider and evaluate. At this slower pace, transitions and repetitions may seem appropriate. But if you reread at your readers' swifter pace, you may discover that momentum will carry you smoothly from one idea to the next without transitions or repetition. Cut unnecessary words.

highway route markers to tell them they're on the right road. For example, consider the following paragraphs in which Pulitzer prize–winning poet and journalist Donald Murray explains how experienced nonfiction writers create voice. Note how often Murray repeats the word *voice* and related words (emphasis added).

Experienced writers rarely begin a first draft until they **hear** in their heads—or on the page—a **voice** that may be right. **Voice** is usually the key element in effective writing. It is what attracts the reader and communicates to the reader. It is that element that gives **the illusion of speech. Voice** carries the writer's intensity and glues together the information that the reader needs to know. It is the **music** in writing that makes meaning clear.

Writers keep rehearsing possible first lines, paragraphs, or endings, key scenes or statements that will reveal how what is to be **said** may be **said** best. The **voice** of a piece of writing is the writer's own **voice,** adapted in written language to the subject and audience. We **speak** differently at a funeral or a party, in church or in the locker room, at home or with strangers. We are experienced with using our **individual voices** for many purposes. We have to learn to do this same thing in writing, and to **hear a voice** in our head that may be polished and developed on the page.

The **voice** is not only rehearsed but practiced. We should **hear** what we're writing as we write it. I **dictate** most of my writing and monitor my **voice** as I'm **speaking,** so that the **pace,** the **rhythm,** the **tone** support what I'm trying to **say.**

("Tricks of the Nonfiction Trade," *The Writer,* July 1985)

From paragraph to paragraph, sentence to sentence, repeated key words lead readers from a definition of voice to a description of its effects and the way it is created.

How to . . .

How to Repeat Key Words

To create coherence between paragraphs, repeat key words frequently, especially key words from your thesis and topic sentences. Create variety with synonyms and other related words. To develop an idea within a paragraph, use related words that refer to part of the subject expressed by key words, as Donald Murray does in his third paragraph. Murray refers to the "pace, the rhythm, the tone" of his written "voice," his primary key word.

7b Write transitions to connect ideas

Coherent writing not only repeats key words to develop its subject; it also links topics, sentences, and paragraphs with **transitions.** The word *transition* comes from a word that means "going across." Transitional words, phrases, and sentences are like bridges that enable writers and readers to "go across" from one idea to the next. They make the following connections:

- Addition: *additionally, again, also, and, as well, equally important, first (second, third), for one thing, further, moreover, next, and so forth*

- Alternation: *or, otherwise, nor, rather, instead*

- Comparison: *also, in the same way, likewise, similarly*

- Concession or agreement: *granted, it is true, of course, to be sure*

- Contrast: *after all, and yet, but, conversely, even so, however, in contrast, instead, nevertheless, nonetheless, on the contrary, on the other hand, yet*

- Examples: *as an illustration, for example, for instance, specifically*

- Explanation and logical relation: *as a result, because, consequently, for, for this reason, so, that being the case, therefore, thus, since*

- Place: *above, at this point, below, beyond, close, elsewhere, farther, here, near, next, on the other side, opposite, outside, within, there*

- Summary, emphasis, or conclusion: *accordingly, in conclusion, in other words, in short, in summary, indeed, on the whole, that is, therefore, thus*

- Time: *after, as, at last, at once, at the same time, by degrees, eventually, gradually, immediately, in a short time, in the future, later, meanwhile, promptly, soon, simultaneously, suddenly, then, when, while*

Consider transitions in the following excerpt, in which the writer uses his childhood to make a point about the value of living with risks. Transitions weave action and description into a story, compare the past to the present, and signal conclusions. (Transitions linking paragraphs, sentences, and clauses are emphasized.)

Time transition	**When** I was a boy skating on Brooks Pond, there were no grown-ups around. Once or twice a year, on a weekend day or a holiday, some parents might come by with a thermos of hot cocoa. Maybe they would build a fire (which we were forbid-
Addition	den to do), **and** we would gather around.
Contrast	**But for the most part** the pond was the domain of children. In the absence of adults, we made and enforced our own rules. We had hardly any gear—just some borrowed hockey gloves,
Logical relation	some hand-me-down skates, maybe an elbow pad or two—**so** we played a clean form of hockey, with no high-sticking, no punching, and almost no checking. A single fight could ruin
Emphasis	the whole afternoon. **Indeed,** as I remember it, thirty years later, it was the purest form of hockey I ever saw—until I got to see the Russian national team play the game.
Time, contrast	**But before we could play,** we had to check the ice. We be- came serious junior meteorologists, true connoisseurs of cold. We learned that the best weather for pond skating is plain, clear cold, with starry nights and no snow. (Snow not only mucks up the skating surface but also insulates the ice from the
Addition	colder air above.) **And** we learned that moving water, even the gently flowing Mystic River, is a lot less likely to freeze than
Logical relation	standing water. **So** we skated only on the pond. We learned all the weird whooping and cracking sounds that ice makes as it
Logical relation	expands and contracts, **and thus** when to leave the ice.
Question link	**Do kids learn these things today?** I don't know. How
Contrast	would they? We don't let them. **Instead** we post signs. Ruled by lawyers, cities and towns everywhere try to limit their legal
Contrast	liability. **But try as they might,** they cannot eliminate the un- derlying risk. Liability is a social construct; risk is a natural fact. When it is cold enough, ponds freeze. No sign or fence or ordinance can change that.
Conclusion	**In fact,** by focusing on liability and not teaching our kids how to take risks, we are making their world more dangerous.
Time	**When we were children,** we had to learn to evaluate risks and

Logical relation

handle them on our own. We had to learn, quite literally, to test the waters. **As a result,** we grew up to be savvier about ice and ponds than any kid could be who has skated only under adult supervision on a rink.

(Adapted from Christopher B. Daly, "How the Lawyers Stole Winter," *The Atlantic,* March 1995)

7c | Link sentences with pronouns

Pronouns substitute for nouns and noun phrases (the antecedents of pronouns). The result is smoother reading. In the following example, consider how pronouns substitute for key words and, by so doing, link one sentence to another. Also imagine how much choppier the paragraph would seem if the writer had used only nouns. (Pronouns and antecedents are emphasized.)

In the folklore of the country, numerous superstitions relate to winter weather. Back-country **farmers** examine **their** corn husks—the thicker the husk, the colder the winter. **They** watch the acorn crop—the more acorns, the more severe the season. **They** observe where white-faced **hornets** place **their** paper nests—the higher **they** are, the deeper will be the snow. **They** examine the size and shape and color of the spleens of butchered hogs for clues to the severity of the season. **They** keep track of the blooming of dogwood in the spring—the more abundant the blooms, the more bitter the cold in January.

(Edwin Way Teale, from *Wandering Through Winter*)

How to . . .

How to Link with Transitions and Pronouns

Transitions

Use transitions sparingly. If you organize effectively, your writing will lead naturally from one topic to the next. You'll need few transitions; more would be distracting.

Choose transitions that accurately signal the relationship between ideas and paragraphs—not ones that mean almost what you intend. For example, *and* may mean either "in addition" or "consequently."

Choose transitions that suit the formality of your writing. For example, you may use *so* or *but* in informal writing and *therefore* or *nevertheless* in more formal writing.

Pronouns

Repeat pronouns frequently to substitute for nouns and noun phrases. As reminders, occasionally repeat the nouns or phrases to which pronouns refer.

7d Write "old/new" sentences: include material from preceding sentences in each new sentence

■ Fluent sentences repeat "old business" from earlier sentences—words, ideas, or structural patterns—and add "new business" to develop a topic one step further. Read the following paragraph and consider how each sentence is linked to those that precede it. (Sentences are numbered; "old business" in each sentence is emphasized.)

(1) Be willing to make radical changes in your second draft. (2) If your thesis **changed** while you were writing your first draft, you will base your **second draft** on this new subject. (3) **Even if your thesis** has not **changed,** you may need to shift paragraphs around, eliminate paragraphs, or add new ones. (4) Inexperienced writers often suppose that **revising** a paper means **changing** only a word or two or adding a sentence or two. (5) **This kind of editing** is part of the writing process, but it is not the most important part. (6) **The most important part of rewriting** is a willingness to turn the paper upside down, to shake out of it those ideas that interest you the most, to set them in a form where they will interest the reader, too.

(Adapted from Richard Marius, "Writing Drafts," from *A Writer's Companion.*)

Sentences 1 and 2	*Changes/changed . . . second draft* are key words used in both sentences.
Sentences 2 and 3	*If . . .* in sentence 2 is grammatically parallel with *Even if . . .* in sentence 3 (parallel structure), and the words *thesis . . . chang*ed are key words used in each sentence.
Sentences 3 and 4	*Revising* in sentence 4 connects with *shift paragraphs around, eliminate paragraphs, and add new ones* in sentence 3 (key words).
Sentences 4 and 5	The key words *This kind of editing* in sentence 5 refer to an activity described in sentence 4.
Sentences 5 and 6	In sentence 6, *The most important part* repeats key words from sentence 5, and a dramatic description of revision reminds readers of the key words *radical changes* in sentence 1.

As you rewrite, examine your sentences to see whether they repeat words, ideas, and patterns from earlier sentences. Without these links, your sentences will seem to jump around, disconnected. With them, your sentences will flow.

A note on needless repetition: If you repeat words or sentence patterns unnecessarily, your writing will sound choppy or wordy. (See 21b and 28a–c.)

Sentence Editing

part II. Sentence Editing

Identifying Grammar

Editing Grammar and Usage

Identifying Grammar

Grammar describes how native speakers and writers of a language produce their sentences. It is not so much a list of do's and don'ts as it is a portrait of the way people speak and write. But this description is not what people have in mind when they say, "Watch your grammar!" What they mean is a precise set of language rules known as usage. **Usage** refers to the conventions and language etiquette followed by the members of specific language groups. Grammar says, in effect, "This is what a native speaker or writer does." Usage says, "This is what a speaker or writer ought to do."

The grammar presented in books like this one is actually a combination of the grammar and usage for one version or dialect of English, **Standard Written English.** This is the dialect generally written in schools, the professions, the business world, and the media—and worth knowing because it is so widely shared.

Another reason for learning the grammar presented here is the same one musicians have for learning to read music. Some musicians, unable to read a note, play beautifully, but most have to learn to read music to play well. Like musicians, some writers have an ear for language and write well with seldom a thought for grammar. But most find their writing becomes more accurate, powerful, and expressive the more they know about language. If you're just starting out as a writer, if you doubt you have an "ear" for language, this section will help you develop that ear.

Parts
of Speech

The term **parts of speech** refers to a system for grouping and labeling English words according to their functions in sentences. Traditionally,

How to . . .

How to Identify Key Parts of Speech

Use the following tips to help you identify words as you edit your writing. Recognizing the parts of speech will help you choose the right words to say what you intend.

Nouns

1. Nouns may be preceded by *a, an,* or *the*: *a computer, an apple, the president.*
2. Most nouns may be singular, plural, or possessive: *horse* [singular], *horses* [plural], *horse's* [possessive].
3. Nouns formed from other words end in *-ance* (*guidance*), *-ation* (*donation*), *-dom* (*freedom*), *-ence* (*reference*), *-hood* (*neighborhood*), *-ice* (*justice*), *-ion* (*incision*), *-ist* (*tourist*), *-ity* (*generosity*), *-ment* (*judgment*), *-ness* (*business*), *-ship* (*friendship*).

Verbs

1. If you change the time of an action, a verb changes its form (known as **tense**): *Aaron opened the book. Aaron is opening the book.* (For more on tense, see 8c3.)
2. Verbs formed from other kinds of words end in *-ize* and *-ify*: *realize, identify.*

A note on adverbs: The adverbs *already, always, ever, not, often, only,* and *very* are sometimes placed in the middle of verbs to

words have been divided into eight parts of speech: nouns, pronouns, verbs, adjectives, adverbs, prepositions, conjunctions, and interjections. But some words change classes as their functions change. Consider the uses of the word *present.*

- A verb that describes action: *A geologist will present the next report.*
- A noun that describes an object: *Larry gave his sister a present.*
- An adjective that describes a feature: *This verb is in the present tense.*

8a | Nouns

■ **Nouns** identify persons, places, or things, including ideas, activities, qualities, conditions, and materials.

■ 1 Proper nouns

A **proper noun** is capitalized and names a specific person, place, or thing: *Harriet Beecher Stowe, the Sudan, the Holy Grail.* (See also 40b.)

provide additional information: *Larry has already written the report.* Do not mistake adverbs for verbs.

Adjectives

1. Adjectives answer the questions *Which one? What kind? How many?*: *A fast car* [what kind?].
2. Adjectives formed from other words end in *-able* (*enjoyable*), *-ar* (*spectacular*), *-ent* (*dependent*), *-ful* (*powerful*), *-ial* (*colonial*), *-ible* (*responsible*), *-ing* (*disgusting*), *-ish* (*foolish*), *-ive* (*inventive*), *-less* (*useless*), *-ly* (*kindly*), *-ous* (*generous*), *-y* (*leafy*).
3. Adjectives can be compared using *-er/-est, more/most, less/least*: *happier, most beautiful.*

Adverbs

1. Adverbs answer the questions *How? When? Where? Why?*: *She smiled slyly* [How?].
2. Many adverbs end in *-ly*: *happily, evenly, smoothly.* But adverbs also have other forms: *far, fast, first, not, very,* and *well.* And not all *-ly* words are adverbs: *She gave him a friendly* [adjective] *glance.*
3. Most adverbs can be compared using *-er/-est, more/most, less/least* (*faster, more slowly*): *The couple walked more slowly the closer they came to the front door.*

■ 2 Common nouns

A **common noun** names a general category of person, place, or thing: *pilot, desert, gemstones.*

■ 3 Abstract nouns

An **abstract noun** refers to an intangible, something not perceived by our senses: *joy, mercy, prudence, democracy.* (See also 26b.)

■ 4 Concrete nouns

A **concrete noun** refers to something perceived by our senses: *glove, computer, book, mountain, voter.* (See also 26b.)

■ 5 Count nouns

A **count noun** refers to something that can be counted: *an apple, twenty-nine cents, three cookies, billions of stars.* (See also 30a.) An ESL note: Do not omit the *-s/-es* endings of plural count nouns: *suits, potatoes.*

■ 6   Noncount nouns

A **noncount noun** refers to a mass or quantity that cannot be counted: *pepper, snow, air, iodine, peace.* (See also 30b.)

■ 7   Collective nouns

A **collective noun** names a group acting as a unit: *jury, class, team, community.* (See also 14g and 15c.)

■ 8   Compound nouns

A **compound noun** is made up of more than one word and may be written as separate words (*attorney general*), closed (*makeup, grandfather*), or hyphenated (*brother-in-law*). (For more on hyphens and compounds, see 44b.)

8b | Pronouns

■   A **pronoun** refers to a noun, called its **antecedent,** that gives the pronoun its meaning. Pronouns change form to signal their function in a sentence.

	personal	possessive	reflexive
antecedent	pronoun	pronoun	pronoun

The little boy boasted that he could tie his shoes for himself.

■ 1   Personal pronouns

Personal pronouns refer to specific persons, places, or things. (See also 17a–d.) Singular: *I, me, you, he, she, him, her, it.* Plural: *we, us, you, they, them.*

■ 2   Possessive pronouns

In contrast to possessive nouns, **possessive personal pronouns** have no apostrophe. Singular: *my, mine, your, yours, his, her, hers, its.* Plural: *our, ours, your, yours, their, theirs.* (See also 17d; for ESL, see 32d.)

■ 3   Demonstrative pronouns

A **demonstrative pronoun** (*this, that, these, those*) points to the noun it replaces.

pronoun   antecedent

These are the grapes that make the best jelly.

■ 4 Indefinite pronouns

An **indefinite pronoun** refers to a nonspecific person or thing. (See also 14f and 15d.)

all	anything	everyone	nobody	several
another	both	everything	none	some
any	each	few	no one	somebody
anybody	either	many	nothing	someone
anyone	everybody	neither	one	something

■ 5 Interrogative pronouns

An **interrogative pronoun** begins a question: *who(ever), which(ever), whom(ever), whose, what(ever). Who wrote this poem?*

■ 6 Relative pronouns

A **relative pronoun** (*who, which, whom, whose, that, whoever, whomever*) connects a relative clause to a noun in the main clause. (See also 16d.)

antecedent pronoun   relative clause

We asked directions from a man who was selling newspapers.

■ 7 Intensive and reflexive pronouns

Intensive and **reflexive pronouns** consist of a personal pronoun + *-self* or *-selves*: *myself, yourself, himself, herself, itself, ourselves, yourselves, themselves.* (See also 17g.)

- Intensive pronouns. An **intensive pronoun** emphasizes a noun: *Joan designed the house herself.*

- Reflexive pronouns. A **reflexive pronoun** identifies the receiver of an action as identical to the doer of the action: *Peter rewarded himself with a day off.*

■ 8 Reciprocal pronouns

A **reciprocal pronoun** (*each other, one another*) refers to an individual part of a compound subject: *Pedro and Jack read each other's essays.*

$8c$ | Verbs

■ Verbs express action or state of being: *run, wish, is, appear, become, taste.*

Carol Morales **is campaigning** for a seat in the legislature.

He **seems** content.

■ 1   Helping verbs

Twenty-six **helping verbs** (also called **auxiliary verbs**) help to complete the meaning of verbs: *They have arrived. Have, do,* and *be* may also stand alone as verbs: *I have the answer.* **Modals** act only as helping verbs: *We might leave early.* (See also 13d; for ESL, see 31a–c.)

HAVE, DO, BE	MODALS
have, has, had	can, could, may, might, must, shall,
do, does, did	should, will, would, ought to, had better, had to
be, am, is, are, was, were, being, been	

■ 2   Main verb forms

Except for the verb *to be,* the main verb of a sentence has five forms:

- Base or infinitive form: *I often (play, speak).*
- *-s/-es* or third person form: *He often (plays, speaks).*
- Past tense: *Then I (played, spoke).*
- Past participle: *I have (played, spoken) before.*
- Present participle: *I am (playing, speaking) now.*

A note on participles: When accompanied by helping verbs, participles act as verbs: *They are playing my song.* When they stand without helping verbs, participles act as nouns or adjectives: *Playing is sometimes hard work. Playing softly, the guitarist sang a sad song.* (See 8c8, Verbals, and 10a2, Verbal Phrases; for ESL, see 31f.)

■ 3   Tense

Helping verbs and main verb forms combine to create **tense,** the time when an action occurs. Standard English has six tenses, and each tense has a progressive *-ing* form to indicate continuous action. (See also 13b; for ESL, see 31a.)

- **Present tense:** action that takes place now. *I sigh. He speaks. You/we/they are working.*
- **Past tense:** past action. *I sighed. He spoke. You/we/they were working.*
- **Future tense:** action that will take place. *I will sigh. He will speak. You/we/they will be working.*
- **Present perfect tense:** past action continuing or completed in the present. *I have sighed. He has spoken. You/we/they have been working.*

- **Past perfect tense:** past action completed before another past action. *I had sighed. He had spoken. You/we/they had been working.*

- **Future perfect tense:** action that will begin and end in the future. *I will have sighed. He will have spoken. You/we/they will have been working.*

■ 4 Transitive, linking, and intransitive verbs

Verbs can be classified by their function in a sentence.

- Transitive verbs. A **transitive verb** acts upon someone or something, called the *direct object.* (See 9c.)

  transitive verb   direct object

  The player kicked the ball into the net.

- Linking verbs. A **linking verb** links a subject to a noun, pronoun, or adjective, called the *complement,* that describes the subject. (See also 9d1 and 14c.) Common linking verbs are *be, appear, become, feel, grow, look, remain, seem, smell, sound,* and *taste.*

  linking verb   complement

  Abidjan is the capital of the Ivory Coast.

- Intransitive verbs. An **intransitive verb** does not require an object or complement to complete its meaning, although it may be followed by other words.

  The engine **hummed.** The mechanic **hummed** softly.

■ 5 Voice

Voice identifies whether the subject of a verb commits the action of the verb or is acted on.

- Active voice. In the **active voice,** the subject is active; it performs the action of the verb: *Jane mailed the letter.* The subject, *Jane,* performs the action.

- Passive voice. In the **passive voice,** the subject is passive; it is acted on or receives the action of the verb: *The letter was mailed.* The subject, *letter,* is acted on. To form the passive voice, use a form of the helping verb *be* + the past participle of the main verb: *was mailed.*

Do not confuse passive voice with past tense. A verb in the passive voice may appear in any tense. Present tense: *The letter is being mailed.* Past tense: *The letter was mailed.* Future tense: *The letter will be mailed.* (For more on voice, see 20a and 28c4; for ESL, see 31d.)

▪6 Mood

Mood identifies the kind of statement a verb makes: an expression of fact, a command, or a hypothetical statement.

- Indicative mood. The **indicative** mood expresses facts or opinions, makes assertions, asks questions: *She looked happy. They would have won. Are you sad?*

- Imperative mood. The **imperative** mood makes commands or direct requests: *Come home. Try again.*

- Subjunctive mood. The **subjunctive** mood makes hypothetical statements, including wishes, speculations, assumptions, recommendations, and indirect requests: *If I were you, I would apply for the job.* (See 13f.)

▪7 Regular and irregular verbs

Verbs can be classified by their past tense and past participle forms. (See also 13a.)

- Regular verbs. **Regular verbs** form their past tense and past participle forms in regular ways, by adding *-d* or *-ed*: *believe* [present tense], *believed* [past tense], *believed* [past participle]; *play* [present tense], *played* [past tense], *played* [past participle].

- Irregular verbs. **Irregular verbs** form their past tense and past participle in "irregular" ways: *begin* [present tense], *began* [past tense], *begun* [past participle]; *eat* [present tense], *ate* [past tense], *eaten* [past participle].

▪8 Verbals

Verbals are verbs acting as other parts of speech: nouns, adverbs, or adjectives.

- Gerunds. A **gerund** is the *-ing* verb form standing alone and acting as a noun: *Writing is both a craft and an art.* The gerund *writing* is the subject of the sentence. (See also 10a2; for ESL, see 31f.)

- Participles. A **participle** is the verb form ending with *-ing, -d, -ed, -en, -n,* or *-t.* When a participle stands alone, it acts as an adjective to modify or provide information about nouns and pronouns. (See also 10a2.)

  Please give me **written** instructions.

  Writing rapidly, she completed the letter in fifteen minutes.

- Infinitives. An **infinitive** consists of *to* plus the base form of the verb: *to write.* It may act as a noun, adjective, or adverb. (For ESL, see 31f.)

  infinitive as a noun (the subject of the sentence)
  ┌─────────┐
  To write effortlessly is the goal of every writer.

infinitive as an adjective modifying *assignment*

Here is your assignment to write for next week.

infinitive as an adverb modifying *use*

Use a computer to write your essay.

■ 9 Two-word verbs

A **two-word verb** (also called a **phrasal verb**) consists of a verb and a preposition-like word called a *particle*. The meaning of a two-word verb differs from the meanings of its individual words: *Please put out* [extinguish] *your cigarette. I put the book away* [*put away* means to remove to a proper place]. *Let's put off* [postpone] *our date until next week.* (For ESL, see 31g.)

8*d* Adjectives and articles

■   An **adjective** modifies a noun or pronoun. It answers the questions *Which one? What kind?* or *How many?* (See also 18a, c, and d; for ESL, see 32e.)

which one

That rock may contain a fossil.

what kind   what kind

The dark clouds warned of a dangerous storm.

how many   how many

Lacrosse is played by two teams of ten players each.

A note on adjective series: When two or more adjectives are used together without commas separating them, they must be arranged in a particular order. (See 32e3.)

■ 1 Comparisons

In comparisons, adjectives change form by adding *-er* or *-est* or are preceded by *more, most, less, least.* (See also 18d.)

POSITIVE	COMPARATIVE	SUPERLATIVE
happy	happier	happiest
beautiful	more beautiful	most beautiful
intelligent	less intelligent	least intelligent

■ 2 Articles

The **articles** *a, an,* and *the* are considered adjectives. *The* is a **definite article** referring to specific persons, places, or things: *the dancer, the house. A* and *an* are **indefinite articles** referring to indefinite persons, places, or things: *a lawyer, an apple.* (For ESL, see 30.)

8e Adverbs

■ An **adverb** modifies verbs, adjectives, or other adverbs. It answers the questions *How? When? Where? Why? Under what circumstances? To what extent?* (See also 18a and c; for ESL, see 32e.)

an adverb modifying an adverb: how

The old man whispered very softly.

an adverb modifying the verb *revise*: when

Revise your paper later.

an adverb modifying the verb *are camping*: where

The scouts are camping nearby.

Comparisons

In comparisons, adverbs change form by adding *-er* or *-est* or are preceded by *more, most, less, least.* (See also 18d.)

POSITIVE	COMPARATIVE	SUPERLATIVE
fast	faster	fastest
slowly	more slowly	most slowly

8f Prepositions

■ A **preposition** usually precedes a noun or pronoun called the *object of the preposition.* Together they form a **prepositional phrase** that modifies other words in a sentence. (See also 10a1; for ESL, see 32f.)

preposition object   preposition object

The children ran into the room and knelt before the fire.

COMMON PREPOSITIONS

about	along	at	beside	by
above	among	before	besides	concerning
across	around	behind	between	considering
after	as	below	beyond	despite
against	as well as	beneath	but	down

during	into	opposite	than	underneath
except	like	out	through	unlike
for	near	over	throughout	until
from	next	past	till	up
in	of	respecting	to	upon
in addition to	off	round	toward	with/within/
instead of	on	since	under	without

A note on two-word prepositions: Prepositions may also consist of two or more words: *according to, as many as, different from, in spite of, together with,* and so forth.

8g | Conjunctions

■ A **conjunction** links words, phrases, or clauses and signals their relationship as grammatically equal or unequal.

■1 Coordinating conjunctions

Coordinating conjunctions (*and, but, for, so, or, nor, yet*) link grammatically equal words and word groups. (See also 11b7, 14d, 15a, and 19a; for ESL, see 32b3.)

Kim **and** Jean played their best tennis of the season, **but** they lost to superior opponents.

■2 Correlative conjunctions

Correlative conjunctions are word pairs (*both/and, either/or, neither/nor, not/but, not only/but also, whether/or*) that link grammatically equal words and word groups. (See also 14e, 15b, and 19c.)

Both the Earl of Oxford **and** Ben Jonson have been proposed as the true author of William Shakespeare's plays.

■3 Subordinating conjunctions

Subordinating conjunctions begin adverb clauses and link them to independent clauses. (See also 10b2.)

after	even if	since	until
although	even though	so	when
as	how	than	where
as if	if	that	wherever
as though	in order that	though	whether
because	rather than	till	while
before	once	unless	why

```
┌──── subordinate clause ────┐ ┌──────── independent clause ────────┐
```
After they finished breakfast, the campers began loading their gear into
the canoes.

▪4 Conjunctive adverbs

A **conjunctive adverb** is used with a semicolon to link independent
clauses. (See also 12b3 and 35b.)

also	furthermore	likewise	otherwise
anyhow	hence	meanwhile	similarly
anyway	however	moreover	still
besides	incidentally	nevertheless	then
consequently	indeed	next	therefore
finally	instead	nonetheless	thus

It has rained five inches in the last week; **however,** the drought is far
from over.

8*h* | Interjections

▪   An **interjection** is a strong expression of feeling or call for attention, followed by a comma or exclamation point: *Oh, I'm sorry to hear that.*
Ouch! I've pinched my hand in the door.

9 | Sentence Parts ▪

A sentence has two parts: a *subject* and a *predicate.* Together they make
a complete statement, question, exclamation, or command. In most commands, the subject *you* is not stated.

```
          ┌─ subject ─┐ ┌──────── predicate ────────┐
```
- A statement: The sonnet has two forms, the Italian and the Elizabethan.

```
                          ┌──────── predicate ────────┐
```
- A command with an unstated subject *you:* Be sure to bring the volley-
ball to the picnic!

9*a* | Subjects

▪   The **subject** of a sentence names the person, place, or thing that
acts, is acted on, or is described. Subjects may precede or follow the predicate, but usually precede it.

9a   agr/frag

Algae produce their food through photosynthesis.

The batik technique for dyeing fabric was developed in Malaya.

In a box under the porch slept **four tiny kittens.**

How to Identify Sentence Parts

How to . . .

Use the following tips to help you identify sentence parts as you edit your writing. Recognizing sentence parts will help you write complete sentences and arrange the parts for greatest effect.

Subjects

Ask *Who* or *What* + the verb + the remainder of the sentence. *Algae produce their food through photosynthesis.* What produce their food through photosynthesis? *Algae.* (Note that not all sentences open with the subject.)

Direct objects

To identify direct objects, locate the subject and verb. Use them in a question ending with *whom?* or *what? Judy is growing a new variety of hosta in her garden.* Judy is growing what? The answer is the complete direct object: *a new variety of hosta.* The simple direct object is a noun or pronoun: *variety.*

Indirect objects

Indirect objects occur with certain verbs: *ask, bring, buy, find, give, get, hand, lend, offer, pay, pour, promise, read, sell, send, show, take, teach, tell, throw, write.* To identify indirect objects, look for the words *to* or *for,* or see whether you can insert them before the person to or for whom an action is done. You may have to rearrange the sentence: *Dr. Watson gave Sherlock Holmes a clue.* [Dr. Watson gave a clue to Sherlock Holmes.]

Subject complements

Subject complements are nouns or adjectives that appear with linking verbs such as *appear, become, be, feel, grow, look, taste, seem, smell. The bread smells delicious* [the complement *delicious* modifies the subject *bread*].

Object complements

Object complements are nouns or adjectives that modify the direct objects of verbs such as *appoint, call, choose, consider, color, elect, find, make, name, ordain, paint, think: The umpire called the runner safe* [the adjective *safe* modifies the direct object *runner*].

■ 1   Simple subjects

The **simple subject** of a sentence is the noun or pronoun by itself, without modifying words, phrases, or clauses: *algae, technique, kittens.*

■ 2   Complete subjects

The **complete subject** includes the noun or pronoun and all of its modifiers: *the batik technique for dyeing fabric, four tiny kittens.*

■ 3   Compound subjects

A **compound subject** consists of two or more simple subjects linked by a conjunction.

Muscle strength and aerobic efficiency are essential to physical fitness.

9*b* Predicates

■ 1   Simple predicates

The **simple predicate** of a sentence consists of a verb and its helping verbs, if any.

The locksmith **is resetting** the tumblers of the lock.

■ 2   Complete predicates

A **complete predicate** consists of the simple predicate and all words associated with it: modifiers, objects, and complements.

       ┌── verb ──┐┌──── object ────┐
The locksmith is resetting the tumblers of the lock.

■ 3   Compound predicates

A **compound predicate** consists of two or more predicates with the same subject.

┌── Subject ──┐┌──── predicate ────┐   ┌── predicate ──┐
The locksmith reset the tumblers of the lock and made a new key.

Objects

■ 1 Direct objects

A **direct object** is the person, place, or thing that receives the action of a transitive verb. (See also 8c4.)

┌── verb ──┐ ┌──── direct object ────┐
Judy is growing a new variety of hosta in her garden.

■ 2 Indirect objects

An **indirect object** occurs with certain verbs to identify to whom or for whom an action occurs.

┌ subject ┐ ┌ verb ┐┌ indirect object ┐ ┌ direct object ┐
Dr. Watson gave Sherlock Holmes a clue.

9d Complements

■   **Complements** complete the meaning of a verb and provide additional information about a subject. (See also 14c and 18b.)

■ 1 Subject complements

A **subject complement** is a noun or adjective that describes the subject of a linking verb such as *become, be, feel, taste.* Subject complements are sometimes called *predicate adjectives* or *predicate nouns.* (For more on linking verbs, see 8c4.)

┌ subject complement: an adjective ┐
The sunset is beautiful.

┌ subject complement: a noun ┐
The prince will soon become king.

■ 2 Object complements

An **object complement** is a noun or adjective that follows a direct object and describes it.

┌ subject ┐ ┌ verb ┐ ┌ direct object ┐ ┌ object complement: an adjective ┐
The jury found the defendant guilty.

$9e$ | Basic English sentence patterns

English sentences can be grouped into five basic patterns according to their parts. Knowing these patterns will help you construct effective sentences. (For more on writing effective sentences, see Chapters 20 and 21.)

Pattern 1: Subject + verb

subject verb
Writers write.

Pattern 2: Subject + verb + direct object

subject verb   direct object
Some writers write books.

Pattern 3: Subject + verb + indirect object + direct object

subject   verb indirect object direct object
Many writers write their friends letters.

Pattern 4: Subject + verb + subject complement

subject verb subject complement
Writers are creative.

Pattern 5: Subject + verb + direct object + object complement

subject   verb   direct object   object complement
Envious writers call successful writers lucky.

chapter 10 Phrases, Clauses, and Sentence Types

To add detail to your writing, you can expand the five sentence patterns just described using single words, phrases, or clauses.

$10a$ | Phrases

A **phrase** is a grammatically related group of words lacking a subject, a verb, or both. Within a sentence it may act as a noun, verb, adjective, or adverb.

phrase as a noun   phrase as an adjective

Kevin's decision to return the lost wallet was not very difficult to make.

1 Prepositional phrases

A **prepositional phrase** consists of a preposition + a noun or pronoun (called the *object of the preposition*) + any related words. (See also 8f; for ESL, see 32f.)

preposition modifiers object

at the morning roll call

Prepositional phrases may act as adjectives (telling which one or what kind), as adverbs (telling how, when, or where), or as nouns.

prepositional phrase as an adjective: which one

The man in the gray suit is my father.

prepositional phrase as an adverb: where

Sally is studying in the biology lab.

prepositional phrase as a noun: subject complement

The best time to see your instructor is before class.

2 Verbal phrases

A **verbal phrase** is a verb and its related words acting as a noun, adjective, or adverb. (See 8c8.)

■ Gerund phrases. A **gerund phrase** consists of the *-ing* form of a verb (the present participle) and any related words: *campaigning for office, swimming in the ocean, exercising regularly*. In a sentence, a gerund phrase acts as a noun. (For ESL, see 31f.)

gerund phrase as a subject

Campaigning for office requires energy and money.

gerund phrase as a direct object

I enjoy swimming in the ocean.

gerund phrase as a complement

One key to good health is exercising regularly.

- Participial phrases. A **participial phrase** consists of the *-ing, -d, -ed, -en, -n,* or *t* form of the verb (the present or past participle) and any related words. A participial phrase always acts as an adjective modifying a noun or pronoun. (See also 8c8 and 11b3.)

participial phrase modifying a subject

Gazing at the painting, she was reminded of the house where she was born.

participial phrase modifying a direct object

The soldier put on a uniform covered with ribbons and medals.

- Infinitive phrases. An **infinitive phrase** consists of the word *to* + the base form of the verb + any related words. It may act as a noun, adjective, or adverb.

infinitive phrase as a noun: direct object

Paul wanted to learn silk screening.

infinitive phrase as an adjective modifying place

Unfortunately, the library is no longer a place to find peace and quiet.

infinitive phrase as an adverb modifying *use*

Use a spell checker to help you proofread your writing.

■ 3 Appositive phrases

An **appositive phrase** describes a preceding noun or noun phrase. It acts like a noun or noun equivalent.

noun   appositive phrase

Shiraz, the ancient capital of Persia, is now a pilgrimage center for Shiite Muslims.

■ 4 Absolute phrases

An **absolute phrase** consists of a noun or noun phrase + the participle of a verb (the *-ing, -d, -ed, -en, -n,* or *-t* form) preceded or followed by a comma. An absolute phrase modifies an entire sentence or clause.

Hands waving, the children clamored for the teacher's attention.

The sailors raised the sails eagerly, **their minds filled with dreams of home.**

10*b* | Clauses

■ A **clause** is a group of words with a subject and a predicate: *roses are red, where the buffalo roam, which is best.*

- Independent clauses. An **independent clause** (often called a **main clause**) can stand alone as a complete sentence: *Roses are red.*
- Dependent clauses. A **dependent clause** cannot stand alone: *where the buffalo roam, which essay is best.* Within a sentence a dependent clause may act as a noun, an adjective, or an adverb: *We were told to decide which essay is best.* The dependent clause *which essay is best* acts as a noun, the direct object of the sentence.

(To distinguish between independent and dependent clauses, see 11b1, the "yes/no" question test.)

■ **1** Noun clauses

Noun clauses may act as subjects, objects, complements, or appositives. They usually begin with *how, that, which, who, whoever, whom, whomever, what, whatever, when, where, whether, whose, why.*

┌─── subject ───┐
Where he went is a mystery to me.

┌─── direct object ───┐
Researchers have discovered what causes depression.

■ **2** Adverb clauses

An **adverb clause** (often referred to as a **subordinate clause**) begins with a subordinating conjunction such as *after, because, since, when.* (See 8g3 for a list.) Adverb clauses modify verbs, adjectives, or adverbs, and tell how, when, where, why, or under what conditions. (See also 11b4.)

┌── adverb clause that tells when ──┐
After the hailstorm had ended, the farmers inspected their damaged crops.

■ **3** Adjective clauses

An **adjective clause** (also called a **relative clause**) begins with a *relative pronoun* (*who, whoever, which, that, whose, whom, whomever*) or, occasionally, with a *relative adverb* (*when, where, why*). Relative clauses act as adjectives and tell which one or what kind. (See also 11b5.)

We plan to hire someone **who can do technical writing.**

The land **where the buffalo roam** has been shrunk to a few national parks and preserves.

10c Sentence types

Sentences can be identified by the clauses they contain or by their purposes. Knowing these sentence types will help you create sentences that are emphatic, varied, and interesting to read. (For more on emphasis and variety, see Chapters 20 and 21.)

■ **1** Classifying sentences by their clauses

■ Simple sentences. A **simple sentence** has one independent clause and no dependent clauses. It may also have compound subjects or predicates, and one-word or one-phrase modifiers.

> ┌──────── independent clause ────────┐
> The Roman poet Virgil is the author of the *Aeneid*.

> ┌──────────── independent clause ────────────┐
> Adam and Eve left the Garden of Eden and entered a treacherous new world.

■ Compound sentences. A **compound sentence** has two or more independent clauses and no dependent clauses. Its clauses may be linked by the coordinating conjunction *and, or, but, yet, so, for, nor* or by a semicolon. (See also 34a and 35a.)

> ┌──────── independent clause ────────┐ ┌──────── independent clause ────────┐
> A penny saved may be a penny earned, but the earnings don't amount to much.

■ Complex sentences. A **complex sentence** has an independent clause and at least one dependent clause.

> ┌──────── dependent clause ────────┐ ┌──────── independent clause ────────┐
> When the wind changed direction, the temperature began to drop.

■ Compound-complex sentences. **A compound-complex sentence** has at least two independent clauses and at least one dependent clause.

> ┌──────── independent clause ────────┐ ┌──────── independent clause ────────┐
> ┌─ dependent clause ─┐ ┌─ dependent clause ─┐
> Imran knew that he should help, but he wasn't sure what he should do.

■ **2** Classifying sentences by their purpose

■ Declarative sentences. A **declarative sentence** makes a statement: *Bumblebees hummed in the doorway of the abandoned house.*

■ Interrogative sentences. An **interrogative sentence** asks a question: *Where is Lake Agassiz located?*

■ Imperative sentences. An **imperative sentence** issues a command, makes a direct request, or gives advice: *When you come to the meeting, bring your copy of the annual report.*

■ Exclamatory sentences. An **exclamatory sentence** makes an exclamation of excitement or emotion: *That's the best performance of* Othello *I've seen!*

Editing Grammar and Usage

chapter 11

Editing Sentence Fragments

How to Edit Sentence Fragments

Sentence fragments break the thread that ties related ideas together. The result can be writing that feels choppy or too informal for the occasion. Answer these questions to see whether you're likely to write fragments:

1. Do you write in an informal, conversational style?
2. Do you punctuate by length, putting in a period when you feel a pause or when the sentence seems too long?
3. Are you unsure what makes a complete sentence?
4. Have readers pointed out that you write fragments?

If you answer yes to any of these questions, look for sentence fragments in your writing.

How to look for fragments:

1. Beginning at the end of your paper, read each sentence aloud. Isolating each sentence in this way will help you hear the incomplete thoughts that signal fragments.
2. Look for clue words that sometimes signal sentence fragments: (a) -*ing* verbs without accompanying helping verbs (see 11b3); (b) opening subordinating conjunctions such as *although, because, when, after, if,* and so forth (see 11b4); (c) relative pronouns—*who, which, whom, that*—at the beginning of statements that are not questions. (See 11b5.) A computer tip: Use the Find or Search and Replace commands in your word-processing program to look for these clue words.

How to identify fragments: Use the "yes/no" question test. (See 11b1.) If a word group is not already a question, turn it into a yes or no question. If it makes sense and sounds complete, it is a complete sentence; if not, it is a fragment.

Fix fragments by connecting them to nearby complete sentences or by rewriting them as complete sentences, with subjects, verbs, and, if necessary, helping verbs. (See 11a.)

What to study: Chapter 9, Sentence Parts, and Chapter 10, Phrases, Clauses, and Sentence Types.

11*a* | Connect fragments to complete sentences or rewrite them as complete sentences

■ A **sentence fragment** is an incomplete sentence. To be complete, a sentence must have an independent clause—a subject and verb that can stand alone. (See 9a and b, 10b.) In the following examples, fragments are italicized.

> The individual most responsible for making Texas part of the United States was Sam Houston. *War hero, president of Texas, and its first senator.*
>
> [The italicized word group is a series of noun phrases without a verb.]

> Last night I opened my window to enjoy the autumn air. *Which unfortunately was filled with ragweed pollen from the vacant lot next door.*
>
> [The italicized word group has a subject and verb, *which . . . was filled,* but *which* cannot be the subject of an independent clause.]

If readers indicate that you sometimes write fragments, you can teach yourself to identify and rewrite them as complete sentences. Most can be fixed in one of two ways.

■ **1** Connecting fragments

Connect the fragment to a nearby complete sentence. Repunctuate if necessary. Use this method if your main idea is in the complete sentence rather than in the fragment.

> The individual most responsible for making Texas part of the United
>
> States was Sam Houston/~~War~~ ^, war^ hero, president of Texas, and its
>
> first senator.

■ **2** Rewriting fragments

Rewrite the fragment as a complete sentence. Add words or change word forms; if necessary, rearrange for clarity or emphasis. Use this method to emphasize an idea in the fragment or to create two sentences where one would be too long.

> Last night I opened my window to enjoy the autumn air. ^*Unfortunately, it*^ ~~Which unfor-~~
>
> ~~tunately~~ was filled with ragweed pollen from the vacant lot next door.
>
> [The relative pronoun *which* cannot be the subject of a sentence. The revision substitutes the personal pronoun *it,* which can be a subject, and rearranges for emphasis.]

11*b* Learn the clues that signal sentence fragments

■ 1   The "yes/no" question test

If you're unsure whether a word group is a complete sentence, try the **"yes/no" question test.** If it is not already a question, turn the word group into a yes or no question. Rearrange words if necessary. If the question makes sense and sounds complete, you have an independent clause, which can be punctuated as a complete sentence. If not, you have a fragment.

English has borrowed many words from Native American languages.

[A "yes/no" question: *Has English borrowed many words from Native American languages?* The question makes sense and sounds complete. The original is, therefore, an independent clause and may be punctuated as a sentence.]

Borrowing many words from Native American languages.

[*Is borrowing many words from Native American languages?* This question sounds incomplete. The original is, therefore, a fragment.]

Because English has borrowed many words from Native American languages.

[*Has because English borrowed many words from Native American languages?* The question doesn't make sense; the original is, therefore, a fragment.]

Certain word groups are sometimes written and punctuated as complete sentences. Learn to recognize them as sentence fragments. (See 11b2–8.)

■ 2   Noun phrases without verbs

Look for noun phrases called **appositives** that describe a word at the end of the preceding sentence. If you find a noun phrase without an accompanying verb, you've found a fragment. Usually you can connect these fragments to the preceding sentence with a comma. (See also 10a3.)

The first African-American to earn widespread fame for his novels was
, *author*
Richard Wright/~~Author~~ of <u>Native Son</u> and <u>Black Boy</u>.

[A "yes/no" question: *Has the author of* Native Son *and* Black Boy? It sounds incomplete and is, therefore, a fragment.]

■ 3   Phrases with *-ing* verbs and no helping verbs

Phrases with *-ing* verbs and no helping verbs are participial phrases that cannot be punctuated as complete sentences. They lack subjects and complete verbs. (See 10a2.) Usually you can connect these fragments to the preceding sentence.

> The greatest environmental threat to equatorial Africa is the Sahara
> *, spreading*
> Desert⁄ S̶p̶r̶e̶a̶d̶i̶n̶g̶ southward during ten years of severe drought.
>
> [A "yes/no" question: *Is spreading southward during ten years of severe drought?* It sounds incomplete, and the original is, therefore, a fragment.]

■ 4 Word groups beginning with subordinating conjunctions

Subordinating conjunctions such as *after, because,* and *when* link dependent to independent clauses. (See 8g3 for a complete list.) Although a dependent clause has a subject and verb, it cannot stand alone as a complete sentence. If you find one standing by itself, you've found a fragment. Connect it to a sentence nearby. If necessary, move it next to the words it modifies, as in this example.

> *Because his paintings appeal to nostalgia and sentimentality,*
> ⁄ Norman Rockwell is an artist admired by many. B̶e̶c̶a̶u̶s̶e̶ ̶h̶i̶s̶ ̶p̶a̶i̶n̶t̶i̶n̶g̶s̶
>
> a̶p̶p̶e̶a̶l̶ ̶t̶o̶ ̶n̶o̶s̶t̶a̶l̶g̶i̶a̶ ̶a̶n̶d̶ ̶s̶e̶n̶t̶i̶m̶e̶n̶t̶a̶l̶i̶t̶y̶.
>
> [A "yes/no" question: *Is because his painting appeals to nostalgia and sentimentality?* This is a nonsense question, and the original is, therefore, a fragment.]

A note on punctuation: Introductory phrases and clauses are usually set off from the main part of the sentence with a comma. (See 34b.)

■ 5 Word groups beginning with relative pronouns

Relative pronouns (*who, whom, which, that*) link a group of words—an adjective clause—to an independent clause. (See 10b3.) Although it has a subject and verb, a relative clause cannot stand alone as a complete sentence. If you find a capitalized relative pronoun at the beginning of a word group that is not a question, you've probably found a fragment.

> *, who*
> Each judge gave a long speech praising the contestants⁄ W̶h̶o̶ stood
>
> near the podium, smiling nervously, waiting for the winner to be
>
> announced.
>
> [A "yes/no" question: *Is who stood near the podium smiling nervously, waiting for the winner to be announced?* The result is a nonsense question, and the original is, therefore, a fragment.]

■ **6** Lists punctuated as sentences

Connect fragmentary lists to the clause that introduces them. Use a colon, a dash, or an introductory phrase: *for example, such as, including,* and so forth. (See 36a and 39a.)

Plans for rehearsing the play should be precise$\overset{: two}{\underset{\wedge}{/\text{Two}}}$ weeks for

memorizing the script, two weeks for learning the music, one month for

practicing the dance routines.

[To hear the fragment, apply the "yes/no" question test to the list.]

■ **7** Disconnected compound predicates

Compound predicates are verbs linked by the coordinating conjunctions *and, but, so, for, or, yet, nor,* or the adverb *then.* (See 9b3.) If one part of a compound predicate is separate from the other and punctuated as a complete sentence, it is a fragment. Connect the fragment to the preceding sentence.

Most viewers praise the artistry in <u>Birth of a Nation</u>$\overset{but}{\underset{\wedge}{/\text{But}}}$ condemn the

movie for its racism and distortions of American history.

Their engines groaning, several cars slowly climbed the steep mountain

road$\overset{, then}{\underset{\wedge}{/\text{Then}}}$ disappeared over the summit.

[To hear the fragments in these examples, apply the "yes/no" question test to each statement punctuated as a sentence. You'll be able to distinguish complete sentences from fragments.]

■ **8** Long prepositional phrases

Look for phrases beginning with *during, concerning, except, in addition to, instead of.* (See 8f for a list of prepositions.) If the phrase is disconnected from an independent clause, it is a fragment. Connect it to the preceding sentence.

Senator Stevens proposed that all welfare recipients receive job training

or education$\overset{in}{\underset{\wedge}{/\text{In}}}$ addition to welfare checks.

[To hear the fragment, apply the "yes/no" question test to each statement punctuated as a sentence.]

11*c* Exception: in certain situations, you may write fragments for special effect

Most writing for school, business, and the professions requires complete sentences. But occasionally, in personal, informal, or emotionally charged writing, you may write fragments to emphasize an idea, avoid repetition, or create speech rhythms. To decide whether a fragment is appropriate, consider whether the situation permits informal or emotionally charged writing. Write fragments sparingly. (Fragments are italicized in the following examples.)

■ **1 A fragment for emphasis and economy**

A beautiful woman, we say in English. *But a handsome man.* "Handsome" is the masculine equivalent of—and refusal of—a compliment which has accumulated certain demeaning overtones, by being reserved for women only.

(Susan Sontag, "A Woman's Beauty: Put-down or Power Source?")

■ **2 Fragments for emphasis, feeling, and speech rhythms**

Family language, my family's sounds: the voices of my parents and sisters and brother. Their voices insisting: You belong here. We are family members. *Related. Special to one another.* Listen! *Voices singing and sighing, rising and straining, then surging, teeming with pleasure which burst syllables into fragments of laughter.* At times it seemed there was steady quiet only when, from another room, the rustling whispers of my parents faded and I edged closer to sleep.

(Richard Rodriguez, "Aria: A Memoir of a Bilingual Childhood," *American Scholar*)

12 Fixing Comma Splices and Fused Sentences

12*a* Fix comma splices by repunctuating or rewriting

A **comma splice** is two or more independent clauses (grammatically complete word groups) linked by a comma. They are "spliced" together as if they were parts of one sentence instead of being punctuated as the separate statements they actually are. Consider the examples on page 78. Independent clauses are italicized.

How to Edit Comma Splices

Comma splices are errors that blur the boundaries between separate ideas and may make your sentences difficult to read. Answer these questions to see whether you're likely to write comma splices:

1. Do you come from a background where British English is written or speak a first language other than English?
2. Are you unsure how to recognize independent clauses?
3. Do you rarely use semicolons in your writing, relying instead on commas to signal pauses?

If you answer yes to any of these questions, reread your writing and look for comma splices.

How to look for comma splices:

1. Look for commas. A computer tip: Use the Find or Search and Replace command in your word-processing program to locate commas automatically.
2. Following a comma, look for personal pronouns (*he, she, it, we, they*). (See 12b2.)
3. Following a comma, look for two kinds of linking words: transitions (*for example, in addition,* and so forth) and conjunctive adverbs (*however, therefore*). (For a complete list of these words, see 12b3.)

To identify comma splices, answer these questions about the word groups before and after a comma:

1. Do both word groups contain their own subject and verb? (See 12b1.)
2. If so, can you replace the comma with a period and make a complete sentence of each? If you answer yes, you've written a comma splice. (See 12b1.)
3. Have you joined two word groups with a comma and a linking word other than *and, but, or, for, so, yet, nor*? If each word group can be a complete sentence by itself, you've written a comma splice. (See 12b3.)

Fix comma splices by repunctuating with a period, semicolon, colon, or dash; rewrite, turning one independent clause into a dependent clause or a phrase. (See 12a.)

What to study: 9a and b, Subjects and Predicates; 10b, Clauses; 10c, Sentence Types; 35, The Semicolon; 36, The Colon; and 39a, The Dash.

Ramon performed well on the first test, *he expected to do even better* on the second.

[*Ramon performed well* is one independent clause with its own subject and predicate; *he expected to do even better* is a second.]

In Standard Written English, independent clauses are separated by more than a comma. If readers indicate that you write comma splices, you can learn to identify them and fix them. Choose the solution that helps you emphasize the point you want to make.

A note on ESL and dialects: Some languages and English dialects permit comma splices; Standard Written English does not.

■ 1 Repunctuating

■ Periods. Use periods to turn each clause into a separate sentence.

Ramon performed well on the first test/ ~~he~~ _{. He} expected to do even better on

the second.

■ Semicolons. Use a semicolon (;) to join related independent clauses when they are nearly equal in importance. (See 35a.)

Ramon performed well on the first test/ _; he expected to do even better on

the second.

■ Colons. Use a colon (:) to join independent clauses when one introduces or explains the other. (See 36a.)

Professor Li is the best instructor I've had/ _: he knows his subject and how

to present it in an imaginative way.

■ Dashes. Use a dash to join independent clauses when the second makes a surprising or abrupt response to the first. (See 39a.)

Alison asked Betsy if she knew where the car keys were/ —she didn't.

■ 2 Adding a coordinating conjunction

Add a coordinating conjunction (*and, but, or, nor, so, yet, for*) following the comma that joins two independent clauses. The result is a compound sentence. (See 10c1.)

Ramon performed well on the first test, _{*and*} he expected to do even better on

the second.

■ 3 Rewriting to create one complete sentence

- Adding a subordinating conjunction. Add a subordinating conjunction (*because, although, when,* and so forth) to one clause to connect it grammatically to the other. (See 8g3.) The result is a complex sentence that emphasizes one clause and deemphasizes the other. (See 10c1.)

Because
Ramon performed well on the first test, he expected to do even better on
ʌ
the second.

- Turning a clause into a phrase. Turn one clause into a phrase that modifies the remaining independent clause. The result is a simple sentence. (See 10c1.)

       After performing   *Ramon*
~~Ramon performed~~ well on the first test, ~~he~~ expected to do even better on
          ʌ   ʌ

the second.

12b | Learn the clues that signal comma splices

■ 1 Independent clauses on both sides of a comma

Study the words on both sides of a comma. If you can put a period after both passages, you've found two independent clauses and a comma splice. Fix the comma splice by repunctuating or rewriting.

                                                     ;
I'm not going to college because my parents told me to/there are subjects
                                                ʌ

I want to study.

[To the left of the comma, *I'm not going to college* is an independent clause; to the right, *there are specific subjects* is an independent clause.]

To identify independent clauses, use the "yes/no" question test. (See 11b1.) The first word group in the preceding example becomes *Am I going to college because my parents told me to?* The second becomes *Are there specific subjects I want to study?* Both questions sound complete and make sense; they are, therefore, independent clauses joined by a comma—a comma splice.

■ 2 A second clause that begins with a pronoun

In some comma splices the subject of the second independent clause is a pronoun referring to the subject of the first.

Julian refused the award for heroism, ~~he~~ said he had only done what

anyone would.

[The *he* following the comma is the subject of the second independent clause; it also refers to the subject of the first, *Julian*.]

■ 3   Independent clauses joined by a comma and a transition or conjunctive adverb

Transitions and conjunctive adverbs link words and word groups. Here are the most common:

accordingly	conversely	in fact	otherwise
after all	even so	in other words	similarly
also	finally	in the first place	specifically
anyhow	for example	likewise	still
anyway	for instance	meanwhile	subsequently
as a matter of fact	furthermore	moreover	then
as a result	hence	nevertheless	therefore
at any rate	however	next	thus
at the same time	indeed	now	that is
besides	instead	of course	
certainly	in addition	on the contrary	
consequently	in conclusion	on the other hand	

These words appear similar to the coordinating conjunctions *and, but, for, nor, or, so,* and *yet.* But they are grammatically different kinds of words. Joining independent clauses with a comma + a transition or conjunctive adverb produces a comma splice. Use a semicolon instead.

Mass transit offers many environmental benefits; for example, the

nitrogen emissions responsible for smog are greatly reduced.

[Two independent clauses linked by a comma and the transition *for example* produce a comma splice. To join independent clauses, use a semicolon before a transition.]

John did not enjoy mathematics; however, if he was going to study

economics, he had to understand statistics.

[Two independent clauses linked by a comma and the conjunctive adverb *however* produce a comma splice. To join independent clauses, use a semicolon before a conjunctive adverb.]

A note on other uses of conjunctive adverbs: A comma + a transition or conjunctive adverb does not always signal a comma splice: *Both parents may work part-time, however, to share the care of their children.* The group of words before *however* is an independent clause that can stand alone. But the second is a phrase. The commas before and after *however* signal pauses in a single independent clause. (See also 34f.)

12c Fix fused sentences by punctuating or rewriting

How to Edit Fused Sentences

How to . . .

Fused sentences are hard to read because readers can't easily see where one thought ends and the next begins. Answer these questions to see whether you're likely to write fused sentences:

1. Are you unsure what makes a complete sentence?
2. Are you unsure how to punctuate related ideas?
3. Do you sometimes write so fast you don't pay attention to how your ideas go together?
4. Do you string ideas together to make your sentences look long enough?
5. Have readers said you write "run-on" sentences?

If you answer yes to any of these questions, reread your writing and look for fused sentences.

How to look for fused sentences: Read your writing aloud at a steady pace. If you've written a fused sentence, you may stumble where two separate thoughts come together.

How to identify fused sentences:

1. Study the words before and after the spot where you stumble, or where two ideas seem to blur together.
2. Can each word group be punctuated as a complete sentence? To find out, use the "yes/no" question test. (See 11b1.) If each word group is not already a question, try to turn it into a yes or no question. If each question sounds complete and makes sense, and if no punctuation separates your original word groups, you've written a fused sentence.

To fix fused sentences, put a period, semicolon, colon, or dash between independent clauses. Or rewrite to create one complete sentence.

What to study: Chapter 9, Sentence Parts; 10b, Clauses; and 10c, Sentence Types.

A **fused sentence,** sometimes called a **run-together** or **run-on,** is two or more grammatically complete sentences with no punctuation between them. They are joined ("fused") so tightly that, at a glance, they appear to be a single sentence, not two sentences. Consider this example:

Soon the holidays will be here once more many will miss an opportunity to share themselves and their possessions with the less fortunate.

Did you stumble as you read this example? If so, you've experienced the effect of fused sentences. If readers indicate that you write fused sentences, you can learn to identify and rewrite them, usually by adding punctuation or making one sentence subordinate to the other.

■ 1 Adding punctuation

■ Periods. Use a period to separate one independent clause, which can stand alone as a complete sentence, from another.

Soon the holidays will be here *. Once* ~~once~~ more many will miss an opportunity

to share themselves and their possessions with the less fortunate.

[In this example, *the holidays will be here* is one independent clause; *many will miss an opportunity* is the second.]

■ Semicolons and colons. Use a semicolon to link related independent clauses roughly equal in importance. (See 35a.) Use a colon to link independent clauses when one clause introduces or explains the other. (See 36a.)

The Grand Canyon is not the first choice of travelers familiar with

canyon scenery ; that honor goes to Zion National Park or Bryce

Canyon.

It all began like this : I had a new computer and needed help installing

the software.

■ A comma + a coordinating conjunction. Insert a comma before a coordinating conjunction (*and, but, or, nor, so, yet, for*) to link related independent clauses.

I enjoy cooking , but cleaning up afterward is another matter.

- A semicolon + a transition or conjunctive adverb. Insert a semicolon before a transition or conjunctive adverb linking independent clauses. (For a list of transitions and conjunctive adverbs, see 12b3.)

The Jensens knew that starting a business would not be easy ; however ,

they did not imagine how difficult it would be.

[The semicolon links two independent clauses; the comma is added following *however* to signal a pause. For more on punctuating transitional words and phrases, see 34f.]

■ 2 Rewriting to make one clause subordinate to the other

Add a subordinating conjunction (*because, although, when, since,* and so forth) to an independent clause to make it a dependent clause. Connect it to the remaining independent clause to make one complete sentence. (For a list of subordinating conjunctions, see 8g3.)

The witness did not understand the lawyer's question about South
because   *there*
Carolina he had never been to South Carolina.

[The second independent clause, beginning with *he had,* has been turned into a dependent clause by adding the subordinating conjunction *because.*]

■ 3 Compressing two independent clauses into one sentence

Omit words or change word forms to make one shorter sentence out of two independent clauses.

Travelers
~~The Grand Canyon is not the first choice of travelers~~ familiar
                                                        prefer
with canyon scenery ~~that honor goes to~~ Zion National Park or
            to the Grand Canyon
Bryce Canyon.

The Jensens ~~knew that starting a business would not be easy~~

~~however they~~ did not imagine how difficult it would be / *to start a*

business.

13 Choosing Verb Forms

chapter

How to . . .

How to Edit Verbs

Using the right verb forms will make your ideas clearer and easier to follow. Overall, your writing will sound more professional, less conversational. Answer these questions to see whether you should pay attention to verbs as you edit:

1. Do you feel that your writing is supposed to be different from the way you talk?
2. Are you sometimes unsure about the right way to express complicated actions?

If you answer yes to either question, reread your writing and look for verbs.

How to identify verbs:

1. To find the verbs in a sentence, change the time of the action, from present to past, past to present, and so forth. The verb will change form. (See 8c3.)
2. A computer tip: Use your spell checker to look for verbs with confused or incorrect endings. They often show up as misspellings.

How to choose correct verb forms:

1. To identify the correct forms of irregular verbs like *lay, lead,* and *set,* see the list in 13a3.
2. If you're unsure of the right tense to identify the time of an action, see the survey of tenses in 8c3. For special situations, see 13b; for ESL, see 31a.
3. If you have a computerized grammar checker, it may help you identify nonstandard verbs and some problems of tense. Use the warnings as flags to look at specific words and sentences. Then use this book to make your own diagnosis.

What to study: 8c, Verbs; 9b, Predicates; and 10a2, Verbal Phrases; for ESL, see Chapter 31.

13a
Use the standard forms of irregular verbs

■1 Identifying main verb forms

Except for the verb *to be,* the main verb of a sentence has five forms:

- Base or infinitive form: *I often* (*play, speak*).
- *-s/-es,* or third person form: *He often* (*plays, speaks*).
- Past tense: *Then I* (*played, spoke*).
- Past participle: *I have* (*played, spoken*) *before.*
- Present participle: *I am* (*playing, speaking*) *now.*

■2 Identifying regular and irregular verbs

Regular verbs form the past tense and past participle in regular ways, by adding *-d* or *-ed.* **Irregular verbs** are "irregular" because they form the past tense and past participle in a variety of ways.

	PRESENT TENSE	PAST TENSE	PAST PARTICIPLE
Regular verbs	play believe	played believed	played believed
Irregular verbs	begin eat	began ate	begun eaten

Regular and irregular past tense verbs stand alone: *The pianist played softly. The pianist began her solo.* When they act as the main verb of a sentence, regular and irregular past participles require a helping verb like *is, has, had, were,* or *does* to complete their meaning: *She had played this song many times before. The concert has begun.*

■3 Identifying frequently used irregular verbs

If you're unsure how to write an irregular verb or whether a verb is, in fact, irregular, consult this list of frequently used irregular verbs or your dictionary.

PRESENT TENSE	PAST TENSE	PAST PARTICIPLE
awake	awoke, awakened	awakened
be	was, were	been
beat	beat	beaten
begin	began	begun

PRESENT TENSE	PAST TENSE	PAST PARTICIPLE
bend	bent	bent
bite	bit	bitten, bit
blow	blew	blown
break	broke	broken
bring	brought	brought
build	built	built
burst	burst	burst
buy	bought	bought
catch	caught	caught
choose	chose	chosen
come	came	come
cost	cost	cost
do	did	done
draw	drew	drawn
drink	drank	drunk
drive	drove	driven
eat	ate	eaten
fall	fell	fallen
find	found	found
flee	fled	fled
fly	flew	flown
forget	forgot	forgotten
freeze	froze	frozen
get	got	gotten
give	gave	given
go	went	gone
grow	grew	grown
hang (suspend)	hung	hung
hang (execute)	hanged	hanged
hear	heard	heard
hide	hid	hidden
hold	held	held
keep	kept	kept
know	knew	known
lay (to place something)	laid	laid
lead	led	led
leave	left	left
lend	lent	lent
lie (to recline, to rest on a surface)	lay	lain
lose	lost	lost
pay	paid	paid
ride	rode	ridden
ring	rang	rung
rise	rose	risen
run	ran	run
say	said	said

see	saw	seen
set (to place)	set	set
shake	shook	shaken
shrink	shrank	shrunk
sing	sang	sung
sink	sank	sunk
sit (to be seated)	sat	sat
slide	slid	slid
speak	spoke	spoken
spend	spent	spent
spring	sprang	sprung
stand	stood	stood
steal	stole	stolen
strike	struck	struck
swim	swam	swum
take	took	taken
teach	taught	taught
tear	tore	torn
tell	told	told
throw	threw	thrown
wear	wore	worn
weave	wove	woven
write	wrote	written

■ 4 Avoiding switched verb forms

A note on dialect: Some speakers of English use verb forms different from those of Standard English. They add regular endings to irregular verbs (*blowed* instead of *blown*), treat regular verbs as if they were irregular (*drug* instead of *dragged*), or use the past participle in place of the past tense (*seen* instead of *saw.*)

NONSTANDARD ENGLISH	STANDARD ENGLISH	NONSTANDARD ENGLISH	STANDARD ENGLISH
brung	brought	drived	drove
binded	bound	drug	dragged
blowed	blew	growed	grew
catched	caught	snuck	sneaked
creeped	crept	sweared	swore
costed	cost	had went	had gone
drawed	drew		

In your writing, use the appropriate standard forms for the past tense and past participle of regular and irregular verbs.

dragged
They ~~drug~~ the sandbags onto the levee.
$\wedge$

[Drag is a regular verb that forms the past tense with *-ed*.]

blew
The wind ~~blowed~~ from the northeast for fourteen days.
                 ^

[As an irregular verb, *blow* forms the past tense irregularly.]

saw
We ~~seen~~ him in his garage last night.
        ^

[The past tense of *see* is *saw,* not *seen,* which is the past participle.]

given
My brother had ~~gave~~ his keys to the mechanic so he could start the car.
                    ^

[The past participle is required for action begun and completed in the past.]

■ 5 Using *lie/lay, sit/set, rise/raise* correctly

The words in each of these pairs are often confused. One is an intransitive verb, the other transitive. Intransitive verbs do not take direct objects; they indicate states or conditions: *The basket is sitting on the table.* Transitive verbs take direct objects; they do something to something: *The boy set the basket on the table.* Avoid confusing one kind of word with the other. (See also 8c4.)

- *Lie, lay, lain, lying* (intransitive) means to rest on or to recline: *He lay down to take a nap. The book is lying on the table. The cat had lain in the basket for an hour.*

- *Lay, laid, laid, laying* (transitive) means to put or place something: *I will lay the pillow on the bed. He laid the book on the table.*

- *Sit, sat, sat, sitting* (intransitive) means to be seated: *She sat down at the piano.*

- *Set, set, set, setting* (transitive) means to put or place something in a particular position: *The student set the pen on the desk.*

- *Rise, rose, risen, rising* (intransitive) means to get up from a lying, sitting, or kneeling position: *She rose from the chair.*

- *Raise, raised, raised, raising* (transitive) means to move something to a higher position: *He raised his hand to speak.*

■ 6 Spelling irregular verbs correctly

Because of their similarity to other words, the following are sometimes misspelled.

- *Laid/"layed."* The past tense of *lay* is *laid,* not "layed."

  laid
  He ~~layed~~ the book on the table.
      ^

- *Led/lead.* The past tense of the verb *to lead* is *led,* not "lead."

led
The leader ~~lead~~ the soldiers into battle.
                ^

[When *lead* is pronounced like "led," it refers to the soft gray metal or to pencil lead.]

■ *Lose/loose. Lose* is a verb; *loose* is an adjective.

lose
If he doesn't improve his grades, he may ~~loose~~ his scholarship.
                                          ^

■ *Paid/"payed." The past tense of *pay* is *paid,* not "payed."

paid
The workers were ~~payed~~ weekly.
                  ^

13*b* Choose verb tenses that put events in sequence

Tense refers to the form a verb takes to indicate the time of an action: present (*she is studying*), past (*she studied*), and so forth. Sometimes it is difficult to know which tense to choose to describe an action, especially if more than one action is involved. The following guidelines will help you decide. (To review the six tenses of English verbs and the way they are created using helping verbs and main verb forms, see 8c3. For ESL, see 31a.)

■ **1** Using the present tense in special situations

■ Writing about literature. Authors of fiction, poetry, and nonfiction usually write in the past tense. For example: *When Paul went down to dinner, the music of the orchestra came floating up the elevator shaft to greet him* [Willa Cather]. But to summarize action in a literary paper, use the present tense. (See 59f2.)

goes   *hears*
When Paul ~~went~~ down to dinner, he ~~heard~~ the orchestra through the
            ^   ^

elevator shaft.

■ Introducing quotations, summaries, and paraphrases. In research writing, use present tense verbs such as *reports, suggests,* and *argues* in signal phrases that introduce quotations, summaries, and paraphrases. Follow this convention whether the writer you cite is living or dead. (See also 50c1 for a list of these verbs.)

argues
In the essay "Violent Crime," Bruce Shapiro ~~argued~~ that current
                                              ^

anticrime legislation is based on a "delusion, a myth" about criminals.

A note on APA style: If you include a date in the text of your writing, as the American Psychological Association style requires, use the past tense to introduce your borrowing: *In the essay "Violent Crime," Shapiro (1995) argued that current anticrime legislation is based on "a delusion, a myth" about criminals.* (See also 54a1.)

■ Describing scientific principles and general truths. Use the present tense to describe accepted scientific principles or general truths.

> *describes*
> Ohm's law ~~described~~ the amount of resistance in an electrical circuit.

> *declares* *are*
> The Declaration of Independence ~~declared~~ that all people ~~were~~ created equal.

■ 2 Using the present perfect for past action continuing in the present

Use the present perfect tense (*has/have* + the past participle: *has laughed, have eaten*) when actions begin in the past and continue in the present or occur at no specific time.

> *have never forgotten*
> I ~~never forgot~~ my mother's words of wisdom.

[Because the writer still remembers these words, the present perfect tense is appropriate.]

■ 3 Using the past perfect for past action completed before other past action

Use the past perfect tense (*had* + the past participle: *had laughed, had eaten*) when a past action begins and is completed before another past action.

> *had been*
> The police officer stated that my brother ~~was~~ in an accident.
> [The accident occurred before the officer informed the writer.]

> *had*
> When the hikers reached the lake, they found that someone camped
> there recently.
> [Others had camped there before the hikers arrived.]

13*c* -s/-es

■ 4 Using infinitives and participles in a sequence of events

Use infinitives and participles to refer to actions related in some way to the action of the main verb.

■ Simultaneous actions: the present infinitive. Use the present infinitive (*to* + the base verb form: *to laugh, to eat*) for actions occurring at the same time or immediately after the action of the main verb.

Park officials tried to ~~have~~ *spray* ~~sprayed~~ for mosquitoes after every rain.

[The action of the infinitive *to spray* occurred at the same time as the action of the main verb *tried*.]

■ One action and then another: the present perfect infinitive. Use the present perfect infinitive (*to have* + the past participle: *to have laughed, to have eaten*) for actions occurring before the action of the main verb.

The Mayor would like to ~~give~~ *have given* a speech before the council's decision.

[The speech would have occurred in the past before the Mayor's wish. Therefore, the present perfect infinitive (*to have given*) is required.

■ Simultaneous actions: the present participle. Use the present participle (*-ing*) for an action occurring simultaneously with that of the main verb: *Pulling into the parking lot, he saw a thief smashing a car window.*

■ One action and then another: the past participle or present perfect participle. Use the past participle (*laughed, eaten*) or the present perfect participle (*having* + the past participle: *having laughed, having eaten*) for actions occurring before that of the main verb.

Having finished
~~Finishing~~ his exam before the period was half over, Kim asked to be

excused.

13*c* | Use *-s/-es* on present-tense verbs that have third person singular subjects

■ A note on dialect and ESL: Some speakers of English drop the *-s* or *-es* from third person singular verbs in the present tense: *he works* becomes *he work.* In your writing, take care to add *-s* or *-es* to third person singular verbs following the words listed on the next page. (See also 13d.)

- Singular nouns: *Joan hikes. The baby cries.*

- Singular personal pronouns: *She hikes. He sings. It falls.*

- Indefinite pronouns, which are usually singular: *Everyone hikes. Each sings.*

  tries   *keeps*
  He ~~try~~ to come home early, but his job often ~~keep~~ him out late.
     ^   ^

13*d* Use the Standard English forms of *be, have,* and *do*

A note on dialect: Some speakers of English use the forms of *be, have,* and *do* in ways different from Standard English. In your writing, use Standard English verb forms.

■ 1 *Be*

The eight forms of *be* (*be, am, is, are, were, was, been, being*) make it the most complex English verb.

	SINGULAR	PLURAL
First person	I am/am being/ was/have been	we are/are being/ were/have been
Second person	you are/are being/ were/have been	you are/are being/ were/have been
Third person	she is/is being/ was/has been	they are/are being/ were/have been

To use *be* in its Standard English forms, follow these guidelines:

- Events in progress or habitual events. Use the third person singular *-s* form (*is*) + the present participle (*-ing*) to indicate events in progress and habitual or continuous events: *is laughing.*

  is
  He going to school.
     ^
  [He is on his way to school.]

  is
  He ~~be~~ going to school.
         ^
  [He is currently attending school.]

- Using *am, is,* and *was* with first person and third person singular verbs. Use *am, is,* and *was* with first person and third person singular verbs; use *are* and *were* with all others.

  was
  She ~~were~~ trying to get her essay published in the campus magazine.
       ^
  [*She* takes a third person singular verb, *was.*]

■ Omitted verbs. In informal Standard English, verbs are sometimes contracted with their subjects: *I'm, you're, she's, we're, they're*. But these verbs may not be omitted entirely. (See also 31a2.)

am
I working forty hours a week.
^

         is
The actress on stage now.
       ^

■ 2 *Have*

Use the *-s* form *has* for the third person singular (*John has*); use *have* for all other present tense and present perfect forms (*we have*). Do not omit *has* or *have* when these forms are used as helping verbs: *John has worked, we have lived*. (See also 31a2.)

   has
She ~~have~~ come to every meeting of the drama club.
 has ^
He been a successful businessman for twenty years.
 ^*have*
They been going to Canada every summer for five years.
  ^

■ 3 *Do*

Use the *-es* form *does* for the third person singular (*she does*); use *do* for all other present tense forms. (See also 31b.)

    doesn't
Merrilee ~~don't~~ want to go to the party this weekend.
Does   ^
~~Do~~ he ever consider other people's feelings?
 ^

13e Beware of dropped or confused verb endings in words like *used*, *supposed*, *asked*, and *would have*

■ Influenced by the sound of spoken English, writers occasionally omit or confuse verb endings. Follow these guidelines to Standard English verb endings:

■ 1 *Use* and *suppose*

"Use to" and "suppose to" are nonstandard. Write *used to* and *supposed to*.

    supposed
Polly was ~~suppose~~ to fly to Memphis at the beginning of the month.
   ^

used
Scientists ~~use~~ to believe that outer space was filled with ether.
^

■ 2 Past and past perfect endings

Signal the past and perfect tenses of regular verbs with *-d* and *-ed* endings.

frightened
The little boy ~~frighten~~ the ducklings.
^

asked
My mother has ~~ask~~ me to call her every week.
^

developed
Robert Goddard was the American who ~~develop~~ the rocket engine.
^

■ 3 *Would, could, should*

"Would of," "could of," and "should of" are nonstandard. Write *would've* or *would have, could've* or *could have, should've* or *should have*.

have
We would ~~of~~ won the tournament if we had practiced harder.
^

13*f* Use the subjunctive mood for wishes and other nonfactual statements

■ The **subjunctive mood** of verbs is used for statements contrary to fact: wishes, speculations, assumptions, recommendations, indirect requests, and hypothetical situations. (See 8c6.)

- Present tense subjunctive. To form the present tense subjunctive, use the base form of the verb (*be, give, arrive*): *It is necessary that everyone arrive by nine o'clock.*

- Past tense subjunctive. To form the past tense subjunctive, use *were* not *was*: *If I were better organized, I would get more done.*

Although slowly disappearing from English, the subjunctive still remains in certain phrases and situations.

■ 1 Wishes and desires

Use the subjunctive to express wishes and to follow verbs expressing wish or desire: *ask, insist, move, recommend, request, suggest,* and *urge*.

award
We recommend that the Dean ~~awards~~ an honors certificate to Carlos
^

Montoya.

[present tense]

were
Gena wished that the instructor ~~was~~ finished with his lecture.
[past tense]

■ 2 Nonfactual statements

Use the subjunctive after *if* or *as if* to express hypothetical or nonfactual situations.

were
If I ~~was~~ you, I would study harder for tomorrow's quiz.

■ 3 Indirect requests

Use the subjunctive to express indirect requests.

be
It is important that you ~~are~~ in your seat before the concert begins.

[present tense]

■ 4 Speculation

Use the subjunctive to make a speculation.

were
James looked as though he ~~was~~ enjoying the movie.

[past tense]

14 Making Subjects and Verbs Agree

Agreement refers to the forms that words take to express their relationships. When subjects and verbs *agree*, they match in number (singular or plural) and person (first, second, and third), as in the following examples.

	SINGULAR	PLURAL
First person	I run	we run
Second person	you run	you run
Third person	he/she/it runs,	they run
	Pauline runs	

third person singular agreement
On weekends Penny volunteers at a homeless shelter.

third person plural agreement
Two homeless shelters were opened during last month's severe weather.

How to . . .

How to Edit for Subject-Verb Agreement

Making subjects and verbs agree (by using matching forms) is one way to improve the precision and accuracy of your sentences. Answer these questions to see whether you may have an occasional problem of subject-verb agreement:

1. Are you unsure how to identify the subject of a sentence?
2. Do you sometimes write long, complex sentences?

If you answer yes to either of these questions, reread your writing and look for subjects and their verbs.

How to find problems of subject-verb agreement:

1. Look for long sentences.
2. Look for clue words that may accompany agreement errors: the sentence openers *There is/are, Here is/are* (14b); the conjunctions *and, or, nor* (14d and e); indefinite pronouns, such as *every, anyone, everybody* (14f); collective nouns, such as *team, committee, group, number* (14 g); plural nouns considered as a single unit, such as *economics* and *glasses* (14h); and the relative pronouns *who, which, that* (14i). A computer tip: Use your Find or Search and Replace commands to locate these words.

To decide whether subjects and verbs agree, first identify the subject and verb. (See 8c and 9a for guidelines.) Then read the subject and verb without the words that come between. Rewrite if they do not have the same number (singular or plural) and person (first, second, or third person).

What to study: 8a and b, Nouns and Pronouns; 8c, Verbs; and 9a and b, Subjects and Predicates.

14*a* | Make separated subjects and verbs agree

Subjects and verbs are sometimes separated by other words. But no matter how far apart the two are, subjects determine the person and number of their verbs.

plural subject   plural verb
The tapestries on the walls of the palace were woven by children.

To decide whether separated subjects and verbs agree, first identify the subject and verb. (See 8c and 9a.) Then read the subject and verb without the words that come between: *tapestries . . . were woven* (a plural subject and verb agree). Rewrite when necessary.

believes
Not one of the scientists investigating AIDS ~~believe~~ a cure will soon be
    ^

found.

[The subject of the sentence is *one*. *Scientists* is the object of the preposition *of* and cannot be the subject of a sentence.]

are
The beneficial effects of her enthusiastic work ~~is~~ apparent everywhere.
    ^

[The subject is the plural *effects*. *Work* is the object of the preposition *of* and cannot be the subject of a sentence.]

A note on prepositional phrases: Prepositional phrases that begin *accompanied by, along with, as well as, except, in addition to, including, no less than, together with,* or *with* do not add to a subject to make it plural. Identify the noun, pronoun, or noun phrase that is the true subject.

was
The valedictorian, together with her major professors, ~~were~~ asked to
    ^

stand for the audience's applause.

[The subject, *valedictorian*, is singular; *her major professors* is the object of the preposition *together with* and is not part of the subject. To form a plural subject, use a coordinating conjunction: *the valedictorian and her major professors.*]

14*b* Make the subject and verb agree when the subject follows the verb

■   Normal English word order is subject + verb: *The geese were flying.* Occasionally, however, normal word order is inverted, and the subject follows the verb (verb + subject): *On the pine branch sat two large bluejays.* Whatever its position, the subject determines the number of the verb. Compare these two examples:

plural verb plural subject
Seated in the front row were the parents of the bride and groom.

are
In his backpack ~~is~~ enough food and clothing for two weeks of camping.
    ^

[*Backpack* is the object of the preposition *in*; it is not the subject of the sentence. The subject is a compound, *food and clothing,* so the verb must be plural.]

A note on *there* and *here:* In sentences beginning *there is, there are, here is,* and *here are,* the subject follows the verb. Compare these two examples:

plural verb plural subject
There are three reasons to elect Alice Brown to the Student Council.

were
Last night there ~~was~~ a dictionary and a thesaurus on my desk.
    ^

[The compound subject, *a dictionary and a thesaurus,* is plural, so the verb must be plural.]

14*c* | Make a linking verb agree with its subject, not with a subject complement

■ Linking verbs (*am, is, are, was, were, seem, become, appear, feel, smell, sound, taste*) link a subject to an adjective or a noun, called a *subject complement*, that describes the subject: *Becky is a social worker.* Do not confuse the subject with the subject complement. In most sentences, the subject precedes a linking verb. (See 8c4 and 9d1.)

A loving family, loyal friends, and interesting work ~~is~~ *are* my definition of

happiness.

[The three-part subject is plural and so the verb must be plural, even though the subject complement, *definition*, is singular.]

The most attractive feature of the house ~~are~~ *is* the large, arched windows.

[The subject, *feature*, is singular, so the verb must be singular.]

If grammatically correct sentences seem awkward, rewrite to turn the subject complement into the subject: *My definition of happiness is a loving family, loyal friends, and interesting work. The large, arched windows are the most attractive feature of the house.*

14*d* | With most compound subjects, use a plural verb

■ Compound subjects are linked by the coordinating conjunctions *and, but, or, so, for, yet, nor.*

plural subject   plural verb
Cairo and Alexandria are the two largest cities in Egypt.

The dress and equipment for racquetball ~~is~~ *are* similar to that for tennis.

A note on unit compounds and compounds headed by *each* or *every*: If a compound subject is thought of as a unit, refers to one person, or is headed by *each* or *every*, use a singular verb.

The **horse and buggy is** the primary mode of transportation among the Amish.

The **company's president and chief operating officer has announced** her retirement.

Fortunately, **every man, woman, and child was rescued** from the sinking ship.

14e With compound subjects linked by *or* or *nor*, make the verb agree with the closer subject

■ When both parts of a compound subject joined by *or* or *nor* are singular or plural, agreement is an easy match of subject and verb forms.

singular subject *nor* singular subject = singular verb

Neither Alice nor Gary plays chess well enough to be on the chess team.

plural subject *or* plural subject = plural verb

Either tulips or daffodils are a good choice for early spring flowers.

But when one subject is singular and the other is plural, the subject closer to the verb determines its number as singular or plural. When the closer subject is singular, the verb is singular. When the closer subject is plural, the verb is plural.

was
Neither the children nor their mother ~~were~~ happy when the parade
                                        ∧

ended.

[The singular *mother* is closer to the verb, so the verb must be singular.]

have
Either the lawyer or her clients ~~has~~ been available each day for
                                   ∧

interviews.

[The plural *clients* is closer to the verb, so the verb must be plural.]

To avoid awkwardness, rewrite using *and*: *The children and their mother were unhappy when the parade ended.* But note that *or* may be necessary to signal alternates, either one subject or the other: *The children or their mother carries an umbrella to every parade.*

14f Treat indefinite pronouns as singular

■ Indefinite pronouns refer to indefinite, unspecified persons or things. (See 8b4.) The following indefinite pronouns usually take singular verbs.

anyone	either	everything	someone
anybody	everyone	neither	something
each	everybody	none	

These words may seem to be plural and are often treated as such in speech. *Everybody* seems to refer to more than one person. But because their form is singular—there is only one *body* in *everybody*—indefinite pronouns take singular verbs. (See also 15d.) Compare these examples:

Each of the flowers **is** blooming.

Anyone who wants to be a good writer must also be a good editor.

has
None of the students in our dorm ~~have~~ signed up for intermural sports.

[*None* means not one, so the verb must be singular.]

is
Either of the mechanics ~~are~~ able to repair the car.

[*Either* means one or the other, so the verb must be singular.]

A note on *all, any, most, some:* These indefinite pronouns may be singular or plural, depending on the sense of the sentence or the words they refer to.

All of the volunteers **have** arrived.
[*All* refers to more than one volunteer; the sense is plural.]

All that she has left **is** twenty-five dollars.
[*All* refers to the twenty-five dollars as a unit; the sense is singular.]

Most of the speakers **have supported** the proposal.
[The sense of *most* is plural.]

Most of the snow **has** melted.
[*Most* refers to snow, which is usually singular.]

14g Treat collective nouns as singular, unless their individual members act separately

Collective nouns are words like *class, committee, couple, dozen, family, group, herd, jury, number, public, remainder,* and *team.* If their members act collectively, as a unit, collective nouns take a singular verb. If their members act separately, they take a plural verb. Compare these examples:

The senior **class is** about to sing the national anthem.

are
The class ~~is~~ in their seats.

[In the first example, the class sings together as one, and the verb is singular. In the second, the individual members of the class take their own seats, the sense of the subject is plural, and the verb must be plural.]

The **jury is deliberating.**

are
The jury ~~is~~ divided over the verdict.

[In the first example, the jury deliberates together as one, and the subject is singular. In the second, the individual members of the jury hold separate opinions, the sense of the subject is plural, and the verb must be plural.]

An ESL note on noncount nouns: Noncount nouns referring to things as a whole (*advice, crime, coffee, luggage, machinery,* and so forth) appear similar to collective nouns. But noncount nouns are almost always singular and require singular verbs: *Our luggage is in the trunk of the car.*

A note on *the number, a number: The number* is singular in meaning and takes a singular verb; *a number,* referring to individuals acting separately, is plural and takes a plural verb.

The number of students who prepare writing portfolios **is** increasing.

A number of these students **have** prepared portfolios.

14*h* With plural nouns singular in meaning, use singular verbs

Some plural nouns are singular in meaning or understood as a unit: *athletics, economics, mathematics, measles, news, physics, statistics.* These words take singular verbs. Compare these examples:

After last night's dinner, **three dollars was** all he had in his wallet.

Fifteen miles is a long way to hike through mountainous terrain.

Mathematics sometimes ~~cause~~ *causes* a disturbance known as "math anxiety."

The measles ~~have~~ *has* affected half the third graders.

A note on units of measure: If units of measure refer to separate persons or things, use a plural verb. Otherwise, the verb is singular.

Three-fourths of the students **are** doing A or B work.

Three-fourths of the school year **has** passed.

[In the first example, the students work individually, the sense of the subject is plural, and the verb is plural. In the second, *three-fourths* refers to one part of the year, and the verb is singular.]

A note on unit plurals: Some plural words thought of as a unit take a plural verb: *glasses, scissors, tweezers, jeans.*

The **scissors were** lying on the table.

14*i* With *who, which,* and *that,* use verbs that agree with their antecedents

To decide whether a relative pronoun is singular or plural, identify its **antecedent,** the noun or pronoun it refers to. (To learn to recognize nouns and pronouns, see 8a and b.)

noun   pronoun verb

The Atlas Mountains, which extend from Morocco to Tunisia, are among the highest in western Africa.

[The relative pronoun *which* refers to the Atlas Mountains, a plural noun, so the verb *extend* must be plural.]

■ 1 One of the . . . who/which/that

The construction *one of the . . . who/which/that* usually precedes a plural verb. Compare these examples:

plural   plural   plural

Leslie is one of the few members of this class who understand quadratic equations.

[*Who* refers to members, not *Leslie* or *one*; therefore, *who* is plural and the verb *understand* is plural.]

have

White Pines is one of many state parks that ~~has~~ scenery worth a

second visit.

[*That* refers to *parks*; therefore, the verb must be plural.]

■ 2 Only one of the . . . who/which/that

The construction *only one of the . . . who/which/that* usually precedes a singular verb. Compare these examples:

singular   singular   singular   singular

Leslie is the only one of these students who understands quadratic equations.

lives

The manatee is the only one of the elephant's relatives that ~~live~~

under water.

[*Which* refers to *one*, not *relatives*. Only one relative lives under water.]

Note another version of the same construction: *I am the only person I know who actually enjoys airports.*

14j With titles and words mentioned as words, use singular verbs

When I was a child, *Alice's Adventures in Wonderland* **was** one of my favorite books.

[One book, singular, takes a singular verb.]

Wharves **is** the plural of *wharf.*
[A word used as a word takes a singular verb.]

Tales of the Grotesque and Arabesque ~~were~~ *was* written by Edgar Allan Poe.

Procter and Gamble ~~are~~ *is* one of the United States' largest corporations.

15 Making Pronouns and Antecedents Agree

A pronoun refers to a noun or another pronoun, called the **antecedent.** (See 8b.) Whether appearing in the same or different sentences, pronouns and antecedents must match (agree) in person (first, second, or third), number (singular or plural), and gender (masculine, feminine, or neuter).

third person singular feminine agreement

The **mother** cradled **her** child in **her** arms.

third person plural agreement

The **students** exchanged **their** essays to read and discuss.

The **Colorado River** flows from northern Colorado to the Gulf of

third person singular neuter agreement

California. During **its** 1450-mile journey, **it** loses most of **its** water.

15a With compound antecedents linked by *and*, use plural pronouns

David and **Darrell** congratulated **themselves** for their good luck.

15b With compound antecedents linked by *or* or *nor*, make the pronoun agree with the closer antecedent

Neither **Alicia** nor **Louise** uses a computer to write **her** papers.
[*Neither* means not one or the other; the pronoun must be singular.]

How to Edit Noun-Pronoun Agreement

How to . . .

Making nouns and pronouns agree (by using matching forms) is one way to improve the precision and accuracy of your sentences. Answer these questions to see whether you may have an occasional problem of noun-pronoun agreement:

1. Do you tend to write informally, the way you talk?
2. Are you unsure how to identify nouns or indefinite pronouns?
3. Do you sometimes write long sentences or lose the thread of your ideas from one sentence to the next?

If you answer yes to any of these questions, consider pronouns and their antecedents as you edit your writing.

How to find pronouns and antecedents that may need editing for agreement:

1. Look for long sentences or passages in which your ideas are complex.
2. Look for the antecedents that may cause noun-pronoun disagreement: nouns linked by _and, or, nor_ (15a and b); nouns referring to groups, such as _committee_ or _audience_ (15c); words referring to individuals without regard to gender, such as _student_ or _everyone_ (15d); the names of organizations (15e). A computer tip: Use the Find or Search and Replace commands to locate _and, or, nor_ and pronouns containing _-body, every-, -one._
3. To hear noun-pronoun disagreement, read a pronoun and its antecedent without the words between.

How to fix noun-pronoun disagreement: Use singular pronouns to refer to singular antecedents; use plural pronouns to refer to plural antecedents.

What to study: 8a, Nouns; and 8b, Pronouns.

Either the **Cardinals** or the **Cubs** have a chance to win the World Series if **they** improve **their** pitching.

[Both antecedents are plural; the pronoun must be plural.]

Neither **Mrs. Newton** nor her **daughters** visit as often as **they** would like.

[The second antecedent, _daughters,_ is closer to the pronoun than _Mrs. Newton;_ the pronoun must be plural, _they._]

A note on awkwardness and ambiguity: When one antecedent is singular and the other plural, put the plural last to avoid awkwardness, as in the third example here: _Neither Mrs. Newton nor her daughters._ If one antecedent is male and the other female, rewrite to avoid awkwardness or ambiguity. *Either Paul or June will share her notes* is unclear. An alternative: *Paul and June will share their notes.*

15*c* With collective nouns, use singular pronouns unless individual members act separately

■ Collective nouns are words like *audience, class, committee, couple, crowd, dozen, group, herd, jury, number, public, remainder,* and *team.* Compare these examples:

The **audience** gave **its** approval.

[The audience acted together, as a unit, and so the pronoun is singular.]

The *jury* refused to discuss **their** opinions of the defendant.

[Each member of the jury had a separate opinion, and so the pronoun that refers to *jury* is plural.]

                                                        its
The jury delivered ~~their~~ verdict.
                                ^
[The members of the jury function together, as a unit, and so the pronoun that refers to *jury* must be singular.]

An ESL note on noncount nouns: Noncount nouns referring to things as a whole (*advice, crime, coffee, luggage, machinery,* and so forth) appear similar to collective nouns. But noncount nouns are almost always singular and require singular pronouns: *We brought our luggage out to the car, and my father packed it in the trunk.*

15*d* With generic nouns and indefinite pronouns, avoid disagreement and stereotyping

■ **Generic nouns** and **indefinite pronouns** refer to individuals without regard to gender.

SAMPLE GENERIC NOUNS	SAMPLE INDEFINITE PRONOUNS
person, student, professor, lawyer, chemist, secretary, doctor, athlete, bicyclist, firefighter, flight attendant	anyone, each, everybody, nobody, none, someone, something, and so forth (For a complete list, see 8b4.)

Using singular pronouns (*he, she, his, her,* and so forth) to refer to generic nouns and indefinite pronouns can create gender stereotyping, as in *A doctor owes his primary loyalty to his patients* [the pronouns in this sentence suggest that all doctors are male]. In casual speech we avoid such stereotyping by using plural pronouns: *A person who goes out of their way to help others is a Good Samaritan. Did everybody remember to bring their skis?* In this way, *person* and *everybody* may refer to male or female. But in your writing, pronouns and antecedents should agree. To make pronouns agree with generic nouns and indefinite pronouns—and to avoid gender stereotyping—follow these guidelines:

- Using plural nouns and pronouns. When possible, use plural nouns and pronouns.

  Good Samaritans are people
  A Good Samaritan is a person who ~~goes~~ out of their way to help others.
  go

  [The plural generic noun *people* takes a plural pronoun, *their.*]

  the students
  When ~~everyone~~ had finished studying, they picked up their books and left.

  [Replacing the indefinite pronoun *everyone* with a plural generic noun *students* makes the plural personal pronoun *they* agree.]

- Omitting pronouns. When possible, omit the generic noun or the pronoun.

  Good Samaritans make sacrifices to help others.
  ~~A Good Samaritan is a person who goes out of their way to help others.~~

  [With rewording, this sentence omits the pronoun *their.*]

  a
  Someone had walked off and left ~~their~~ backpack under a tree.

- Using *he or she.* When the sense of a sentence must be singular, use *he or she, his or her, him or her* to refer to a singular generic noun or an indefinite pronoun.

  his or her
  A Good Samaritan is a person who goes out of ~~their~~ way to help others.
  his or her
  Someone had walked off and left ~~their~~ backpack under a tree.

  [Avoid awkward chains of paired pronouns: *Everyone in the building was angry when he or she received his or her latest rent increase.* In public writing do not use the slash to link pronouns, as in *he/she, his/her,* and so forth. (See 39e.)]

15e | With nouns that name organizations, use singular pronouns

It may be logical to think of an organization in terms of its members and to refer to it with a plural pronoun. But use *it* and *its* to refer to a single organization.

It *has*
A good library contains more than books and periodicals. ~~They~~ also ~~have~~
audiovisual materials of all kinds.

[The pronoun *it* refers to the organization *library.*]

Mercy Hospital cares for ~~their~~ *its* patients' emotional as well as physical

health.

[*Its* refers to the organization *Mercy Hospital*.]

Making Pronoun Reference Clear

How to . . .

How to Edit Unclear Pronoun Reference

In accurate, precise writing, pronouns refer clearly to their antecedents, the nouns or other pronouns that give them meaning. In the process of writing and revising, however, nearly every writer has an occasional problem with unclear reference. As you rewrite, carefully consider your pronouns and their antecedents.

To identify unclear pronoun reference:

1. If readers indicate that your writing is vague or hard to follow, locate your pronouns and see whether each has a specific noun or pronoun it refers to. (See 16a.)
2. Look for nouns that refer to organizations and for possessive nouns (ending -'s or -s'). Then look for nearby pronouns and decide whether they can logically refer to these nouns. (See 16a1 and 2.)
3. Look for the pronouns *you, it, this, who, which,* and *that,* especially at the beginning of sentences or clauses. A computer tip: Use the Find or Search and Replace commands to locate these words. Decide whether they have clear, specific antecedents.
4. To decide whether pronoun reference is faulty, substitute the antecedent for the pronoun and reread. You'll hear the problem. (See 16a and b.)

To fix unclear pronoun reference:

1. Add a specific noun, indefinite pronoun, or noun phrase to be the antecedent for a pronoun.
2. Rewrite to replace an unclear pronoun with a clarifying word or phrase.

What to study: 8a and b, Nouns and Pronouns.

A pronoun refers to a noun or other pronoun called the antecedent, which gives the pronoun its meaning.

As *Stephanie* watched quietly, **she** saw a red *fox* emerge from **its** den.

Because pronouns can substitute for nouns and other pronouns, they enable writers to avoid monotonous repetition and create close relationships between sentences and paragraphs. Consider how pronouns (italicized for emphasis) add variety and link sentences in this example:

> Writers must learn to be *their* own best enemy. *They* must accept the criticism of others and be suspicious of *it; they* must accept the praise of others and be even more suspicious of *it.* Writers cannot depend on others. *They* must detach *themselves* from *their* own pages so that *they* can apply both *their* caring and *their* craft to *their* own work.
>
> (Donald Murray, "The Maker's Eye: Revising Your Own Manuscripts")

But when writers use pronouns without specific antecedents or use too many pronouns, the result is faulty pronoun reference and writing that is vague and sometimes hard to understand. To help make your writing clear, follow these guidelines.

16*a* | Make pronouns refer to specific antecedents

You should be able to point to the antecedent that a pronoun refers to. If you can't identify the specific word or phrase, rewrite to supply the missing antecedent or to omit the pronoun.

My grandfather may have been seriously ill, but he declared that he

wasn't dead yet and wasn't afraid of ~~it~~.
                                    dying
                                    ^

[The pronoun *it* cannot refer to the adjective *dead.* To hear the faulty reference, try rereading the sentence using *dead* in place of *it.* The revision substitutes the noun *dying,* which completes the meaning of the sentence.]

                                        prisoners are squeezed
American prisons are now so crowded that in some states ~~they squeeze~~
                                                                ^

~~them~~ in, four or five to a cell.

[In this sentence, *they* and *them* have no antecedents. The revision omits *they,* replaces *them* with the noun *prisoners,* and changes the verb form.]

■ **1** Using *they*, *them*, and *their* to refer to organizations

A pronoun that takes the place of an organization should refer to the organization (*it, its*), not to its members (*they, them, their*).

On May 3, 1996, The *Careful Shopper* announced that **it** was closing **its** last store.

To revise faulty references to organizations, omit the faulty pronoun, substitute the appropriate pronoun, or add the name of the organization.

Tarbell's Café is popular because of ~~their~~ *its* atmosphere and delicious food.

[The revision omits a pronoun that refers to people and replaces it with a pronoun referring to the restaurant itself.]

In the last decade ~~they~~ *manufacturers* have begun to build televisions with superior sound systems.

[The revision replaces a pronoun with an identifying noun.]

■ 2 Using pronouns that refer to possessive nouns

Nouns that end in -'s or -s' act as adjectives and cannot be the antecedents for pronouns. Rewrite to supply a noun antecedent for each pronoun or to correct faulty pronoun reference.

As Lucy admired ~~the motorcycle's~~ *its* sleek design, she knew she wanted to own ~~it~~ *the motorcycle.*

[*Motorcycle's* cannot be the antecedent of *it*. To hear the faulty reference, reread the sentence replacing *it* with *motorcycle's*.]

Jill bent to hear the old woman'~~s voice, who was~~ mumbling of old friends long dead.

[*Woman's* cannot be the antecedent of *who*. To hear the problem, try replacing *who* with *woman's*.]

■ 3 Using *you* as an indefinite pronoun

You is a personal pronoun, not an indefinite pronoun referring to persons in general. In public writing, use *you* only to address readers directly. To refer to people in general, use *people* or *one*. If these words make your writing sound stuffy, rewrite to omit the pronoun.

Even in remote wilderness, ~~you can find~~ *one can find* pollution, litter, and environmental damage.

Even in remote wilderness, ~~you can find~~ pollution, litter, and environmental damage *can be found*.

■ **4** **Using *it* to refer to authors or their writing**

In summarizing, do not use the personal pronoun *it* to refer to authors or their writings in phrases such as *it says that*.

argues
~~In~~ Henry David Thoreau's *Walden*, ~~it says~~ that people should simplify
                              ^

their lives.

[Logically, the author does the saying, not the book. This revision emphasizes the book. Another revision emphasizes the author: *In* Walden, *Henry David Thoreau argues that people should simplify their lives.*]

16*b* | Avoid ambiguous reference

■ Pronoun reference is ambiguous when a pronoun seems to refer to more than one possible antecedent. Rearrange or rewrite so that each pronoun has one specific antecedent.

When abusive *are angry, they*
~~Abusive~~ parents often hit their children ~~when they are angry~~.
         ^   ^

[In the original sentence, it is unclear who is angry. The revision clarifies the antecedent for *they*.]

To polish the watches, the   *them*
~~The~~ jeweler removed ~~the watches~~ from the display cases ~~to polish them~~.
  ^   ^

[In the original, it is unclear whether the jeweler intended to polish the watches or the display cases. The revision clarifies the antecedent of *them*.]

16*c* | Generally avoid using *it*, *this*, *that*, and *which* to refer to whole sentences

■ If you use *it*, *this*, *that*, and *which* to refer broadly to whole sentences or clauses, you may confuse readers. Replace these pronouns with their antecedents or rewrite to clarify meaning.

When prices rise, consumers purchase less and production decreases.
pattern
This leads to higher unemployment.
   ^

[In the original, the antecedent for *this*, the cause of higher unemployment, is unclear.]

In Everglades National Park, hundreds of species of nonnative plants
                              . Such carelessness illustrates
grow from seeds scattered by picnickers, ~~which is~~ why antilittering
                                          ^

regulations are needed.

[In the original, the pronoun *which* does not identify the reason regulations are needed: the number of nonnative plants, the actions of picnickers, or both.]

16d Use *who*, *that*, *whose*, or *whom* to refer to people and to animals with names

Many early blues musicians, few of ~~which~~ *whom* could read or write music, are remembered today only because of the historians ~~which~~ *who* recorded them.

A note on references to objects and unnamed animals: Use *that*, *which*, and *whose* to refer to objects and unnamed animals.

The planets **that** orbit farthest from the sun are Neptune and Pluto.

The deer, **whose** food was threatened by drought, began foraging in suburban backyards.

17 Choosing Pronoun Case Forms

Nouns and pronouns change what is known as **case form** to signal their functions as subjects, objects, and possessives. Deciding the correct form of nouns is rarely a problem because they change form only in the possessive.

- Subject and object forms: *That little dog just bit your dog on the tail.*
- The possessive form: *My dog's bark is worse than his bite.*

Personal pronouns, however, change forms to signal each of their functions.

SUBJECT FORMS	OBJECT FORMS	POSSESSIVE FORMS
I	me	my
you	you	your
he/she/it	him/her/it	his/her/its
we	us	our
they	them	their
who/whoever	whom/whomever	whose

To choose the pronoun form that matches its function in a sentence, use the following guidelines.

How to . . .

How to Edit Pronoun Case Forms

Using pronouns that fit their roles as subjects or objects will give your sentences the accuracy and polish readers expect in public writing. To identify pronouns that may not fit their roles in a sentence, do the following:

1. When a pronoun is part of a compound or identifies a preceding noun, use the "drop" test. Drop everything from the compound except the pronoun in question, or drop the nearby noun. Reread the sentence and trust your ear to hear the correct form. (See 17a–c.)

2. When you're trying to decide between *who/whom* or *whoever/ whomever*, follow a four-step formula: (a) Consider the words following *who/whom*. (b) Rearrange the words into a complete sentence, leaving a blank where the pronoun should go. (c) Put *he, she, him, her, they*, or *them* in the blank, whichever is correct. (d) Use *who* or *whoever* in place of *he, she, they*; use *whom* or *whomever* in place of *him, her, them*. (See 17e.)

3. When a pronoun follows *than* or *as* in a comparison, mentally complete the thought to hear the correct form. (See 17f.)

To choose the correct pronoun:

1. Use subject forms (*he, she, we, who*, and so forth) for subjects and pronouns that refer to subjects. (See 17a.)

2. Use object forms (*him, her, us, whom*, and so forth) for direct objects, indirect objects, objects of prepositions, and the subjects and objects of infinitive (*to* +) verbs. (See 17b and c.)

3. Use the possessive forms (*my, your, her, our*, and so forth) for nouns and pronouns preceding gerunds (*-ing* verbs used as nouns). (See 17d.)

4. Use *who/whoever* for subjects, *whom/whomever* for objects. (See 17e.)

5. Use reflexive pronouns (*myself, yourself*, and so forth) only when the receiver of an action or the object of a preposition is identical to the doer of an action: *I did it myself*. (See 17g.)

What to study: 8b, Pronouns; 9a, Subjects; 9c, Objects; 9d, Complements; 10a1, Prepositional Phrases; and 10a3, Appositive Phrases.

17a | Use the subject form for subject pronouns and for pronouns that identify subjects

■ Singular pronoun subjects seldom cause a problem.

When **she** saw her nephew playing with the puppy, **she** laughed so hard **she** almost cried.

■ 1 Using pronouns in compound subjects

To determine the correct pronoun in a compound subject, use the "drop" test. Drop everything from the compound except the pronoun in question, say the sentence, and trust your ear to guide you.

Kim and ~~me~~ *I* spent spring vacation in Vancouver.

[Drop *Kim* to hear the error in *me spent.* The first person subject pronoun *I* is correct.]

We took this path because ~~me and him~~ *he and I* were told it was open to

bicyclists.

[Drop one half of the compound at a time to hear the errors in *me . . . were told* and *him were . . . told.* In a compound construction, put the other person before yourself.]

■ 2 Using pronouns as subject complements

Use the subject form for pronouns that identify the subject of a linking verb like *be, is, was,* or *were.* (See also 9d1.)

The only one to read the complete report was ~~me~~ *I*.

[*One* is the subject of the verb *was. I* complements—identifies—the subject and is in the subject form.]

In Standard English, subject complements are always in the subject form, but if this sounds stuffy, try another version of the sentence: *I was the only one to read the complete report.*

■ 3 Using pronoun appositives that identify subjects

An **appositive** describes a preceding noun. (See 10a3.) Use the subject form for pronoun appositives that describe subjects.

At the end, only two spectators, Sally and ~~me~~ *I*, remained to mourn our

team's loss.

[Use the "drop" test to remove everything from the subject and appositive except the pronoun: *only . . . me remained. I* is the correct form.]

■ 4 Using *we* or *us* before subjects

Use the subject form *we,* not the object form *us,* to precede and identify a subject.

we
Does Professor Desai know that ~~us~~ students want to postpone the exam?
        ^

[Use the "drop" test to omit the subject and hear the error in *that us . . . want to post-pone the exam. We* is correct.]

17b | Use the object form when pronouns are objects

■ Single direct objects, indirect objects, or objects of prepositions seldom cause a problem.

Lisa's parents saw **her** sitting on the porch.

To choose the correct pronouns for compound objects, use the "drop" test. Drop everything from the object except the pronoun, read the sentence, and trust your ear to guide you.

■ 1 Using pronouns in compound direct and indirect objects

When pronouns act as direct or indirect objects to complete the meaning of a verb, use the object form. (See 9c.)

me
Please help my friend and ~~I~~ with this calculus problem.
                        ^

[Drop *my friend and* to hear the error in *help . . . I. Me* is correct.]

■ 2 Using pronouns as objects of prepositions

Use the object form for pronouns following prepositions. (See 10a1.)

me
I wish someone would settle a friendly debate between my father and ~~I~~.
                                                                   ^
[*Between* is a preposition. Drop *my father and . . .* to hear the error in *between . . . I. Me* is correct.]

us
Among ~~we~~ Southerners are many who prefer Yankee pot roast to fried
        ^

chicken.
[*Among* is a preposition. Drop *Southerners* to hear the error in *Among we. . . . Us* is correct.]

■ 3 Using pronoun appositives that describe direct or indirect objects

Appositives follow a noun and describe it. (See 10a3.) Use the object form for pronouns in an appositive that describes a direct or indirect object.

me
Professor Konewski chose two new research assistants, John Park and I.
^

[Drop *two new research assistants, John Park and* to hear the error in *chose . . . I. Me* is correct.]

17c ⎸ Use the object form in the compound subjects and objects of infinitives

■ An **infinitive** consists of *to* plus the base form of the verb: *She asked me to bake a chocolate cake.* But the *to* is sometimes omitted: *She helped me bake a cake.* (See 10a2.) To hear the correct pronoun form for the compound subjects and objects of infinitives, use the "drop" test. Drop everything from the compound except the pronoun in question, reread the sentence, and trust your ear.

me
Our English instructor has asked Oscar and I to critique each other's
^

essays.

[Drop *Oscar and* to hear the error in *has asked . . . I* to critique. The object form in *has asked . . . me* is correct.]

me
Penny volunteered to tutor John and I.
^

[Drop *John and* to hear the error in *to tutor . . . I.* The object form in *to tutor . . . me* is correct.]

17d ⎸ Use the possessive form for nouns and pronouns before gerunds

■ A gerund is an *-ing* verb used as a noun: *Flying is safer than driving.* (See 10a2.) Use the possessive form for nouns and pronouns that precede gerunds: noun + *-'s/-s'* or the pronouns *my, your, his, her, its, our, their* (*the pilot's flying, his flying*).

Celeste's
Roger appreciated Celeste helping him learn Spanish.
^

his
Dorothy received the credit for him being elected to the senate.
^

A note on participles and gerunds: Do not confuse participles with gerunds. A participle is an *-ing* or *-ed* verb used as an adjective: *Flying low, the hawk searched for prey.* Here *flying* is an adjective describing *hawk.* Do not use the possessive form before participles.

■ No possessive before a participle: *Kevin observed a hawk flying above the field.*

■ A possessive before a gerund: *Amelia Earhart's flying made her an American hero.*

A note on possessive pronouns and the apostrophe: Possessive pronouns do not contain apostrophes: *yours, hers, its, ours, theirs,* and *whose.* (See 37a.)

17*e* | Use *who* and *whoever* for subjects and subject complements, *whom* and *whomever* for objects

■ This guideline for the correct use of relative pronouns is sometimes difficult to follow. There is, however, an easy four-step formula to help you decide which words are correct.*

- Step 1: Consider the words following *who/whom.* In the sentence *The reporter was uncertain who/whom she should interview,* consider *who/whom she should interview.*

- Step 2: Rearrange the words you're considering to make a complete sentence. Leave a blank where the pronoun should go: *She should interview _____ .*

- Step 3: In the blank put *he, she, him, her, they,* or *them,* whichever is correct: *She should interview him.*

- Step 4: Replace *he, she,* or *they* with the subject form *who* or *whoever.* Replace *him, her,* or *them* with the object form *whom* or *whomever*: *The reporter was uncertain whom she should interview.*

Other examples:

Voters want to know who/whom the Democratic candidate will be.

[Step 1: Consider the words following *who/whom.* Step 2: Rearrange them to make a sentence, with a blank where the pronoun should be: *The Democratic candidate* will be _____ . Step 3: In the blank, put *he, she, him, her, they,* or *them,* whichever is correct: *The Democratic candidate will be she* (Use the subject form *she* for a subject complement following the linking verb *be*). Step 4: Replace *he, she, they* with *who* or *whoever*; replace *him, her, them* with *whom* or *whomever*: *Voters want to know who the Democratic candidate will be.*]

Who/whom do you think should receive the award?

[Step 1: Consider the words following the pronoun. Step 2: Rearrange them to make a sentence, with a blank where the pronoun should be: *Do you think _____ should receive the award?* Step 3: In the blank, put *he, she, him, her, they,* or *them,* whichever is correct: *Do you think they should receive the award?* Step 4: Replace *he, she, they* with *who* or *whoever*; replace *him, her, them* with *whom* or *whomever*: *Who do you think should receive the award?*]

---

*For the formula to discover pronoun case, I am grateful to Maxwell Nurnberg, *Questions You Always Wanted to Ask about English* (New York: Pocket Books, 1972).

17f For the correct form in comparisons using *than* or *as*, mentally complete the sentence

■ Informal spoken English often uses an object pronoun after *than* and *as*: *Brenda likes jazz more than me.* But this construction is ambiguous. Does it mean Brenda likes jazz more than I like jazz, or Brenda likes jazz more than she likes me? In your writing, use the subject or object forms following *than* or *as* to make your meaning clear. To choose the correct form, complete the thought: *Brenda likes jazz more than I [like jazz]*.

Fran may be younger than her supervisor, but she is as qualified as ~~him.~~ *he*

[*He* is the subject of the unstated verb *is qualified: as qualified as he [is qualified]*. If it sounds stuffy to end a sentence with *he*, add the verb: *she is as qualified as he is.*]

I think my art history professor likes old buildings more than ~~we~~ *us*

students.

[*Us* is the direct object of the verb *likes: more than [she likes] us students.*]

17g Use reflexive (-*self*) pronouns only to refer to a preceding noun or pronoun

■ **Reflexive pronouns** are formed by adding -*self* to possessive or object pronouns: *myself, yourself, itself, himself, herself, ourselves, themselves.* They name the receiver of an action or the object of a preposition as identical to the doer of the action: *The baby scratched himself. I am going for a walk by myself.* (See also 8b7.) When a reflexive pronoun is part of a compound, use the "drop" test to hear the correct form. Drop everything from the compound except the pronoun in question, reread, and trust your ear.

Judy and ~~myself~~ *I* have operated our antique store for only a year.

[Drop *Judy and* to hear *myself have operated. I have operated* is correct.]

Maria and Carlos invited Barbara and ~~myself~~ *me* to the concert.

[Drop *Barbara and* to hear *invited myself. Invited me* is correct.]

A dialect note on nonstandard forms: *Hisself, themself, theirself,* or *theirselves* are not correct forms of Standard English. Use *himself, herself,* or *themselves.*

chapter 18

Choosing Adjectives and Adverbs

How to Edit Adjectives and Adverbs

Using adjectives and adverbs correctly will give your sentences the accuracy and polish readers expect of public writing. Answer these questions to see whether you should pay special attention to these words as you edit:

1. Do you feel that your writing is supposed to be different from the way you talk?
2. Are you unsure how to distinguish adjectives from adverbs?

If you answer yes to these questions, look for adjectives and adverbs as you rewrite.

How to identify and edit adjectives and adverbs:

1. Adjectives answer the questions *Which one? What kind? How many?* They modify (provide information about) nouns and pronouns. Adverbs answer the questions *How? When? Where? Why?* They modify verbs, adjectives, and other adverbs. (See 18a.)
2. Look for linking verbs (*be, appear, become, feel, grow, look, prove, remain, smell, seem, sound, taste, turn*) that are often followed by complements, words describing the subject of the sentence. Be sure that these complements are adjectives or nouns, not adverbs. (See 18b1.)
3. Look for the verbs *call, consider, create, elect, find, keep,* and *make.* Use adjectives, not adverbs, to modify their direct objects. (See 18b2.)
4. Look for *good, bad, well, badly.* Use *good* and *bad* as adjectives, especially after linking verbs like *be, look, smell,* and so forth. Use *well* as an adjective to refer to health; otherwise, use *well* as an adverb. Use *badly* as an adverb. A computer tip: Use the Find or Search and Replace commands to locate these words. (See 18c.)
5. Look for comparative statements. Use comparative forms (*-er, more, less*) to compare two subjects; use superlative forms (*-est, most, least*) to compare three or more. Use one comparative form at a time, *-er* or *more, -est* or *most.* (See 18d.)
6. Look for absolutes, words like *unique, perfect,* or *priceless* that cannot be compared. Omit the comparative or rewrite to make your meaning clear. (See 18d4.)
7. Look for negative words. Use one negative word at a time. (See 18e.)

18*a* | Use adjectives with nouns and pronouns; use adverbs with verbs, adjectives, and other adverbs

■ 1 Using adjectives

Adjectives modify—provide information about—nouns and pronouns by indicating which one, what kind, or how many. (See 8d.)

    which one   **what kind**
That tall, heavyset man is an excellent dancer.

A note on adjectives in sequence: When two or more adjectives are used without commas separating them, they must be arranged in a specific order. (See 34d; for ESL, see 32e3.)

■ 2 Using adverbs

Adverbs modify verbs, adjectives, or other adverbs, indicating how, when, where, why, or under what conditions: *She spoke enthusiastically.* (See 8e.) Many adverbs, as in this example, end in -*ly*, but not all: *always, here, nearby, there,* and *very.* And some -*ly* words are adjectives: *friendly* and *lovely.*

In casual speech adjectives are sometimes substituted for adverbs, usually by dropping the -*ly* from the end of an adverb. In writing, however, use adverbs to modify verbs, adjectives, and other adverbs.

                      surely
Stock market investors in 1929 ~~sure~~ did not expect the market to crash.

[*Surely* is necessary to modify the verb *expect*.]

                   rapidly
Second-parent adoption is a ~~rapid~~ growing phenomenon.

[*Rapidly* is necessary to modify the verbal adjective *growing*.]

    very
It was a ~~real~~ beautiful morning, perhaps the best of the summer.

[In casual speech *real* is sometimes used to modify adjectives like *beautiful*. But in Standard English use *very*.]

18*b* | Use adjectives as complements

■   Adjectives usually appear before nouns. But they may also follow certain verbs as complements, words that complete the meaning of a noun or pronoun. Sometimes it is difficult to decide whether to use an adjective complement modifying a noun or an adverb modifying a verb.

▮ 1 Using subject complements

Subject complements describe or rename the subjects of the linking verbs *be, appear, become, feel, grow, look, prove, remain, smell, seem, sound, taste, turn.* (See 9d1.) Use an adjective as a subject complement following a linking verb. Compare these examples:

She *appears* **angry.**

Does anything smell as ~~sweetly~~ *sweet* as a freshly mowed lawn?
                      ^

[*Sweet,* an adjective, modifies the subject *anything,* not the linking verb *smell.* It describes a thing, not an action.]

▮ 2 Using object complements

Object complements give information about the direct objects of the verbs *call, consider, create, elect, find, keep,* and *make.* (See 9c1 and 9d2.) Use adjectives to modify noun and pronoun direct objects. Compare:

A safety deposit box will keep valuable *papers* **safe.**

The personnel manager considered the applicants ~~equally~~ *equal.*
                                                ^

[*Equal* is an adjective describing the direct object *applicants.* In the original sentence, *equally* modifies *considered* and describes the action of the manager.]

18c Use *good/well* and *bad/badly* correctly

▮ Some writers find these words troublesome because of the influence of casual speech; others may try too hard to use them correctly. Follow these guidelines to the correct use of *good, well, bad,* and *badly:*

▮ 1 Using *good* and *bad* as adjectives

Use *good* and *bad* as adjectives after linking verbs (see the list in 18b1): *The fresh bread smelled good. The music from those speakers sounds bad.*

As the coach studied her players, she thought how ~~well~~ *good* everyone
                                                  ^

looked.

[*Good* is a subject complement accompanying the linking verb *looked* and describing the appearance, not the health, of the subject *everyone.*]

Bill felt ~~badly~~ *bad* about his behavior.
          ^

[Following the linking verb *felt, bad* is an adjective, a subject complement describing the subject *Bill.* It does not describe the act of feeling.]

■ 2 Using *well* as an adjective or an adverb

Use *well* as an adjective to refer to health or well-being. Otherwise, use it as an adverb modifying verbs, adjectives, and other adverbs.

well
After three weeks' rest, I feel ~~good~~ again.
                              ^

[Here *well* is an adjective following a linking verb and modifying the subject *I*.]

well
After its tuneup, the car runs ~~good~~.
                               ^

[Here *well* is an adverb modifying the verb *runs*.]

■ 3 Using *badly* as an adverb

Use *badly* as an adverb: *The team played badly.*

18*d* To compare two things, use the comparative form; to compare three or more things, use the superlative

■ 1 Forming comparatives and superlatives

Adjectives and adverbs have three forms to indicate degree or intensity: **positive, comparative,** and **superlative.**

POSITIVE	COMPARATIVE	SUPERLATIVE
good	better	best
bad	worse	worst
happy	happier	happiest
beautiful	more beautiful, less beautiful	most beautiful, least beautiful

To form comparatives and superlatives, follow these guidelines:

- One-syllable adjectives and adverbs. One-syllable adjectives and adverbs generally use *-er* and *-est* (*taller, tallest; faster, fastest*).

- Two-syllable adjectives. Two-syllable adjectives accented on the first syllable use *-er* and *-est* (*happier, happiest; lovelier, loveliest*).

- Three-syllable adjectives. Three-syllable adjectives use *more/most, less/least* (*more beautiful, most beautiful; less beneficial, least beneficial*).

- Two- and three-syllable adverbs. Two- and three-syllable adverbs, especially those ending *-ly*, use *more/most, less/least* (*more slowly, most slowly; less happily, least happily*).

- Irregular adjectives and adverbs. Memorize these irregular words: *good/better/best; bad/worse/worst; far/farther/farthest; far/further/furthest; little/less/least.*

■2 Confusing comparative and superlative forms

Do not use one form where the other is required.

Although Ernest Hemingway and William Faulkner are considered

major novelists, Hemingway has been ~~most~~ *more* influential.

[Two writers are compared; the comparative is necessary.]

My chores were weeding, planting, and, ~~worse~~ *worst* of all, emptying garbage.

[Three activities are compared; the superlative is necessary.]

■3 Repeating comparative or superlative forms unnecessarily

Avoid unnecessary repetition. Use one form, *-er/-est* or *more/most,* not both.

Increasing the number of pedestrians will lead to a ~~more~~ healthier

environment.

That was the most ~~unkindest~~ *unkind* remark I have ever heard.

■4 Comparing absolutes

Absolutes are words describing characteristics that cannot be compared. *Unique* means one of a kind; something cannot be more unique ("more one of a kind") or most unique ("most one of a kind"). If an object is *priceless,* it is without price. It cannot be "more priceless" or "most priceless." Other absolutes: *absolute, boundless, circular, complete, definite, empty, eternal, enough, favorite, final, full, inevitable, mutual, perfect, perpendicular, round, square, sufficient, supreme, total, triangular, universal, vacant.* Avoid the comparison of absolutes.

Your story will be ~~more~~ complete when you add an exciting ending.

Of all the old jazz bands, the Count Basie Orchestra is my ~~most~~ favorite.

18e Avoid double negatives

A note on dialect: A **double negative** says no twice and seems to contradict itself: *Eighteen-year-olds without jobs don't have nothing to lose by joining the army.* A logical person might say that if these young people

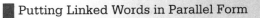
do *not* have *nothing* to lose, then they must have *something* to lose. One negative cancels the other and turns a negative statement into a positive. Of course, no one misunderstands double negatives in this way. In many dialects of English the double negative is a way of saying no emphatically.

But Standard English tends to be logical. Therefore, avoid double negatives in writing. Avoid using *not, never,* or *no* with other negative words, such as *no one, nobody, neither, none, nothing, barely, hardly,* and *scarcely.*

Eighteen-year-olds without jobs ~~don't~~ have nothing to lose by joining the

military.

    can barely
She ~~can't hardly~~ swim a stroke.
   ^

                                       a
Despite what some may think, welfare recipients don't live ~~no~~ life of
                                        ^

ease.

An exception: You may use a double negative to soften the intensity of a positive statement or to suggest irony: *Karen was not unhappy to learn she would graduate with honors.*

Putting Linked Words in Parallel Form

Parallel form (also known as *parallelism* or *parallel structure*) refers to linked words that match grammatically as nouns, verbs, prepositional phrases, clauses, and so forth. *Rosario and Maria* is a pair of linked nouns (noun and noun). *Revise and edit* is a pair of linked verbs (verb and verb). Abraham Lincoln's *government of the people, by the people, for the people* is a series of prepositional phrases. And from President John Kennedy's inaugural address, *ask not what your country can do for you—ask what you can do for your country* is a pair of clauses. Parallelism is a way to join and emphasize equally important ideas.

Faulty parallelism occurs when linked words do not have the same grammatical form. *Rosario and who has a sister named Maria* links a noun and a clause (noun and clause). *To hike or skiing* links a verb and a noun (verb and noun). *Tall, dark, handsome, and with a sly wit* links three adjectives to a prepositional phrase (adjectives and prepositional phrase). To make your sentences emphatic and grammatical, put linked words in parallel form. (See also 20c.)

How to...

How to Edit for Parallel Form

Putting linked words in parallel (or matching) grammatical form will emphasize their relation and make them stand out for your readers. Answer these questions to see whether you should look for parallel forms as you edit:

1. Are you unsure of the parts of speech (nouns, verbs, adjectives, and so forth) or how to identify phrases and clauses?
2. Do you sometimes write long sentences?
3. Do you sometimes add details to make your meaning clear?

If you answer yes to any of these questions, look for linked words as you rewrite.

How to identify and fix faulty parallelism:

1. Look for the conjunctions *and, or, but, yet, so, for, nor.* A computer tip: Use the Find or Search and Replace commands to locate these words. Be sure the linked words before and after them have parallel form. (See 19a–c.)
2. Look for comparisons. Be sure that the items being compared have the same grammatical form. (See 19d.)

What to study: Chapter 8, Parts of Speech; 10a, Phrases; 10b, Clauses; and 20c, Coordination.

19a Put words linked by coordinating conjunctions in parallel form

Coordinating conjunctions (*and, but, yet, for, so, or, nor*) link grammatically equal words. (See 8g1.) Use parallel forms before and after these conjunctions.

Among her favorite sports, Jill likes ~~to jog~~ *jogging* and racquetball the most.

[In the original, the verb *to jog* is linked to a noun, *racquetball.* The revision links a noun to a noun.]

Nearing thirty-five and ~~with~~ *having* only a high school diploma, Alan is

pessimistic about his future.

[In the original, an adjective phrase, *nearing thirty-five,* is linked to a prepositional phrase, *with only a high school diploma.* The revision links two adjective phrases, *nearing thirty-five* and *having only a high school diploma.*]

for running

We enjoyed everything about the trip except ~~when we ran~~ out of gas in
∧

Wyoming and a violent sandstorm in Arizona.

[In the original, a clause, *when we ran out of gas in Wyoming,* is linked to the noun phrase, *a violent sandstorm in Arizona.* The revision links two noun phrases as objects of the preposition *for.*]

19b Put words in series in parallel form

■ Words in series may be linked by a conjunction, or they may be a list. In either case, make each item in the series grammatically parallel to the others.

As I plan this semester, I am dividing my life into three categories:

school

~~academic~~, work, and pleasure.
∧

[In the original, the adjective *academic* is linked with two nouns. The revision links three nouns.]

Representative Cairns criticized her opponent as soft on crime,

quick to raise taxes

indifferent to voters, and ~~a tax-and-spend politician~~.
∧

[The original links two adjective phrases (*soft on crime, indifferent to voters*) to a noun phrase (*a tax-and-spend politician*). The revision links three adjective phrases.]

19c Put words linked by correlative conjunctions (*either . . . or*) in parallel form

■ Correlative conjunctions are linking phrases that come in two parts: *either . . . or, neither . . . nor, not only . . . but also, both . . . and, whether . . . or.* (See 8g2.) Make words linked by correlative conjunctions grammatically parallel. Do not use a comma after the first part.

When it comes to fast food, I love not only old favorites like hamburgers

but also ethnic foods like falafel ~~make my mouth water~~.

[The original links a noun phrase *old favorites like hamburgers* to a clause *ethnic foods like falafel make my mouth water.* The revision links two noun phrases, *old favorites like hamburgers* and *but also ethnic foods like falafel.*]

camping

Cassie was undecided whether to go white water rafting or ~~camp~~.
∧

[The original links a verbal noun called a gerund, *rafting,* to the verb *camp.* The revision links two gerunds, *rafting* and *camping.*]

19d Put comparisons using *than* or *as* in parallel form

Many students find it easier to write a research paper than ~~composing~~ a *to compose* poem.

[The original links the infinitive *to write* and the participle *composing*. The revision links two infinitives, *to write . . . than to compose*.]

The Anasazi ruins of Mesa Verde are as impressive as in Athens ~~at the Acropolis~~. *the Acropolis*

[The original links the noun phrase *the Anasazi ruins* to a prepositional phrase, *in Athens at the Acropolis*. The revision links two noun phrases.]

19e Repeat function words to signal parallel form

Readers depend on function words to signal grammatical forms and relations. Function words are prepositions (*to, by, in,* and so forth), articles (*a, an, the*), the infinitive *to,* and introductory words at the beginning of clauses (*that, who, which, because, when, if,* and so forth). If readers may misunderstand you, repeat function words before parallel statements. To see the effect of repetition, read the following examples in their original versions and then in revision.

The climbers deserved praise for risking their lives to save their injured friend but not *for* the recklessness that led to his fall.

The keys to academic success, Jana decided, were to attend class as if she were going to work and *to* study as if she were playing a sport.

Senator Cohen said that he opposes the Cartwright Dam project and *that* the Fremont River must remain unobstructed.

Crafting
Sentences,
Choosing
Words

Crafting Sentences

How to Edit for Emphasis and Variety

Sentences that are emphatic in design and varied in rhythm are a pleasure to write and read. More important, they convey their meaning clearly and powerfully. Read your writing aloud. Do you hear monotonous sentences, too many short or long sentences? Edit to give your writing the rhythm and emphasis of speech.

Count the number of words in your sentences. If you find passages in which sentences fall repeatedly within a few words of one another, you may have found a choppy or monotonous passage to rewrite. (See 21a–c.)

As you rewrite, consider your readers' knowledge and reading skills. The greater they are, the longer or more sophisticated your sentences can be. But remember that readers always value conciseness and directness.

Decide on your most important ideas:

1. Place them in a main clause or at the beginning or end of a sentence. (See 20b and e.)
2. Link related important ideas in a coordinate structure. (See 20c.)
3. Repeat important words for emphasis. (See 20d.)

To combine short, choppy sentences:

1. Identify the ideas you want to keep.
2. Deemphasize less important ideas in subordinate phrases or clauses. (See 20b.)
3. Look for words to cut: forms of the verb *to be*, needless repetitions, pronouns, conjunctions, and transitions. (See 28a–c.)

Divide long, rambling sentences. The most readable sentences usually have one main idea or set of related ideas and one purpose. (See 21c.)

20

Writing Emphatically

In emphatic sentences, important ideas stand out. Not only do they appear where readers expect them, they have been arranged to attract attention. The following guidelines will help you give your sentences this kind of impact.

20a | Use the active voice when possible

■ *Voice* refers to verb forms that show whether a subject performs an action or is acted on. In the **active voice,** an active subject—an actor—performs the action of its verb.

subject verb   direct object

Jane mailed the letter.

In the **passive voice,** a passive subject receives the action of the verb.

subject   verb

The letter was mailed.

■ 1 Using the active voice for emphasis

In the active voice, a sentence becomes a little story. Someone or something does something. This kind of sentence is usually the simplest to write, the shortest, and the easiest to read. And simplicity and brevity usually make main ideas stand out. Consider the italicized subjects and active voice verbs in the following passage. Note how they bring ideas to life and emphasize them.

> A fertilized female *tarantula lays* from 200 to 400 eggs at a time; thus it is possible for a single tarantula to produce several thousand young. *She takes* no care of them beyond weaving a cocoon of silk to enclose the eggs. After *they hatch*, the *young walk* away, *find* convenient places in which to dig their burrows and *spend* the rest of their lives in solitude. *Tarantulas feed* mostly on insects and millipedes. Once their appetite is appeased, *they digest* the food for several days before eating again.
>
> (Alexander Petrunkevitch, "The Spider and the Wasp," *Scientific American,* emphasis added)

■ 2 Changing the passive to active voice

As you edit your writing, look for passive voice sentences. When you find one, rewrite it in the active voice whenever possible. Make the actor into the subject of the sentence or, if necessary, identify the actor. (See also 8c4 and 5.)

Many doctors oppose children's
~~Children's~~ sports leagues ~~are opposed by many doctors.~~

[The phrase *many doctors*, referring to the actors, has become the subject of the verb *oppose*.]

The Board of Trustees is considering tuition
~~Tuition~~ increases of ten percent ~~are being considered~~ for next year.

[The revision adds the actors who perform the action of the sentence.]

20*b* sub

■ 3 Using the passive voice effectively

Two situations require the passive voice:

- Unknown actors. Use the passive voice when the actor is unknown or irrelevant.

  Nearly half of the world's fresh water **is locked** in the Antarctic ice sheet.

- Unimportant actors. Use the passive voice when the receiver of the action is more important than the actor.

  During the last Ice Age, the landscape of Wisconsin and northern Illinois **was gouged and shaped** by a gigantic moving ice sheet.

To put a verb in the passive voice, use a form of the helping verb *be* + the past participle of the main verb: *is mailed, was loved, will be chosen.* Don't confuse voice and tense; as these examples illustrate, the passive voice may appear in any tense. (See also 31d.)

20*b* Subordinate less important ideas

■ To emphasize important ideas, put them in an independent clause, the main part of a sentence. To deemphasize less important ideas, subordinate them in dependent clauses or phrases connected to the independent clause. What you choose to emphasize will depend not only on what is most important about your topic but also on the way one sentence fits with those that precede and follow. (For more on subordination, see 21b and 28c.)

■ 1 Subordinating with dependent clauses

You can deemphasize an idea by expressing it in a dependent clause, a group of words with a subject and verb that cannot stand by itself as a complete sentence.

- Dependent clauses headed by subordinating conjunctions. Add a subordinating conjunction such as *after, although, because, when,* and so forth, to create a dependent clause. Connect it to a related independent clause. (For a list of subordinating conjunctions, see 8g3.)

Because
 ˰Oahu was once a social center for Hawaii's kings, ~~so~~ it is now called

"The Meeting Place."

[By subordinating the first half of the sentence as a dependent clause, the revision emphasizes the title given to Oahu.]

■ Dependent clauses headed by relative pronouns. Add a relative pronoun such as *who, which,* and *that* to act as the subject of a dependent clause. Use it to modify a word in the main clause or to act as part of the main clause. (See also 10b1 and 3.)

, which
Oahu⌃was once a social center for Hawaii's kings, ~~so it~~ is now called

"The Meeting Place."

[The dependent clause deemphasizes the history of Oahu; the independent clause emphasizes the title based on that history.]

■ 2   Subordinating with phrases

You can reduce the importance of an idea further by putting it into a **phrase,** a word group lacking a subject, a verb, or both. Here are two kinds of phrases useful for subordinating ideas.

■ Appositive phrases. Put a less important idea in an appositive, a nounlike word or phrase that describes a nearby noun.

,
Oahu⌃~~was~~ once a social center for Hawaii's kings, ~~so it~~ is now called

"The Meeting Place."

■ Participial phrases. Put a less important idea in a phrase headed by the *-ing* or *-ed* participial forms of the verb. Put the phrase near the noun or pronoun it modifies.

Called "The Meeting Place,"
⌃Oahu was once a social center for Hawaii's kings, ~~so it is now called~~

~~"The Meeting Place."~~

[By deemphasizing the second half of the sentence in a participial phrase, the revision emphasizes Oahu's history, now part of an independent clause.]

20c | Use coordination to emphasize equal ideas

■ **Coordination** (also called **parallel form**) refers to linked words having the same grammatical form. It is a way to emphasize the equality of related words and ideas.

■ 1   Coordinating with a conjunction

Use a coordinating conjunction (*and, but, or, so, for, yet, nor*) to link and emphasize equally important words and phrases.

┌── linked words ──┐
Horns and sirens announced the ship's arrival.

┌──────────────── linked phrases ────────────────┐
The violin evolved from ancient Asian fiddles and medieval stringed
└──────────────┘
instruments.

■ 2 Coordinating with a comma and coordinating conjunction

Use a comma and coordinating conjunction to link equally important
independent clauses. (See also 34a.)

, but its
The old cabin looked warm and cozy. ~~Its~~ roof leaked, even in a gentle
 ^

rain.

■ 3 Coordinating with a semicolon and a transition or conjunctive adverb

You may also use a semicolon and a transition or conjunctive adverb
such as *however* or *therefore* to link related and equally important independent clauses. (For a list of transitions and conjunctive adverbs, see 12b3;
see also 35b.)

; however, they
Some say American workers are unproductive. ~~They~~ now work more
 ^

than forty-five hours per week.

■ 4 Coordinating with a semicolon alone

Use a semicolon standing alone to balance equally important clauses
that are similar in structure. (See 35a.)

; artificial
Natural air pollutants include dust, gases, spores, and pollens. ~~Artificial~~
 ^

air pollutants include smoke and gases from industries, vehicles, and

households.

A note on faulty coordination: Avoid stringing coordinate word
groups together into loose, rambling, unemphatic sentences. (See 21c.)
Also avoid the faulty parallelism that occurs when grammatically unequal
words are linked. (See 19a–c.)

20d | Repeat key words to emphasize ideas

To affirm your beliefs, express feelings, or give special emphasis, repeat key words in grammatically equal (parallel) structures. Parallel structures are italicized in the following passages.

> If all you saw of life was the Iowa State Fair on a brilliant August day, when you hear those incredible crops ripening out of the black dirt between the Missouri and Mississippi rivers, you would believe that this is surely the best of all possible worlds.
>
> You would have *no* sense of the destruction of life, only of its rich creativeness: *no* political disasters, *no* assassinations, *no* ideological competition, *no* wars, *no* corruption, *no* atom waiting in its dark secrecy to destroy us all with its exploding energy.
>
> > (Paul Engle, "The Iowa State Fair," *Holiday,* emphasis added)

> Twice in my life I have seen the expression on the face of a person who was soon to die by suicide. *It was* not the look of depression or despair. *It was* more the look of a person watching life from a great distance. *It was* an absorbed attention, as if the person were reviewing an elaborate show, of which he or she had once been the star. I hope I never see it again.
>
> > (Hugh Drummond, "The Masked Generation," *Mother Jones,* emphasis added)

In the first example, each repeated *no* helps emphasize just how safe the writer believes Iowa to be from the threats of the modern world. In the second, the repeated *it was* links the ideas in three sentences and emphasizes the contrast between the despair readers might expect to see and what the writer actually saw.

A note on excessive repetition: Excessive repetition will make your writing sound choppy or overemotional. (See 21b and d.)

20e | Place important ideas in emphatic positions

Beginnings and endings—especially endings—are emphatic positions. Consider:

> Stars, like people, do not live forever. But the lifetime of a person is measured in decades; the lifetime of a star in billions of years.
>
> > (Carl Sagan, from *The Cosmic Connection: An Extraterrestrial Perspective*)

The writer might have begun *Like people, stars do not live forever.* But because he is more interested in the age of stars than of people, he begins and ends with stars and their lifetime.

■ 1 Putting emphasis at the beginning

To emphasize a topic at the beginning of a sentence, make it the subject and open with the main clause. Compare these examples:

> *The lightning was no longer forking now but illuminating the entire sky,* flashing a dead strobe white, turning the bay fluorescent and the islands black, as if in negative.
>
> (Joan Didion, from *Miami*, emphasis added.)

[In the main clause that opens the sentence, the topic—*the lightning*—is the subject and the compound verb—*no longer forking now but illuminating*—states the main idea, which is then described in modifying phrases at the end.]

> *The* *was hit by a swerving truck.*
>
> ~~The truck swerved and hit the~~ ancient elm standing in front of my house.

[The revision makes the direct object of the original sentence—*the ancient elm*—into the subject.]

■ 2 Putting emphasis at the end

Design your sentences so that the main idea comes in the final phrase or word. Compare these examples:

Nothing can prepare you for the experience of **being laid off.**

The transformation of American horror movies began with

Alfred Hitchcock's <u>Psycho</u> ~~began the transformation of American horror~~

~~movies~~.

You can create an especially emphatic ending by writing a **periodic sentence.** Open with modifying phrases or clauses that lead to a closing main clause and, often, to an important idea that comes in the last word.

> Having laid waste the wilderness, skunked the waterways with toxics, and decimated animal and Indian alike in the name of economic progress, *we now indulge ourselves in an orgy of sentimentalism for whatever comes labeled "natural."*
>
> (Jonathan Evan Maslow, "Stalking the Black Bear," *Saturday Review,* emphasis added)

> When our voices are finally mute, when we have finally suppressed the natural instinct to complain, whether the vexation is trivial or grave, *we shall have become automatons, incapable of feeling.*
>
> (William F. Buckley, "Why Don't We Complain," *Esquire,* emphasis added)

When you occasionally add a periodic sentence to your writing, you delay your readers' understanding momentarily, heighten suspense, and emphasize the main clause at the end.

■ 3 Ordering items in series from least to most important

To develop suspense in a series, place the most important item or most impressive image last. To protest boxing's brutality, the writer of the following example builds to a final italicized description of a boxer punishing his injured opponent.

> It is nonsense to talk about prize fighting as a test of boxing skills. No crowd was ever brought to its feet screaming and cheering at the sight of two men beautifully dodging and weaving out of each other's jabs. The time the crowd comes alive is *when a man is hit hard over the heart or the head, when his mouthpiece flies out, when blood squirts out of his nose or eyes, when he wobbles under the attack and his pursuer continues to smash at him with poleax impact.*
>
> (Norman Cousins, "Who Killed Benny Paret?"
> *Saturday Review,* emphasis added)

chapter **21**

Adding Variety

21*a* | Vary the length of your sentences

Effective writing is like music. Repeated words and sentence patterns create an emphatic rhythm, and varied patterns make a melody that adds surprise, moves readers ahead, and prevents monotony. One of the most important creators of this musical style is variety in sentence length. Long sentences, short sentences, sentences in between—like musical notes, they give writing a varied tempo, a pace that makes reading easier and more interesting.

Consider the following example. The numbers to the left indicate the number of words per sentence:

19	The point of going somewhere like the Napo River in Ecuador is not to
8	see the most spectacular anything. It is simply to see what is there. We are
18	here on the planet only once, and might as well get a feel for the place. We
60	might as well get a feel for the fringes and hollows in which life is lived,
	for the Amazon basin, which covers half a continent, and for the life that—
	there, like anywhere else—is always and necessarily lived in detail: on the
	tributaries, in the riverside villages, sucking this particular white-fleshed
	guava in this particular pattern of shade.

(Annie Dillard, "In the Jungle," from *Teaching a Stone to Talk*)

Opening with a sentence of average length (the average English sentence runs seventeen to twenty words), the writer takes issue with the reason many people give for traveling. Then, in eight emphatic words, she offers a better reason. The next sentence, average in length, explains her point. The long final sentence describes some of the details that, for her, are the point of travel. Varying sentence length enables this writer to emphasize her main idea and to create at the same time the conversational rhythms that give voice to her writing.

As you write and revise, use short sentences to emphasize important ideas. The topic sentences of paragraphs are often shorter than those that follow; so are emotionally charged sentences and climactic sentences that make a closing point. Use longer sentences to explain, describe, and restate. The following guidelines will show you how to create this variety.

21*b* | Combine short, choppy sentences

■ One or two short sentences will emphasize important ideas, but several choppy ones may create a monotonous, singsong effect. To combine choppy sentences: eliminate unnecessary words, reword, rearrange, and repunctuate.

■ 1 Subordinating less important ideas

Combine choppy sentences by reducing one sentence to a subordinate phrase or clause. (See 20b.)

Although many
ˆ ~~Many~~ people try to avoid jury duty, ~~But~~ those who serve often praise

for the
their experience, ~~They speak of~~ new insights into human nature they

have gained.

[The revision combines three sentences into one, subordinating the first sentence as a dependent clause and the third as a phrase.]

■ 2 Coordinating equal ideas

Use parallel forms to coordinate related, equally important ideas. (See 20c.)

Most high school students watch television several hours a day, ~~They~~

spend little time on homework, ~~They~~ seldom read, and never write for

pleasure.

[The revision eliminates pronouns and repunctuates to link the uses of high school students' time into an emphatic series.]

■3 Rearranging and combining sentences

To emphasize what is most important, you may have to rearrange ideas.

Because they *, jurors*
~~Jurors~~ often come from vastly different backgrounds~~, Before beginning~~

~~their deliberations, they~~ must spend time learning one another's values
before beginning their deliberations
and attitudes.

[To emphasize the time jurors spend becoming acquainted, the revision subordinates the first sentence as a dependent clause, combines sentences, and moves the opening phrase of the second sentence to the end.]

21*c* Divide loose, rambling sentences into two or more separate sentences

■ Carefully crafted long sentences can be as clear, emphatic, and easy to read as shorter sentences. But long, rambling sentences may obscure important ideas and be tiresome to read.

■1 Dividing loose sentences at conjunctions or transitions

Omit conjunctions or transitions if possible. Then check to see that your revised sentences are varied and emphatic.

Some cigarette advertisements use cartoons to make smoking a playful
;
activity~~, and~~ others present attractive models to make smoking
. But if
glamorous~~, but if~~ you examine these ads closely, you will discover more

complicated messages about smoking.

■2 Dividing sentences at subordinating conjunctions or relative pronouns

Too many dependent clauses in a sentence make reading difficult, especially when they come at opposite ends of the sentence. Rewrite dependent clauses as complete sentences.

As the soil of privately owned tree farms in the Pacific Northwest has

become less fertile, lumber companies have turned to federal lands and

. *Once*

their prime stands of old-growth timbe̸r̸, ̶a̶l̶t̶h̶o̶u̶g̶h̶,̶ ̶o̶n̶c̶e̶ logging begins,

however,

‸these forests will last less than a decade.

[To create two sentences, the revision omits a subordinating conjunction, *although,* and adds a conjunctive adverb, *however,* as a transition.]

At the upper edge of earth's atmosphere, chlorine atoms attack the

. *This*

ozone laye̸r̸, ̶w̶h̶i̶c̶h̶ ̶i̶s̶ ̶a̶ form of oxygen (O_3) ̶t̶h̶a̶t̶ collects in a thin band

above the stratosphere̸/ and ̶w̶h̶i̶c̶h̶ protects the earth from ultraviolet

radiation.

[To make two sentences, this revision turns a clause, *which is a form of oxygen,* into a phrase, *this form of oxygen,* that becomes the subject of a second sentence and then omits two relative pronouns, *that* and *which,* to create the main verbs.]

21*d* | Vary your sentence types

■ Sentences can be classified according to the clauses they contain. (See also 10c1.)

- A simple sentence contains one independent clause and no dependent clauses: *Randy fell in love.*

- A compound sentence contains two or more independent clauses and no dependent clauses: *Randy fell in love, and he planned to live happily forever.*

- A complex sentence contains an independent clause and one or more dependent clauses: *When Janet walked through the door, Randy fell in love.*

- A compound-complex sentence contains two independent clauses and at least one dependent clause: *Randy, who had other things on his mind, didn't expect to fall in love, but he did the moment Janet walked through the door.*

One sentence type is not better than the others. But too many of one type may create monotony or obscure important ideas. Varying types will help you emphasize important ideas and vary sentence length and rhythm. Consider the varied sentences in the following example.

Compound	The Puritans were a daring lot, but they had a mean streak.
Simple, simple	They hated the theater and banned Christmas. They punished
Complex	people in a cruel and inhuman manner. They killed children
	who disobeyed their parents. When they came in contact with
Complex	those whom they considered heathens or aliens, they behaved
	in such a bizarre and irrational manner that this chapter in the

Compound-
complex

American history comes down to us as a late-movie horror film. They exterminated the Indians, who taught them how to survive in a world unknown to them, and their encounter with the calypso culture of Barbados resulted in what the tourist guide in Salem's Witches' House refers to as the Witchcraft Hysteria.

(Ishmael Reed, "America: The Multinational Society," from *Writin' Is Fightin'*)

21e | Vary the structure of your sentences

■ 1 Varying sentence openers

Most sentences, like this one, open with their subjects. The most common sentence opener, it is also the one readers most expect and the easiest to read. But too many of these sentences in a row can be monotonous. Vary your sentence openers occasionally to create new rhythms and to direct readers to the ideas you want to emphasize.

- Adverbs and adverbial openers. Known as *free modifiers,* adverbs can be moved almost anywhere in a sentence.

Slowly, the
 ∧The bicyclist pedaled ~~slowly~~ up the steep hill.

When runners   *exercise, they*
 ∧~~Runners~~ and bicyclists∧ should not wear portable stereos ~~when they~~

~~exercise.~~

- Participial openers. Open with a participial phrase headed by the *-ing* or *-ed* form of the verb. Follow it with the noun or pronoun that it modifies.

Churning the brown river, the
 ∧The paddle-wheel steamer/ ~~churning the brown river/~~ pulled from the

dock.

- Prepositional phrases. Open with a prepositional phrase, often a modifier of the main verb of the sentence.

In November, the
 ∧The city of Bloomington opened its first homeless shelter∧ ~~in November~~.

- An introductory series. Open with an introductory series in order to move important ideas to the end of a sentence. Use a dash to connect the series to the main clause. (See also 39a3.)

Flipping burgers, stocking shelves, tearing ticket stubs—these are the ways many
 ∧~~Many~~ high school students spend valuable homework time ∧~~flipping~~

~~burgers, stocking shelves, and tearing ticket stubs.~~

- An appositive. Open with a noun or noun phrase that modifies a nearby noun.

The loneliest of athletes, ultramarathon   *compete*
ʌ~~Ultramarathon~~ runners ~~are the loneliest of athletes, competing~~ in events

with few prizes and even fewer spectators.

- An absolute phrase. Open with a modifier containing a subject and part of a verb.

His hand trembling, the
ʌ~~The~~ graffiti artist~~, his hand trembling,~~ began to spray-paint the station

wall.

■ 2 Inverting sentence order

The most common English word order is subject + verb + object, complement, or verbal modifier. If you invert this order, putting the verb or other later words before the subject, you will change the rhythm of a sentence and create variety.

On the east wall hung a
ʌ~~A~~ small painting of a French river ~~hung on the east wall~~.

[This revision moves the verb and a prepositional phrase to the beginning.]

Among
ʌ~~The Chippewas of central Minnesota are among~~ the first Native
                                    are the Chippewas of central Minnesota
Americans to govern themselves outside federal government authority.ʌ

[This revision moves the subject and verb to the end of the sentence.]

A note on overusing the inverted order: Too many inverted sentences will make your writing sound awkward or pretentious.

21f Ask an occasional question or address readers directly

■ Most sentences you write are declarative sentences that provide information. (See 10c2.) But you can increase sentence variety and attract readers if you alternate declarative sentences with questions and sentences of direct address. (These strategies are italicized in the following examples.)

■ 1 Using questions that begin paragraphs

Placed at the beginning of a paragraph, questions give direction to your writing and involve readers in a search for answers.

But does imprisonment deter crime? Deterrence requires that potential offenders think about the consequences of their actions, as many fail to do. More important, deterrence requires that those who do think about the consequences see some real risk that they will be caught and punished—a risk that must outweigh the benefits they expect from the crime. Unfortunately for deterrence, potential offenders think that the threat of capture and punishment applies to others but not to them.

(Paul H. Robinson, "Moral Credibility and Crime,"
The Atlantic Monthly, emphasis added)

■ 2 Using rhetorical questions

Rhetorical questions, assertions phrased as questions, vary the expression of your ideas and opinions.

We need to recognize that ideas have consequences. By granting a special status to children, we go far toward ensuring that they will be self-occupied and all too often, irresponsible. *If children are fundamentally different from you and me, how could we possibly expect them even to begin to measure up to the same standards? How can you discipline them when, by definition, they are supposed to be creative, natural, and free?*

(R. Keith Miller, "The Idea of Children," *Newsweek,*
emphasis added)

■ 3 Using direct address

Addressing readers directly as *you* or *we* involves them and invites their response to your ideas.

Old men, old women, almost 20 million of them. They constitute 10 percent of the total population, and the percentage is steadily growing. Some of them, like conspirators, walk all bent over, as if hiding some precious secret, filled with self-protection. The body seems to gather itself around those vital parts, folding shoulders, arms, pelvis like a fading rose. *Watch and you see how fragile old people come to think they are.*

(Sharon R. Curtin, "Aging in the Land of the
Young," *The Atlantic,* emphasis added)

Avoiding Mixed and
Incomplete Messages

No matter how vivid, insightful, or stylish your writing, if your sentences don't make sense or say what you intend, the virtues of your writing will be lost on readers. The following guidelines will help you express your meaning accurately.

How to Edit to Say What You Mean

If the parts of your sentences don't fit together logically and say what you intend, your readers will not get your meaning. As you edit your writing, reread from their point of view. How will your readers understand your sentences? Read to see what you've actually written instead of what you meant to write.

As you reread, ask "What's happening here?" Rewrite so that actions and events make sense.

1. Identify actors and their actions, subjects and their verbs. Do they go together logically? As you rewrite, try to keep your subjects and verbs as close together as possible. Your meaning will be clearer. (See 22a and b. To learn to identify subjects and verbs, see 8c and 9a.)

Study your sentences, asking "What goes with what?" Rewrite to create logical relationships.

1. Consider comparisons. Be sure they are logical and complete. (See 22c.)
2. Study your sentences to see whether they have all the words necessary to express your meaning accurately. (See 22d.)
3. Consider words that precede and follow commas. If one word group modifies the other, be sure the relation is logical. (See 23a and b.)
4. Check to see that pronouns are consistent in their reference and verbs are consistent in their forms. (See 24a–e.)

22a Write subjects and predicates that make sense together

■ Subjects must fit logically with their predicates, consisting of the main verb and any associated words. When they do not, the error is known as **faulty predication.** Subjects must be able to do what their verbs say they are doing. Subjects and the complements that modify them must fit together naturally and appropriately. Rewrite so that all the parts of your sentence make sense together.

has been neglected by
The ideal of national service ~~has dwindled among~~ many young

Americans.

[Logically, an ideal cannot dwindle, which means to become smaller. The problem is not the size of the ideal but people's awareness of or opposition to it.]

■ 1 Using a subject that does not fit part of a compound predicate

A subject must make sense with all of its verbs.

Hot air ballooning experienced a renaissance
~~The renaissance of hot air ballooning came~~ in the early 1960s and has

since then grown increasingly popular.

[The original version says that a *renaissance . . . came . . . and has grown . . . popular.* But the renaissance did not grow popular. The writer means to say that hot air ballooning has grown popular.]

■ 2 Using an illogical subject complement

An adjective or noun that follows a verb must logically describe or re-name the subject of the sentence.

A   *is an organization*
~~The hospice~~ ~~concept is a program~~ that provides skilled and

compassionate care to dying patients.

[The original says that a concept is a program. The assertion is illogical, and neither word accurately describes a hospice.]

■ 3 Using *is when, is where*

These phrases are common in casual speech, but often, especially in definitions, they create statements that are not grammatical or logical.

the
Algophobia is ~~when a person has~~ excessive fear of pain.

[*When* is an adverb of time, but *algophobia* is a condition. The revision connects the term to its definition.]

in which
Cubism was an early twentieth-century artistic style ~~where~~ painters

presented multiple perspectives of three-dimensional objects.

[*Where* is an adverb of place, but Cubism was an artistic movement.]

22b | Avoid mixed constructions that say one thing in two ways

■ Many ideas can be expressed in more than one way. A **mixed construction** occurs when two ways of saying the same thing are combined in one sentence. To rewrite a mixed construction, identify the two patterns of expression and choose the one that best fits the surrounding sentences and most clearly expresses your ideas.

The   *has*
~~According to a report by the~~ Center for U.S.-Mexican Studies ʌuncovered

changed immigration patterns in California.

[In the original, a prepositional phrase, *according to a report*, seems to be the subject of the sentence—a grammatical impossibility. The revision uses a noun phrase, *the Center for U.S.-Mexican Studies*, as the subject. Another revision might follow the pattern begun by the original opening: *According to a report by the Center for U.S.-Mexican Studies, immigration patterns in California have changed.*]

22c Make comparisons logical and complete

■ 1 Comparing noncomparable items

You know the old saying people use to identify faulty comparisons: "That's like comparing apples to oranges." To be logical, compare subjects that are genuinely comparable.

Cosmetic manufacturers have experimented with rabbits because they

eyes.
have eyes similar to ~~the membrane of the~~ human ʌeyeʌ

[The original sentence compares eyes to a membrane: *eyes similar to the membrane of the human eye.* The revision compares eyes with eyes.]

■ 2 Using incomplete formulas

Comparisons are made using certain verbal formulas. To be logical, supply all words necessary to complete the formula.

that of
Foreign cars often have a warranty longer than ʌAmerican cars.

[The original seems to compare a warranty to a car: *a warranty longer than American cars. That of*, supplied in the revision, completes the comparison between *foreign cars* and *American cars.*]

they spend with
Alcoholics often spend more time drinking with friends than ʌtheir

families.

[The original seems to say that alcoholics drink with friends and families alike. Inserting *they spend with* distinguishes time spent with friends from time spent with families.]

■ 3 Making incomplete comparisons

To be complete, comparisons must include all items being compared.

than the Chicago Bears

The Miami Dolphins are not only a bigger and faster football team. Man

for man, they are also more experienced.

■ 4 Mixing comparative and superlative forms

Use the comparative *-er/more* form to compare two items, the superlative *-est/most* form to compare three or more items. (See also 18d2.)

a higher

The United States has ~~the highest~~ divorce rate than any other country.

[The original sentence uses the superlative form to compare the United States to any other country. The revision uses the correct form for comparing two items.]

22d | Include all necessary key words and function words

■ 1 Checking for omitted key words

As they reread their writing, writers often see what they meant to say instead of what they've actually written. As a result, they don't see the illogical statements produced by omitted key words. As you rewrite, be sure your sentences have all the words necessary to express your ideas completely.

for teachers

High school homeroom periods last just long enough to take attendance

for students to

and hear announcements.

[The original says, illogically, that the homeroom periods take attendance and hear announcements. The revision adds the subjects for these actions, *teachers* and *students*.]

When we reached a clearing in the forest, we found ourselves knee-deep

lost in six-foot   ,   blinded by

in green slime, weeds ~~six feet tall~~ and clouds of flying insects.

[In the original, the hikers improbably appear to be knee-deep in six-foot weeds and clouds of insects, as well as slime. The added verb phrases describe their situation accurately.]

22d **mixed**

■ 2 Checking for omitted function words

Function words help to identify the grammatical functions performed by the key words of sentences. Include all the function words necessary to signal the direction your sentences are taking.

- The articles *a, an,* and *the.* Include articles before nouns to make series or compounds grammatically complete.

  Onto the stage walked a doctor,⌃*an* astronaut, and⌃*the* president of the

  university.

  [It is necessary to add *an* before a word beginning with a vowel and the definite article *the* before the title of a specific person.]

- The subordinating conjunction *that.* You may often omit *that* from your sentences: *Leslie stuffed her backpack with all [that] she would need for two weeks.* But include *that* if readers may not see that a clause follows a verb instead of a direct object.

  Kevin found⌃*that* the historic house he wanted to photograph had been

  demolished.

  [Adding *that* indicates that the historic house is the subject of a clause, not the direct object of *found.*]

- Verbs in compound structures. Even though a verb may be common to both parts of a compound structure, you must repeat the verb to signal tense changes.

  Without generous scholarships, our university has not⌃*recruited* and never will

  recruit the best students.

  [The original is ungrammatical: *has not . . . recruit. Recruited* is necessary to signal that the tense of the first verb differs from that of the second.]

- The relative pronouns *who* and *whom.* If a relative pronoun changes case from one part of a compound structure to another, use both case forms. (See 17e.)

  Arthur Ashe was a man⌃*whom* many thought the greatest male tennis player of

  his generation but who should be remembered more for his social

  activism.

  [*Whom* must be added to the first half of the compound to signal that it is in the object case as the direct object of the verb *thought.* In the second half, *who* is in the subject case as the subject of the verb *should be remembered.*]

Placing Modifiers

23a | Move misplaced modifiers near the words they modify

A **misplaced modifier** is a word or phrase that is located incorrectly in relation to the words it modifies. The result may be an illogical sentence that is difficult to follow. If you spot a misplaced modifier, rearrange the sentence to make sense and make reading easier.

, which hummed quietly,
A small fan‸stood on the desk‸~~which hummed quietly~~.

[In the original, the desk appears to hum quietly. The revision moves the modifier next to the word it modifies, *fan*.]

, driving through eastern Pennsylvania,
I knew I was near my destination when‸I tuned in a New York radio

station‸~~driving through eastern Pennsylvania~~.

[In the original, the New York radio station appears to be driving through Pennsylvania. Locating the modifier next to *I* makes clear who is driving.]

■ 1 Using limiting modifiers correctly

Limiting modifiers restrict or limit the meaning of the words they modify: *almost, even, exactly, hardly, just, merely, nearly, only, scarcely, simply.* To make your meaning clear and unambiguous, place these modifiers before the words they modify.

only
Barry ~~only~~ chose‸the chocolate-covered caramels.

almost
On average, Americans ~~almost~~ work‸as many hours per week as the

Japanese.

■ 2 Avoiding squinting modifiers

Squinting modifiers appear to modify both preceding and following words, creating ambiguous meaning. Move the modifier before the word it modifies or rewrite to eliminate ambiguity.

Because she wanted to work for the National Park Service, Nancy

seriously
∧considered ~~seriously~~ studying for a degree in botany.

[The original seems to say that Nancy considered doing some serious studying. The revision says that the way she considered was serious.]

in the evening
The owner required his tenants ~~in the evening~~ to play their music quietly∧.

[The original seems to say that the landlord made his requirement in the evening. The revision says that the tenants must be quiet in the evening.]

■ 3 Avoiding split infinitives

An infinitive is the *to* form of a verb: *to run*. **Split infinitives** occur when a modifier comes between *to* and the verb: *to quickly run*. Avoid split infinitives when they sound awkward or when readers may be confused.

quickly
Dean's mother told him to ~~quickly~~ run∧to the store and buy a newspaper.

without much preparation
Sheri hoped to~~, without much preparation,~~ pass her French final exam∧.

It is, however, appropriate to write split infinitives in some circumstances:

■ To avoid ambiguity. Consider the difference between these two sentences, the first containing a split infinitive: *The President proposed to further delay agricultural reforms. The President proposed to delay further agricultural reforms.* In the first sentence, the President proposed to increase the delay. In the second, the President proposed to delay more reforms.

■ To avoid awkwardness. Consider this sentence containing a split infinitive: *With more practice, the relay team was able to nearly equal their best time.* This version is clearer and more natural than *With more practice, the relay team was able nearly to equal their best time.*

23b │ To connect dangling modifiers, rewrite or add missing words

■ A **dangling modifier** has no words to modify. It "dangles" disconnected or appears to make an illogical connection.

■ 1 Rewriting dangling participles

A participle is the *-ing* or *-ed* verb form acting as an adjective. A **dangling participle** "dangles" because it has no logical actor to perform the action that it names. Rewrite to identify the actor; note that you will also have to change the form of the verb.

As I pedaled
ᴧ ~~Pedaling~~ around a sharp curve on the steep mountain road, the warning

of other bicyclists echoed in my head.

[In the original, the warning itself seems to be pedaling around a curve. The revision adds a subject and changes the verb to turn a phrase into a dependent clause.]

we had drifted
After ᴧ ~~drifting~~ down the river for another hour, the bridge came into

view.

[In the original, the opening phrase seems to modify *bridge*. Adding a subject, *we*, and turning the opening phrase into a dependent clause clarifies the meaning of the sentence.]

■ 2 Rewriting a modifier that appears to modify a possessive

Modifiers that provide information about nouns or pronouns cannot modify possessive -'s words, which act as adjectives rather than nouns. Rewrite to omit the possessive or to supply a noun or pronoun.

Although recognized by many for her fundraising, Lucille Allen ~~'s name~~

didn't become well known until she married the mayor.

[In the original, the opening phrase seems illogically to modify *Lucille Allen's name*. Dropping the possessive -'s and *name* makes all parts of the sentence fit together.]

■ 3 Rewriting dangling appositives

A noun or noun phrase functioning as an appositive must stand near the noun or equivalent form that it can logically modify. Rewrite to create logical relations.

to be
The actress's sensitive performance revealed the mother ~~'s character~~ ᴧ a

strong, courageous person.

[In the original, the appositive *a strong, courageous person* illogically modifies *character*. Adding *to be* turns the appositive into a complement describing *mother*.]

Avoiding Faulty Shifts

24*a* | Maintain a consistent point of view

■ **Point of view** is the perspective of a piece of writing: **first person** point of view (*I* or *we*), **second person** (*you*), or **third person** (*he, she, it, one,* or *they*). A faulty shift in point of view frequently involves a shift from first or third person to second person, for example, from *I* or *they* to *you*. As you write, settle on a point of view appropriate to the subject and occasion. For informal writing, first person point of view is usually appropriate, but for more formal writing, third person is more often appropriate. Once you've decided on your point of view, maintain it consistently.

My job washing dishes may be damp and dirty, but at least no one ever
bothers ~~you~~ *me* while ~~you are~~ *I am* working.

Pedestrians stared suspiciously at the Jeffreys as they searched for the
right address. Wherever ~~you~~ *they* turned, ~~you~~ *they* were inspected from head to

foot.

A note on direct address: Write *you* only when you mean to address readers directly, as in instructions or advice: *When you finish a rough draft, let it sit for a while before you begin revising.* (See 16a3.)

24*b* | Avoid inconsistent shifts in number

■ If you begin writing about a subject using the plural, stick to the plural; if you begin in the singular, stick to the singular.

Televised violence has made many viewers afraid to leave their ~~home~~ *homes* at

night.

24*c* | Stay in one tense unless the time of the action changes

When you use more than one verb to describe an action, put all verbs in the same tense. A faulty tense shift between past and present sometimes occurs in narratives about past events.

When General Picket was ordered to prepare his men to charge, the
could not
young officer ~~cannot~~ contain his anticipation.

[The original version shifts from the past tense, *was ordered*, to the present, *cannot contain*. The revision makes both verbs past tense.]

At the beginning of Shirley Jackson's short story, Mr. Johnson leaves his
wants
house in love with the world. He ~~wanted~~ to make others feel as good as
does
he ~~did~~.

[The original, from a student paper about a short story, shifts from present to past tense. The revision makes all the verbs present tense, the appropriate tense for writing about literature and the events that take place in individual stories, novels, and plays. (See also 13b1.)]

24*d* | Maintain a consistent mood and voice

■ 1 Avoiding shifts in mood

Mood identifies the kind of statement a verb makes: an expression of fact (**the indicative mood**), a command or advice (**the imperative**), and wishes or speculation (**the subjunctive**). Stick to one mood unless you have reason to change. (See also 8c6 and 13f.)

plant marigolds
For best growth and color, ~~it is important that marigolds be planted~~ in

full sun. Water them often and pinch back the blooms to encourage

further growth.

[The original shifts from the subjunctive mood in the first sentence, *be planted*, to the imperative mood in the second, *water . . . and pinch back*. The revision puts both sentences in the imperative mood appropriate for instructions.]

■ 2 Avoiding shifts in voice

Voice refers to the relationship between a subject and verb. (See 8c5.) In active voice expressions, an active subject performs the action of the verb: *The child hit the ball.* In passive voice expressions, a passive subject is acted on: *The ball was hit.* Maintain a consistent voice unless you have reason to change. (See also 20a.)

she had achieved
Jane congratulated herself because ꞈall of her goals ꞈhad been achieved ̷

[The original shifts from the active voice, *congratulated*, to the passive, *had been achieved*. The revision maintains the active voice throughout.]

24e | Avoid inconsistent shifts from indirect to direct discourse

■ **Direct discourse** consists of word-for-word quotations and questions addressed directly to listeners or readers. **Indirect discourse** summarizes quotations and questions. Be consistent in the form of discourse you use. (For ESL, see 32c.)

Last week Dr. Lambert told us that we were behind schedule ̶,̶ ̶a̶n̶d̶
and would   *our*
"̶Y̶o̶u̶'̶l̶l̶ have to our finish ̶y̶o̶u̶r̶ report by the end of the month.̶"̶

[The original shifts from summary to direct quotation. The revision maintains indirect discourse throughout. An alternative revision would quote all of Dr. Lambert's remarks: *Last week Dr. Lambert told us, "You're behind schedule. You'll have to finish your report by the end of the month."*]

Doctors of the nineteenth century were uncertain whether the causes of
whether they should
mental illness differed for men and women and ̷ ̶i̶f̶ ̶s̶o̶,̶ ̶s̶h̶o̶u̶l̶d̶ ̶t̶h̶e̶y̶ be

treated differently ̷.̶?̶

[The original opens with an indirect question and shifts to a direct question. The revision maintains indirect discourse throughout.]

Choosing Words

How to . . .

How to Choose the Right Words

As you plan your writing, consider the seriousness of your subject and your audience's knowledge. The more serious the subject, the more formal your vocabulary should be. The less informed your audience, the less technical your vocabulary should be and the more definitions you should provide. (See 27a.)

You'll write most accurately and vividly if you choose words that tell the truth as you know it. The right words state facts, ideas, and feelings exactly as you understand them.

Whenever possible, choose words you know well. Look up words outside your everyday vocabulary. To decide which word best fits the context of your writing, use the list of synonyms after many dictionary entries, a thesaurus, or Chapter 29, A Guide to Usage: Troublesome Words and Phrases.

Create metaphors and similes to describe your subject, make judgments, or express your feelings. Use the figurative language formula on p. 163 to get you started: "If _____ were a _____ , it would/would not be a _____ ." (See Chapter 26.)

Experiment as you write. When you come to a word that doesn't seem exact, try several alternatives. If you don't find the exact word, put a ✓ in the margin as a reminder to reconsider your choice as you revise.

Chapter 25

Choosing Exact Words

25a Denotation: Choose words that say exactly what you mean

■ The **denotation** of a word is its literal, dictionary definition. Although writers don't intend to choose the wrong word, even the best occasionally end up choosing a word that is not quite right. As you write and revise, look for the following mismatches between what you mean to say and what your words actually mean.

As you begin revising, ask yourself these questions:

1. Am I writing about an unfamiliar subject?
2. Does the occasion feel especially formal or serious?

If you answer yes to either of these questions, reread to be sure your words are accurate and appropriate.

Follow these guidelines as you edit:

1. When possible, use concrete and specific "pictorial" words. (See 26a and b.)
2. Unless you have reason to change, maintain a consistent formality or informality and a consistent positive, negative, or neutral attitude toward your subject. (See 27a and 25b.)
3. Provide definitions for technical words your readers may not understand. (See 27c.)
4. In referring to groups of people, choose words the members of those groups will accept: *disabled person* rather than *crippled person*. Check the personal pronouns *he, she, him, her, his, hers*. If any words could refer to both men and women, rewrite your sentence to include both sexes. (See 27e.)
5. Study your metaphors and similes. If you've read or heard them elsewhere, they may be *clichés*. Create fresh alternatives. (See 26d1.)

■ 1 Checking for ambiguous words

Writers sometimes choose words that, in the context of their writing, may have multiple, or ambiguous, meanings. To write unambiguously, choose specific words that express only the meaning you intend. (See 26a.)

Although many were dissatisfied with Judge Tanaka's decision, they did

     impartial
agree that it was ~~fair~~.

[*Fair* may mean that the judge ruled without favoritism, the meaning of *impartial*. But *fair* may also mean in the best interests of each person involved or without self-interest. The exact meaning of *fair* is unclear in the original sentence.]

■ 2 Checking for approximate words

Some words are near synonyms of other words. But, as Mark Twain observed, the difference between the right word and the almost-right word is the difference between lightning and a lightning bug. To distinguish between words with similar meanings, use the synonym section of dictionary entries or a thesaurus. (See 25c and d.)

~~quietly~~ ~~weakly~~ faintly

At dawn, the cardinal's song echoed ~~feebly~~ over the roof tops.

■3 Checking for confused words

One word may be confused with another that is similar in appearance, sound, or meaning. (For more on frequently confused words, see 25e and 29.)

principles

The ~~principals~~ of good journalism are truth, skepticism, and dramatic

stories.

[As a noun, *principal* refers to one who holds a high position; *principle* refers to a basic truth or standard, the meaning here.]

25b | Connotation: Choose words that convey appropriate feelings and attitudes

■ The **connotation** of a word consists of its emotional associations and attitudes. Words similar in dictionary definition often differ widely in connotative meaning; one may be positive, another neutral, a third, negative. Consider the connotations of the word pairs in the following sentences. The words in each pair are similar in denotation but differ in connotations. Is each word positive, negative, or neutral?

On the dining room table was a vase filled with *artificial/fake* flowers.

The old *cabin/shack* stood near the edge of a forest.

Political parties aim to *educate/indoctrinate* voters.

■1 Matching connotation and the writer's attitude

Choose words whose positive, neutral, or negative connotation matches your attitude toward your subject. Find the right word in the synonym section of a dictionary entry or in a thesaurus. (See 25c and d.)

scent

The ~~odor~~ of burning leaves reminds me of childhood.

[*Odor* generally has negative, unpleasant associations. If the writer's memories are positive, *scent*, associated as it is with perfume, is the better choice.]

■2 Expressing connotation in public writing

Decide whether words with strong connotations are suitable for the occasion. Not all situations permit such expressions of feeling or attitude, either positive or negative. Informative writing in school and on the job usually requires neutral or subdued words.

    crowd   *rushed to*

A ~~mob~~ of reporters ~~stormed~~ the rooming house where President Lincoln

lay dying.

[The strong negative connotations of the original words are inappropriate for writing from an objective perspective.]

25c | Learn to use all parts of a dictionary entry

■ A good college desk dictionary—such as *The American Heritage Dictionary* (3rd edition), *The Random House College Dictionary, Webster's Tenth New Collegiate Dictionary,* or *Webster's New World Dictionary*—does more than give spelling, pronunciation, and basic definitions. To choose the exact words for your meaning, you need to know—and use—all that a dictionary entry contains. Here is an entry from *The American Heritage Dictionary.*

        Pronunciation   Grammatical labels   Word endings

Spelling —— **af·fect**[1] (-ə-fĕkt´) *tr.v.* **-fect·ed, -fect·ing, -fects. 1.** To have
and word   ┌ an influence on or effect a change in: *Inflation affects the buying*
division   *power of the dollar.* **2.** To act on the emotions of; touch or
       move. **3.** To attack or infect, as a disease: *Rheumatic fever can* ┐
Definitions — *affect the heart.* —**affect** (ăf´ĕkt´) *n.* **1.** *Psychology.* **a.** A ├—**Usage label**
     feeling or emotion as distinguished from cognition, thought, ┘
     or action. **b.** A strong feeling having active consequences.
  └ **2.** *Obsolete.* A disposition, feeling, or tendency. [Latin *affi-* —**Etymologies**
    cere, affect- : *ad-* + *facere,* to do; see **dhē-** in Appendix.]   **(word**
                                         origins)

     SYNONYMS: affect, influence, impress, touch, move, strike. These ┐
     verbs are compared as they mean to produce a mental or
  ┌ emotional effect. To *affect* is to act upon a person's emotions:
     The adverse criticism the book received didn't affect the author one
     way or another. Influence implies a degree of control or sway
Examples   over the thinking and actions, as well as the emotions, of an-
illustrating other: *"Humanity is profoundly influenced by what you do"* (John
the contexts Paul II). To *impress* is to produce a marked, deep, often endur-
appropriate ┤ ing effect: *"The Tibetan landscape particularly impressed him."* ├—**Synonyms**
for each (Doris Kerns Quinn). *Touch* usually means to arouse a tender   **(related**
synonym response, such as love, gratitude, or compassion: *"The tributes*   **words)**
     [to the two deceased musicians] *were fitting and touching"*
     (Daniel Cariaga). *Move* suggests profound emotional effect
     that sometimes leads to action or has a further consequence:
     The account of her experiences as a refugee moved us to tears. Strike
     implies keenness or force of mental response to a stimulus: *I*
  └ *was struck by the sudden change in his behavior.* ┘
Usage ——— *USAGE NOTE: Affect*[1] and *effect* have no senses in common.
     As a verb *affect*[1] is most commonly used in the sense of "to in-
     fluence" (*how smoking affects health*). *Effect* means "to bring
     about or execute": *layoffs designed to effect savings.* Thus the
An example —— sentence *These measures may affect savings* could imply that the
of appropriate measures may reduce savings that have already been real-
usage ized, whereas *These measures may effect savings* implies that the
     measures will cause new savings to come about.

▇ 1 Locating spelling, word division, and pronunciation

Words are divided by syllables: **af·fect.** Two words with the same spelling but different meanings are numbered to signal their difference. Compounds are written as one word (*multimedia*), with a hyphen (*multiple-choice*), or as two words (*multiple sclerosis*). When two or more spellings or pronunciations are correct, the preferred appears first. The phonetic alphabet (as in ə-fĕkt´) is explained in the dictionary's introduction and in the pronunciation key usually found at the bottom of the page. Accent marks (´) indicate the most heavily stressed character or syllable.

▇ 2 Locating grammatical labels and word endings

Labels indicate the grammatical function (part of speech) of a word and its various endings: *tr.v.* **-fect·ed, -fect·ing, -fects.**

adj. adjective	*interj.* interjection	*prep.* preposition
adv. adverb	*n.* noun	*pron.* pronoun
aux. auxiliary	*pl.* plural	*sing.* singular
conj. conjunction	*pl. n.* plural noun	*tr.* transitive
def. art. definite article	*pref.* prefix	*intr.* intransitive
indef. art. indefinite article	*suff.* suffix	*v.* verb

Whenever a word changes grammatical function, alternatives are listed in boldface accompanied by a grammatical label:—**affect** (ăf´ ĕkt´) *n.* All abbreviations are defined in the dictionary's introduction (see the table of contents after the title page).

▇ 3 Locating definitions and etymologies

Definitions are numbered and arranged by frequency of use or according to meaning clusters. Letters following numbers identify closely related definitions. Examples occasionally illustrate a word's use. The **etymology** of a word (its origin or history) is often an important guide to its meanings and associations. **Affect,** for example, comes from Latin words (Latin *afficere, affect-* : *ad-, ad-* + *facere,* to do).

▇ 4 Locating usage labels

Labels preceding a definition tell under what conditions that definition is appropriate: *Informal, Slang, Nonstandard, Offensive, Archaic, Obsolete, Chiefly British.* Field labels identify special areas such as music, art, computer science, and medicine where specific definitions apply (see *Psychology* in the sample entry).

▇ 5 Locating synonyms and usage

Following the main entries of many words are notes that distinguish among related words (see the synonyms of *affect*) or that compare actual uses of words with what experts consider correct uses (see the Usage Note on *affect* and *effect*).

25*d* Use a thesaurus to find the exact word, not necessarily the biggest or fanciest

■ A **thesaurus** (from the Latin word for "treasure") lists words together with their synonyms, antonyms, and related words. A thesaurus may be a printed reference work such as *Roget's II; The New Thesaurus,* or *Webster's Collegiate Thesaurus,* or a data file accompanying a computer word processor. Here is an entry from *Webster's Collegiate Thesaurus.*

Headword   Grammatical label   Numbers identifying different senses of the headword

believe *vb* **1** to have a firm conviction in the reality of something — Illustration of the core meaning of the headword

Synonyms listed   < *believes* in ghosts >

syn accept, ‖ buy, swallow

Related words that are not synonyms — *rel* accredit, credit, trust; admit

Idiomatic equivalents — *idiom* have no doubts about, hold the belief that, take (*or* accept) as gospel, take at one's word, take one's word for

Contrasting words that are not antonyms — *con* discredit, distrust, doubt, mistrust, question, suspect; challenge, dispute; reject, turn down — Cross reference number

Antonyms — *ant* disbelieve, misbelieve

2 *syn* FEEL **3.** consider, credit, deem, hold, sense, think — A signal to check usage labels in a dictionary

3 *syn* UNDERSTAND **3.** assume, expect, gather, imagine, ‖ reckon, suppose, suspect, take, think

■ 1 Matching words to contexts

Although a thesaurus groups words having related meanings, it cannot identify the specific contexts in which each word is appropriate. As you decide between synonyms or related words, consider the denotation and connotation of each word, your readers' vocabulary, and the formality of the occasion. (See 27a and b.) In most contexts, synonyms are not interchangeable with one another.

~~anxious~~ ~~desirous~~ eager
We were ~~dying~~ to share our experiences from our vacation in Egypt.

[*Dying* is too informal for academic and most public writing. *Desirous* sounds too stuffy. And *anxious* suggests apprehension. *Eager* combines the senses of anticipation and desire in a word appropriate for public writing.]

■ 2 Choosing exact words instead of impressive words

Many writers use a thesaurus because they doubt that their words sound educated, polished, or impressive enough. But consider how you've responded to people who have tried to impress you with their vocabularies. Use a thesaurus to help you find exact but familiar words. (See 27a and d1.)

           interest   *began*   *a vacation*
My ~~absorption~~ in archaeology ~~commenced~~ with ~~an excursion~~ in Egypt.

25e Distinguish between frequently confused words

Writers confuse one word with another for several reasons.

- **Homophones** sound alike but are spelled differently and have different meanings: *there, their, they're; affect, effect; complement, compliment.*

- **Near homophones** sound enough alike to be confused with each other: *adapt, adopt; allusion, illusion, delusion; ambiguous, ambivalent; lie, lay.*

- **False synonyms** are related but different words often used in similar contexts: *imply, infer; fewer, less; contagious, infectious; number, amount.*

- Some words have similar roots but differing prefixes or suffixes: *disinterested, uninterested; empathize, sympathize; incredulous, incredible; assume, presume; nauseous, nauseate; sensuous, sensual.*

To avoid confusion, look up words outside your everyday vocabulary and memorize differences between words that you have confused. (For a listing of many frequently confused words, see 29, A Guide to Usage.)

                     integral
Movies have become an ~~intricate~~ part of American culture.

[*Intricate,* meaning complex or elaborate, and *integral,* meaning essential or necessary, are near homophones differing greatly in their denotations.]

25f Use words idiomatically

An **idiom** is a word or expression given special meaning by native speakers of a language. It cannot be understood by the meanings of individual words alone. For example, native speakers of English say "Good evening" as a greeting but "Good night" as a farewell. Although they appear synonymous, these phrases are idiomatic expressions, each with its own meaning. Generally, idioms take three forms.

■ 1 Misusing individual words

Individual words are frequently used in some situations but not in others that may appear similar.

                buried
The murderer ~~lodged~~ his victims in the crawl space beneath his house.

[*To lodge* may mean to place, leave, or deposit an item, as in *The bone lodged in his throat.* Living persons may be "lodged," as in *We lodged our uncle at our neighbor's house.* But in idiomatic English, people are not "lodged" in anything but a residence.]

■2 Using stock phrases

Stock phrases are verbal formulas such as *sitting pretty, comes in handy, travel light, take your time, as good as, heavy-handed, make do, take stock, keep company, change of heart.* Such phrases are often overused. (See 26d1.)

■3 Misusing prepositions

Prepositions (*in, by, on,* and so forth) and preposition-like words called **particles** following verbs (*agree with/to, abide by, according to, argue with/about*) are especially idiomatic, appearing only in specific situations and with certain words.

A quiet walk through autumn leaves is always preferable ~~than~~ weaving $\overset{to}{\wedge}$

~~in~~ the crowded aisles of some department store.
$\overset{through}{\wedge}$

[Idiomatic English uses *better than* but *preferable to. Weaving through* is necessary to describe a person's path through a crowd.]

An ESL note: Native speakers of a language seldom use words unidiomatically, but nonnative speakers and native writers who choose words outside their everyday vocabularies may have difficulties.

- If you're uncertain of a word or phrase check usage notes in Chapter 29 and in dictionary entries.

- For stock phrases unlisted in dictionaries, check special dictionaries of idioms or phrase books in libraries or where English as a Second Language books are sold. (See the introduction to the ESL Editing Guide in Part IV.)

- For prepositions, look up the word preceding the preposition (*preferable* and *weaving* in the example earlier) in a dictionary. (See also 31g and 32f.)

Chapter 26

Choosing Vivid Words

If you're like most writers, you not only want words that say what you mean, you also want powerful words that will make readers pay attention to your ideas. These words transform writing into what the English poet Sir Philip Sidney called "a speaking picture." They are vivid, descriptive words that bring ideas to life in readers' imaginations.

26*a* When possible, choose specific rather than general words

■ Words can be classified as specific, general, or somewhere in between. **General words** are umbrella terms that refer to many things. **Specific words** refer to individual persons, places, things, actions, or qualities.

GENERAL WORDS ◀—————————————▶ SPECIFIC WORDS				
artist		painter		Mary Cassatt
urban area		city		Calcutta
vegetation	tree	evergreen	fir	spruce
observe		look		stare
textured	uneven	rough	coarse	scratchy

Because they are precise in meaning and feeling, specific words tend to be more pictorial than general words and to make a subject clearer and easier to grasp. Choose them for these reasons. Consider the italicized specific words in this passage from a memoir of childhood.

> The bodies of the men I knew were twisted and maimed in ways visible and invisible. The *nails* of their *hands* were *black* and *split,* the *hands* tattooed with *scars.* Some had lost *fingers.* Heavy lifting had given many of them *finicky backs* and *guts* weak from *hernias.* Racing against *conveyor belts* had given them *ulcers.* Their *ankles* and *knees* ached from years of *standing on concrete.* Anyone who had worked for long around machines was *hard of hearing.* They *squinted,* and the *skin of their faces* was *creased like the leather of old work gloves.* There were times, studying them, when I dreaded growing up.
>
> (Scott Russell Sanders, from *The Paradise of Bombs*)

As good writing often does, this passage opens with general words that announce the topic and set the scene: *bodies . . . twisted and maimed in ways visible and invisible.* The specific words that follow describe individual parts of those bodies and their special injuries.

As you write, create the rhythm of general and specific language illustrated by the preceding passage. Use general words to identify a subject, make assertions, and provide background. Use specific words to support assertions and bring ideas to life.

Drivers are becoming increasingly ~~dangerous.~~ *hostile. They tailgate at seventy miles an hour, drag race from stop signs, curse, and honk at whatever they think threatens their sacred right to the road.*

[*Dangerous* is a general word that may refer to unskilled drivers or, as the writer intended, to driver hostility. The added specific examples prove the point and dramatize it.]

by developers and commercialization,   *is now a protected historic site*
Once threatened, Henry David Thoreau's Walden Pond ~~now appears to~~
 ^   ^

~~be safe~~.

[The additions specify the threats to Walden Pond and the reason it is now safe.]

26b | When possible, choose concrete rather than abstract words

■ **Concrete words** refer to things you see, hear, taste, touch, and smell: *rock, trumpet, tomato, fur, rose.* **Abstract words** refer to conditions, qualities, and ideas: *democracy, justice, mercy, misery, hope, independence.* Prefer concrete words for the same reason you prefer specific words: their vivid, pictorial quality. You need abstract words to express ideas, but add concrete words to bring them to life. In the following passage, consider the emphasized concrete words that explain and illustrate *entropy,* the principle of disorder.

> Because of its unnerving irreversibility, entropy has been called the *arrow* of time. We all understand this instinctively. *Children's rooms,* left on their own, tend to get messy, not neat. *Wood rots, metal rusts, people wrinkle* and *flowers wither.* Even *mountains wear down;* even the *nuclei of atoms decay.* In the *city* we see entropy in the *rundown subways* and *worn-out sidewalks* and *torn-down buildings,* in the increasing disorder of our lives. We know, without asking, what is old.
>
> (K. C. Cole, "Entropy," *The New York Times*)

■ 1 Using concrete words for description

As you write and revise, think of concrete nouns to describe your subject and concrete verbs to dramatize its actions.

offers a sensory feast:
An autumn bicycle tour in western Wisconsin ~~is a wondrous sensory~~
 ^
~~journey~~. *the intense red and yellow of maples, musty aromas of just-harvested corn and*

beans, sounds of cattle and roosters, and the texture and taste of apples mounded in baskets

at roadside stands.

■ 2 Avoiding the seven deadly nouns

When possible avoid *area, experience, factor, field, situation, thing,* and *type,* words so abstract and vague that they deaden almost any idea.

the unequal distribution of local property taxes.
Urban public schools suffer from ~~a lack of funds, a situation caused by~~
 ^
~~unfortunate property tax factors~~.

planted her feet before her swing and followed through after her shot.
Lisa would improve her tennis game if she ̭~~changed a few things in her~~

~~swing.~~

■ 3 Choosing alternatives to *to be* verbs

Whenever you can find alternatives to abstract verbs like *is, was, were,* and so forth, the more vivid and pictorial your writing will become.

 protest
Americans ~~are concerned about~~ dwindling natural resources only when
lines of autos jam *soar*
 ̭~~there are long lines at~~ gas stations, home construction costs ~~are high,~~ and
 run into the hundreds of dollars.
monthly utility bills ̭~~are also high.~~

26c | Use figurative language to dramatize ideas, opinions, and feelings

■ **Figurative language** (also called **figures of speech**) uses words imaginatively and nonliterally to describe, evaluate, and express feelings. The most frequently used figure of speech is **figurative comparison,** which reveals hidden similarities between dissimilar subjects by transferring the features of one subject, called the **vehicle,** to the writer's true subject, called the **tenor.** Consider these lines from Robert Burn's famous love poem:

O, My Luve's [love's] like a red, red rose

That's newly sprung in June.

| My luve | is like | a red, red rose |
| [tenor] | | [vehicle] |

⬆ ⌐ The features of the rose: its
 │ beauty, soft petals, freshness,
 │ and the feelings associated
 └ with its color and fragrance

In two short lines, the poet has described his beloved, praised her beauty, and expressed his feeling for her. Because figurative comparisons say so much in so few words, they are an especially vivid use of language, one that can make your writing colorful and powerful, a pleasure for you and your readers.

■ 1 Using similes

As in the preceding example, a **simile** explicitly compares two unlike subjects using *like, as, as if,* or *as though.* Describing an early morning walk

How to . . .

How to Create Similes and Metaphors

Metaphors and similes provide vivid word pictures that help readers see and understand; they are also a compact and powerful way to express feeling and opinion. Use them in all kinds of writing, but carefully consider your purpose—whether to help readers understand an idea or to express a feeling—and adapt your figurative language accordingly.

If you're unsure how to create a metaphor or simile, use the following figurative language formula. Try several alternatives until you find one that is accurate, original, and appropriate to the situation. Then, as you write and revise, omit the formula and work the figure of speech into the context of your sentences.

If ___*(my subject)*___ were ___*(choose from one of the following categories)*___ , it would/would not be ___*(make up a term to complete the formula)*___ .

a movement	a food	a musical instrument
a place	a road	a piece of furniture
a toy	a shape	an article of clothing
a person	a sound	a means of transportation
a smell	a work of art	an animal
a color	a beverage	the weather
an object	a building	vegetation
		music

If *skydiving* were a *movement*, it would be a *dandelion seed drifting in the wind.*

When the parachute opened above me, I lost my prejump jitters, relaxed, and felt how graceful I was, floating as gently as a dandelion seed drifting in the wind. [a simile]

(Nancy Lee, student)

If *grammar* were *a musical instrument*, it would be *a piano played by ear.*

Grammar is a piano I play by ear, since I seem to have been out of school the year the rules were mentioned. All I know about grammar is its infinite power. [a metaphor]

(Joan Didion, "Why I Write," *New York Times Book Review*)

As you edit figurative language, avoid clichés (unoriginal figures of speech) and mixed metaphors (two or more figures of speech about the same subject that clash with each other). (See 26d.)

on an ocean beach, essayist David Black tells how "the waves, as they slid up the sand, foamed and hissed like butter sizzling in a frying pan" (waves = sizzling butter). Along the way, he fills his pockets with water-polished rocks "shaped as perfectly as eggs" (rocks = eggs) and pauses to watch seagulls that "stood in crowds, each gazing over the heads of the others, like guests at a chic party on the lookout for celebrities" (gulls = guests). Here similes describe concrete subjects by adding details of sound, shape, texture, appearance, and action. But they may also describe less tangible subjects, as in this description of how Pueblo people speak:

> The structure of Pueblo expression resembles something like a spider's web—with many little threads radiating from a center, crisscrossing each other. As with the web, the structure will emerge as it is made and you must simply listen and trust, as the Pueblo people do, that meaning will be made.
>
> (Leslie Marmon Silko, "Language and Literature
from a Pueblo Indian Perspective," in Leslie A.
Fiedler and Houston A. Baker, Jr., eds,. English Literature: Opening Up the Canon)
>
> [Comparing the structure of Pueblo speech (tenor) to a spider web (vehicle) dramatizes the organization of the language but also suggests something of its delicacy and sensitivity.]

■ 2 Using metaphor

A **metaphor** compares implicitly: not *X is like Y*, but *X is Y*. Tenor and vehicle are fused; one becomes the other.

> Superstition seems to run, a submerged river of crude religion, below the surface of human consciousness.
>
> (Robertson Davies, "A Few Kind Words for Superstition," Newsweek)
>
> [*Superstition* (tenor) becomes *a submerged river* (vehicle) and acquires the river's traits: depth, darkness, cold, and power.]

> The bristlecone pine of American Indians, Hopis live where almost nothing else will, thriving long in adverse conditions: poor soil, drought, temperature extremes, high winds. Those give life to the bristlecone and the Hopi.
>
> (William Least Heat Moon, Blue Highways, 1982)
>
> [The *Hopis* (tenor), described as *bristlecone pine* (vehicle), acquire the bristlecone's traits of hardiness, longevity, and the ability to thrive in adverse conditions.]

■ 3 Using personification

Personification is a special form of metaphor that describes something nonhuman as if it were human. Here travel writer James Traub describes Guatemalan volcanoes by giving them human personalities.

> For all their stolidity [showing little emotion], the volcanoes lead a moody life: peaceful and protective in the clear light of the morning; brood-

ing and withdrawn when afternoon clouds sail in from the north, creeping up the shoulders of the peaks toward their summit; and at night, in the rainy season, when the sheet lightning flashes across the surface of the lake, splendid and terrifying in a moment of white light.

("God and Man in Guatemala," *Saturday Review*)

26d | Avoid clichés and mixed metaphors

■ 1 Avoiding clichés

Clichés are overused, worn-out figures of speech or other expressions that have lost their power to communicate. Here are a few; how many do you recognize?

avoid it like the plague	the ladder of success	a sneaking suspicion
beat around the bush	last but not least	since the dawn of time
blind as a bat	the last straw	a step in the right direction
the bottom line	life is just a bowl of cherries	stop and smell the roses
burning the midnight oil	light as a feather	stubborn as a mule
crystal clear	off the beaten path	water over the dam
dead as a doornail	on the brink	without a shadow of a doubt
fresh as a daisy	playing with fire	white as a ghost
get a life	rude awakening	
	sadder but wiser	

The simile *stubborn as a mule* and the metaphor *life is just a bowl of cherries* were once lively expressions of stubbornness and life's sweetness. But after decades—centuries, even—of popularity, the mule has died and cherries come packed in freezer cartons. Dead, frozen, drained of color and flavor, clichés may not convey your exact thoughts and feelings, and readers may dismiss them the way they do an old story heard too many times.

If you write a catchy metaphor or simile you've heard others use, chances are it is already a cliché. Create your own fresh, original figurative language. The figurative language formula on p. 163 will help.

■ 2 Avoiding mixed metaphors

A **mixed metaphor** combines two or more comparisons that don't make sense together and often causes unintended humor. To write effective metaphors and similes, make a single figurative comparison.

The <u>Abbey Road</u> album ~~was the springboard that~~ reignited the Beatles' musical career.

[According to the original, the album is compared to a springboard and, through the verb *reignited,* to something that could start a fire. But a springboard cannot start a fire. The revision omits the illogical metaphor.]

Choosing
Appropriate Words ■

27 *a* | Choose words that fit the occasion

■ Choose an informal or a formal vocabulary, depending on your subject and the occasion. An **informal vocabulary** will make your writing personal and give it a conversational style. A **formal vocabulary** will express a serious and more objective attitude. Once you've decided what vocabulary is appropriate for a specific situation, use the following as checklists to guide your writing and editing.

FEATURES OF INFORMAL VOCABULARIES	FEATURES OF FORMAL VOCABULARIES
Contractions: *can't, shouldn't, won't,* and so forth	No contractions
Slang and regional expressions: *broke, strapped, dirt poor, beat my brains, brainy,* and so forth	No slang, few regional expressions: *poor, destitute, concentrate, study, intelligent,* and so forth
Frequent use of *I, we, us,* and *you* to express the writer's closeness to the reader	*I, we, us,* and *you* seldom used; emphasis on the subject rather than the writer or audience
Familiar words used in conversation: *poor, smart, my place, my house, think,* and so forth	Words that appear more frequently in writing; words with Latin roots: *impoverished, intelligent, residence, speculate,* and so forth
Words with obvious connotative meaning: *fake, phony, bright,* and so forth	Words with subtle connotations: *artificial, clever,* and so forth

■ 1 Choosing words in academic writing

Generally use a formal vocabulary for informative or persuasive writing about serious subjects. You shouldn't sound stuffy or use words you're uncomfortable with, but choose words that express the importance of the occasion. Refer to yourself as *I* if you are involved with your subject, but focus on your subject rather than yourself. Avoid slang and most contractions. Use an informal vocabulary for personal narratives, nonserious informative writing, and humorous writing.

■2 Choosing words in job-related writing

For business letters, memos, and reports addressed to strangers or superiors, write with some formality. Choose familiar words to avoid sounding stuffy or pretentious, but consider words subdued in connotation that fit the seriousness of the occasion. For memos and reports addressed to co-workers, less formal words will express your close professional relationship. Aim to sound as if you're talking to them about a subject of mutual concern. (See also 61a–d.)

■3 Maintaining consistent formality

Maintain a consistent attitude toward your subject and a consistent relationship with readers. As you edit, look for shifts from one vocabulary to another. Because you talk more than you write, take special care in serious writing to look for shifts from formal to informal words.

Contemporary religious philosophers have ~~come down hard on~~ *severely criticized*

American society as selfish and materialistic.

[*Come down hard on* is slang. Its conversational tone makes this expression inappropriate for academic writing on serious subjects.]

~~Right now, though~~, compressed natural gas has several ~~bugs~~ in its
Currently, however,   *problems*

storage that prevent its wide use as an alternative to gasoline.

[*Right now, though,* is too conversational and imprecise for serious academic writing. *Bugs* is slang and a cliché, inappropriate in objective writing.]

27b In most academic and public writing, avoid slang, regionalisms, and nonstandard words

■ The larger or more diverse your audience, the more careful you should be to choose words that all your readers will understand and feel comfortable with. You may speak a social or regional dialect of English rich with its own vocabulary, but for diverse readers, such words are inappropriate. Use a widely understood vocabulary instead.

■1 Avoiding slang

Slang is the informal vocabulary of a group or subculture. It is colorful, rapidly changing, strong in feeling, and often not understood by outsiders. Consider the slang popular among young Americans during the last fifty years; note how dated some words sound: *cool, hot, downer* (to describe bad news), *dank, schwag, geek, groovy, gizmo, heavy* (meaning "serious"), *later* (for "goodbye"), *out of sight, razzle-dazzle, I read you.*

Some slang becomes widely accepted and proves so durable that it becomes part of the language: *movie, muckraker, handout.* More often slang is incomprehensible to outsiders, has a life of only a few months or years, and is more often spoken than written. For these reasons it is appropriate only for informal writing to readers you know well.

■ 2 Avoiding regionalisms

A note on dialect: **Regionalisms** are words and expressions used by speakers from a specific geographic region. For example, in the south central Midwest *considerable* means a large amount. In the upper Midwest *eat razor soup* means to make a wisecrack. In the eastern United States, cottage cheese is frequently called *smearcase.* In some parts of Texas, *borrego* (borrowed from Spanish, "a young lamb") is used to refer to sheep and to fleecy-looking clouds. Like slang, regional expressions are often colorful and strong in feeling. But because their use is restricted and they may be misunderstood, you should avoid them in serious writing for diverse audiences.

■ 3 Avoiding nonstandard words

A note on dialect: **Nonstandard words** such as *nowheres, done told, theirselves,* and *don't never* appear in English dialects spoken by certain ethnic or social groups. Each dialect has its own grammar and vocabulary, and both are correct for speakers of that dialect. However, because these nonstandard words tend to be spoken rather than written and because they are not shared by speakers of other dialects, they are inappropriate for academic writing and other writing to diverse audiences. Use standard English words. (See Chapter 29. See also 13c–e, 17g, and 18e.)

27_c_ Use jargon and neologisms only with specialized audiences

■ In its technical sense, **jargon** refers to the technical language of a profession, craft, trade, or activity. Computer operators, for example, use acronyms like *VGA;* metaphors like *motherboard* and *parking a hard drive;* words derived from people's names, like *baud;* compounds like *on-line* and *log in;* shortened words like *e-mail* and *modem;* and old words with new meaning, like *server.*

A **neologism** is a newly invented word. Often neologisms begin their lives as jargon, slang, or media expressions: *vaporware, cyberspace, CAT* *scan, morphing, disco.* Many neologisms, such as *radar* and *scuba,* prove useful and eventually become part of standard English; the rest disappear.

Jargon and neologisms enable members of special interest groups to communicate with one another clearly, economically, and efficiently. They cause problems, however, when addressed to outsiders. Therefore, follow these guidelines:

■ 1 Writing for nontechnical audiences

When writing to nontechnical audiences, avoid jargon and neologisms. Choose accurate, widely understood words. If no other words will say what you mean, provide definitions.

With new computer-imaging technology, movie makers are now able to
transform
~~morph~~ one image into another, for example, fading the head of a man
^
into that of a lion.

■ 2 Academic writing

In academic writing for readers who understand your subject, choose words appropriate to the field or discipline. You are expected to demonstrate your knowledge of technical language. But avoid technical words merely to impress. If in doubt about the proper vocabulary, check with your instructor.

■ 3 Technical writing

In technical writing for knowledgeable readers, for example, in on-the-job memos and reports, a technical vocabulary is appropriate. But carefully consider your audience's knowledge. (See also Chapter 61, Business Writing.)

A note on jargon: Jargon is sometimes used broadly to refer to difficult or flowery words used to impress readers. These words are never appropriate. See the following section.

27d Avoid pretentious words, "doublespeak," and most euphemisms

■ 1 Avoiding pretentious words

Writers who put effort into their writing want it to be admired. But some, doubting their natural style or hoping to impress, choose words more for their "intelligent" or "artistic" appearance than their meaning. The pretentious writing that results is often called *jargon* or "gobbledygook." You know how annoying it is to you; others will be just as annoyed if you write pretentiously. Avoid the following words:

- Unfamiliar "big" words, often with Latin roots.

Some ~~educators in the~~ humanities *teachers* have been ~~dilatory in their cognizance~~ *slow to recognize how* ~~of the pedagogical ramifications of~~ new instructional technologies *can improve their teaching*.

- Flowery words.

The warm sunrise promised ~~Rising into azure heavens flecked with billowy clouds, the warm sun~~ ~~foretold a wondrous autumnal~~ *a fine autumn* day.

- Scientific-sounding words that aren't really scientific.

Increasing ~~the interface~~ *communication* between technicians and supervisors will ~~permit~~ *enable them* ~~the input necessary~~ to ~~determine the parameters affecting~~ *decide what changes will improve* production.

■ 2 Avoiding doublespeak

Doublespeak, a term invented by George Orwell in his novel *1984,* refers to words and expressions that deliberately mislead. Doublespeak aims to create a favorable impression opposite that of the truth. It is an essential feature of political propaganda, but you can find it wherever writers disguise the truth: in advertisements; in government, military, and business writing; even, occasionally, in academic writing. Some examples of doublespeak:

downsizing or
   rightsizing = layoffs

excessed or
   terminated = fired

final solution = kill

Peacekeeper = the
   name of a missile

preowned = used

resource recovery facility
   = incinerator

revenue enhancements
   = tax increases

sanitize = censor

substandard housing = slum

tanker accident = oil spill

Although doublespeak may mislead readers momentarily, its ultimate effect is almost always cynicism and mistrust. Remember Abraham Lincoln's axiom that you can't fool all the people all the time. Avoid misleading language.

■ 3 Avoiding euphemisms

Like doublespeak, euphemisms hide the truth. But **euphemism,** from Greek words meaning "good speech," refers to pleasant-sounding words that don't mislead so much as soften what some may consider distasteful, ugly, or difficult to speak of. Euphemisms usually concern emotionally charged subjects like death (*to pass away, expire*), economic status (*disadvantaged* for *poor, affluent* for *rich*), job titles (*custodian* for *janitor, educator* for *teacher*), the body (*limbs* for *legs, derrière*), bodily functions (*go to the bathroom*), and sex (*X-rated, make love, sleep together, adult entertainment*).

Most readers expect you to avoid vulgarity but to write clearly and directly. Unless your audience would be offended or hurt by the direct truth, avoid euphemisms. They will make you seem prudish or mealy mouthed.

27e Avoid sexist and other offensive words

■ Ethical writing recognizes the dignity and individuality of all people, regardless of background, race, gender, or physical capacities. Choose words that respect the equality of men and women, nationalities, and regional and ethnic groups. Avoid words that belittle, abuse, or deny individual traits.

■ 1 Avoiding sexist and racist words

Sexist words describe men or women, especially women, in demeaning, often physical terms (*chick, broad*) or deny men and women equal status (*gals, the girls in the office, lady astronaut*). **Racist words** and **ethnic slurs** belittle or abuse members of races, nationalities, or ethnic groups (*dago, spic, polack, chink, gook, mick, kike, nigger,* and so forth). Every group has the right to decide what it wants to be called. Some Americans, for example, refer to themselves as *African-American*, others as *persons of color,* and still others as *Black;* most reject *Negro* or *colored.* Fairness obliges you to adopt the words each group uses to describe itself.

■ 2 Avoiding stereotypes

Stereotypes are occupational titles, generic terms, or common expressions that exclude women or men, involve a person's gender where it is irrelevant, deny equality, or describe restrictively. Omit biased language or replace stereotypes with nonrestrictive substitutes.

STEREOTYPE	ACCEPTABLE SUBSTITUTE
businessman	businessperson, executive
chairman	chair, head, moderator, chairperson
congressman	representative, legislator
fireman	firefighter
foreman	supervisor

STEREOTYPE	ACCEPTABLE SUBSTITUTE
handicapped	physically disabled
landlord/landlady	owner, manager
mailman	letter carrier, postal worker
mankind	humankind
policeman	police officer
salesman	salesclerk, salesperson
steward/stewardess	flight attendant
workman	worker

Two special problems of stereotypes:

1. Writers may unintentionally stereotype audiences. As you write, keep in mind the differences in your readers' gender and background.

   Employees are invited to bring their ~~wives~~ *spouse or a friend* to the company picnic.

   [Not all employees may be men; not all may be married. The revision recognizes the diversity of the audience.]

2. A second problem involves the use of *he, him,* and *his* to refer collectively to men and women. Because many women don't see themselves referred to when these pronouns are used to imply *he and she, him and her, his and hers,* use masculine and feminine pronouns or, when possible, change the sentence from singular to plural. (See also 15d.)

   Each candidate must write an essay explaining ~~his~~ *his or her* qualifications for admission.

   When ~~a teenager~~ *teenagers* first ~~receives his~~ *receive their* driver's license, ~~he wants~~ *they want* to drive everywhere.

Editing Wordiness

Except for those who like to hear themselves talk, most people aren't wordy on purpose. But for writers, finding what to say and choosing the best words are often roundabout, messy processes of trial and error. They often end up with more words than readers need to get their message. And so they have to rewrite, cutting unnecessary words that in a final draft might cloud meaning or waste readers' time. To make your writing clear, forceful, and direct—and to earn readers' gratitude—say all that you have to say but in as few words as possible.

28a wdy/rep

How to Edit Wordiness

Don't be concerned about wordiness as you plan and write a first draft. But if you're having trouble saying what you mean, look for words that get in the way of your message. Cutting extra words often clarifies meaning.

As you edit, ask yourself, "What do my readers need to understand me, share my feelings or experiences, or accept my opinions?"

1. Do not omit words containing key facts, information, description, and feelings.
2. Do not omit function words like conjunctions that are necessary to understand the meaning of your sentences. (See 22d2.)

Look for these clues to wordiness and begin cutting where they occur.

1. Needless words, sentences, or extra paragraphs at the beginning or end of your writing.
2. Needlessly repeated words or ideas (*the reason why is because*). (See 28a.)
3. Empty sentence openers (*In my opinion* . . .), needless intensifiers (*really, very*) or qualifiers (*somewhat, seems*), and unnecessary impersonal constructions (*there is, there are, it is*). (See 28b.)
4. Padded transitions that link sentences or sentence parts (*because of the fact that*), unnecessary clause openers (*which is/are, who is/are*), and nouns ending in *-ence, -ance, -ment,* and *-tion* that could be transformed into the main verb of the sentence. (See 28c.)

If a wordy passage contains essential words, replace inflated expressions with concise synonyms, rewrite indirect expressions to make them direct or combine two wordy passages into one. (See 28c3.)

See whether you can cut at least one word from each sentence. If a word or passage seems wordy, bracket it and reread without it. If you don't lose any meaning, cut.

Each of these quilts is unique; no pattern has been duplicated [~~twice~~].

[If something is duplicated, there is one copy. If it is duplicated twice, there are two copies. Each quilt is unique because it has not been copied. *Twice* is wordy and can be cut.]

28a | Eliminate redundancy

■ **Redundancy** refers to unnecessary repetition, as in *blue sky, first and foremost,* or *crisis situation*. One word in each of these examples implies the meaning of the other. Eliminate redundant words from your writing, but remember that sometimes you need to repeat for emphasis or clarity. (See 20d and 22d.) Here are repetitions to avoid:

■ 1 Needlessly repeated words

As I watched her skate, ~~the impression that was most impressed on~~ me *what most impressed*

was her athletic grace.

The man turned the pages of the magazine for a moment or two, then

laid ~~the magazine~~ on the end table. *it*

[Use pronouns to avoid unnecessary repetition of nouns and to create variety.]

■ 2 Needlessly repeated ideas

Cut unemphatic words that merely repeat the meaning implied by other, more important words.

The roots of the ancient elm had grown entangled ~~together.~~

[If the roots are entangled, they twist together; *together* is redundant.]

~~The reason why airline~~ hijackings seldom occur in the United States ~~is~~ *Airline*

because the federal government has improved passenger screening

~~procedures~~.

[*Reason, why,* and *because* mean the same thing in this sentence; two of the three words can be cut. *Passenger screening* implies *procedures;* this word can be omitted.]

■ 3 Redundant pairs

Writers sometimes pair words with the same meaning: *first and foremost, hopes and aspirations, hopes and desires, goals and objectives, honest and true,* and so forth. If you pair redundant words, cut one.

Ellen's ~~hopes and desires were~~ to graduate from college in three years. *hoped*

The ~~basic and~~ fundamental right to free speech is guaranteed by the U.S.

Constitution.

■ 4 Redundant modifiers

Some modifiers are unnecessary because their meaning is contained in the words they modify: *basic fundamentals, the color blue, crisis situation, end result, past memories, period of time, personal opinion, shiny appearance, square in shape, true facts,* and so forth.

According to statistics, a ~~new~~ baby is born in the United States every three minutes.
[When born, all babies are new; the modifier is unnecessary.]

If the supplier expedites our order ~~as quickly as possible~~, we will

~~completely~~ finish the project before the deadline.
[*To expedite* means to speed a process, and to finish something is to complete it; *as quickly as possible* and *completely* are redundant.]

28b | Cut empty words and phrases

■ 1 Cutting empty sentence openers

The meaning of an opening phrase may be implied by the rest of the sentence. Generally cut openers such as *I think that, In some ways, Needless to say, In some respects, For the most part, As everyone knows, The fact is, Obviously,* and *As we see.*

Murders
~~In my opinion, murders~~ are often committed by people too enraged to

consider the consequences of their actions.
[In making an assertion, writers give their opinion. They do not need to state that their opinion is their opinion.]

The meeting will
~~The purpose of the meeting is to~~ inform employees about changes in

their benefits.
[Information about the subject of the meeting identifies its purpose.]

■ 2 Cutting empty qualifiers and intensifiers

Intensifiers and **qualifiers** are modifiers that express degree: *very, definitely, really, truly, uniquely, wonderfully, apparently, may, seems, perhaps, probably, somewhat, quite,* and so forth. You may need them to indicate the strength of a statement or shade your meaning. More often, they suggest that writers doubt the force of their ideas. Prefer the plain truth.

To a Midwesterner like me, the Rocky Mountains are ~~truly~~ breathtaking.

After two semesters, ~~it seems~~ I now feel like ~~something of~~ a veteran

college student.

■ 3 Cutting unnecessary impersonal constructions

Impersonal constructions begin *there is/are* or *it is.* They enable writers to move ideas to the end of a sentence or to emphasize actions that lack actors: *There are four reasons that General Lee lost the Battle of Gettysburg,* or *It is raining.* But when impersonal constructions are unnecessary, cut them and rewrite.

> $\quad\quad\quad$ *Some*
> ~~There is some~~ urban land ~~that~~ is set aside each year for new parks but
>
> not enough to equal the acres buried under new subdivisions and
>
> shopping centers.
>
> $\quad\quad\quad\quad$ *Businesses*
> ~~It is clear that businesses~~ have a social obligation to support nonprofit
>
> organizations in their communities.

28c │ Compress padded writing

■ $\quad$ Wordiness sometimes involves more than extra words here and there. The writing is padded with inflated or indirect expressions. Look for the following wordy expressions in your writing.

■ 1 Cutting padded phrases

Look for inflated phrases to compress to one or two words.

INFLATED	CONCISE	INFLATED	CONCISE
as a matter of fact	in fact	for the reason that	because
at the present time	now, currently	have the ability to	be able to
at this point in time	now, then	in order to	to
because of the fact that	because	in spite of the fact that	although, even though
		in the event that	if
by means of	by	in the final analysis	finally
considering the fact that	because, since	in the neighborhood	approximately, about
due to the fact that	because	in today's world	now, today
for the purpose of	for, to	prior to	before
		with regard to	about

We were impressed ~~by the fact~~ that the courthouse had been renovated

so quickly.

The stagehands erected the scaffold *to paint* ~~for the purpose of painting~~ the set.

■ 2 Cutting padded clauses

Look for padded dependent clauses to compress to a phrase or word. (To learn to recognize clauses, see 10b.)

In front of the troops stood their duffle bags, ~~which had been~~ packed

with all their gear for the next twelve months.

Unable
~~Because they don't know how~~ to handle their new freedom, some recent

high school graduates have difficulty adjusting to college life.

■ 3 Cutting padded sentences

Look for two padded sentences to combine. (For sentence-combining strategies, see 21b.)

The most scenic tour of Mammoth Cave is a four-mile *, four-hour* walk that ~~lasts~~

~~about four hours. This tour~~ includes lunch in the Snowball Room and

ends at Frozen Niagara.

Home fires have three common *causes:* ~~causes. The first cause is~~ the careless use

of smoking *materials,* ~~materials. The second and third are~~ faulty wiring, and

defective furnaces.

■ 4 Avoiding indirect use of the passive voice

As a grammatical term, voice refers to the relation between a subject and verb.

- In the active voice, an active subject commits the action of the verb: *Jane mailed the letter.*

- In the passive voice, a passive subject is acted upon or receives the action of the verb: *The letter was mailed by Jane.*

As these examples reveal, the passive voice often requires more words than the active. Use the active voice to make your writing concise and direct. (To learn when the passive voice is appropriate, see 20a3.)

The judges   *first prize*
~~First prize was~~ awarded ~~by the judges~~ to a poem, "Violet Voices."

■ 5 Avoiding indirect use of nominals

A **nominal** is a noun derived from a verb, often ending *-ence, -ance, -ment, -tion: dependence/depend, guidance/guide, argument/argue, adaptation/ adapt.* Nominals often appear in wordy, indirect writing. When you can do so, transform a nominal into its verb form, eliminate empty words, and rewrite.

donated generously
At a large meeting in Bryan Hall, several alumni ~~made generous~~

~~donations~~ to the building fund.

[Turning *donations* into a verb eliminates the vague verb *made* and emphasizes the action of the sentence.]

The can be repaired only after it is removed
~~Repairs to the~~ compressor ~~are possible only after its removal~~ from the

refrigerator.

[Turning two nominals, *repairs* and *removal,* into verbs eliminates the empty verb *are,* and the sentence becomes direct and emphatic.]

A Guide to Usage: Troublesome Words and Phrases

This glossary contains commonly confused words (such as *less* and *fewer*); words frequently misused (such as *aggravate*); nonstandard words (such as *hisself*); pretentious or needlessly technical words, often referred to as jargon (such as *parameters*); wordy phrases (such as *end result*); and colloquialisms inappropriate for formal writing (such as *okay*).

a, an. Use *a* before words beginning with a consonant sound or an *h* that is pronounced: *a student, a sparrow, a happy man, a hospital.* Use *an* before words beginning with a vowel sound (*a, e, i, o, u*) or silent *h: an apple, an investment, an honor, an honorable person.*

a lot (not alot). *A lot* is two words, not one. *We have had a lot of rain this spring.*

a while, awhile. *A while* is an article and a noun that mean "a period of time": *Stay with us for a while. Awhile* is an adverb and means "a short time": *He visited awhile and then left. Awhile* is never preceded by a preposition such as *after, for, in.*

accept, except. *Accept,* a verb, means "to receive, agree, or believe": *The singer accepted the bouquet from an admirer.* As a preposition, *except* means "but" or "other than": *Everyone is here except James.* As a verb, *except* means "to leave out, exclude": *The last three names were excepted from the list.*

adapt, adopt, adept. *Adapt,* a verb, means "to adjust or to become accustomed": *Some wild animals have adapted to urban environments. Adopt,* also a verb, means "to take up and make one's own": *Many childless parents wish to adopt children. Adept,* an adjective or noun, means "very skilled": *He was adept at the violin.*

advice, advise. *Advice* is a noun, *advise,* a verb: *The lawyer advised her client to accept her advice.*

affect, effect. *Affect* is usually a verb meaning "to influence or act on." *Effect* is usually a noun meaning "a result"; occasionally it is a verb meaning "to bring about." *Smoking affects the body in many ways. Smoking has many harmful effects. Negative advertising may effect a decrease in tobacco use.*

aggravate. *Aggravate* means "to make worse or more troublesome": *High sugar diets often aggravate childhood misbehavior.* In formal writing, avoid the colloquial use of *aggravate,* "to annoy or irritate." *The traffic was irritating* [not *aggravating*].

agree to, agree with. *Agree to* means "to consent": *The lawyers agreed to the proposed settlement. Agree with* means "to be in accord or to match": *She didn't agree with him about the causes of the problem.*

ain't. *Ain't* is nonstandard. Use *am not, is not, has not, have not,* and so forth: *They have not* [not *ain't*] *repaired the motor yet.*

aisle, isle. *Aisle* refers to a passageway, usually between seats: *The bride walked down the aisle. Isle* refers to an island: *He dreamed of retiring to a tropical isle.*

all ready, already. *All ready* means "fully prepared." *Already* means "before or by this time." *By the time everyone was all ready to leave, it was already too late.*

all right (not alright). *All right* is two words; *alright* is nonstandard.

all together, altogether. *All together* means "in a group": *They stood all together near the doorway. Altogether* means "entirely, completely, totally": *They were altogether drenched by the sudden rain.*

alleys, allies. *Alleys* is the plural of *alley,* meaning "a narrow street or passageway." *Allies* is the plural of *ally,* meaning "one who is united with another."

allusion, illusion, delusion. An *allusion* is an indirect reference: *Writers and speakers make frequent allusions to Shakespeare.* An *illusion* is a false perception of reality: *A mirage is an optical illusion created by alternate layers of hot and cool air.* A *delusion* is a false belief or opinion, especially as a symptom of mental illness: *People who are paranoid suffer the delusion that others are persecuting them.*

a.m., p.m. Use these abbreviations with numerals: *7:30 a.m., 9 p.m.* Do not use them as substitutes for morning or evening: *I want to take classes in the early morning* [not *a.m.*].

among, between. Use *among* to refer to three or more things, *between* to refer to two: *There was little agreement among the members of the jury. It is so difficult to choose between strawberry and butter pecan ice cream.* When pronouns follow *between,* they must be in the objective case: *Between you and me* [not *between you and I*], *that is the worst show on television.* (See 17b2.)

amount, number. Use *amount* with things that cannot be counted; use *number* with things that can: *The amount of happiness people enjoy is often related to the number of their friends.*

and. You may begin a sentence correctly using *and.* However, be clear about which ideas *and* joins.

and etc. *Etcetera* (etc.) means "and so forth"; *and etc.* is wordy. (See also *etc.*)

and/or. Avoid *and/or* except in technical writing, where it may be necessary for precision.

angry at, angry with. *Angry at* is nonstandard; use *angry with. I was angry with* [not *at*] *him because he cheated.*

ante-, anti-. *Ante-* means "prior to, earlier, before, in front of": *antebellum, anteroom. Anti-* means "opposed to, against": *antipoverty, antislavery.*

anxious, eager. *Anxious* means "uneasy or worried." In formal writing, avoid using *anxious* to mean "eager." *We are eager* [not *anxious*] *to meet our new president.*

anymore. *Anymore* means "at the present, any longer, or from now on." Use *anymore* only in negative statements: *We will not listen to them anymore.* In formal writing, avoid the colloquial use of *anymore* to mean "nowadays." *Americans spend so much time working nowadays* [not *anymore*] *that they have little time to consider the value of their labor.*

any one, anybody, anyone. *Any one* refers to a specific person or thing in a group: *Any one of our staff will help you. Anybody* and *anyone* mean "any person at all": *I have not found anyone who knows the answer. Anybody* and *anyone* are singular.

anyplace. *Anyplace* is appropriate for informal writing. For formal writing, use *anywhere.*

any way, anyway. *Any way* means "by whatever means or manner." *Any way you choose to travel will bring you unimagined adventures. Anyway* means "nevertheless, at least": *We asked them not to bother us, but they did anyway.*

anyways, anywheres. *Anyways* and *anywheres* are nonstandard forms of *anyway* and *anywhere.*

as, as if, like. *As if* is a subordinating conjunction that joins a subordinate clause to a main clause: *The last runners to finish looked as if they were in a trance. Like* is a preposition that should be followed only by a noun or noun phrase: *The last runner looked like a zombie.* In informal speech, *like* is often substituted for *as* or *as if,* but in formal writing, use *as: As* [not *like*] *the Bible says, it is easier for a camel to pass through a needle's eye than for a rich man to enter heaven.*

ascent, assent. *Ascent* refers to the act or process of rising or going upward: *The climbers began their ascent to the summit. Assent* means "agreement or consent": *The crowd cheered their assent.*

average, mean, median. *Average* refers to the sum of a series divided by the number of members in it: *The average of 3, 4, and 8 is 5. Mean* refers to the midpoint in a range of numbers: *The mean of 20 and 40 is 30. Median* refers to a point in a series at which half the numbers are on one side, half on the other: *The median of 5, 10, 15, 20, and 25 is 15.*

awful, awfully. The precise meaning of the adjective *awful* is "inspiring awe," but it also has the colloquial meaning of "extremely bad or terrible": *Modern technology has increased the awful power of military weapons. Julia was involved in an awful accident.* As an adverb, *awfully* has the colloquial meaning of "very"; avoid this sense of the word in formal writing: *Most unwed teenage mothers are very* [not *awfully*] *poor.*

awhile, a while. See *a while.*

bad, badly. *Bad* is an adjective that often follows linking verbs: *A bad storm is approaching. I feel bad today. Badly* is an adverb that modifies verbs, adjectives, and other adverbs: *He played badly.* (See 18c.)

bare, bear. As a noun, *bare* means "naked," as a verb, "to uncover, to reveal": *I want to bare my soul to someone.* As a verb, *bear* means "to hold up, support, carry, endure, or exhibit": *I can't bear to listen to his complaints.*

basis, bases. *Basis* is singular, *bases,* plural.

being as, being that. *Being as* and *being that* are nonstandard; use *because* or *since: Because* [not *being that*] *I work overtime every day, I have almost no social life.*

beside, besides. *Beside* is a preposition meaning "at the side of or next to": *They walked beside the river. Besides* is a preposition meaning "in addition to or except for": *Besides jazz, I also enjoy bluegrass and gospel music. Besides* is also an adverb meaning "also or furthermore": *My pen has run out of ink; besides, my mind has run out of ideas.*

better, had better. *Had better* is a modal helping verb; be sure to include *had: They had better* [not *they better*] *finish their project this week.* (See 8c1; for ESL, see 31c.)

between, among. See *among.*

brake, break. As a verb, *brake* means "to reduce speed or to apply a brake": *Brake lightly on slippery streets.* Among its many meanings as a verb, *break* means "to divide, fracture, vary, force one's way out of, to smash into pieces, to reduce in rank, to violate, and to give up": *I have tried for a year to break my smoking habit.*

breath, breathe. *Breath* is a noun, *breathe* a verb: *Relax; take a breath; now breathe again.*

bring, take. Use *bring* when the action is toward the speaker: *Please bring me a cup of coffee.* Use *take* when the action moves away from the speaker: *Be sure to take traveler's checks on your vacation.*

burst, bursted; bust, busted. *Burst* is an irregular verb meaning "to open, fly apart, or express suddenly." Its base form, past tense, and past participle are the same, *burst. Bursted* is a nonstandard form of the past tense. *Bust* and *busted* are colloquial. Do not use *bursted*; in formal writing, avoid *bust* and *busted*: *When he lost the game, he burst* [not *busted*] *into tears.*

but. You may begin a sentence correctly using *but.*

but what, but that. *But what* and *but that* are colloquial phrases following expressions of doubt; use *that* instead: *I do not doubt that* [not *but what*] *they intend to do the right thing.*

can, may. *Can* expresses ability, knowledge, or capacity: *I can speak. May* expresses possibility or permission: *It may snow tomorrow. You may borrow my calculator.* In formal writing, avoid using *can* to mean permission: *May* [not *can*] *we send you a brochure?*

capital, capitol. *Capital* refers to a city, *capitol* to a building.

censor, censure. As a verb, *censor* means "to remove or eliminate something objectionable": *Some people want to censor the news.* As a verb, *censure* means "to criticize severely, to blame: *The senate censured the senator for official misconduct.*

center around. Nonstandard; use *center on, center in, center at: The dispute centered on* [not *centered around*] *issues of wages and benefits.*

cite, site. The verb *cite* means "to mention as proof or to quote as an authority": *If you wish to be believed, cite your sources.* As a noun, *site* means "a place or setting for something": *They visited famous battlefield sites.*

climactic, climatic. *Climactic* means "relating to or constituting a climax": *The climactic scene of the play was incredibly violent. Climatic* means "of or pertaining to climate": *Climatic conditions can change suddenly in the Great Plains.*

cloth, clothe. *Cloth* is a noun, *clothe,* a verb: *The best cloth for sportswear pulls perspiration away from the skin. A compassionate government will feed, clothe, and house citizens who cannot care for themselves.*

coarse, course. *Coarse* means "rough in texture or unrefined": *The coarse fabric of his jacket scratched his skin. Course* usually refers to a unit of study, a direction of movement, a playing field, or part of a meal. *Of course* means "naturally or certainly." *Next semester I plan to take a course in Asian art. Of course, we are coming to the party.*

compare to, compare with. Use *compare to* when showing that two things are similar or belong in the same category: *In height, the Alps compare to the Rocky Mountains.* Use *compare with* when you intend to examine things side by side to discover similarities and differences: *Compared with the defense budget, the United States foreign aid budget is quite small.*

complement, compliment, complementary, complimentary. *Complement* means "to go with or complete" or "something that makes up a whole": *His artistic skill complements his creativity. A complement of marines led the attack. Compliment* means "to praise or flatter": *She complimented him for his tact. Complementary* means "completing or offsetting": *She chose complementary colors for the design. Complimentary* means "expressing a compliment or given freely, as an act of courtesy": *He received complimentary software with his new computer.*

conscience, conscious. *Conscience* refers to "moral awareness or the source of moral judgment": *Lying gave him a guilty conscience. Conscious* means "mentally aware or alert": *Before my morning coffee, I am barely conscious.*

contact. Some readers object to the informal use of contact as a verb meaning "to get in touch with." They insist that *contact* is a noun meaning "the coming together of two objects." Therefore, in formal writing, use a more precise alternative: *Call* [not *contact*] *me next week, after you return.*

continual, continuous. *Continual* means "recurring regularly or frequently": *The dog's continual bark kept him awake. Continuous* means "uninterrupted in time or sequence": *The siren rose and fell in a continuous wail.*

could care less. People generally use *could care less* when they really mean *couldn't care less.* The latter expression is logical and correct: *She couldn't care less* [not *could care less*] *about the lives and loves of Hollywood celebrities.*

could of. Nonstandard for *could have* or *could've*: *With his talent, John could have* [not *could of*] *been very successful.*

council, counsel. *Council* is a noun referring to an assembly of people or their discussion: *The city council voted to support the mayor.* As a noun, *counsel* refers to a lawyer: *The counsel for the defense rose to speak.* As a verb, *counsel* means "to advise": *His teacher counseled him to take an advanced writing course.*

criteria. *Criteria* is the plural of criterion, which refers to the standard or rule for a decision or judgment. *One criterion for success is hard work. Two other important criteria are preparation and imagination.*

data. *Data* is the plural of *datum,* meaning "a fact or piece of information used to make a decision." Some readers object when *data* is used with singular verbs and modifiers; use plural verbs and modifiers instead: *These* [not *this*] *data show* [not *shows*] *that soil erosion is increasing.*

desert, dessert. *Desert* is the place; *dessert,* the course served at the end of a meal. *The desert flowers bloomed. For dessert I would like a dish of sherbet.*

different from, different than. *Different from* is always correct: *Is a man's thinking process different from a woman's?* You may use *different than* when it is followed by a clause: *Television has made our thinking process different than it was fifty years ago.*

differ with, differ from. To *differ with* is to disagree with someone: *The student differed with her professor about the meaning of the poem.* To *differ from* is to contrast or be unlike: *The student's interpretation differed from her professor's.*

disinterested, uninterested. *Disinterested* means "unbiased, impartial, objective": *An umpire is supposed to be a disinterested observer. Uninterested* means "without interest": *He was uninterested in their opinion.*

dominant, dominate. *Dominant* means "exercising the most influence or control, most prominent": *Human beings are the dominant species on earth. Dominate* means "to control, govern, or rule": *A miser is dominated by greed.*

done. In formal writing, avoid the imprecise use of *done* to mean "finished or complete": *By 1914, work on the Panama Canal was nearly complete* [not *done*].

don't. *Don't* is the contraction for *do not.* Avoid using *don't* as a contraction for *does not,* which is *doesn't*: *She doesn't* [not *don't*] *waste any time.*

dual, duel. *Dual* means "double or composed of two usually equal parts": *She performed dual roles as teacher and counselor. Duel* means "a prearranged combat or to oppose actively": *Aaron Burr killed Alexander Hamilton in a duel.*

due to. *Due to* means "because of." It is correct when used to introduce a subject complement following a linking verb: *The airplane's crash was due to icy weather.* However, some readers object to the use of *due to* as a preposition: *The airplane crashed because of* [not *due to*] *icy weather.*

each. *Each* is singular. (See 14f and 15d.)

easy, easily. *Easy* is an adjective: *She makes a mile run look easy.* Do not use *easy* as an adverb modifying a verb; use *easily*: *She won the race easily* [not *easy*].

effect, affect. See *affect.*

e.g. *E.g.* is short for *exempli gratia,* "for example." Do not abbreviate in the text of formal writing. *Radical weather changes have occurred in the last decade, for example* [not *e.g.*], *changes in the time of the seasons.*

either. When used as an indefinite pronoun, *either* is singular. (See 14f and 15d.)

elicit, illicit. *Elicit* means "to draw out or bring out": *With a little coaxing, she was able to elicit the right answer. Illicit* means "unlawful": *He was convicted of the illicit use of drugs.*

emigrate from, immigrate to. To *emigrate from* means "to leave one country or area for another: *During the 1840s many people emigrated from Ire-*

land because of famine. To immigrate to means "to enter and settle in another country or region": *During the 1840s many Irish immigrated to the United States.*

eminent, imminent. *Eminent* means "prominent or standing above others": *She was an eminent biologist. Imminent* means "impending, about to occur": *They left quickly because a hurricane was imminent.*

end result. Wordy. Generally, a *result* is the end of a process; omit *end*: *The result* [not *end result*] *of racial segregation is economic inequality.*

enthused, enthusiastic. Some readers object to the use of the informal *enthused* as an adjective. In formal writing, use *enthusiastic*: *I am an enthusiastic* [not *enthused*] *collector of 1950s movie posters.*

-ess. Many people object to the female suffix *-ess* as sexist. Write *actor,* not *actress; waiter* or *server,* not *waitress.*

etc. Avoid *etc.* (*et cetera,* "and so forth") in formal writing; end a list with a specific example or *and so forth.* (Also see *and etc.*)

eventually, ultimately. *Eventually* means "occurring at an unspecified time in the future": *Something worth doing will get done eventually. Ultimately* means "at last, in the end": *Ultimately, most battles are won by the largest army.*

every one, everyone. *Every one* is the pronoun *one* preceded by the adjective *every,* meaning "each individual or thing in a particular group": *Every one of the students was prepared for the exam. Everyone* is an indefinite pronoun meaning "every person": *Everyone was prepared for the exam.* Both are singular. (See 14f and 15d.)

every body, everybody. See *every one.*

every day, everyday. *Every day* is the noun *day* preceded by the adjective *every*: *I try to exercise every day. Everyday* is an adjective meaning "appropriate for ordinary days or routine occasions": *Wear your everyday clothes to the party.*

except, accept. See *accept.*

expect. In formal writing, avoid using *expect* in its colloquial meaning of "to presume, think, or suppose": *I suppose* [not *expect*] *we will take our vacation in June.*

explicit, implicit. *Explicit* means "fully and clearly expressed, with nothing implied": *I was given explicit instructions. Implicit* means "not directly expressed but understood": *We made an implicit agreement to avoid the issue.*

farther, further. *Farther* refers to physical distance: *I can run farther now than I could six weeks ago. Further* refers to quantities or degree and means "more or to a greater extent": *When we inquired further, we found he had changed jobs twice within a year.*

female, male. Some readers object that *female* and *male* unnecessarily restrict the identities of women and men to physical gender. Except where gender is significant, use *woman* and *man.* Compare: *Scholarships have been awarded equally to female and male athletes. A man and two women stood patiently in line.*

fewer, less. Disregard the supermarket signs that say "Ten items or less." Use *fewer* with items that can be counted, *less* with things that are not counted: *Fewer* [not *less*] *students now major in business. We had less snow this winter than last.*

figure. Some readers object to the colloquial use of *figure* to mean "suppose or think"; in formal writing, use more precise terms instead: *I think* [not *figure*] *we will arrive about noon.*

finalize. Many readers object to *finalize*, meaning "to put into final form, complete or conclude," as jargon. Find more precise alternatives: *The baseball players' union completed* [not *finalized*] *negotiations for a new contract.*

firstly. *Firstly* sounds pretentious, as do *secondly, thirdly,* and so forth; use *first, second, third.*

folks. Informal for "parents, family, or people in general." In formal writing, use a more precise alternative: *My parents* [not *folks*] *plan to retire to Arkansas.*

fun. Many readers object to the use of *fun* as an adjective meaning "enjoyable or amusing": *We spent an enjoyable* [not *a fun*] *week in Mexico City.*

further, farther. See *farther.*

get. Because *get* has so many uses, it can be vague or ambiguous. Whenever possible, especially in formal writing, find a more precise word: *We might be able to persuade* [not *get*] *him to help us.*

goes. *Goes* is nonstandard for *says*: *When he says* [not *goes*], *"Folks, I'm not making this up," I know that he is making it up.*

good, well. *Good* is an adjective: *This salsa tastes good. Well* is an adverb: *This old watch still runs well.* Use *well* to refer to someone's health: *After a long rest, he is well again.* (See 18c.)

got, have. *Got* is the past tense of *get.* Do not use the colloquial *got* in place of *have: They have* [not *got*] *the best reputation for reliability.* Do not use *got, got to, has got to,* or *have got to* in place of *must: They must* [not *have got to*] *change their priorities.*

hanged, hung. Use *hanged* to refer to executions, *hung* to refer to what is attached or suspended: *The criminal was hanged at dawn. The coat was hung in the closet.*

hardly, scarcely. Avoid the colloquial double negatives *can't hardly, not hardly, can't scarcely, not scarcely: I can hardly* [not *can't hardly*] *explain what it felt like.* (See 18e.)

has got, have got. Redundant; write *has* or *have* instead: *We have* [not *have got*] *to find more information.*

have, got. See *got.*

have, of. Use *have* following the modal verbs *could, should, may, might, must,* and *would: They should have* [not *of*] *received an invitation.* (See 13e3.)

he. Do not use *he* to mean "he or she." (See 15d and 27e2.)

he/she, his/her. Many readers object to the awkward expressions *he/she, his/her;* use *he or she* or one of the alternatives in 15d.

hisself. *Hisself* is nonstandard; use *himself.*

hopefully. *Hopefully* means "in a hopeful manner": *He looked hopefully toward the clock.* Many readers object to its use, especially at the beginning of a sentence, to mean "it is to be hoped": *Hopefully, job opportunities for graduates will soon improve.* Indicate instead who is doing the hoping: *We hope job opportunities for graduates will soon improve.*

i.e. Avoid *i.e.* (the Latin abbreviation for *id est*) in the text of formal papers. Use the English equivalent, *that is,* instead.

if, whether. Use *if* to introduce statements of condition and *whether* to introduce alternatives: *If we have enough volunteers, we can finish; it makes no difference whether they are young or old.*

imminent, eminent. See *eminent.*

impact. Many readers object to the use of *impact* as a verb: *The recent election will have an impact on* [not *will impact*] *proposed antipollution laws.*

implement. Often a pretentious way to say "do," "carry out," or "achieve"; prefer a simpler alternative: *We carried out* [not *implemented*] *his instructions promptly.*

implicit, explicit. See *explicit.*

imply, infer. *Imply* means "to express indirectly": *She glanced at her watch to imply that it was time to leave. Infer* means "to draw a conclusion": *After studying the evidence, we inferred that the fire was caused by lightning.*

incredible, incredulous. *Incredible* means "unbelievable or astonishing"; *incredulous* means "skeptical, disbelieving": *As he told his incredible tale, she gave him an incredulous look.*

individual. Pretentious synonym for *person*: *The police questioned several persons* [not *individuals*].

infer, imply. See *imply.*

ingenious, ingenuous. *Ingenious* means "creatively skillful or imaginative": *His solution to the puzzle was the most ingenious. Ingenuous* means "without sophistication, artless, frank": *To win their trust, he tried to appear ingenuous.*

irregardless. Nonstandard for *regardless.*

is when, is where, is why, is because. Avoid these imprecise and illogical expressions in writing definitions and explanations: *A paceline is a line of cyclists tightly grouped* [not *A paceline is when cyclists group together tightly*] *to reduce wind resistance.*

isle, aisle. See *aisle.*

its, it's. *Its* is the possessive pronoun: *The dog twitched its tail. It's* is the contraction of *it is*: *It's good to hear that they arrived safely.*

kind(s), sort(s), type(s). *Kind, sort,* and *type* are singular: *This kind of words is* [not *these kind of words are*] *known as "fighting words." Kinds, sorts,* and *types* are plural, referring to more than one kind or sort: *These kinds of flowers grow well in the shade.*

kind of, sort of. Avoid using *kind of* and *sort of* to mean "somewhat": *I was somewhat* [not *kind of*] *disappointed by the novel's conclusion.* Do not use *a* following either phrase: *It was the same sort of* [not *sort of a*] *speech politicians always make.*

lay, lie. *Lay,* a transitive verb meaning "to put or set down," always takes a direct object: *Lay the pencil on the table.* Its other forms are *laying, laid, laid. Lie,* an intransitive verb meaning "to rest on a surface or occupy a position," does not take a direct object: *The pencil lies on the table.* Its other forms are *lying, lay, lain.* (See 13a4.)

lead, led. *Lead* (the metal) sounds like *led* (the past tense of the verb *to lead*); do not confuse them: *The officer led* [not *lead*] *his men into battle.*

learn, teach. *Learn* means "to gain knowledge"; *teach* means "to instruct": *Michael said he would teach* [not *learn*] *his brother to play the guitar.*

leave, let. *Leave* means "to go away"; *let* means "to give permission or allow." Do not use *leave* when you mean *let*: *Let* [not *leave*] *him clean up the mess he has made.*

less, fewer. See *fewer.*

like, as. See *as.*

loose, lose, losing. *Loose* is an adjective meaning "not fastened or contained"; *lose* is a verb meaning "to misplace." Do not use one word when you mean the other, and do not write "loosing," which is not a word, when you mean *losing.* (See 13a5.)

lots, lots of. In formal writing, avoid the colloquial expressions *lots* and *lots of,* meaning "many, much, or a lot": *Many* [not *lots of*] *medicines are produced from rain forest plants.*

male, female. See *female.*

mankind. Many readers object that *mankind* excludes women. Use *humankind, humanity, humans,* or *the human race* instead.

may be, maybe. *May be* is a verb phrase: *The computer may be unplugged. Maybe* is an adverb meaning "possibly": *Maybe the computer is unplugged.*

may, can. See *can.*

may of, might of. Nonstandard for *may have* and *might have.* See *have, of.*

mean, median, average. See *average.*

media, medium. *Media* is the plural of *medium: Among the news media, television is the most popular medium but the least informative.*

most. In formal writing, avoid using *most* as a substitute for *almost: Almost* [not *Most*] *everyone arrived on time.*

must of. See *have, of.*

myself, himself, herself, yourself. Do not use the intensive or reflexive pronouns *myself, himself, herself,* or *yourself* where personal pronouns are appropriate: *Cynthia and I* [not *myself*] *will announce the awards, and then Janna and you* [not *yourself*] *will escort the winners to the stage.* (See 17g.)

nauseous, nauseated. *Nauseous* means "sickening": *A nauseous gas filled the room. Nauseated* means "to feel nausea, loathing, or disgust": *I felt nauseated as soon as I smelled the gas.*

neither. When used as an indefinite pronoun, *neither* is singular. (See 14f and 15d.)

none. *None* is usually singular. (See 14f.)

nowhere near. *Nowhere near* is informal. In formal writing, use *not nearly: I was not nearly* [not *nowhere near*] *ready to leave when they arrived.*

nowheres. *Nowheres* is nonstandard for *nowhere.*

number, amount. See *amount.*

of, have. See *have, of.*

off of, off from. *Off of* and *off from* are redundant; write *off: The cat jumped off* [not *off of*] *the table.*

ok, O.K., okay. All three spellings are acceptable, but avoid these colloquial expressions in formal writing. Use the adjectives *acceptable, satisfactory,* or *all right* or the verbs *approve of, agree to,* or *authorize: If my application is satisfactory* [not *okay*], *will you authorize* [not *okay*] *my loan?*

parameters. Pretentious jargon, often confused with *perimeter* to mean "border, boundary, limit, or guideline." Use a simple, precise alternative: *The guidelines* [not *parameters*] *for committee action have been clearly determined.*

passed, past. *Passed* is the past tense of the verb *pass: The sports car passed the truck. Past* refers to a time before the present or a place farther than another: *The old man spoke nostalgically of his past. He lives two houses past the grocery store.*

percent, per cent, percentage. *Percent/per cent* is always used with numbers written as words: *Thirty-four percent of college students favor harsher criminal penalties. Percentage* means "a proportion or amount" and is used with descriptive words like "large," "small," and "greater" rather than a number: *A large percentage of students take more than four years to earn a BA degree.*

phenomena. *Phenomena* is the plural of *phenomenon,* "a perceptible event, happening, or occurrence": *Many supposedly supernatural phenomena are easily explained natural occurrences. One such phenomenon is the aurora borealis, or northern lights.*

plus. In formal writing, avoid using *plus* to mean "and," "in addition," or "as well as": *Culture consists of the shared knowledge and beliefs of a human community, as well as* [not *plus*] *the tools that use and express culture.*

precede, proceed. *Precede* means "to come before"; proceed means "to go forward": *Preceded by her parents, the bride proceeded down the aisle.*

presently. *Presently* means "in a short time, soon"; do not use it to mean "now": *Currently* [not *presently*], *factory output is ninety percent of capacity. We will arrive presently.*

principal, principle. As a noun, *principal* means "the head of a school or organization" or "a sum of money"; as an adjective it means "first or most important." *Principle* is a noun meaning "a basic truth or law": *My principal taught me the principle known as the Golden Rule.*

proceed, precede. See *precede.*

quote, quotation. *Quote* is a verb, *quotation* a noun. Do not use *quote* as a substitute for *quotation*: *I have several good quotations* [not *quotes*] *supporting my opinion.*

rarely ever. Redundant; write *rarely* or *hardly ever*: *They rarely* [or *hardly ever*, not *rarely ever*] *come to visit anymore.*

real, really. *Real* is an adjective, *really* an adverb. In formal writing, do not use *real* as a substitute for *really*: *He was really* [not *real*] *pleased to receive the award.*

reason is because, reason why. *Reason is because* is illogical; use *that* instead of *because*: *The reason they lost was that* [not *because*] *they rarely ever practiced. Reason why* is redundant: *The reason* [not *reason why*] *the economy has improved is technological advance.*

relation, relationship. *Relation* refers to a connection between two or more things: *The relation between drinking and auto accidents is clear. Relationship* refers more specifically to a relation between people: *Their relationship grew from friendship into love.*

revolve around. In formal writing, avoid using *revolve around* as a substitute for "concern," "involve," or "associated with": *The causes of the war involved* [not *revolved around*] *ethnic hatreds.*

saw, seen. *Saw* is the past tense of *see; seen* is the past perfect and is always used with a helping verb. Do not substitute *seen* for *saw*: *We saw* [not *seen*] *them only a week ago.*

scarcely, hardly. See *hardly.*

sensual, sensuous. *Sensual* means "gratifying physical appetites, erotic, lustful": *Many religions condemn the pursuit of sensual pleasure. Sensuous* means "pleasing to the senses": *Reading poetry aloud is a sensuous experience.*

set, sit. *Set,* meaning "to put or place," has the principal parts *set, set, set.* It is a transitive verb that takes a direct object: *Set the computer on this desk. Sit,* an intransitive verb meaning "to be seated or to rest," has the principal parts *sit, sat, sat: Sit here next to me.*

shall, will. *Shall* has nearly disappeared as a helping verb used with *I* or *we* to signal action in the future. It now appears mainly in polite requests, legal documents, and emphatic statements: *Shall we go? Both parties shall agree. I shall return. Will* is appropriate for most future statements.

should of. See *have, of.*

since. Some readers object to *since* as a substitute for because. Use *since* to mean "from then until now" or "between then and now": *Because* [not *since*] *it rained so hard last night, the game has been postponed. We have been waiting since six o'clock.*

sit, set. See *set.*

site, cite. See *cite.*

so. In formal writing, avoid using *so* as a substitute for the intensifier *very*: *Lake Constance is very* [not *so*] *beautiful.*

some. In formal writing, avoid *some* as a substitute for words like *remarkable, memorable,* and *impressive*: Schindler's List *is a remarkable* [not *some*] *movie.*

someone, somebody, something. *Someone, somebody,* and *something* are singular. (See 14f and 15d.)

some time, sometime, sometimes. *Some time* is the adjective *some* modifying the noun *time*: *She wants to spend some time with her grandparents. Sometime* is an adverb meaning "at an indefinite or unstated time": *We'll be there sometime soon. Sometimes* is an adverb meaning "at times, now and then": *Sometimes we don't understand each other.*

sort, kind. See *kind(s), sort(s), types(s).*

suppose to, use to. Write *supposed to* and *used to.* (See 13e1.)

sure. In formal writing, avoid using *sure* as an adverb; use *surely* instead: *We were surely* [not *sure*] *pleased by the news.*

sure and. *Sure and* is nonstandard for *sure to*: *Be sure to* [not *sure and*] *bring the blueprints to our next meeting.*

take, bring. See *bring.*

than, then. *Than* is a conjunction that links unequal comparisons: *Harry types faster than Kevin. Then* is an adverb meaning "at that time or next in time": *He turned first one way and then another.*

that. See *who, which, that.*

that, which. Many writers use *that* to introduce essential or restrictive clauses, *which* to introduce nonessential or nonrestrictive clauses. (See 34e.)

that there, this here, these here, those there. *That there, this here, these here,* and *those there* are nonstandard for *that, this, these,* and *those.*

their, they're, there. *Their* is a possessive pronoun: *They received their diplomas. They're* is the contraction of *they are*: *They're good dancers. There* means "at, in, to, or toward that place": *We saw them standing there by the fountain.*

theirself, theirselves, themself. *Theirself, theirselves,* and *themself* are nonstandard for *themselves*: *They decided to go by themselves* [not *theirselves*].

them. Do not use *them* as a substitute for *these* or *those*: *How do you like those* [not *them*] *new hiking boots?*

then, than. See *than.*

they. *They* is nonstandard when it means *their*: *The mechanics left their* [not *they*] *tools all over the garage.*

this kind. See *kind(s), sort(s), type(s).*

tinge, twinge. *Tinge* means "a tint or trace of color": *The morning sky was tinged with red. Twinge* is a sharp, sudden pain: *He felt a twinge of remorse.*

to, too, two. *To* is a preposition; *too* means "very" or "also"; *two* is a number.

toward, towards. *Toward* and *towards* are interchangeable; *toward* is the preferred American usage.

try and. *Try and* is nonstandard for *try to*: *Try to* [not *try and*] *remember where you last saw your keys.*

ultimately, eventually. See *eventually*.

unique. *Unique* is an absolute meaning "one of a kind"; do not use *unique* with qualifiers such as *more* and *most*: *She is a unique* [not *the most unique*] *writer.* (See also 18d4.)

usage. Often a pretentious substitute for *use*: *The use* [not *usage*] *of computer networks has enabled many people to work at home.*

use to, suppose to. See *suppose to*.

utilize. Often a pretentious substitute for *use*: *Tools were widely used* [not *utilized*] *during the Bronze Age.*

virtually. *Virtually* means "almost, in effect, or practically"; do not use it to mean "completely or entirely": *By the 1890s, the buffalo were virtually extinct. By 1914, the passenger pigeon was completely* [not *virtually*] *extinct.*

wait for, wait on. *Wait for* means "to expect or await"; *wait on* means "to serve": *We'll wait for* [not *wait on*] *him for another hour.*

ways. In formal writing, avoid the use of *ways* to mean "distance": *They have come a long way* [not *ways*] *to get where they are today.*

weather, whether. *Weather* refers to climate; *whether* is a conjunction that introduces alternatives: *Football is played whether the weather is fair or foul.*

well, good. See *good*.

where. In formal writing, avoid using *where* to substitute for *that* or *when*: *I recently read that* [not *where*] *the news media is more balanced than critics claim. Surprisingly, Christmas is a time when* [not *where*] *many people are most unhappy.*

where ... at/to. Redundant; omit *at/to*: *Where did they say we would find them* [not *find them at*]?

which. See *that, which*, and *who, which, that*.

while. Avoid using *while* to mean "but," "although," or "whereas": *Although* [not *while*] *they were happy to return home, they had many good memories of their year in Mexico.*

who, which, that. Use *who* to refer to people, *which* to things, and *that* to groups of people or to things: *The man who just left carried a suitcase which was scuffed and dirty. I want a book that tells me something new.* (See 16d; see also *that, which*.)

who, whom. *Who* is used with subjects and subject complements, *whom* with objects. (See 17e.)

whose, who's. *Whose* is a possessive pronoun; *who's* is a contraction of *who is*: *Whose essay is this? Who's ready for dessert?*

will, shall. See *shall*.

would of. See *have, of*.

you. Use *you* only when you mean to address your audience directly. Avoid using *you* to mean "anyone": *Anyone* [not *you*] *can tell that spring is near by the smell of thawing soil.*

your, you're. *Your* is a possessive pronoun: *Your time is up.* *You're* is a contraction of *you are*: *You're our first choice.*

ESL
Editing

part IV

ESL Editing

ESL Editing Guide

ESL Editing Guide

Even advanced speakers of English as a second language are sometimes puzzled by the complex features of English grammar and idiomatic expression. For detailed answers to your questions, see these widely available reference books:

- Dictionaries: *Longman Dictionary of American English* (White Plains, NY: Longman, 1983), *New Horizon Ladder Dictionary of the English Language* (New York: Signet, 1990), or *Oxford Advanced Learner's Dictionary*, 4th ed. (New York: Oxford, 1989).

- Phrasebooks and idiomatic dictionaries: NTC's *American Idioms Dictionary* (Lincolnwood, IL: National Textbook Company, 1994) or NTC's *Dictionary of American English Phrases* (Lincolnwood, IL: National Textbook Company, 1995).

- Practice for advanced ESL speakers and writers: Betty Schrampfer Azur, *Understanding and Using English Grammar*, 2nd ed. (Englewood Cliffs, NJ: Prentice-Hall, 1989) or Len Fox, *Focus on Editing* (White Plains, NY: Longman, 1992).

For immediate answers to your questions about English, see the following chapters of this book. Use them as a review of grammar rules, a quick reference while writing, an editorial checklist for revision, and an index to other sections of the book containing important information for writers of English as a second language.

Articles and Quantifiers

Articles (*a, an, the*) and quantifiers (*a few, many, some,* and so forth) are used in English to introduce nouns, which may follow immediately or be preceded by other words.

article + noun

The snow lay in gentle drifts.

article + adjective + noun

A wet snow bent the boughs of the tree.

quantifier + noun

Some snow fell last night.

How to . . .

How to Edit English Sentences When English Is Your Second Language

Subjects and verbs form the core meaning of a sentence. Reread to be sure subjects and verbs make sense together in each sentence. (See 22a–c.) Use a dictionary or phrasebook to check idioms.

As you revise, be sure that you've used all the words that English sentences require: subject pronouns, expletives like *there* used to begin a sentence, and linking verbs like *was*. But avoid unnecessary repetition of subject pronouns, direct objects, adverbs like *there*, and conjunctions like *although* or *but*. (See 32a and b.)

Reconsider clause, phrase, and single-word modifiers to be sure that they are placed properly and that they make sense with the words they modify. (See 23a and b, 32e3 and 4.)

Reconsider word endings to be sure words show the correct part of speech for their roles as nouns (for example, *response*), verbs (*respond*), adjectives (*responsive*), and adverbs (*responsively*). Use your dictionary to make decisions.

Reconsider word endings to be sure words show the appropriate number (singular or plural), person (first, second, or third), tense, or other verb marker.

Reconsider nouns to be sure they are preceded by an appropriate article, if necessary. (See Chapter 30.)

Reconsider prepositions to be sure they are used idiomatically in two-word verbs and at the beginning of prepositional phrases. Use your dictionary or an English phrase book. (For phrases of place and time, see 32f.)

30*a*   Use *a/an* with nonspecific singular count nouns

■ **Count nouns** refer to persons, places, or things that can be counted numerically. They may be singular or plural: *student/students, forest/forests, computer/computers*. **Nonspecific count nouns** refer to a class of things or to something not specifically identified:

A computer makes writing easier.

As this example illustrates, the indefinite articles *a* and *an* are used to introduce nonspecific singular count nouns.

■ 1 Matching *a* with consonant sounds, *an* with vowel sounds

■ Use *a* before words beginning with a consonant sound: *a book, a happy man, a pen.*

■ Use *an* before words beginning with a vowel sound (*a, e, i, o, u,* or silent *h,* as in *hour*): *an apple, an episode, an impossible task, an operator, an understanding, an honor.*

■ 2 When to use *a* or *an*

Use *a* or *an* in the following situations.

■ One of a certain type. Use *a* or *an* to mean "one of a certain type": *A banana will give you more energy than an apple.*

Most moral issues have $\overset{a}{\wedge}$ gray area where right and wrong become cloudy.

■ Something not specifically identified. Use *a* or *an* to refer to something not specifically identified: *Choose an apple from this bowl.*

I have just received $\overset{an}{\wedge}$ exciting job offer.

■ First mention. Use *a* or *an* to mention something for the first time: *A dish* [first mention] *fell from the shelf and broke. The dish* [second mention] *belonged to my grandmother.*

A note on exceptions requiring *the*: *The* is used in a generic sense with certain nonspecific singular count nouns to mean "one of a certain type of thing."

■ Species of animals: *The woolly mammoth lived in Siberia 6,000 years ago.*

■ Inventions: *The computer is indispensable for most students.*

■ Musical instruments: *The koto, a stringed instrument similar to the zither, is important to Japanese sacred music.*

30*b* | Never use *a/an* with noncount nouns

■ Noncount nouns refer to things as a whole that are not counted in English and cannot be made plural. They are never preceded by *a* or *an.*

■ Whole groups of similar items: *baggage, clothing, equipment, food, fruit, furniture, garbage, hardware, jewelry, junk, luggage, machinery, mail, makeup, money/cash/change, postage, scenery, traffic,* and so forth.

When I return home next time, I will take only ~~a~~ luggage.
one piece of

[To refer to countable units of noncount nouns, use quantifiers like *one piece* or *a little*. See 30e3.]

■ Abstractions: *advice, beauty, courage, education, grammar, happiness, health, homework, honesty, importance, information, knowledge, laughter, music, news, peace, progress, sleep, time, violence, wealth, work, vocabulary,* and so forth.

On American television, ~~a~~ violence is presented as attractive and

exciting.

■ Liquids: *water, coffee, tea, milk, oil, soup, gasoline, blood,* and so forth.

■ Solids: *ice, bread, butter, cheese, meat, gold, iron, silver, glass, paper, wood, cotton, wool,* and so forth.

■ Gases: *steam, air, oxygen, hydrogen, smoke, smog, pollution,* and so forth.

■ Particles and powders: *rice, chalk, corn, dirt, dust, flour, grass, hair, pepper, salt, sand, sugar, wheat,* and so forth.

■ Languages: *Arabic, Chinese, English, Polish, Sanskrit, Spanish, Urdu,* and so forth.

■ Fields of study: *chemistry, engineering, history, mathematics, psychology,* and so forth.

■ Recreation: *baseball, bridge, chess, soccer, tennis,* and so forth.

■ General activities: *driving, studying, traveling,* and other gerunds (*-ing* words).

■ Natural phenomena: *darkness, dew, electricity, fire, fog, gravity, hail, heat, humidity, lightning, rain, sleet, snow, thunder, weather, wind,* and so forth.

A note: Some nouns may be considered either count or noncount nouns: *Please bring us two coffees* [count noun]. *African coffee* [noncount noun] *is especially dark and strong.* Nouns of this kind must be learned; see your dictionary.

30c | Use *the* with nouns whose specific identity your readers know

■ The definite article *the*, indicating "this" or "that," introduces a specific person, place, or thing singled out from others. Use *the* in the following situations.

■ Known identity. Use *the* when readers know the identity of the noun: *I enjoy going out late in the evening.*

Many societies have abandoned *the* death penalty.

■ Unique persons, places, or things. Use *the* with nouns that refer to a unique person, place, or thing: *Last year, the Pope visited my country.*

In this poem, *the* poet asks us to praise God for His creation.

■ Second mention. Use *the* when you mention a noun for the second time: *Last night I went to a new restaurant* [first mention]. *The restaurant* [second mention] *is called La Chosa.*

■ Specific identity. Use *the* when the words following the noun specify its identity.

The notes on your experiment are detailed and complete.

The student who won the chess championship was David Wu.

■ Superlatives. Use *the* when the statement is a superlative.

The tallest player on the team is Nestor Wozny.

When I finally got married, **the most relieved person in the room** was my mother.

30*d* | Do not use *the* with most proper nouns and statements meaning "all" or "in general"

■ 1 Proper nouns

Do not use *the* before most singular proper nouns, including languages (*Arabic, English*), people (*Juan Ramirez*), organizations (*Environmental Technologies*), holidays (*New Year's*), continents (*South America*), countries (*Mexico*), states (*New Jersey*), cities and towns (*Dallas*), streets and roads (*42nd Street, Fifth Avenue*), squares (*Herald Square*), parks (*Central Park*), single lakes (*Lake Geneva*), bays (*Tampa Bay*), islands (*Easter Island*), and specific mountains (*Mount Kilimanjaro*).

In ~~the~~ Japanese, the saying "Look up into the sky" means "Stop and

smell the roses."

Some exceptions require *the* preceding singular proper nouns:

■ Phrases with the word *language*. Use *the* before phrases containing *language*: *the Chinese language, the Sanskrit language,* and so forth.

■ The names of certain countries. Use *the* before the names of certain countries: *the United States, the Philippines, the Ukraine, the People's Republic of China, the Commonwealth of Independent States.*

- Geographic terms. Use *the* before regions (*the East Coast*), deserts (*the Sahara*), peninsulas (*the Malay Peninsula*), and bodies of water other than lakes (*the Pacific Ocean, the Mediterranean Sea, the Mekong River*).

- Plural proper nouns. Use *the* before plural proper nouns, such as *the United Nations, the Himalayan Mountains, the Great Lakes, the Sunda Islands.*

■2 General statements

Do not use *the* before plural or noncount nouns used in a general sense.

       Students
~~The students~~ today are drinking less but smoking more.

In dangerous situations, ~~the~~ courage may not be as important as ~~the~~

patience.

■3 Certain place expressions

Do not use *the* before general uses of the words *school, class, work, church, town,* and *bed.*

This semester I go to ~~the~~ school three days each week.

■4 Games

Do not use *the* before the names of games: *chess [not the chess], baseball, soccer.*

■5 Subjects of study

Do not use *the* before subjects of study: *economics* [not *the economics*], *history, mathematics, political science, sociology,* and so forth.

When I took ~~the~~ art history, I studied both Western and Asian painters.

30*e* | Match quantifiers with appropriate count or noncount nouns

■ Quantifiers are words or phrases that tell how much or how many of something: *two inches of rain, a few students.* Use certain quantifiers with certain kinds of nouns.

30e art/adj

■ 1 Using quantifiers with singular count nouns

Use *one, each,* and *every* with singular count nouns: *one apple, each student, every computer.*

■ 2 Using quantifiers with plural nouns

Use the following quantifiers with plural nouns to tell "how many": numbers of two or more, *both, a couple of, a few, many, a number of* (the), *a percentage of* (the), *quite a few, several, too many.* For example: *two apples, many apples, a majority of the students, a number of computers.*

■ 3 Using quantifiers with noncount nouns

Use *a little, much,* and *a great deal of* with noncount nouns to tell "how much": *a little baggage, much snow, a great deal of progress.*

■ 4 Using quantifiers with plural and noncount nouns

Use the following quantifiers with plural and noncount nouns to tell "how many" or "how much": *all, almost all, almost no, a lot of, enough, hardly any, lots of, a majority/minority of* (the), *most, not any/no, plenty of, some.* For example: *all the apples, all the snow, hardly any students, hardly any progress, some computers, some fog.* When count nouns follow these quantifiers, be sure to make them plural.

universities
Some ~~university~~ make an extra effort to help international students feel

at home.

A note on articles + quantifiers: In general, do not use an article preceding a quantifier.

The zoo in my hometown had ~~a~~ one large animal, an old bear.

A favorite pastime of ~~the~~ many older people is going out to eat and

talk.

Exceptions include *a few, a little, the most, all the, a number of, a majority of,* and so forth: *a few days ago, the most important discovery, all the time, a number of students, a majority of women.*

Verbs

This chapter focuses on features of English verbs frequently trouble-some to nonnative speakers of English. Features that may be troublesome to native and nonnative speakers alike are treated elsewhere in this book.

- Irregular English verbs: See 13a.
- Specific uses of English verb tenses: See 13b.
- Subject-verb agreement: See 13c and 14.
- The helping verbs *be, have,* and *do*: See 13d.
- *-d, -ed,* and *-ve* verb endings: See 13e.
- The subjunctive mood for wishes and nonfactual statements: See 13f and 24d.
- Voice: See 20a, 24d2, 28c4.

31*a* | To express tense correctly, match appropriate helping and main verb forms

■ 1 Forming tenses

Tense refers to the time of an action: past, present, and so forth. English has six tenses and a progressive form for each (using a form of *be + ing*) to indicate continuous or ongoing action. To form each tense correctly, use the following combinations of helping verbs and main verbs.

- Present tense: action that takes place now. Use the base or *-s/-es* form of the main verb: *I sigh. He speaks. I am working. He is working. You/we/they are working.*

- Past tense: past action. Use the past tense *-d/-ed* form of the main verb: *I sighed. He spoke. I/he/she was working. You/we/they were working.*

- Future tense: action that will take place. Use *will +* the base form of the main verb: *I will sigh. He will speak. You/we/they will be working.*

- Present perfect tense: past action continuing or completed in the present. Use *has/have +* the *-d/-ed/-n/-en/-t* past participle form of the main verb: *I have sighed. He has spoken. He/she has been working. I/you/we/they have been working.*

- Past perfect tense: past action completed before another past action. Use *had +* the *-d/-ed/-n/-en/-t* past participle form of the main verb: *I had sighed. He had spoken. I/he/you/we/they had been working.*

- Future perfect tense: action that will begin and end in the future. Use *will* + *have* + the *-d/-ed/-n/-en/-t* past participle form of the main verb: *I will have sighed. He will have spoken. I/he/you/we/they will have been working.*

As you revise, be sure that you have used the correct combination of helping and main verbs to express tense.

changing
She is ~~change~~ her major from biology to botany.

[The progressive *-ing* verb form is necessary to form the present progressive tense, indicating present ongoing action.]

have
Scientists ~~had~~ now demonstrated that some animals are capable of

reason.

[*Has* or *have* is necessary to form the present perfect, indicating past action completed in the present.]

A note on tense consistency: When two or more verbs refer to the same action, they must be in the same tense. (See 24c, Faulty Shifts, Tense.)

■ 2   Including omitted helping verbs

Always include helping verbs even when the meaning or verb tense seems clear without them.

are
So far, they the friendliest students in my dorm.

[The helping verbs *be*, *have*, and *do* may stand alone as main verbs. Here *are* is necessary to connect the subject *they* to its modifier, *the friendliest students*.]

has
She been a member of Amnesty International for five years.

[*Has* is necessary to create the present perfect tense.]

■ 3   Identifying verbs that lack progressive forms

The following verbs do not generally appear in the progressive *-ing* forms.

- Verbs referring to mental states: *believe, doubt, feel, forget, imagine, intend, know, mean, need, prefer, realize, recognize, remember, suppose, understand, wish.*

have known
I ~~am knowing~~ the Patel family for seven years.

- Verbs referring to emotional states: *appreciate, care, dislike, envy, fear, hate, like, love, mind.*

- Verbs referring to the act of possessing: *belong, have, own, possess. Have,* an exception, is sometimes used in an active sense: *She is having a baby.*

- Verbs referring to sense perceptions: *feel, hear, see, smell, taste.* Exceptions: These verbs may appear in progressive tenses with a change of meaning. For example, in *I can feel the soft ground beneath my sleeping bag, feel* refers to tactile experience. But in *I'm feeling good this morning, feeling* refers to the speaker's mood.

31*b* After the helping verbs *do*, *does*, and *did*, use only the base form of the verb

The helping verb *do* appears in questions, in negatives with *not* or *never,* and in emphatic statements. Use the appropriate form to signal tense and number (singular or plural): *do* = the base form, *does* = *-s* form (third person singular), *did* = past tense. Following *do, does,* or *did,* use the base form of the main verb. Do not omit these helping verbs even if the meaning is clear without them. (See the exception in summarized quotations, 32c1.)

- A question: *Do you have the videotape I requested?*

- A negative statement: *He doesn't* [present tense: *does not*] *know what he wants for dinner.*

- An emphatic statement: *We did* [past tense] *offer to help whenever we could.*

31*c* Use modal verbs to indicate your attitude toward the action of a main verb

The modal helping verbs *can, could, may, might, must, shall, should, will, would, ought to, had better,* and *had to* express the writer's attitude toward an action.

- Capability: *I can help you with your calculus.*

- Intention: *I will finish by tomorrow.*

- Possibility: *They might go to the party.*

- Probability: *She must have gone home already.*

- Permission: *You may leave when you finish the exam.*

- Advisability: *He should edit his writing more carefully.*

- Necessity: *We must finish the book by this weekend.*

Use only one modal before a main verb.

They might ~~could~~ take a Spanish class next semester.

■ 1 Using present/future modals

For action in the present or future, use *can, may, might, must, should, had better, ought to, will* + the base form of the main verb. Do not add an *-s* to the modal, even when the subject is *he, she,* or *it*: *Next semester I will take fewer classes.*

Natasha says she ⌃ come to the party this evening. *[will]*

[The modal verb *will* is required to express future action even though the closing phrase, *this evening,* indicates future time.]

Tamiko assured her supervisor that she ~~cans~~ finish the project by *[can]*

Tuesday.

[Modal verbs never take the *-s* verb ending.]

With a little encouragement, Henry might ~~volunteers~~. *[volunteer]*

[To signal future action, the modal *might* is followed by the base form *volunteer.*]

Lucia might ~~to play~~ a Chopin sonata at her next recital. *[play]*

[Following the future tense modal *might,* the base form of the main verb *play* is required rather than the infinitive *to play.* (For uses of the infinitive, see 31f.)]

■ 2 Using past modals

For past action, use *would, could, might, had to* + the base form of the main verb. Do not use the past tense of the main verb: *Carlos had to leave early in order to be home by midnight.*

As she listened to their explanation, she ~~can~~ understand their motives. *[could]*

When I saw how pale she was, I thought she might ~~been~~ sick. *[be]*

■ 3 Using past perfect modals for potential past action

For past action that did not actually occur, use *could (not) have, should (not) have, would (not) have* + the past participle of the main verb: *Edgardo should have covered his roses to protect them from frost.* (See also 31e.)

With regular feeding, the fish would not have ~~die~~. *[died]*

They should ⌃ waited a week or two before planting the flowers. *[have]*

31*d* Use the passive voice when a subject receives the action of a transitive verb

■ In passive voice expressions, a passive subject receives the action of a transitive verb. The subject is acted on instead of performing an action.

a subject being acted on

In ancient Ethiopia, coffee was consumed as a food rather than a beverage.

■ 1 Confusing voice and tense

Do not confuse the passive voice with the past tense. A passive voice verb may appear in the past, present, or future. To form the passive, use the appropriate form of *be* to signal number and tense + the past participle of the main verb (usually ending *-ed, -d, -en, -n,* or *-t*). Note that *be, being,* and *been* must be preceded by another helping verb.

Present passive: *The music is played.*
Present progressive passive: *The music is being played.*
Present perfect passive: *The music has been played.*
Past passive: *The music was played.*
Past progressive passive: *The music was being played.*
Past perfect passive: *The music had been played.*
Future passive: *The music will be played.*
Future perfect passive: *The music will have been played.*

■ 2 Misusing the passive

- To form the passive voice, use the past participle form of main verbs, not the base or past tense forms.

  released
  The movie will be ~~release~~ in China early next year.

  driven
  The emigrants who left Ireland in the 1840s were ~~drove~~ by famine.

- Include the appropriate form of *be* in all passive voice expressions.

  is
  In our culture today, too much emphasis placed on material goals.

- Use the passive voice sparingly. (See 20a and 28c4.)

31*e* Use correct verb tenses in conditional (*if . . .*) sentences

Conditional sentences usually consist of two parts, an *if* dependent clause stating conditions and a main clause stating results.

┌── conditions ──┐┌──────── results ────────┐
If we have time, we'll go bicycling this weekend.

┌──────── results ────────┐┌──── conditions ────┐
We used to go bicycling when we had the time.

┌─────────── results ───────────┐┌──── conditions ────┐
We would go bicycling this weekend if we had enough time.

┌────── conditions ──────┐┌─────────── results ───────────┐
If we had had enough time, we would have gone bicycling last weekend.

These examples illustrate three features of conditional sentences: (1) the *if* clause may appear before or after the main clause stating results; (2) not every conditional sentence contains *if*; and, most important, (3) the kind of conditional statement determines the tenses of the verbs.

■ 1 Describing habitual past and present conditions

For conditions that occur again and again in the past or present, use the same tense in the *if* clause and the "results" main clause.

┌── present tense (*if* clause) ─┐┌── present tense (*results* clause) ─┐
If we have enough time, we go bicycling on weekends.

┌──── past tense (*if* clause) ────┐┌──── past tense (*results* clause) ────┐
When we had enough time, we went bicycling on weekends.

■ 2 Describing possible future conditions

To predict future conditions and results:

- In the *if* clause, use *if* or *unless* + the present tense (not the future tense).

- In the "results" clause, use *can, may, might, should,* or *will* + the base form of the verb.

┌── present tense (*if* clause) ─┐┌── *may* + base form (*results* clause) ──┐
If we have enough time, we may go bicycling this weekend.

┌────── *will* + base form (*results* clause) ──────┐ ┌── present tense (*if* clause) ──┐
We will go bicycling this weekend unless it rains.

■ 3 Speculating about present or future conditions

To speculate about imagined conditions in the present or future:

- In the *if* clause, use *if* + the past tense (not the present tense). A note on *be*: If you use a form of the verb *be* in the *if* clause, use *were* instead of *was*, whether the subject is singular or plural. (See also 13f.)

- In the "results" clause, use *could, might,* or *would* + the base form of the verb.

past tense (*if* clause)   *would* + base form (*results* clause)

If the weather were better today, we would go bicycling.

might + base form (*results* clause)   past tense (*if* clause)

We might go bicycling if it stopped raining.

■ 4 Speculating about past conditions

To speculate about what might, could, or should have happened in the past:

- In the *if* clause, use *if* + the past perfect tense (*had* + *-ed, -d, -en, -t* past participle).

- In the "results" clause, use *could have, might have,* or *would have* + the past participle.

past perfect tense (*if* clause) — *would have* + past participle

If it had stopped raining, we would have gone bicycling.

could have + past participle (*results* clause)   past perfect tense (*if* clause)

We could have gone bicycling if the weather had been better.

31_f_ Learn which verbs may be followed by infinitives, gerunds, or either verb form

An infinitive is the base form of a verb preceded by *to*: *to study.* A gerund is the *-ing* form of a verb used as a noun: *Studying is difficult after a full day's work.* Following certain verbs, infinitives and gerunds may appear as objects.

■ 1 Verb + infinitive

- Some verbs are followed by an infinitive (*to* + base form) but not a gerund:

agree	claim	deserve	offer	refuse
appear	come	hope	plan	seem
arrange	decide	intend	pretend	wish

The group agreed **to study** [not *studying*] in the library after dinner.

- When used in the active voice, a related group of verbs follows this pattern: verb + noun/pronoun + infinitive:

advise	convince	force	permit	tell
allow	encourage	instruct	persuade	urge
ask	expect	invite	remind	want
cause	forbid	order	require	warn

verb + noun + infinitive

We have invited Gary to join us for dinner.

verb + pronoun + infinitive

Brigit advised me to apply for a scholarship.

- A small group of verbs may be followed by either an infinitive or a noun/pronoun + an infinitive:

allow	cause	get	promise
ask	expect	help	want
beg	force	need	would like

verb + infinitive

The lawyer asked to address the court.

verb + noun + infinitive

Mercedes asked Luis to bring his laptop computer to class.

- When the verbs *have* ("cause"), *let* ("allow"), and *make* ("force") are followed by a noun or pronoun + infinitive, the *to* is omitted:

Please have the carpenters finish [not *to finish*] their work by Thursday.

■ 2 Verb + gerund

- These verbs may be followed by a gerund but not an infinitive:

admit	deny	imagine	postpone	resist
appreciate	discuss	keep	practice	risk
avoid	enjoy	mention	put off	suggest
consider	escape	mind	quit	tolerate
delay	finish	miss	recall	

Keiko recalled **leaving** [not *to leave*] her gloves in the car.

- The following expressions with prepositions often take a gerund or a possessive noun/pronoun + a gerund:

accuse someone of	approve of	be capable of
apologize for	be accustomed to	be excited about

be fond of	dream of	look forward to
be interested in	feel like	object to
be responsible for	forgive someone for	prevent someone from
be tired of	get around to	stop someone from
be used to	have an influence on	succeed in
believe in	help in	talk about
concentrate on	insist on	think about
depend on	keep someone from	

verb + preposition + gerund

For more than a year Anne and Judy have dreamed of traveling to Italy.

verb + preposition + pronoun + gerund

I depend on his arriving on time.

■ 3 Verb + infinitive or gerund

- Certain verbs may be followed by infinitives or gerunds with little or no change of meaning: *begin, continue, hate, like, love, prefer, start.*

  Ali **loves playing** the guitar.

  Ali **loves to play** the guitar.

- After the verbs *forget, remember, stop,* and *try,* the infinitive and gerund have different meanings:

  A Good Samaritan is someone who **stops to help** those in need. [provides assistance]

  Concerned with his own problems, Felix **has stopped helping** those in need. [no longer provides assistance]

31_g_ | Use two-word verbs correctly

■ **Two-word verbs** (also called *phrasal verbs*) consist of a verb and a preposition that together mean something different from the meanings of their individual words. Consider two-word verbs using *call*:

I promise to **call up** my parents this weekend. [to telephone]

When I get the information, I'll **call** you **back.** [to return a telephone call]

The Army **is calling up** its reserves. [to report for service]

The instructor **called** the student **in** for a conference. [to ask to come to a specific place for a specific purpose]

I'm going to **call on** you tomorrow. [to ask to speak, to visit]

The umpire **called off** the game because of darkness. [to cancel]

■ 1 Using a dictionary or phrase book

Because English two-word verbs are so numerous and their meanings are almost always idiomatic, use a dictionary or phrase book of idioms as you write and edit. Check to see that you've used the correct verb + preposition combination for the meaning you intend.

■ 2 Placing objects and prepositions following the verb

The preposition in a two-word verb, called the *particle,* is either inseparable or separable.

■ Inseparable particles. **Inseparable particles** follow the verb immediately.

The instructor **called on** Jigna to answer the question.

Today's college students often **drop out** of school for a few years and then return.

Rosendo decided **to go out** to dinner to celebrate his promotion.

■ Separable particles. **Separable particles** may be separated from transitive verbs according to two patterns:

Noun objects. If the object of a separable two-word verb is a noun, place it after the particle or between the verb and particle: *The umpire called off the game* (verb + particle + noun). *The umpire called the game off* (verb + noun + particle).

Pronoun objects. If the object of a separable two-word verb is a pronoun, place it between the verb and particle: *The umpire called it off* (verb + pronoun + particle).

More Grammar

■ 1 Including subjects

Except for imperatives, all English sentences must have a subject. Be especially careful to include personal pronoun subjects that refer to antecedents in preceding clauses or sentences. Compare these examples:

The Hindu god Brahma is considered equal to Vishnu and Siva. However, **he** has had only one temple dedicated to him, at Pushkar in India.

Because Carlos practices speaking into a tape recorder, *he* has excellent

pronunciation.

Takao is such an optimist. ~~Says~~ *She says* that problems are only clouds hiding the

sun.

■ 2 Including the expletives *it*, *here*, and *there*

Expletives are words used primarily for grammatical purposes. They provide a subject for a sentence that doesn't logically have one or introduce a subject following the verb. Usually an expletive is followed by a form of *be*.

It *is* raining again.

delayed subject

There *are* many Andean mountains higher than 6,700 meters.

Do not omit *it*, *here*, and *there* even though they contribute little meaning to your sentences, and be sure the verb agrees with its actual subject. (See also 14b.)

It is
~~Is~~ necessary to take health precautions before traveling in tropical

countries.

[*It* is required to introduce the subject of the sentence, *to take health precautions*.]

, there
Ten years ago was a severe drought in my country.

[The subject of the sentence is not *ten years ago* but *a severe drought* following the verb *was*. *There* is required to introduce it.]

Here are
~~Is~~ two solutions to the problems created by illegal immigration.

[The subject of the sentence, *two solutions*, requires the plural verb *are*.]

32*b*
Avoid unnecessary repetition

■ 1 Avoiding unnecessary subject repetition

Do not repeat a subject within its own clause, even when the subject and verb are separated.

American cigarette manufacturers ~~they~~ now advertise heavily

throughout Asia.

The Wei River, at flood stage for nearly three weeks, ~~it~~ began to recede

at last.

■ 2 Avoiding unnecessary object and adverb repetition

Do not repeat an object or adverb in an adjective clause beginning
with a relative pronoun (*who, which, whom, whose, that*) or relative adverb
(*where, when*).

Ahmed is the one person whom I can always trust ~~him~~ to tell the truth.

[The relative pronoun *whom* is also the object of the verb *trust*; the objective pronoun *him* is unnecessary. Even if *whom* were omitted, *him* would be unnecessary:
Ahmed is the one person I can always trust to tell the truth.]

Marrakech sits on a high plain where the air is thin and the sun is

brilliant ~~there~~.

[*There* repeats the meaning of the relative adverb *where* and is, therefore, unnecessary.]

■ 3 Repeating conjunctions unnecessarily

Conjunctions link words, phrases, and clauses. Coordinating conjunctions (*and, or, but,* and so forth) link words of equal value. Subordinating
conjunctions (*although, because, if, when,* and so forth) link dependent clauses
to main clauses. To link clauses, use only one conjunction. (See also 8g.)

Although I'm happy here, ~~but~~ I miss the sweet sounds and smells of

home.

[The subordinating conjunction *although* links the first clause, *I'm happy here,* to the
following main clause; *but* is unnecessary. To emphasize the clauses equally, the
writer would omit *although* and retain *but*: *I am happy here, but I miss the sweet sounds
and smells of home.*]

32c | Follow these guidelines to summarize
         | questions and speech

■ 1 Summarizing questions

Summarized questions (also called *indirect questions*) are usually part
of a longer statement of fact; therefore, they follow the word order and
punctuation of declarative sentences. (See 10c2.)

- Subject + verb. After the question word (*who, which, when, why, where, how,* and so forth) that introduces the summarized question, place the subject before the verb.

  The panel considered where ~~is~~ air pollution the most severe.
  (is inserted above, caret below "pollution")

- Using *whether* for "yes/no" and "or" questions. Use *whether* to introduce summarized "yes/no" questions and "or" questions that pose alternatives.

  whether I will
  I have not decided ~~will I~~ go home for the summer or attend summer

  school.

- Omitting *do, does, did.* Omit *do, does, did* from summarized questions; signal tense (the time of the action) with the correct form of the main verb.

  whether   needed
  He asked me ~~did~~ I ~~need~~ help with my experiment.

  [*Needed* matches the past tense form of the main verb *asked.*]

- Punctuation. Punctuate summarized questions in a way appropriate to the complete sentence.

  The judge asked the jury whether it had reached a verdict~~?~~.

■2 Summarizing speech

In **summarized speech** (also called *reported speech* or *indirect quotation*), a writer restates a direct quotation in his or her own words, without quotation marks, in the following formats.

- Summarizing in a noun clause. Write the summarized speech as a noun clause within your own sentence.

DIRECT QUOTATION	SUMMARIZED SPEECH
She said, "A monsoon is a strong seasonal wind."	She said that a monsoon is a strong seasonal wind.

  [*That* may be omitted from certain noun clauses. (See 22d2.)]

- Changing present to past tense and present progressive to past progressive. Change the present tense or present progressive of direct quotations to the past tense or past progressive in summarized speech. An exception: Use the present tense if the summarized speech is a general truth or habitual action, as in the preceding example.

DIRECT QUOTATION	SUMMARIZED SPEECH
She said, "My report is finished."	She said that her report was finished.
She said, "I am finishing my report."	She said that she was finishing her report.

- Changing the past tense or present perfect to past perfect. Change the past tense or present perfect of direct quotations to the past perfect of summarized speech.

DIRECT QUOTATION	SUMMARIZED SPEECH
She said, "They arrived an hour ago."	She said that they had arrived an hour ago.
She said, "I have tried to help him."	She said that she had tried to help him.

- Changing modal verbs. When summarizing speech, change *can* to *could, will* to *would, may* to *might, must* to *had to*.

DIRECT QUOTATION	SUMMARIZED SPEECH
She said, "I will call him next week."	She said that she would call him next week.

- Summarizing commands. To summarize commands, use *to* + the base form of the verb (the infinitive).

DIRECT QUOTATION	SUMMARIZED SPEECH
She told her students, "Go to the lab."	She told her students to go to the lab.

32*d* Show possession with an apostrophe or an *of* phrase

■ English signals a possessive noun with an apostrophe or a phrase using *of*: *India's president, the president of India*. In some cases, as in the preceding examples, the forms are interchangeable; often they are not.

■ 1 Indicating possession with an apostrophe

To make a singular noun or indefinite pronoun possessive, usually add *-'s*: *the student's book, someone's book*. To make a plural noun ending in -s possessive, usually add only an apostrophe: *the students' request*. An apostrophe is generally used with nouns referring to persons and other living beings: *the president's address, the lions' roar*. (For more on the possessive form and the apostrophe, see 17d and 37a.)

■ **2** **Indicating possession with** *of*

To signal possession when referring to things, you would typically use an *of* phrase: *the body of the car, the soles of my feet.* An *of* phrase may also be used to emphasize what is possessed: *the novels of Chinua Achebe.* Do not use possessive *of* phrases with personal pronouns: *her book,* not *the book of her.*

Many parents do not consider the TV violence ~~effect~~ on their children.
_{effect of}

Without ~~the~~ help ~~of him~~, we could not have afforded the trip.
_{his}

Exceptions: The apostrophe form of the possessive appears frequently in references to time (*an hour's drive, a month's time*), natural phenomena (*the sun's rays, Earth's atmosphere*), political organizations (*the city's parks, the nation's tax system*), and groups of people working together (*the ship's crew, the company's employees*).

32e
Use adjectives and adverbs with care

■ **1** **Forming adjectives**

Adjectives modify nouns by telling which one, what kind, how many: *the tall man, a new student, four flowers.* (See 8d and 18a.) Some languages add singular and plural endings to adjectives so that they match the nouns they modify, but in English adjectives are neither singular nor plural. Do not add *-s* to adjectives even when they precede plural nouns:

After only four full**s** days of work, Zahid knew this job was the one he

wanted.

■ **2** ***-ing* and *-ed* adjectives**

To form some adjectives, English uses present participle (*-ing*) verbs and past participle (*-ed, -en, -n, or -t*) verbs: *a terrifying story, a crowded street.* Both kinds of participles may appear before a noun or following a linking verb: *The terrifying story is completely true. The story is terrifying. The terrified child could not speak. The child was terrified.* But present and past participles may not be used interchangeably.

■ Present participle adjectives. Use present participle adjectives (ending in *-ing*) to describe something causing or stimulating an experience: *The survivors told a terrifying story to their fearful listeners* [the story caused terror in the listeners].

They jumped in surprise at the sound of ~~broken~~ glass.
_{breaking}

■ Past participle adjectives. Use past participle adjectives (ending in *-ed, -d, -en, -t*) to describe a person or thing undergoing an experience: *The listeners shuddered, terrified by the survivors' story* [the listeners experienced terror].

embarrassed
I felt ~~embarrassing~~ when my instructor read my paper aloud.
                      ^

■ 3 Arranging cumulative adjectives

Cumulative adjectives are two or more adjectives unseparated by commas that modify the whole phrase following them: *the large round Persian rug.* To use cumulative adjectives correctly, arrange them in this order:

1. Article, possessive, or quantifier: *the, my, Teresa's, some, four,* and so forth.
2. Comparative and superlative: *younger, older, best, worst, least.*
3. Evaluator (a word that can be preceded by *very*): *beautiful, courageous, responsible.*
4. Size: *large, small, gigantic, tall.*
5. Length or shape: *long, round, oval, square, triangular.*
6. Age: *young, old, new, antique, modern, twentieth-century.*
7. Color: *green, yellow, violet.*
8. Nationality: *Peruvian, Iranian, Polish, Canadian.*
9. Religion: *Baptist, Buddhist, Christian, Hindu, Muslim, Protestant.*
10. Material: *wood, walnut, metal, gold, wool.*
11. Noun used as an adjective: *guest* (as in *guest room*), *history* (as in *history class*).
12. Noun modified: *room, class, truck, table.*

Compare these examples:

Four old wooden clocks will be sold at the auction.

two
The baby was being entertained by her older ~~two~~ sisters.
                                          ^

A note on adjective series: Avoid long series of cumulative adjectives. Generally use no more than two or three between an article, possessive, or quantifier and the noun they modify: *an old Hindu temple, Kevin's famous buttermilk pancakes, several well-known European scientists.*

■ 4 Placing adverbs

Adverbs used to modify verbs may appear at the beginning, end, or in the middle of a sentence. However, do not place an adverb between a verb and a direct object. (See also 23a.) Compare these examples:

Carefully, she took her daughter's hand.

He turned the dial **carefully.**

He walked **carefully** along the ledge.

To complete my art history project, I examined ~~carefully~~ *carefully* Mayan

architecture.

32_f_ | Choose the appropriate preposition for expressions of place and time

English expressions of place and time using *at*, *in*, and *on* can be troublesome. Here are guidelines to their use. Note, however, that exceptions do exist. Consult an ESL dictionary, such as the *Longman Dictionary of Contemporary English* or the *Oxford Advanced Learner's Dictionary.*

■ 1 Indicating place

- *At.* Use *at* before a location, meeting place, the edge of something, the corner of something, or a target: *arriving at school, seated at the table, turning at the corner of Fifth and Maple streets, aiming at the bull's eye.*

- *In.* Use *in* before an enclosed space or geographic location: *growing in the garden, standing in the phone booth, hiking in the desert, living in Mexico City.*

- *On.* Use *on* before a surface or street: *lying on the table, hanging on the wall, walking on Fifth Avenue.*

■ 2 Indicating time

- *At.* Use *at* before specific expressions of time: *She arrived at 2:30. They left at dawn.*

- *In.* Use *in* before a month, year, century, period of time, or part of a twenty-four-hour period: *in May, in 1865, in the twentieth century, in an hour, in the morning.*

- *On.* Use *on* before a day or date: *on July 20th, on Thursday.*

■ 3 Arranging place and time phrases

In most English expressions, *place* comes before *time*: *My relatives arrived at my house in the early morning.* However, a prepositional phrase of time may appear at the beginning of a sentence: *In the early morning, my relatives arrived at my house.*

Punctuation
and
Mechanics

Punctuation and Mechanics

Punctuating

How to Identify and Correct Common Punctuation Errors

How to...

Read your writing aloud to hear punctuation errors. Answer these questions:

1. Do I hear frequent pauses that make my writing sound choppy?
2. Does my punctuation cause me to stumble or reread?

If you answer yes to either of these questions, rewrite or repunctuate. Use as little punctuation as possible to make your writing correct and easy to read. A computer tip: Use the Find or Search and Replace command in your word-processing program to locate punctuation.

Periods. Search for unnecessary periods following

1. the titles of your papers
2. abbreviations that end a sentence
3. question marks and exclamation points
4. all-capital abbreviations. (See 33a4.)

Exclamation points. Look at your writing. Have you overused exclamation points? If so, your writing may sound melodramatic or false. Use periods wherever possible. (See 33c.)

Commas. Add required commas

1. before a coordinating conjunction like *and* or *but* joining independent clauses
2. following introductory words
3. between items in a series
4. between coordinate adjectives
5. before and after word groups that interrupt the flow of a sentence. (See 34a–g.)

(continued)

How to ...

How to Identify and Correct
Common Punctuation Errors *(continued)*

Omit unnecessary commas

1. between subjects and verbs
2. between verbs and the remainder of the predicate
3. before indirect quotations
4. before the comparative *than*
5. following subordinating conjunctions like *although* and phrases like *such as* to introduce a list
6. surrounding essential modifiers and items in a series
7. before parentheses or brackets and following question marks or exclamation points. (See 34k.) Look for commas joining independent clauses, an error called a *comma splice.* (See 12b.) Add a coordinating conjunction like *and* or *but* or replace the comma with a period or semicolon.

Semicolons. If you have used a comma before a transition or conjunctive adverb (*for example* or *however*) that links independent clauses, use a semicolon instead. (See 12b3.) To identify independent clauses, use the "yes/no" question test. (See 11b1.) If items in series contain internal commas, use semicolons between items. (See 35c.) Do not use semicolons between

1. dependent and independent clauses
2. modifiers and the words they modify
3. lists and the words that introduce them. (See 35d.)

Colons. Look for lists, quotations, and explanations preceded by an independent clause; use a colon to link them. (See 36a.) To identify independent clauses, use the "yes/no" question test. (See 11b1.)
Look for places where colons are unnecessary:

1. after words like *such as, like,* or *including*
2. between verbs and the remainder of the predicate, subordinating conjunctions and the clauses that follow, or prepositions and objects. (See 36c.)

Apostrophes. In most cases, if a noun ends in *s* and precedes another noun, add an apostrophe before the *s* if the word is singular, after the *s* if the word is plural. (See 37a.) A computer tip: If your word-processing program permits partial-word searches, look for nouns ending in *s.*

If you're unsure whether a noun is possessive, try to create an *of* phrase (*the students paper = the paper of the student*). If you can do this, the original word takes an apostrophe. (See 37a.) Possessive pronouns (*his, hers, its, your, yours,* or *whose*) do not take apostrophes. (See 37d.) A computer tip: Use the Find or Search and Replace commands to locate apostrophes.

Quotation marks. Use double quotation marks around quotations, no matter how brief. Use single quotation marks only for quotations of quotations. (See 38a and d.)

Periods and commas go inside double and single quotation marks. Semicolons and colons go outside quotation marks. Question marks and exclamation points go inside if they are part of the quotation, otherwise outside. (See 38b.)

Use quotation marks around the titles of short works. (See 38e.) Use underlining or italics for the titles of long works. (See 41a.)

Omit unnecessary quotation marks around indented quotations, the titles of your own writing, slang, and indirect or summarized quotations. (See 38c and g.)

A computer tip: Use the Find or Search and Replace commands to locate quotation marks used alone and with other punctuation.

The dash. Look at your writing. Many dashes may make it too informal or difficult to read. Rewrite, using other punctuation as necessary. (See 39a.)

Parentheses and brackets. Look at your writing. If you've used excessive parentheses or brackets, your writing will be difficult to read. Rewrite as necessary. (See 39b and c.) Use brackets, not parentheses, to insert clarifying words into a direct quotation. Put commas, semicolons, and colons after parentheses and brackets, not before them.

End Punctuation

33*a* | Use a period to mark sentences, abbreviations, and conventional divisions

■ 1 Marking sentences

Use a period to end all sentences except direct questions and genuine exclamations. Use a period to end sentences that summarize questions, make polite requests not phrased as questions, and give commands that are not exclamations.

Edyta called the ticket office to ask whether the concert had been canceled.

Please respond to the memo as soon as possible.

Return the rental car by Friday at noon.

- Periods and quotation marks. Place periods inside all quotation marks, single or double, whether the quotation is a word, phrase, or complete sentence. (See 38b1.)

  According to Joy Williams, many hunters consider wild animals a " 'resource' to be 'utilized.' "

- Periods and the ellipsis. When a quoted sentence ends with an ellipsis (three evenly spaced periods . . .), it usually requires an additional fourth period: " '*Tis better to have loved and lost. . . .*" (See 39d.)

■ 2 Marking abbreviations

Punctuation of abbreviations varies. When in doubt, consult a dictionary, style manual, or publication guide appropriate to your subject or audience. The Modern Language Association provides these guidelines.

- Initials in names. Use a period followed by a space after initials used for personal names:

  Susan B. Anthony, H. G. Wells, J. Pierpont Morgan

- Abbreviations ending in lower case. Use a period after most abbreviations ending in lower-case letters. Do not put a space between lower-case letters that each represent a word.

Mr.	Inc.	Capt.	a.m.
Mrs.	Jan.	Maj.	p.m.
Ms.	Feb.	etc.	e.g.
Dr.	Sept.	introd.	i.e.

- Abbreviations that end sentences. When an abbreviation ends a sentence, do not add a second period.

- All-capital abbreviations. Do not use a period in all-capital abbreviations or following US Postal Service abbreviations of states.

ALL-CAPITAL ABBREVIATIONS				US POSTAL SERVICE ABBREVIATIONS
NATO	FBI	IQ	CAT scan	CA
UNESCO	USA	COD	BA	MA
NAACP	NRA	IOU	PhD	TX

■ 3 Marking related items

Use periods to mark conventional divisions between related items.

- Money and decimals. Use a period between dollars and cents (*$29.25*) and before decimals (*3.141592*).

- Computer file names and addresses. Use a period (usually referred to as a *dot*) between computer file names and extensions and to separate the parts of an e-mail address: *grammar.doc, cjones@aol.com*

- Lists. Use a period and two spaces after numbers or letters that precede items in a list. Use a period following items in a vertical list only when one or more items is a complete sentence.

In the middle of the nineteenth century, birds and animals that are now endangered or extinct were plentiful.

1. More than 13 million bison were divided into two vast herds, one in the northern plains, one in the south.
2. Over 100,000 grizzly bears roamed the western United States.
3. Flocks of passenger pigeons more than 100 miles long were not uncommon.

■ Writing about literature. To cite a passage from a literary work, use a period with no intervening spaces between the divisions of the work.

Hamlet 3.2.16–23 or *Hamlet* III.ii.16–23 [act, scene, lines]

Paradise Lost 10.55–57 or *Paradise Lost* X.55–57 [book, lines]

■ 4 Avoiding unnecessary periods

■ Paper titles. Do not use a period after the titles of your papers, even if they are complete sentences. Except for run-in headings, do not use periods after section headings in your papers. (See 46b1.) Use question marks and exclamation points when appropriate.

■ Acronyms. Do not use a period after acronyms (CD-ROM), all-capital abbreviations (DNA), or US Postal Service abbreviations (NJ, OK, WA).

■ Second periods. When an abbreviation ends a sentence, do not add a second period.

The shipment will be delivered by 9 a.m./

■ A sentence within a sentence. Do not use a period after a sentence within a sentence.

"Cure the disease and kill the patient" was a statement made by Francis Bacon, not Benjamin Franklin.

By 1893, fewer than a thousand buffalo remained in the United States (at the beginning of the century there had been 20 million).

■ Lists. Do not use a period following items in a vertical list unless one or more items are complete sentences.

33*b* | Use a question mark to signal questions, requests, and doubts

■ 1 Signaling questions

Use a question mark after direct questions.

How long did Henry David Thoreau live at Walden Pond?

A note on indirect or summarized quotations: Do not use a question mark after indirect or summarized questions. (See 38a; for ESL, see 32c1.)

She asked when the order would be delivered?
                                             ∧

A note on questions in series: You may use question marks following questions in a series even when they are not complete sentences.

Will reducing income taxes stimulate savings? Encourage investment? Weaken social programs? Enlarge the federal budget deficit?

▪ **2** Signaling expressions of doubt

Use a question mark to signal doubt.

Professor Isaacs is not giving a final exam this semester?

▪ **3** Signaling polite requests

Use a question mark following a polite request phrased as a question.

Will you please send me an admissions application?

▪ **4** Questions and quotation marks

Place question marks inside quotation marks when the quotation is a question; otherwise, put them outside.

The ticket agent asked, "Is this your suitcase?"

What famous philosopher said, "I think; therefore, I am"?

A note: When a question within a sentence is followed by other words, put a question mark after the question and a period at the end of the sentence.

"What time does the play begin?" he asked.

33c Use an exclamation point for an outcry, emphasis, and irony

▪ **1** An outcry

"A horse! A horse! My kingdom for a horse!" cried the desperate king.

▪ **2** An expression of emphasis

Alderman Paddy Bauler became famous for declaring, "Chicago ain't ready for reform!"

■ 3 An expression of irony

Standing in the mud, shivering in the rain, she muttered, "I keep reminding myself that this is the vacation of a lifetime!"

A note on unnecessary exclamations: Avoid overusing exclamation points. They rarely appear in academic writing, especially in serious informative writing. Even in personal or narrative writing, too many will create a melodramatic or false tone, as essayist and surgeon Lewis Thomas playfully illustrates:

> Look! they say, look at what I just said! How amazing is my thought! It is like being forced to watch someone else's small child jumping up and down crazily in the center of the living room shouting to attract attention. If a sentence really has something of importance to say, something quite remarkable, it doesn't need a mark to point it out. And if it is really, after all, a banal sentence needing more zing, the exclamation point simply emphasizes its banality!

> ("On Punctuation," from *The Medusa and the Snail*)

The Comma

34*a* | Use a comma before a coordinating conjunction (*but, and*) that links independent clauses

When the coordinating conjunctions *and, but, or, nor, so, for,* and *yet* link independent clauses—word groups that can be punctuated as complete sentences—they are preceded by a comma. (To identify independent clauses, use the "yes/no" question test, 11b1; also see 12c.)

Groups of sharks attack their prey ferociously, but they never bite one another.

Jill loves animals, so it's natural that she's majoring in veterinary medicine.

A note on short independent clauses: If the meaning of a compound sentence is clear and the independent clauses are short, you may omit the comma before the conjunction.

The whistle bellowed once and the boat left the dock.

A note on conjunctions that link phrases or dependent clauses: Do not use a comma before conjunctions that link phrases or dependent clauses. (To learn to identify phrases and dependent clauses, see 10a and b.)

The musicians played sad songs marching to the funeral / but joyful

songs on their return.

[The *but* in this sentence joins two phrases, *sad songs . . . but joyful songs . . .* , so the comma is unnecessary.]

Paiute Ghost Dancers believed that their magical shirts would protect

them from harm / and that their dances would bring back the nearly

extinct buffalo.

[The *and* in this sentence joins two dependent clauses opening with the subordinating conjunction *that: that their magical shirts would protect them . . . and that their dances would bring back the nearly extinct buffalo.* Neither clause can be punctuated as a complete sentence, so the comma is unnecessary.]

34b | Use a comma after introductory words

■ Use a comma to set off an introductory word, phrase, or dependent clause from the rest of the sentence. The comma signals that the main part of the sentence is about to begin. (To learn to identify phrases and clauses, see 10a and b.)

Unfortunately, exotic species introduced to new habitats often threaten native species.

Growing up in Africa, she had been entertained by story tellers of all kinds.

After Harriet Tubman escaped the South, she became a "conductor" on the Underground Railroad that carried slaves north.

A note on brief phrases and clauses: You may omit the comma following a brief introductory phrase or clause.

By noon the storm had passed.

But be sure to use commas to prevent misreading.

When Carol returned , her baby's smile was the greeting that meant the

most.

34*c* | Use a comma between items in a series

■ Use a comma to separate three or more words, phrases, or clauses written as a series.

Winter drivers should carry a scraper, shovel, sand, flares, extra washer fluid, and a blanket.

A note: You may omit the comma before the conjunction preceding the last item in a series, but in some cases the comma may be necessary to prevent misreading.

Julie attended the presidential inauguration with her relatives, a senator, and a judge.
[a comma before the conjunction]

Julie attended the presidential inauguration with her relatives, a senator and a judge.
[no comma before the conjunction]

The first sentence is clear: Julie attended the inauguration with her relatives and a senator and a judge. The second may mean the same as the first, or it may mean that one of her relatives is a senator, the other a judge. To be clear, use a comma before the conjunction in a series.

34*d* | Use a comma between coordinate adjectives but not between cumulative adjectives

■ 1 Using a comma between coordinate adjectives

Adjectives are coordinate if each modifies a noun by itself. Use a comma after each adjective to signal its separate function.

Muhammad Ali was a **skilled, fierce, imaginative** boxer.
[Each adjective—*skilled, fierce, imaginative*—modifies *boxer* by itself.]

■ 2 Avoiding a comma between cumulative adjectives

Adjectives are cumulative if each modifies all the words that follow it, adjectives and noun together. Because meaning accumulates as the phrase unfolds from adjective to adjective, do not separate the adjectives by commas.

Muhammad Ali was **the most famous war** protestor to refuse military service during the Vietnam War.
[*War* modifies *protestor, famous* modifies *war protestor,* and *most* modifies *famous war protestor.* Meaning accumulates as the phrase unfolds.]

■ 3 Identifying coordinate and cumulative adjectives

Two tests will help you distinguish between coordinate adjectives and cumulative adjectives.

- The *and* test. If you can put *and* between the adjectives, they are coordinate and require a comma between them to signal their separate functions. Consider the two preceding examples: *A skilled and fierce and imaginative boxer* signals coordinate adjectives that require commas to separate them. But you would not write *most and famous and war protestor,* so these are cumulative adjectives not separated by commas.

- The reversal test. If you can reverse the order of the adjectives, they are coordinate and require a comma between them (*skilled, fierce, imaginative boxer* may become *fierce, skilled, imaginative boxer*). But you would not write *war famous most protestor.*

34e | Use commas to set off nonessential modifiers; do not use commas to set off essential modifiers

■ 1 Using commas with nonessential modifiers

Nonessential modifiers (also called **nonrestrictive modifiers**) are words, phrases, or clauses that add extra information but are not essential to the basic meaning of a sentence. Omitting these modifiers would not drastically alter the meaning. Use commas to signal their nonessential nature.

Arthur Jensen, **my minister,** has volunteered to head the Heart Fund drive.

[Because it is nonessential, *my minister* is set off by commas.]

The Ferris Wheel, **which is named for the man who invented it,** was first erected in 1892 at the Chicago World's Fair.

[Information about the inventor of the Ferris Wheel is nonessential to a sentence about the wheel's first location and is set off by commas.]

Many nineteenth-century pioneers came first to Kansas City, **where one branch of the Oregon Trail began.**

[Information about the Oregon Trail is important but not essential to a sentence about Kansas City, and so it is set off by a comma.]

■ 2 Avoiding commas with essential modifiers

Essential modifiers (also called **restrictive modifiers**) restrict the meaning of the words they modify to a special sense. If they are omitted, the sentence changes meaning. To signal their essential information, do not set off essential modifiers with commas. Consider how commas change the meaning of these sentences:

My brother **who lives in Little Rock** often comes to visit. [essential modifier]

[The modifier *who lives in Little Rock* identifies which brother often comes to visit. Because it is essential to the basic meaning of the sentence, it is not set off by commas.]

My brother**, who lives in Little Rock,** often comes to visit. [nonessential modifier]

[The writer's only brother, who happens to live in Little Rock, often comes to visit. The brother's location is not essential to the basic meaning of the sentence, and so it is set off by commas.]

■ **3** Identifying nonessential and essential modifiers

Sometimes it is difficult to tell whether a modifier is nonessential or essential. Try reading the sentence without the modifier. If the basic meaning is unchanged, the modifier is nonessential and set off by commas. If the sentence changes or loses meaning, the modifier is essential and should not be set off. Compare:

Ernest Hemingway's story "Hills Like White Elephants" portrays a couple debating the consequences of an abortion.

Ernest Hemingway's story . . . portrays a couple . . .

[Without the title of the story and *debating the consequences of an abortion,* the sentence has no meaning. These are both essential modifiers not set off by commas.]

If after rereading you're still not sure whether a modifier is nonessential or essential, use these clues.

■ Modifiers of capitalized nouns (nonessential). Modifiers of capitalized nouns (known as *proper nouns*) are usually nonessential and set off by commas.

Nimi speaks Hindi**, which is the official language of India.**

■ Clauses beginning *although, even though,* and *whereas* (nonessential). Clauses beginning with these words are usually nonessential and set off by commas.

The burglar was captured within hours**, even though he was sure he had left no clues.**

■ Modifiers of indefinite pronouns such as *anyone* and *something* (essential). Modifiers of indefinite pronouns are usually essential and are not set off by commas.

Anyone **who studies the textbook** can pass this course.

[The clause *who studies the textbook* is essential to identify *anyone* and is therefore not set off by commas.]

- Relative clauses beginning with *that* (essential). If a relative clause begins with *that*, do not punctuate.

  Cars **that require the fewest repairs** have the highest resale value.

- Substituting *that* (essential modifiers). If you can substitute *that* for *who, whom,* or *which,* do not punctuate. (For when to use *that,* see 16d.)

  The painter **whom/that** I admire most is Edward Hopper.

- Omitting *who, whom,* or *that* (essential modifiers). If you can omit *who, whom,* or *that,* do not punctuate.

  The painter **[whom]** I admire most is Edward Hopper.

- Concluding adverb clauses beginning *as soon as, before, because, if, since, unless, until,* and *when* (essential modifiers). Clauses beginning with these words are essential to the basic meaning of a sentence and are not set off by commas.

  Students should sign up for flu vaccinations **as soon as they arrive on campus.**

34f Use commas to set off transitions, parenthetical expressions, and contrast statements

■ 1 Using commas with transitions

Conjunctive adverbs such as *however* and transitional phrases such as *for example* act as bridges carrying readers from one idea to the next. Set these transitions off with commas. (For a complete list of conjunctive adverbs and transitional phrases, see 12b3.)

Most people refuse to think about pain. Some kinds of pain**, however,** are important to recognize and understand.

Some common pain killers have harmful side effects. **For example,** aspirin may cause internal bleeding.

A note on transitions that connect independent clauses: When you connect independent clauses with a transition, use a semicolon before the transition and, usually, a comma following it. (See 35b.)

Professional athletes must often play in pain; **consequently,** they turn to trainers for strong pain suppressants.

If little or no pause follows a transition, you may omit the comma.

We have never planned a long bicycle trip; **therefore** we're asking for your suggestions.

■ 2 Using commas with parenthetical expressions

Parenthetical expressions that add supplemental or explanatory information should be set off with commas.

> Riverboat gambling, **once an example of social decay,** is now a tax resource eagerly sought by politicians.

> Beth was the first to arrive, **as usual.**

A note on *too*: When the word *too*, meaning "also," appears in the middle or at the end of a sentence, it is usually set off with commas.

> Muslims, too, believe that Jesus was born of the Virgin Mary.

■ 3 Using commas with contrast statements

Use a comma to set off statements of contrast or contradiction, usually beginning *not, nor, never, but,* or *unlike.*

> Jan's stepfather, **unlike her father,** is relaxed and jovial.

> Mom gave the last piece of pie to Jerry, **never one to refuse an extra dessert.**

34*g* | Use commas to set off quotation tags, direct address, and mild interjections

■ 1 Using commas with quotation tags

Use a comma to set off quotation tags at the beginning or end of a sentence.

> As George Bernard Shaw wrote, **"In the arts of peace Man is a bungler."**

> **"I'll do it tomorrow,"** Kevin said lazily.

A note on commas and quotation marks: Place commas inside quotation marks, as in the preceding examples. (See 38b1.) Do not use a comma if the quotation is the subject or complement of the sentence.

> "I shall return/" was General MacArthur's vow on leaving the

> Philippines.

■ 2 Using commas in direct address

Use commas to set off words that signal you are addressing readers directly: names or titles, question tags, the words *yes* or *no.*

Thank you, **Professor Thoreson,** for writing a recommendation for me.

The book is better than the movie, **don't you think?**

Yes, the overdue books have been returned to the library.

■ 3 Using commas with mild interjections

Use commas to set off mild expressions of feeling.

Well, I'm not surprised to see her receive a promotion.

34_h_ | Use commas with titles and degrees, dates, addresses, place names, and numbers

■ 1 Titles and degrees

Use commas to set off titles or degrees that follow a person's name.

Martin Luther King, **Jr.,** campaigned for peace as well as civil rights.

The keynote address will be given by Jean Payne, **president of Springfield College.**

■ 2 Dates

In dates, use a pair of commas to set off the year from the rest of the sentence. Do not use commas if the date is inverted or only the month and year are given.

On March 6, **1837,** General Santa Anna defeated the Texans at the Alamo.

In **April 1942** the United States began building the Alaskan Highway.

The blizzard that began **27 January 1967** was the worst in the state's history.

■ 3 Addresses and place names

Use commas following addresses and place names. Do not use a comma before a zip code.

The regional community center is now located at 238 West Spring, Seneca, IL 61370.

The Women's Christian Temperance Union was founded in Cleveland, Ohio, in 1874.

34j $\overset{\wedge}{,}$

■ 4 Numbers

In numbers of four digits or more, use commas to divide numerals into groups of three. In numbers of four digits, the comma is optional.

1,466

186,000

6,286,836

An exception: Do not use commas within street numbers, zip codes, telephone numbers, or years: 1997, 6206 Main Street, 495-7662.

A note on units of measure which have been spelled out: In units of measure written as words, use commas to separate feet and inches, pounds and ounces, and so forth.

My labrador puppy stands **one foot, two inches** and weighs **twenty pounds, four ounces.**

34i Use commas to signal omissions and prevent misreading

The hikers took the right fork in the path; their rescuers, the left.

To Paul, Carlos remained a puzzle.

34j Follow these guidelines to use commas with quotation marks, parentheses, and brackets

■ 1 Using commas with quotation marks

Place commas inside closing quotation marks, single and double, whether the quotation is a word, phrase, complete sentence, or longer. (See 38b.)

It is "time to stop thinking of wild animals as 'resources' and 'game,' " claims Joy Williams in her argument against hunting.

■ 2 Using commas with parentheses and brackets

Place commas outside closing parentheses and brackets.

Caused by an extra number 21 chromosome (three instead of the usual two), Down's syndrome is characterized by mental retardation and a flattened facial profile.

34k | Avoid unnecessary commas

■ Some writers, knowing that commas signal pauses, insert them whenever they hear a pause or a passage seems too long. Such overuse can make for tiresome, even confusing reading. Use commas sparingly.

■ 1 Avoiding unnecessary comma dividers

- **Between a subject and predicate.** Do not use a comma between a subject and its predicate.

  Taxes that communities receive from legalized gambling/ are often offset

  by the losses of local gamblers.

- **Between a verb and its object or complement.** Do not use a comma between a verb and the object or complement that follows.

  Men and women in their thirties often protest/ their increasingly limited

  career choices.

- **Between compound phrases or dependent clauses.** Do not use a comma before conjunctions joining phrases or dependent clauses. (To learn to identify phrases and dependent clauses, see 10a and b.)

  The coach warned her team that their next opponents were not only tall

  and fast/ but also very smart.

- **Before *than*.** Do not use a comma before the conjunction *than* in comparison statements.

  I'd rather visit the ancient ruins of Egypt and Greece/ than go to Disney

  World.

- **Between cumulative adjectives or adjectives and nouns.** Do not use commas between cumulative adjectives or between adjectives and nouns.

  Eddie fished all day but caught only one/ small/ red snapper.

  [*One* and *small* are cumulative adjectives and do not take commas.]

  One wrong turn after another led him into difficult, nearly impassable/

  terrain.

  [*Impassable* is an adjective modifying the noun *terrain,* so no comma separates them.]

- Before indirect quotations. Do not use a comma before a summarized or indirect quotation.

A famous philosopher once wrote/ that anything worth saying can be

said clearly.

■2 Avoiding unnecessary introductory commas

- After *such as* or *like*. Do not use a comma after *such as* or *like* to introduce a list.

Many people, such as/ Arabs, Indians, and southern Europeans, have

personal space requirements different from those of northern Europeans.

- After *although*. Do not use a comma after the subordinating conjunction *although* that introduces an adverb clause.

The mayor continued the sprinkler ban, although/ rain had fallen weekly

for a month.

- After a phrase that opens an inverted sentence. Do not use a comma after a phrase that opens an inverted sentence.

On top of the highest hill/ stands a house designed by Frank Lloyd

Wright.

- Before the first or after the last item in a series. Although you should use commas between items in a series, do not use them before the first or after the last item.

Laura's favorite flowers are/ hollyhocks, day lilies, and irises.

Someone who enjoys camping, hiking, and cycling/ shouldn't mind a

little rain.

■3 Avoiding unnecessary commas to set off essential modifiers

Do not use commas to set off modifiers essential to the basic meaning of a sentence.

The friends/ whom Lacy trusted the most/ repaid her faith in them.

[Readers need the modifier *whom Lacy trusted the most* to know which friends are referred to. It is essential and not set off by commas.]

The wagon train crossed the river/ where it was shallowest.

[Readers need the modifier *where it was shallowest* to know where the wagon train crossed the river. It is essential and not preceded by a comma.]

■ 4 Avoiding unnecessary commas with other punctuation

- Before parentheses. Do not use a comma before parentheses, only afterward.

Although critics of rock and roll often quote Plato/ (who favored the

strict regulation of music), few have examined his argument carefully.

- After a question mark or exclamation point. Do not use a comma after a question mark or exclamation point.

"What's a thousand dollars?"/ asked Groucho Marx. "Mere chicken feed.

A poultry matter."

The Semicolon

35*a* | Use a semicolon to join closely related independent clauses

A semicolon usually links grammatically equal word groups. Use it in place of a comma and coordinating conjunction (*and, but, so, or, nor, for, yet*) to link independent clauses closely related in subject or structure. To identify independent clauses, use the "yes/no" question test. (See 11b1.)

Few people will admit to being superstitious; it implies naiveté or ignorance.

> (Robertson Davies, "A Few Kind Words for Superstition," *Newsweek*)

Gratitude looks to the past and love to the present; fear, avarice, lust and ambition look ahead.

> (C. S. Lewis, from *The Screwtape Letters*)

A note on comma splices: Joining independent clauses with a comma instead of a semicolon creates an error known as a comma splice. (See 12a.)

Students of the 1960s were activists and dreamers; students of the 90s are

less idealistic and more practical.

35b | Use a semicolon before a conjunctive adverb or transitional phrase joining independent clauses

■ Conjunctive adverbs and transitional phrases such as *however* and *for example* are linking words. (For a complete list, see 12b3.) Although they often mean the same as coordinating conjunctions (*and, but, so, or, nor, for, yet*), such linking words must be punctuated differently. Use a semicolon preceding conjunctive adverbs or transitions that link independent clauses. To use a comma instead is to make a comma splice. (See 12a.)

The runner slid into second base certain he was safe; however, the

umpire called him out with a swift jerk of his thumb.

There is still no treatment for smallpox; even so, a vaccination against

the disease has been in use since 1796.

A note: If the conjunctive adverb or transitional phrase comes in the middle of the second independent clause or at the end, use a semicolon between clauses and enclose the conjunctive adverb or transitional phrase with commas.

The runner slid into second base certain he was safe; the umpire, however, called him out with a swift jerk of his thumb.

35c | Use a semicolon between items in a series if one or more items contain internal punctuation

■ Generally, commas are used between items in a series, but if one or more items contain internal punctuation, readers may not be sure where one item ends and the next begins. Use semicolons to separate internally punctuated series.

Exotic species posing severe threats to native American wildlife are the ruffe, which may drive the Great Lakes perch to extinction; the Muscovy duck, which has ousted the Florida mallard; Mute Swans, which kill related species' goslings and ducklings; and the starling, which has displaced flickers, wrens, swallows, and bluebirds.

35*d* | Avoid unnecessary semicolons

Do not use semicolons between grammatically unequal word groups.

■ 1 Avoiding semicolons between dependent and independent clauses

Do not use a semicolon between a dependent clause and the rest of the sentence. Use a comma instead. (See 34b.) To identify dependent and independent clauses, use the "yes/no" question test. (See 11b1.)

Although New Jersey has numerous oceanside resorts*/*,they are too close

to home for most easterners.

■ 2 Avoiding semicolons between a nonessential dependent clause and the rest of the sentence

If a nonessential dependent clause ends a sentence, precede it with a comma, not a semicolon. (See 34e1.)

The smallpox vaccine was developed by Edward Jenner*/*,who discovered

that a mild infection acquired from cows would give immunity to

smallpox.

■ 3 Avoiding semicolons between an appositive and the word it explains

Do not use a semicolon between an appositive (a nounlike modifier) and the word it explains. Use a comma instead. (See 34e1.)

To build furniture, you need a doweling jig*/*,a tool for drilling straight

holes.

■ 4 Avoiding semicolons between a list and the words that introduce it

Do not use a semicolon to introduce a list. Use a colon instead. (See 36a.)

States now employ five methods of execution*/*:hanging, the firing squad,

the electric chair, the gas chamber, and lethal injection.

■ 5   Avoiding semicolons between independent clauses linked by a coordinating conjunction

Do not use a semicolon between independent clauses linked by a coordinating conjunction such as *and* or *but.* Use a comma instead. (See 34a.)

The gap between the highest- and lowest-paid workers has been

increasing for years/so the President has proposed an increase in the

minimum wage.

The Colon

36a | Use a colon following an independent clause to introduce a list, quotation, appositive, or explanation

■ A colon is a kind of un-equals (≠) sign. It signals that what follows depends on what comes before—but is not necessarily less important. A colon is a compressed way of saying "for example," "that is," or "this is what I mean."

■ 1   Using a colon with a list

Use a colon to introduce a list or series.

It is by the goodness of God that we have in our country three unspeakably precious things: freedom of speech, freedom of conscience, and the prudence never to practice either.

(Mark Twain, from *The Perpetual Pessimist*)

■ 2   Using a colon with a quotation

Use a colon to introduce a quotation.

Animal trainer Vickie Hearne describes the brutal brevity of life in the wild: "In Africa, 75 percent of the lions cubbed do not survive to the age of two. For those who make it to two, the average age at death is ten years."

3 Using a colon with an appositive

Use a colon to emphasize an appositive that explains a preceding noun.

Many hyperactive children eat only one kind of food: junk food.

4 Using a colon with an explanation

Use a colon to introduce an explanation of what comes before.

Humanity does not pass through phases as a train passes through stations: being alive, it has the privilege of always moving yet never leaving anything behind.

(C. S. Lewis, from *The Allegory of Love*)

A note on the colon and capital letters: If an independent clause follows the colon, you may begin with either a capital or lower-case letter. If two or more complete sentences follow, begin only with a capital.

36b Use a colon to separate related formal elements

1 Using colons in business letters

Use a colon to separate the salutation from the body of a business letter.

Dear Director of Admissions:

2 Using colons in bibliographic citations

In bibliographic citations, use a colon to separate the title from the subtitle, the city of publication from the publisher.

Lopez, Barry. <u>Arctic Dreams: Imagination and Desire in a Northern Landscape</u>. New York: Scribner's, 1986.

3 Using colons with numbers

Use a colon to separate hours and minutes (9:36 a.m.), ratios (15:1), volume and page numbers (4: 98–115), and biblical chapter and verse (John 3:16).

An MLA note: The Modern Language Association requires a period instead of a colon in Bible verses (John 3.16).

36c | Avoid unnecessary colons

Except for the related formal elements listed in the preceding section, a colon usually follows an independent clause. Here's a test: A colon is appropriate if you can place a period where you intend to use a colon, as with the colon preceding this sentence. Do not use a colon where no punctuation should be used.

■ 1 Avoiding colons after *such as*, *like*, or *including*

Do not use a colon after words that introduce items in a series.

The children took whatever they could eat while they played, such as/

candy bars, carrots, and sandwiches.

[Because the sentence cannot be ended with *such as*, a colon is inappropriate. Do not separate a list from an introductory phrase.]

■ 2 Avoiding colons between a verb and its object or complement

Do not use a colon to separate a verb from its object or complement. (To identify objects and complements, see 9c and d.)

Two unnecessary animal experiments are/ poisoning rats to test drugs

and injuring monkeys to test helmet safety.

■ 3 Avoiding colons between a subordinating conjunction and the clause that follows

Do not use a colon to introduce a clause following a subordinating conjunction. (For a list of subordinating conjunctions, see 8g3.)

Most research reports that/ the death penalty does not reduce murder

rates.

■ 4 Avoiding colons between a preposition and its object

Do not use a colon to separate a preposition and its object. (For a list of prepositions, see 8f.)

Jason slowly packed his collections of/ tapes, posters, and comic books.

37 The Apostrophe

chapter

37a Use an apostrophe to signal possession by nouns and indefinite pronouns

As a grammatical term, possession not only refers to actual possession or ownership, as in *the student's book.* It also signals relationships, associations, amounts, and duration: *the flower's scent, Pike's Peak, your money's worth,* and *two days' journey.* To decide whether a noun should be written as a possessive, use two tests.

- Creating an *of* phrase. Try to turn the words into an *of* phrase: *the scent of the flower, the worth of your money, a journey of two days.* (To learn when to use an apostrophe for the possessive and when to use an *of* phrase, see 32d.)

- Identifying noun + noun. In most cases, if two nouns appear together and the first ends in s, add an apostrophe to the first to make it possessive: *students* (noun) + *book* (noun) = *student's book; Pikes* (noun) + *Peak* (noun) = *Pike's Peak.* (To learn to identify nouns, see 8a.)

■ 1 Forming possessives of singular nouns

To form the possessive of singular nouns, add an apostrophe + s.

the sun's rays	television's influence	Dr. Benton's lecture
the girl's bicycle	Aesop's fables	Arkansas's governor
an hour's work	John Keats's poems	IBM's new computer

Exceptions:

- Awkward pronunciation. Add an apostrophe but no *s* to singular possessive nouns if pronunciation would be awkward: *Moses' commandments, Aristophanes' plays, Achilles' tendon.*

- Institutional and place names. The apostrophe is frequently omitted from institutional and place names: *Nags Head, North Carolina; Grants Pass, Oregon; Governors Island, New York; The Boys Club; Teachers College of Columbia University.* Check a dictionary, atlas, or encyclopedia.

■ 2 Forming possessives of plural nouns

To form the possessive of plural nouns ending in s, add an apostrophe.

the planets' orbits	the players' coach	the drivers' licenses
the machines' noise	the Johnsons' car	the Yankees' uniforms

A note on irregular plurals: To form the possessive of irregular plural nouns, add *'s: children's games, The Women's Health Network, the news media's accuracy.*

■ 3 Forming possessives of indefinite pronouns

Most indefinite pronouns (*everyone, everybody, no one, something*) are singular. To form the possessive, add an *'s.* (For a complete list of indefinite pronouns, see 8b4.)

To **no one's** surprise, the Bears won the championship game.

A democratic government must represent **everyone's** interest.

■ 4 Indicating joint and individual possession

To signal joint possession, make only the last noun possessive. To signal individual possession, make each noun possessive.

- Joint possession.

  Ben and Jerry's Ice Cream
  Carol, Eileen, Martha, and Bill's group project

- Individual possession.

  Betty's and **James's** skis
  Plato's and **Gandhi's** philosophies

■ 5 Forming possessives of compound nouns

To form the possessive of compound nouns, add *'s* or *s'* to the last word.

my **father-in-law's** birthday
the **Board of Supervisors'** report

37b Use an apostrophe to signal contractions

■   Use an apostrophe to signal omissions of letters or numbers.

It's [it is] not easy to read by candle light.

Rock **'n'** [and] roll sounds best when the volume is turned way up.

Dexter Gordon plays the best version of " **'Round** [Around] Midnight."

The blizzard of **'79** [1979] was not as bad as the one back in **'67** [1967].

A note on academic writing: Contractions are inappropriate in most serious academic writing.

A note on possessive pronouns: The possessive pronouns *its* and *your* are not contractions and do not take an apostrophe. (See 37d3.)

its
The tree is losing ~~it's~~ leaves because of a fungus.
                    ^

Your
~~Your'~~ father was the last to hear about the accident.
  ^

37c Use an apostrophe and an *s* with plural letters and words used as words

Conventions vary regarding the use of the apostrophe to form the plural of letters and words used as words. The Modern Language Association guideline is to use an apostrophe and an *s*.

The *A*'s and *B*'s on this assignment outnumber the *C*'s and *D*'s.

Let's finish this project without any more *if*'s, *and*'s, or *but*'s.

A note on italics/underlining: Individual letters and words used as words are italicized or underlined, but the apostrophe and *s* are typed without italics or underlining, as in the preceding examples.

37d Avoiding unnecessary apostrophes

■ 1 Avoiding apostrophes with plural numbers and abbreviations

Conventions vary on the use of apostrophes with plural numbers and abbreviations. The Modern Language Association guideline is to omit the apostrophe.

The winning hand was a pair of **8s** and three **3s.**

This season Berenson has a batting average in the high **280s.**

In the **1990s,** not even people with **MAs, PhDs,** and high **IQs** can be sure of finding jobs.

Two **IDs** are required for customers to pay by personal check.

■ 2 Avoiding possessives that sound like contractions

Do not confuse contractions with similar-sounding pronouns that do not take an apostrophe: *you're* (*you are*) with *your*, *it's* (*it is*) with *its*, *they're* (*they are*) with *their*, *who's* (*who is*) with *whose*.

You're
~~Your~~ going to thank me for this advice.
  ^

■ 3 Avoiding apostrophes with possessive pronouns

Possessive personal pronouns (*hers, his, its, ours, theirs, whose, yours*) do not take an apostrophe.

The hurricane unleashed it's wind and rain on the coastal lowlands.

[*It's* is the contraction of *it is*.]

Whose
~~Who's~~ backpack is sitting under the desk?

[*Who's* is the contraction of *who is*.]

■ 4 Avoiding apostrophes with nouns that are not possessive

Not all nouns that end in *s* take an apostrophe. Use the apostrophe only when it is required to signal possession.

The Bates' family is away on vacation.

[*The Bates* do not possess the family; *Bates* is their name.]

The decision of the judges' will be final.

[Possession is signaled by the *of*; the apostrophe is unnecessary.]

Quotation Marks

38*a* | Enclose direct quotations in double quotation marks (" ")

■ Use double quotation marks at the beginning and end of all word-for-word quotations of speech or writing, whether you quote a word, phrase, sentence, or more.

In his inaugural address President John F. Kennedy redefined citizenship in a democracy: **"Ask not what your country can do for you; ask what you can do for your country."**

Henry David Thoreau emphasizes the message of *Walden* with one word: **"Simplicity, simplicity, simplicity!"**

■ 1 Avoiding quotation marks in indirect quotations

Do not use quotation marks around indirect (summarized) quotations.

According to President Kennedy, Americans should not ask what their country can do for them; they should ask what they can do for their country.

■ 2 Using quotation marks in paragraphing

In writing dialogue, begin a new paragraph to signal a change in speaker, no matter how brief each person's speech.

> "Girl number twenty," said Mr. Gradgrind, squarely pointing with his square forefinger, "I don't know that girl. Who is that girl?"
> "Sissy Jupe, sir," explained number twenty, blushing, standing up, and curtseying.
> "Sissy is not a name," said Mr. Gradgrind. "Don't call yourself Sissy. Call yourself Cecilia."
>
> (Charles Dickens, from *Hard Times*)

A note on multiparagraph speeches: If one person's speech runs for two or more paragraphs, open each paragraph with quotation marks, but do not use closing quotation marks until the end of the speech.

38*b*   To punctuate quotations correctly, follow these guidelines

■ 1 Periods and commas

Put periods and commas inside quotation marks, even when the quotation is less than a sentence.

"Writing is a very painful process," says essayist and novelist Tom Wolfe. "I never understand writers who say it's enjoyable."

The Supreme Court ruled that school integration should proceed "with all deliberate speed."

A note on MLA in-text documentation: When you use the Modern Language Association's in-text documentation format, place the period after the quotation marks and parenthetical documentation. (See 51a.)

Flannery O'Connor's "Greenleaf" is a story dramatizing "the divine harmony that embraces nature, man, and God" (Asals 330).

■ 2 Colons and semicolons

Put colons and semicolons outside quotation marks.

Murphy's Law ought to be called "Murphy's Threat": If something can go wrong, it will.

Shakespeare wrote "All the world's a stage"; if he were a member of today's music video generation, he'd write, "All the world's a sound stage."

■ 3 Question marks and exclamation points

Put question marks and exclamation points inside quotation marks if they are part of the quotation. Otherwise, put them outside.

Mark Twain wrote an essay surprisingly titled "Was Shakespeare Famous?"

What famous mystery writer said, "Where there is no imagination there is no horror"?

A note on MLA in-text documentation: When you use the Modern Language Association's in-text documentation format, punctuate quoted questions and exclamations according to the preceding guidelines, followed by the parenthetical documentation and a period.

Mr. Lengel, the antagonist of John Updike's short story "A & P," gives the hero one last chance when he asks, "Did you say something, Sammy?" (133).

■ 4 Introducing quotations

To introduce a quotation, use a colon, comma, or no punctuation, whichever is appropriate to the context.

- Introductory independent clauses. Use a colon after an introductory independent clause.

   Sue Hubbell explains that bees communicate by dancing: "Bees tell other bees about good things such as food or the location of a new home by patterned motions."

- Opening quotation tags. After opening quotation tags like *he said* or *she observes*, use a comma.

   Scientist Carl Sagan warns, "There are severe and previously unanticipated global consequences of nuclear war—subfreezing temperatures in a twilit radioactive gloom lasting for months or longer."

- Closing quotation tags. When a quotation tag closes a quotation, use a comma after the quotation unless it ends with a question mark or exclamation point.

"The other America, the America of poverty, is hidden today in a way that it never was before," **argues** social critic Michael Harrington.

"Dr. Livingstone, I presume?" **asked** explorer H. M. Stanley when he found the doctor on the shores of Lake Tanganyika in 1871.

- Quotations woven into a sentence. Use no punctuation before a quotation that is the object or complement of a verb, a clause following a subordinating conjunction, a modifying phrase, or the object of a preposition.

The American Psychological Association **notes that** "80% of people who fall victim to depression fail to recognize the illness."

Describing the origins of barbecue, poet Amiri Baraka praises West Africans **for** "developing the best sauce for roasting whole oxen and hogs, spicy and extremely hot."

■ 5 Interrupted quotations

If you interrupt a quotation with a quotation tag in the middle of a sentence, set off the tag with commas.

"God is subtle," **quipped Einstein,** "but he is not malicious."

If you interrupt a quotation at the end of a complete sentence, use a comma before the quotation tag and a period following. Then resume the quotation.

"We are born knowing how to use language," **remarks Lewis Thomas.** "The capacity to recognize syntax, to organize and deploy words into intelligible sentences, is innate in the human mind."

38c | Indent long quotations of prose and poetry

■ 1 Indenting prose quotations

These are the Modern Language Association guidelines for long quotations. (For American Psychological Association guidelines, see 46d4.)

- Length. To make quotations longer than four typed lines easy to read, set them off in an indented block, separate from your words.

- Introduction and punctuation. Introduce the quotation in your own words. If your introduction is an independent clause that could be punctuated as a complete sentence, follow it with a colon. If it is a quotation tag such as *According to philosopher Susan Sontag,* follow it with a comma. If no grammatical break occurs between your words and the quotation, use no punctuation.

- Indentation. Indent one inch or ten spaces from the left margin and none from the right.

- Quotation marks and spacing. Do not enclose indented quotations with quotation marks. The block format signals word-for-word quotation. Doublespace the quotation.

- Paragraphing. If you quote part of a paragraph or only one paragraph, do not indent the first line more than the rest. To quote two or more paragraphs in block format, indent first lines an additional quarter-inch or three spaces (a total of thirteen spaces from the left margin). Following a block quotation, begin a new paragraph of your own writing only if you change subjects.

- Documentation. Two spaces after the quotation, cite the source parenthetically. (For more on MLA in-text documentation, see 51b.)

> The portrait of Thomas Gradgrind that Charles Dickens presents
>
> in <u>Hard Times</u> satirizes defects in the nineteenth-century philosophy
>
> of utilitarianism:

>> Thomas Gradgrind, sir. A man of realities. A man of facts
>>
>> and calculations. A man who proceeds upon the principle that
>>
>> two and two are four, and nothing over, and who is not to be
>>
>> talked into allowing for anything over. . . . With a rule and a
>>
>> pair of scales, and multiplication tables always in his pocket,
>>
>> sir, ready to weigh and measure any parcel of human nature,
>>
>> and tell you exactly what it comes to. (2)

A note on omitted words: If you omit words from a quotation, signal the omission with an ellipsis (. . .). (See 39d.)

■ 2 Indenting quotations of dialogue in fiction

If you quote exchanges of dialogue between two or more speakers, use the indented quotation format and follow the paragraphing of the original, even if you quote fewer than four typed lines. Two spaces after the quotation, cite the source parenthetically. (See 51b9.)

■ 3 Indenting quotations of dialogue in drama and film

If you quote dialogue between two or more speakers, use the indented quotation format. Indent one inch or ten spaces from the left margin. Introduce each speaker by his or her name written in all capitals followed by a period: *OTHELLO.* Use quotation marks only if they appear in the original. Indent subsequent lines in a character's speech an additional quarter-inch or three spaces. When a new character speaks, start a new line one inch or ten spaces from the left margin. Two spaces after the quotation, cite the source parenthetically. (See 51b9.)

> As Iago incites him, Othello plots Desdemona's murder:
>
> OTHELLO. Get me some poison, Iago, this night. I'll not expostulate
>
> with her, lest her body and beauty unprovide my mind again. This
>
> night, Iago!
>
> IAGO. Do it not with poison. Strangle her in bed, even the bed she hath
>
> contaminated. (4.1.200–204)

■ 4 Indenting quotations of poetry

For quotations of more than three lines of poetry, use the indented quotation format.

- **Indentation.** Indent one inch or ten spaces from the left margin, unless the poem would look unbalanced on the page; then indent more or less as necessary.

- **Spacing and formatting.** Doublespace the quotation and arrange the passage to look as much like the original as possible. If a quotation begins in the middle of a line, follow the appearance of the original and do not shift the line to the left.

- **Line length.** If a long line does not fit within the right margin, continue it on the next line, indenting an extra quarter-inch or three spaces.

- **Quotation marks.** Use quotation marks only if they appear in the original.

- **Line numbers.** Include line numbers in parentheses two spaces after the last line.

- **Omissions.** If you omit words or lines from a quotation, use an ellipsis (. . .). (See 39d.)

> William Blake's "The Tiger" questions the origins of that part of creation
>
> which is not innocent but not necessarily evil, either.
>
> > Tiger, Tiger, burning bright
> >
> > In the forests of the night,
> >
> > What immortal hand or eye
> >
> > Could frame thy fearful symmetry? (1–4)

A note on brief quotations: To quote two or three lines of poetry, incorporate them in your text with a slash (/) between the lines. (See 39e.)

38d ■ Use single quotation marks (' ') only to enclose quotations within quotations

As Phillip walked into trigonometry class, he muttered, "Someone should post a sign outside this room that quotes Dante: 'Abandon hope, all ye who enter here.' "

A note on punctuating brief quotations: Some writers assume that quotations of single words or brief phrases should be enclosed with single quotation marks. Not so. Use single quotation marks only for quotations within quotations.

A note on quoting nested quotations: If you must quote a passage that contains a quotation, alternate quotation marks: double, single, double (" ' "..." ' "). Be sure to use as many closing as opening quotation marks.

Kerry continued, "Then Lisa whispered, 'Don't forget the old saying, "If at first you don't succeed, try, try again." ' "

38e Use quotation marks to enclose titles of short works

■ Use quotation marks around the titles of magazine and newspaper articles, essays and book chapters, short stories, poems, songs, and episodes of radio and television programs.

Nathaniel Hawthorne's "Young Goodman Brown" is the story of what happens to a man who is not as good as he thinks.

At next week's church service, our choir will sing "Amazing Grace."

A note on titles of long or complete works: The titles of books, plays, long poems, films, television and radio series, and the names of magazines and newspapers are italicized or underlined. (See 41a.)

38f Quotations may be used to signal words used in a special sense

■ Although italics or underlining is the preferred method to signal a word used as a word or in a special sense, you may use quotation marks. But be consistent throughout your writing.

The word "Dutch" in "Pennsylvania Dutch" refers to the *Deutsche,* people from Germany.

The word *Dutch* in *Pennsylvania Dutch* refers to the *Deutsche,* people from Germany.

A note: Foreign words are underlined or italicized. (See 41c.)

38g Avoid unnecessary quotation marks

■ 1 Avoiding quotation marks around titles of your papers

Do not use quotation marks around your titles unless they are actual quotations.

■ 2 Avoiding quotation marks for emphasis or slang

Do not use quotation marks for emphasis or to set off slang.

Store owners who sell liquor to teenagers often receive only a ⫽slap on the wrist.⫽

■ 3 Avoiding quotation marks with indirect quotations

Do not use quotation marks with indirect (summarized) quotations.

The lawyer warned the team owner that ⫽his players would sue him for breach of contract.⫽

39 Other Punctuation Marks

39a Use a dash for a change of thought, parenthetical remarks, or faltering speech

■ Type a dash as two hyphens, with no space before or after (*word--word*). Use the dash to send the following signals.

■ 1 Indicating an emphatic change in thought or feeling

Use a dash to signal an emphatic change in thought or feeling.

I don't make jokes—I just watch the government and report the facts.
                    (Will Rogers, "A Rogers Thesaurus," *Saturday Review*)

■ 2 Setting off parenthetical material

Use a pair of dashes to set off and emphasize parenthetical material.

It seems possible that more than 2 billion people—almost half of all the humans on earth—would be destroyed in the immediate aftermath of a global thermonuclear war.

> (adapted from Carl Sagan, "The Nuclear Winter," *Parade*)

A note: As the preceding example illustrates, a dash is the strongest mark of parenthetical punctuation. Dashes emphasize what they enclose; parentheses and commas deemphasize. (See 39b.)

■ 3 Displaying lists

Use a dash to introduce a list or to connect a list to the main part of the sentence.

It is almost a ghost forest, for among the living spruce and balsam are many dead trees—some still erect, some sagging earthward, some lying on the floor of the forest.

> (Rachel Carson, from *The Edge of the Sea*)

Choosing, defining, creating harmony, bringing that clarity and shape that is rest and light out of disorder and confusion—the work I do at my desk is not unlike arranging flowers.

> (May Sarton, from *Plant Dreaming Deep*)

A note: A colon may also introduce a list; a dash is less formal but more emphatic.

■ 4 Setting off parenthetical modifiers containing punctuation

Modifiers rename, explain, or add information to nearby words. Often they are set off by commas, but if they contain internal punctuation, commas may be confusing. Use dashes to set off modifiers that contain internal punctuation.

The sun—like a hot, luminous magnet—happened to be shining powerfully that antique afternoon.

> (Al Young, "Java Jive," *Harpers*)

■ 5 Indicating faltering speech

Use a dash to signal faltering speech.

"I—I—don't know how it could have happened," he said, astonished by the accident.

■ 6   Avoiding unnecessary dashes

Avoid the dash unless you want to create an informal tone. In serious academic writing, prefer the comma, colon, or parentheses. Too many dashes will make your writing unclear or choppy.

A majority of students surveyed—71 percent—favored the elimination of

classes beginning at 7 a.m. *(71 percent)*

Shortly after the Civil War—in 1860s and 1870s—bison were *, in the 1860s and 1870s,*

slaughtered—in the millions—by paid hunters—hired by the railroads to

feed their employees.

39*b*   Use parentheses for parenthetical remarks and numbers that mark items in a series

■ 1   Using parentheses for parenthetical remarks

Use parentheses to set off supplemental or explanatory information.

Already we have childproof (and, often, adultproof) containers for virtually everything.

                  (Philip Sellinger, "Mother Hen," *Newsweek*)

A note: Of all the punctuation used to enclose, parentheses signal the greatest separation between material inside and outside the enclosure. Dashes emphasize what they enclose; parentheses deemphasize. (See 39a.)

■ 2   Using parentheses for numbers or letters to mark a series

Use parentheses to enclose letters or numbers that identify items in a series.

Touring bicyclists should carry what they need to cope with unpleasant surprises: (1) a ground cloth for their tent, (2) waterproof matches, (3) water purification tablets, (4) twine and tape, (5) extra flashlight batteries, (6) a folding tire, (7) extra inner tubes.

■ 3   Using parentheses correctly and effectively

■ Parentheses and other punctuation. Put commas and semicolons after parentheses, not before them. (See 34k4.)

Colleges have begun to try new methods of evaluation/(portfolios, self-

evaluation, and peer evaluation)_,_ but teachers' grades are still the most

common.

- A sentence within a sentence. If one sentence contains a second sentence enclosed by parentheses, do not open the parenthetical sentence with a capital or end it with a period.

  Brian Delaney and Rita Kim have the best chances to win the downhill skiing competition (they currently hold the conference records).

- A parenthetical sentence by itself. When a parenthetical sentence stands by itself, open with a capital and close with appropriate end punctuation.

  The nursery rhyme about Little Jack Horner pulling a plum from his Christmas pie has historical sources. (The real Jack Horner was a cunning 16th century Englishman who helped King Henry VIII seize land from the Catholic Church.)

- Unnecessary parentheses. Avoid unnecessary parentheses. Readers tend to skip parenthetical remarks. Parentheses may also make your sentences overly complex and difficult to read.

To test the effects of overpopulation, researchers (in 1991) released a

300-acre
small herd of fifteen deer (15) in a forest preserve (it was 300 acres and

surrounded by subdivisions).

39_c_ | Use brackets for insertions

Use brackets, typed or hand drawn, to insert explanations, clarifications, or corrections within direct quotations and to enclose parentheses within parentheses.

■ 1 Using brackets for explanations

Use brackets to insert information necessary for readers to understand a quotation.

"More than 33,000 cases [of skin cancer] leading to nearly 7,000 deaths are expected this year alone."

■ 2 Using brackets for clarifications

Use brackets to insert the antecedent nouns referred to by quoted pronouns or to take the place of omitted words.

"Many state legislators view this [tax revenues from riverboat gambling] as free money, but it is not."

"French-speaking Canadians believe they will disappear as a distinct people if [Quebec] does not become independent."

[The original of this quotation is *French-speaking Canadians believe they will disappear as a distinct people if the province does not become independent.* For clarity, *the province* was replaced with *[Quebec].*]

■ 3 Using brackets for corrections

Always quote accurately. If a quotation contains an error, insert *sic* (Latin for "so," "thus," "in this manner") in brackets immediately following the error.

"On his second expedition to the New World, in 1943 [*sic*], Columbus made landfall in the Lesser Antilles."

■ 4 Using brackets for parentheses within parentheses

In research papers that follow the Modern Language Association format for in-text documentation, use brackets to enclose documentation within parenthetical remarks.

Where wolves have been released in the wild, their numbers have increased slowly (see National Park Service reports [Johnson 23 and Lopez 29–36]).

39*d* | Use the ellipsis to signal omissions

> ■ Use the ellipsis to signal omissions from direct quotations.

■ Spacing. Type an ellipsis as three evenly spaced periods with a space before and after each period.

"The flock of geese turned . . . in a large circle above the lake."

[The original sentence reads, *The flock of geese turned slowly, sweeping in a large circle above the lake.*]

■ End punctuation. If an ellipsis comes at the end of a quoted sentence, use a period or other end punctuation before the ellipsis points and quotation marks following. No space precedes the period or the quotation marks.

"The flock of geese turned slowly. . . ."

■ Adding punctuation and capital letters. Add punctuation or capitalize to clarify a quotation containing an ellipsis.

"The flock of geese turned . . . , sweeping in a wide circle above the lake."

■ 1 Using ellipses with prose quotations

Use an ellipsis to signal the omission of a word, phrase, sentence, or whole paragraph.

> According to essayist Lewis Thomas, "It begins to look . . . as if the gift of language is the single human trait that marks us all genetically, setting us apart from all the rest of life. . . . Language is, like nest-building or hive-making, the universal and biologically specific activity of human beings."
>
> [The first ellipsis signals the omission of a phrase; the second, with an added period, signals the omission of a complete sentence.]

To use the ellipsis effectively, follow these guidelines:

- Omissions. Use an ellipsis to omit unnecessary words from a quotation. Quote only the words you need. Unnecessarily long quotations are tiresome and confusing.

- Accuracy. An omission must not change or distort the meaning of the original.

- Grammar. A quotation containing an ellipsis must be grammatically correct. You would not write *According to essayist Lewis Thomas, "the gift of language . . . setting us apart from the rest of life."* The quotation is not grammatical. Use brackets to make elliptical quotations grammatically correct: *"the gift of language . . . [sets] us apart from the rest of life."* (See 39c.)

- Omissions at the beginning of a quotation. Do not use ellipsis points at the beginning of a quotation. Use ellipsis points at the end only if you have omitted words from the last sentence quoted.

  > According to essayist Lewis Thomas, "language is the single human trait that marks us all genetically. . . ."

- Fragmentary quotations. Do not use an ellipsis if the quotation is an obviously incomplete sentence.

  > Essayist Lewis Thomas calls language the "biologically specific activity of human beings."

- MLA documentation and the ellipsis. To document a quotation that ends in an ellipsis using the Modern Language Association in-text format, follow this pattern: three spaced periods + quotation marks + parenthetical documentation + a period.

  > According to essayist Lewis Thomas, "language is the single human trait that marks us all genetically . . . " ("Social Talk" 105).

- The ellipsis and end-of-line breaks. Do not put part of an ellipsis at the end of one line and the rest on the next. Put all three periods on a single line.

■ 2 Using ellipses with poetry quotations

When quoting poetry, use three spaced periods to signal the omission of less than a line. To omit a line or more, use a line of spaced periods equal to the length of a complete line.

> The world is too much with us; . . .
>
> Getting and spending, we lay waste our powers;
>
> . . . .
>
> We have given our hearts away, a sordid boon!
> > (William Wordsworth)

■ 3 Using ellipses with pauses, interruptions, or incomplete thoughts

Use an ellipsis in narratives or dialogue to signal pauses, interruptions, or incomplete thoughts. At the end of a sentence left intentionally incomplete, use three periods.

> "It has to be . . . ," he worried, shuffling the papers on his desk. "I'm sure I saw it sitting on top of . . . "

39*e*
Use the slash with poetry and paired words

■ 1 Using slashes with run-in quotations of poetry

Use a slash to separate two or three lines of poetry run into your text. Add a space before and after the slash.

> Boasting of his poetic powers, Shakespeare opens one of his most famous sonnets with "Not marble, nor the gilded monuments / Of princes, shall outlive this powerful rhyme."

A note on indented quotations: To quote more than three lines of poetry, use the indented quotation format. (See 38c4.)

■ 2 Using slashes with paired words

Use the slash to separate paired words or abbreviations: *AC/DC, CAD/CAM, true/false, introvert/extrovert.* Do not use a space before or after the slash. Note that overuse of the slash in this way will make your writing seem finicky or complex. Especially avoid *and/or, he/she, his/hers.*

Mechanics, Spelling, and Formatting

Capital Letters

40a | Capitalize the first word of sentences, deliberate fragments, and lines of poetry

■ 1 Sentences

The wind blew the snow in swirling circles.

A note on quotations: Do not capitalize the first word of a quoted sentence you have woven into your own sentence.

President Harry Truman's motto "~~The~~ *"the* buck stops here" is a vow of

personal responsibility many people admire but seldom practice.

A note on a sentence following a colon: If a complete sentence follows a colon, capitalization is optional.

Stars are not all that twinkle in the night sky: the brightest lights may be reflections from satellites or the space shuttle.

A note on parenthetical sentences: Do not capitalize the first word of a parenthetical sentence contained within another sentence.

Western ranchers claim that wolves reintroduced to the wild will kill

their livestock (~~Conservation~~ *(conservation* groups, however, have pledged to repay

them for losses).

■ 2 Deliberate fragments

Capitalize the first words of deliberately written sentence fragments.

The Pueblo people believe that lightning strikes bring death to evildoers. And magical powers to persons of good will.

■ 3 Poetry

When you quote poetry, capitalize the first word of a line unless the original is uncapitalized.

FIRST WORDS CAPITALIZED
I heard a fly buzz when I died.
The stillness in the room
Was like the stillness in the air
Between the heaves of storm.
(Emily Dickinson)

FIRST WORDS UNCAPITALIZED
Fiesta laughed with me in San Juan
many compas fired their rifles
  at the stars
music played on radios till dawn
where Venus danced the *cumbiá*
  with Mars
(Rex Burwell)

40b Capitalize proper nouns and words derived from them

Proper nouns name specific persons, places, and things (*Confucius, Grand Canyon, the US Constitution*). Proper nouns and their derivatives are capitalized. Common nouns name persons, places, and things in general (*a religious leader, a canyon, a government document*) and are not capitalized unless part of a specific name, as in *Grand Canyon*.

■ 1 Capitalizing the names and titles of people

- The names of people. Capitalize the names, nicknames, and initials of real and imaginary persons, and words derived from names: *William Shakespeare, Shakespearean, Abraham Lincoln, Honest Abe, the Great Emancipator, Lincolnesque, Dwight D. Eisenhower, Ike, Mickey Mouse.*

- Races and nationalities. Capitalize races, nationalities, geographic groupings of people, languages, and words derived from them: *Asian, Spanish, Hispanic, African, English, Native American, Polish-American.*

- Titles of persons. Capitalize civil, military, religious, and professional titles immediately preceding a personal name: *President Lincoln, General Grant, Pope Paul, Queen Victoria, Senator Kassebaum.* Capitalize titles used in place of names in introductions, toasts, and direct address: *Dear Senator.* Do not capitalize titles following a name: *Abraham Lincoln, sixteenth president of the United States; Victoria, queen of England.*

                senator
Nancy Kassebaum, ~~Senator~~ from Kansas, will chair the committee.
                                     director
Patricia McLean has been reappointed ~~Director~~ of the Port Authority
Board.

- Kinship names. Capitalize kinship names followed by a given name or used in place of the name; otherwise, use lower-case letters. Compare these examples:

This year **Aunt Jennifer** is helping to pay my tuition.

When she was first married, ~~mother~~ *Mother* worked in a furniture factory.

Rebecca's ~~Father~~ *father* has just been admitted to the hospital.

- Abstractions. Capitalize abstract words if they have been personified with the attributes of people; otherwise, use lower-case letters.

All Nature wears one universal grin.

> (Henry Fielding, from *Tom Thumb the Great*)

In nature there are no rewards or punishments; there are consequences.

> (Horace Annesley Vachell, from *The Face of Clay*)

■ 2 Capitalizing religious terms

Capitalize the names of religions, deities, holy persons, holy writings, religious groups and movements, religious events and services, and words derived from these terms.

Islam, Islamic	the Bible	Holy Communion
the Lord, our Lord	the Koran	the Sermon on
Christ, the Savior	the Ten	the Mount
the Blessed Virgin	Commandments	Dead Sea Scrolls
Buddha, Buddhism	Catholicism	
the Prophet	the Baptist church	
(Muhammad)	the Crucifixion	

A note: *Bible* is usually not capitalized when used as an adjective (*biblical*) nor when it refers to authoritative books: *When Judy is in the kitchen,* The Joy of Cooking *is her bible.*

■ 3 Capitalizing cultural and historical terms

Capitalization of cultural and historical terms varies; check your dictionary. In general, capitalize the names of historical, political, and cultural events and documents; capitalize historical periods only when proper nouns or to avoid ambiguity.

Boston Tea Party	the Fall of Rome	*but:* ancient Rome
Reconstruction	the Renaissance	*but:* the sixteenth century
Prohibition	the Roaring Twenties	*but:* the twenties
the War on Poverty	the Great Depression	*but:* the thirties

A note on archeological periods: Capitalize time periods recognized by archeologists and anthropologists: *Bronze Age, Neolithic era, Paleolithic times.* Lowercase recent periods: *the space age, the cold war, the civil rights era.*

A note on philosophic and artistic terms: Capitalize philosophic, literary, and artistic terms derived from proper nouns; otherwise, use lowercase letters: *Platonism* but *existentialism;* a *Gothic novel* but a *horror story;* the *Hudson River school, neoclassical, impressionism, jazz, the blues.*

■ 4 Capitalizing geographic regions, place names, and structures

■ Countries, regions, continents. Capitalize geographic names for countries, regions, and continents: *Spain, Europe, the Arctic, the Southern Hemisphere, the South, New England, North Pole, the Badlands of South Dakota, the Texas Panhandle, the New World.* Do not capitalize terms that indicate direction.

south
When they retire, Peter and Becky plan to move ~~South~~.

■ Place names. Capitalize the names of cities, counties, states, empires, colonies, locales, and popular place names: *New York City, New York's Lower East Side, the City of Brotherly Love, the Loop (Chicago), Cook County, Louisiana, the Buckeye State, the Roman Empire, Soweto Township, Land of the Rising Sun, the New Jersey Shore.*

■ Geographic names. Capitalize the names of rivers, lakes, oceans, islands, and other specific geographic places: *the Fox River, Lake Itasca, the Indian Ocean, Long Island, the San Juan Mountains, the Nile Delta, Walden Pond, the Hudson River Valley.*

■ Structures: Capitalize the names of buildings, streets, highways, bridges, and monuments. *the White House, the Capitol, the Pyramids, New York Thruway, Fifth Avenue, Forty-Second Street, Woodfield Mall, London Bridge, the Eiffel Tower.*

Note on generic place names: Generic places names that precede a name or stand alone are usually lowercased.

city
The ~~City~~ of New York sponsors a marathon that attracts 25,000 runners.

■ 5 Capitalizing the names of objects

■ Celestial bodies. Capitalize the names of celestial bodies: *Earth, the North Star, Halley's Comet, the constellation of Orion, the Big Dipper.*

- Means of transportation. Capitalize the names of ships, trains, aircraft, and spacecraft: USS *Constitution, Wabash Cannonball, Spirit of St. Louis, Voyager 2.*

- Trademarks and brand names. Capitalize trademarks and brand names but not the generic products associated with them: *Coca-Cola, Coke,* but *cola; Levi's jeans; Kleenex tissue; Tylenol,* but *aspirin; Xerox photocopier; GMC trucks.*

bicycle
When I was a kid, all I wanted was a Schwinn ~~Bicycle~~.

■ 6 Capitalizing dates and time designations

Capitalize days of the week, months, and holidays: *Tuesday, July, Halloween, Lent, Ramadan, Passover, Yuletide, Labor Day, the Fourth of July, New Year's Day, Veterans Day.* Lowercase the seasons, decades, centuries, or time zones that have been spelled out: *spring, the nineties, the nineteenth century, central daylight time.*

autumn
My favorite season is ~~Autumn~~.

■ 7 Capitalizing the names of organizations

Capitalize the names of companies, civic organizations, institutions, and government agencies: *Hudson's Bay Company, La Chosa Restaurant, the Salvation Army, Chicago Cubs, Boy Scouts, Hampton Institute, the MacArthur Foundation, United States Congress, House of Representatives, Democratic Party, Indianapolis City Council, the Supreme Court.* Lowercase generic organization names and plural generic names that follow organization names: *adoption court, the president's cabinet, the legislative branch, socialism.*

democratic   *fascism*
There is nothing ~~Democratic~~ about ~~Fascism~~.

■ 8 Capitalizing academic terms

Capitalize the names of specific courses: *I'm taking two literature courses, Literature of the Nonwestern World and Fiction 115.* Lowercase school terms (*spring semester*), generic degrees, and the names of academic subjects except foreign languages.

bachelor's   *history*   *political science*
The job requires a ~~Bachelor's~~ degree in ~~History~~ or ~~Political Science~~.

English
I have to take two ~~english~~ classes.

■9 Capitalizing plants, animals, and medical terms

Capitalization is varied; see your dictionary. Generally capitalize proper nouns that are part of a name; otherwise, lowercase them: *Canada thistle, Virginia Creeper, Peace rose, a Morgan horse, an Irish setter, Dalmatian, Hodgkin's disease, Down's syndrome,* but *black-eyed susan, rottweiler, cocker spaniel, anorexia, rheumatic fever.*

■10 Capitalizing acronyms

Acronyms are all-capitals abbreviations formed from the first letters of words. They include the names of organizations, government agencies, companies, and institutions (*OPEC, SPCA, HUD, NOAA, IBM*); technical, scientific, and military terms (*CD-ROM, HIV, AIDS, ICBM*); and radio and television call letters (*WBEZ-FM, KQED-TV*).

40c | Capitalize the first, last, and all major words in the titles of works

■1 General guidelines

- Titles and subtitles. Capitalize the titles and subtitles of written works such as books and essays, performances such as plays, visual works such as painting and sculpture, and media productions such as television and radio programs:

Moby Dick	*Hamlet*
Adam's Task: Calling Animals by Name	the *Mona Lisa*
"The Murders in the Rue Morgue"	*Star Trek*

- First, last, and major words. Capitalize first, last words, and major words. Do not capitalize articles (*a, an, the*), prepositions (*in, of, toward, according,* and so forth), coordinating conjunctions (*and, but, for, yet, so, or, nor*), and the *to* in infinitives (*How to Repair Almost Anything*).

- Compounds. Always capitalize the first word of a compound in a title (*The Modern City-State*); capitalize the second word only if it is important. Compare *Twenty-First Century, A-Bomb,* and *Citizen-Soldier* with *Medium-sized, Spanish-speaking,* and *Re-education* (one word).

- Newspapers and news stories. Do not capitalize, italicize, or underline *the* before a newspaper name.

                     the
  When I can afford it, I buy ~~The~~ *New York Times.*

In news story titles as actually published, usually only first words and proper nouns are capitalized: *"Destruction of the last smallpox virus delayed."* But when you give the title in your writing, capitalize according to the preceding guidelines: *"Destruction of the Last Smallpox Virus Delayed."*

■ 2 APA guidelines

These are the American Psychological Association guidelines for writing in the social sciences.

- Titles in the text of your writing. When you cite titles in the text of your writing, capitalize all words of four letters or more and both words of a hyphenated compound: *"Landscape, History, and the Pueblo Imagination."*

- Short words. Lowercase articles, prepositions, and conjunctions of one to three letters (e.g., lowercase *the* but capitalize *Toward*).

- Titles in references. When citing titles in references, capitalize only the first word of a title, the first word of a hyphenated compound, the first word after a colon, and proper nouns: *"Landscape, history, and the Pueblo imagination"; Modern media: The electronic transformation of America.*

40*d* | Capitalize the pronoun *I*, the interjection *O*, and the first word in the complimentary close of a letter

■ 1 The pronoun *I*

Jill and **I** are editing each other's term papers.

■ 2 The interjection *O*

Who are these coming to the sacrifice?
To what green altar, **O** mysterious priest . . .
(John Keats)

A note on *oh:* Do not capitalize the interjection *oh* unless it is the first word of a sentence.

■ 3 The complimentary close of a letter

Sincerely yours,

40*e* | Avoid unnecessary capital letters

■ 1 Avoiding capitals with *a*, *an*, and *the*

Do not capitalize the articles *a, an,* and *the* before proper nouns unless they are the first or last words of a title. Compare these examples:

Gene Kelly did his best dancing in *An American in Paris.*

Today there are few genuine luxury liners like ~~The~~ *the* Queen Elizabeth II.

■ 2 Avoiding capitals for emphasis

Do not capitalize words for emphasis.

Fantasia is the ~~GREATEST~~ *greatest* cartoon ever produced by the Disney studio.

[Create emphatic sentences by rewording and rearranging: *The greatest cartoon ever produced by the Disney studio is* Fantasia.]

The fairest system of taxation is the ~~Graduated Income Tax.~~ *graduated income tax.*

■ 3 Avoiding capitals with common nouns derived from proper names

Do not capitalize personal, national, or geographic names when used with special meanings.

arabic, roman numerals	french fries	mecca
brussels sprouts	a herculean task	pasteurize
diesel engine	homeric poetry	quixotic
english muffins	india ink	russian dressing
frankfurter	manila envelope	venetian blinds

Italics/Underlining

In typed or handwritten papers, underline whenever italics (e.g., italic type) would appear in printed works. If your computer has the capability and its italic type is easily recognizable, italicize. But note that the Modern Language Association and American Psychological Association recommend underlining. The guidelines for italics and underlining vary, and quotation marks are sometimes used instead. In academic writing, use the following guidelines.

41*a* Italicize or underline the titles of separately produced works

■ **1** Italicizing written works

Italicize or underline the titles and subtitles of books, pamphlets, the names of magazines and newspapers, and long poems.

The Invisible Man or <u>The Invisible Man</u>

Newsweek or <u>Newsweek</u>

the *New York Times* or the <u>New York Times</u>
[Do not italicize or underline "the" before newspaper titles.]

Paradise Lost or <u>Paradise Lost</u>

■ **2** Italicizing visual and performing arts

Italicize or underline the titles and subtitles of movies and plays, television and radio programs, painting, sculpture, and cartoons.

Hamlet or <u>Hamlet</u>

Star Trek or <u>Star Trek</u>
[Specific episodes of television and radio programs are enclosed by quotations and neither italicized or underlined: "The Trouble with Tribbles."]

Grant Wood's *American Gothic* or <u>American Gothic</u>

Picasso's *The Bather* or <u>The Bather</u>

Doonesbury or <u>Doonesbury</u>

■ **3** Italicizing long musical compositions, recordings, and choreographic works

Italicize or underscore long musical compositions, recordings (records, tapes or compact discs), and choreographic works.

Sgt. Pepper's Lonely Hearts Club Band or <u>Sgt. Pepper's Lonely Hearts Club Band</u>

Swan Lake or <u>Swan Lake</u>

A note: Individual song titles are enclosed by quotations: "Heartbreak Hotel." Do not italicize, underline, or use quotations around musical compositions identified by form, number, or key: Beethoven's Symphony no. 5 in C minor.

■ 4 Italicizing titles within titles

An MLA note: If an italicized or underlined title appears within a quoted title, italicize or underline normally: "The Theme and Narrator of *The Great Gatsby*." If an italicized or underlined title appears within another italicized or underlined title, do not italicize, underline, or quote the shorter title.

Twentieth-Century Interpretations of The Scarlet Letter

<u>Twentieth-Century Interpretations of</u> The Scarlet Letter

■ 5 Exceptions

Do not italicize or underline the titles of sacred writings (including all books and versions of the Bible), the titles of legal documents, descriptive titles, or the titles of your own writing.

the King James Version of the Bible	the Constitution
Genesis	the Declaration of Independence
the Talmud	Lincoln's Gettysburg address
the Koran	Kennedy's inaugural address

■ 6 Italicizing title punctuation

Italicize or underline all punctuation that is part of a title.

My favorite Nat King Cole album is *Where Did Everyone Go?*

- Punctuating MLA citations. In Modern Language Association (MLA) documentation, do not underline periods and commas following a title:

Mowat, Farley. <u>Never Cry Wolf</u>. Boston: Little, 1963.

- Punctuating APA citations. In American Psychological Association (APA) documentation, underline periods and commas following a title:

Jung, C. G. (1957). <u>The undiscovered self.</u> New York: New American Library.

41*b* | Italicize or underline the names of ships, trains, aircraft, and spacecraft

Mayflower or <u>Mayflower</u>   *Spirit of St. Louis* or <u>Spirit of St. Louis</u>
Dixie Flyer or <u>Dixie Flyer</u>   *Apollo 8* or <u>Apollo 8</u>

41*c* | Italicize or underline foreign words and phrases

Italicize or underline foreign words or phrases, whether part of a quotation or your own words. Translate or explain foreign words if readers may not know them.

> Special effects in the ancient Greek theater included the *deus ex machina* ("the god from the machine"), an actor suspended above the stage by a crane.

Exceptions: (1) Do not italicize or underline foreign words used frequently in English: ad hoc, cliché, laissez-faire, per diem, sauerkraut, status quo, versus, and so forth. (2) Do not italicize or underline quotations entirely in another language and non-English titles enclosed in quotation marks.

41*d* | Italicize or underline letters, words, and numbers used as themselves

> With grade inflation, *A*'s have become as common as *B*'s and *C*'s.

> Freud's term *narcissism* has nothing to do with the flower; it refers to the myth of the Greek youth Narcissus who fell in love with his reflected image.

> The number *3* has symbolic meaning in many religions.

A note on quotation marks in place of italics or underlining: Quotation marks are sometimes used to set off words used as words: "narcissism." (See 38f.)

A note on italics, underlining, and the plurals of letters, words, and numbers: Do not italicize or underline the apostrophe or *s* following letters, words, and numbers used as themselves: *p*'s and *q*'s or <u>p</u>'s and <u>q</u>'s; *7*'s or <u>7</u>'s; *yea*'s or *nay*'s, <u>yea</u>'s or <u>nay</u>'s. (See 37c.)

41*e* | Italicize or underline for emphasis—but very sparingly

Many travelers are uncomfortable when foreign countries feel like *foreign* countries.

A note: Too many italics or underlines will make your writing sound strenuous or false. Find emphatic words and sentence patterns that emphasize important ideas. (See 20.)

most offensive
The TV announcers ~~I can't stand most~~ are the gushing, friendly types.

Abbreviations

Abbreviations consist of shortened versions of words (*vol., intro., inc.*), words from which the middle is omitted (*Mr., Mrs., Jr., dept.*), and acronyms formed from the first letters of words (*UNICEF, FBI, AFL-CIO, OPEC, CBS*). Because abbreviations and acronyms may be puzzling to readers, generally avoid them in the body of your writing.

42*a* | General guidelines

■ 1 Using abbreviations correctly

■ Parenthetical statements. In the text of most formal writing, use abbreviations only in parenthetical statements. Compare:

The first insecticides were naturally occurring plant products, **for example,** pyrethrum from dried chrysanthemum flowers.

The first insecticides were naturally occurring plant products (**e.g.,** pyrethrum from dried chrysanthemum flowers).

■ Familiar abbreviations. You may use familiar abbreviations in the text of your writing: *MTV, HIV, CAT scan,* and so forth.

■ Repeated terms. Use abbreviations for repeated names and technical terms. For the first use, write out the term completely and include the abbreviation in parentheses. From then on, use the abbreviation alone.

The **Race Across America (RAAM)** is sponsored annually by the **Ultra-Marathon Cycling Association (UMCA).** The **UMCA** sponsors other races as well.

- Visual aids and documentation. Use abbreviations in tables, graphics, notes, and documentation. (See 46b3 and 4. For MLA documentation, see 52a. For APA documentation, see 54b.)

■ 2 Punctuating abbreviations and acronyms

- Personal names. Use a period and a space following initials: *H. L. Mencken.*

- Acronyms. Do not use periods or spaces between the letters of acronyms: *USA, NY, COD, IQ, NAACP, PhD, rpm.*

- Abbreviations ending in lower-case letters. Use a period following most abbreviations that end in lower-case letters: *intro., pag., pp., assn., e.g., fig.*

42b
Titles with personal names

■ Generally avoid titles in academic writing except to give the qualifications of people whose opinions or information you use. You may use titles frequently in other kinds of writing.

■ 1 Abbreviated titles

- Titles always abbreviated. Always abbreviate *Mr., Ms., Mrs.,* as in *Mr. Edward O'Connell* or *Mr. O'Connell, Ms. Judy Chang* or *Ms. Chang.*

- Titles before full names: Abbreviate titles before a full name. *Prof. Elizabeth Hull, Gen. Colin Powell, Dr. Benjamin Spock, Rev. Michael Leslie, St. Joan of Arc, Sen. Paul Simon.* Do not use abbreviations without names; avoid redundant titles.

      professor
My English ~~prof.~~ plans to travel the route of the European Grand Tour.

The speaker at this year's honors convocation will be Dr. Barbara

Hickey~~, Ph.D.~~

- Titles following names. Abbreviate titles and degrees following a name: *William Wrigley, Sr.; Darlene Clark Hine, PhD; Martin Luther King, Jr.; Jessica Stein, MD.*

■ 2 Unabbreviated titles

Spell out titles used with surnames (last names) alone: *Professor Hull, General Powell, Doctor Spock, the Reverend Leslie, Saint Joan, Senator Simon.* Do not abbreviate given names: not *Benj. Franklin* but *Benjamin Franklin.*

42*c*
Dates and time designations

■ 1 Abbreviating conventional date and time markers

Always abbreviate *a.m., p.m., AD, BC, BCE* (*Before the Common Era*), and *CE* (*Common Era*). Place *AD* (*anno Domini,* or "year of our Lord") before the date: *AD 1066*; place *BC* ("before Christ") following the date: *461 BC.* Use conventional date and time abbreviations only with specific figures: *3:30 p.m., 1066 CE.*

I study best in the early ~~a.m.~~, *morning* when everyone else is asleep.

■ 2 Spelling out dates and times

- Months and days. In the text of formal writing, spell out months and days: *Thursday, October 31st.* Exception: In notes and documentation, abbreviate months and days except May, June, and July.

- Holidays: Spell out holidays. not *Xmas* but *Christmas.*

- Other time designations. Spell out other time designations in the text of your writing: not *secs.* but *seconds*; not *hrs.* but *hours*; not *wks.* but *weeks*; not *yrs.* but *years.*

42*d*
Geographic terms and place names

■ 1 Spelling out in-text names and addresses

In the text of your writing spell out the names of continents, countries, states, territories, provinces, commonwealth members, possessions, city prefixes, words in addresses, and place names: *South America, United States, Michigan, New Brunswick, Puerto Rico, Fort Wayne, State Street, Herald Square, the Empire State Building.* The few exceptions are *USA, UK* (United Kingdom), and *BDR* (Germany).

■ 2 Abbreviating place names in notes and documentation

In notes, documentation, and addresses, use postal codes and other standard abbreviations: *MS* for *Mississippi, Ecua.* for *Ecuador, Gr.* for *Greece,* and so forth.

42*e* Organization names

■ 1 Abbreviating familiar organizations

Use familiar organizational abbreviations in the text of your writing: *UPI, IBM, USC, IRS, NBC, YMCA, UPS.*

■ 2 Spelling out unfamiliar organizations

Spell out the names of organizations unfamiliar to your readers: *Littman Brothers, Chicago and North Western Railroad, Eastridge Neighborhood Organization,* and so forth. *Incorporated* is usually written *Inc.* or omitted.

■ 3 Abbreviating notes and documentation

In notes and documentation abbreviate consistently for *Assoc., &, Co., Corp., Bro., Bros., Inc., Ltd., RR,* and so forth: *Capstone Corp., Littman Bros.*

42*f* Units of measure

■ 1 Spelling out in-text units of measure

Spell out most units of measure in the text of your writing: *inches, cubic foot, gallons, kilograms, meter, megabytes, square yards,* and so forth. Exceptions: *mph, mpg, rpm, Hz* (Hertz).

■ 2 Abbreviating in technical writing and notes

Abbreviate in technical writing and notes: *in., kg, sq. yds., cu. ft., gal, MB,* and so forth.

■ 3 Spelling out plural terms

Always spell out the plural terms inches, feet, meters, and gallons: *25 inches, 540 square feet, 47 meters, 300 gallons.*

42*g* Scholarly, technical, and Latin terms

Spell out scholarly, technical, and Latin terms in the text of your writing. Abbreviations are appropriate in parentheses, tables, notes, and documentation. (See also 52a and 54b3.)

c.	*circa,* "about"	misc.	miscellaneous
cf.	*confer,* "compare"	ms., mss.	manuscript, manuscripts
cont., contd.	continued	NB, n.b.	*nota bene,* "note well"
		n.d.	no date of publication
e.g.	*exempli gratia,* "for example"	n.p.	no place of publication, no publisher
et al.	*et aliae,* "and others"	p., pp.	page, pages
		rpt.	reprint, reprinted by
etc.	*et cetera,* "and so forth"	sic	"thus," "so"
		trans., tr.	translated by, translation
ex.	example	UP	University Press
i.e.	*id est,* "that is"	vs., v.	versus, "against"
illus.	illustrated by, illustration		

43
Numbers

43*a* Write numbers as words or figures according to the following guidelines

■ 1 Spelling out numbers that begin a sentence

Spell out numbers that begin a sentence. If the number is large, rewrite or rearrange the sentence. Compare these examples:

Three hundred students visited the state capitol on a field trip.

The strike involves
  465 employees ~~are on strike.~~

■ 2 Using Modern Language Association guidelines for numbers

- Numbers of one and two words. Spell out whole numbers from one to ninety-nine, including zero if the figure "0" would be confusing: *seven, eighteen, twenty-six, two hundred, fifteen thousand.* Use a hyphen for the numbers twenty-one to ninety-nine. An exception: When using numbers frequently in technical or business writing, use figures for all numbers except those beginning a sentence.

- Numbers of more than two words. Use figures for numbers of more than two words: *340; 1,650; 2,989,000.* Use commas to separate groups of three digits, except in addresses, telephone numbers, dates, and page numbers: *22,560* but *7201 South Locust.*

■ 3 Using American Psychological Association guidelines for numbers

- Numbers one to nine. Spell out the numbers one to nine.

- Numbers over nine. Use figures for numbers over nine: *10; 68; 3,462.*

■ 4 Using numbers in addresses

Always use figures in addresses: *PO Box 14, 15 West 43rd Street, 137 North Maplewood, Route 59.*

■ 5 Using numbers for time, dates, and time periods

- Time. Spell out the time except when using *a.m.* or *p.m.*: *seven o'clock in the morning, twelve midnight, half past four, 6:30 a.m., 9:45 p.m.*

- Decades. Spell out decades or use figures: *the nineties, the 90s, the 1990s.*

- Centuries. Spell out centuries; hyphenate when used as adjectives.

  In the **twentieth century,** major wars have been fought in nearly every decade.

  Next semester I'm taking a **twentieth-century** American history course.

- Historical dates with abbreviations. Use figures with AD, BC, BCE (before the Common Era), and CE (Common Era): *AD 1066, 461 BC, 32 BCE, 1456 CE.* A note: *AD (anno Domini)* precedes the date; BC ("before Christ") follows.

- Inclusive dates. For inclusive dates, write both years in full unless they are in the same century: *1895–1910* but *1941–45.*

■ 6 Writing fractions, ordinal numbers, and ratios

- Common fractions and ordinal numbers. Spell out common fractions (*one-half, two-thirds*) and the ordinal numbers *first* to *ninth*.

  Nearly **one-half** of our employees have been sick since the **first** of the year.

- Decimal fractions, numbers followed by fractions, and ratios. Write decimal fractions, numbers followed by fractions, and ratios as figures: *a 3.8 grade average, a hat size of 7 and ⁷/₈ , a ratio of 4:1* [or *four to one*].

■ 7 Writing numbers with abbreviations and symbols

Use figures with abbreviations and symbols.

$29.00	4 MB	62 km
14 mi. (miles)	65 mph	4" × 6"
8 hrs.	9 V battery	32°–43°
18% [18 percent]	50 lbs.	35-mm film

An MLA note: Exceptions. If your writing contains few numbers, spell out one-, two-, and three-word percentages and amounts of money: *twenty-six percent, sixty-nine cents, fifteen dollars, three hundred dollars.*

■ 8 Writing well-known phrases containing numbers

Generally spell out well-known phrases containing numbers: *the Ten Commandments, the Twelve Apostles, the Fourth of July.*

■ 9 Writing page numbers and divisions of written works

Use figures for page numbers, book divisions, and acts, scenes, and lines of plays: *page 7, pag. 47, volume 5, chapter 16;* Hamlet *3.2.46* or Hamlet *III.ii.46.*

An MLA note: To cite inclusive page numbers, give the second number in full, through *99: 7–23, 85–96.* For larger numbers, give the last two digits of the second number unless more are necessary to prevent confusion: *122–34, 200–05, 1220–32* but *98–103, 287–303, 1238–1342.*

An APA note: When citing inclusive numbers, give all the digits of both numbers: *23–32, 458–467, 1152–1158.*

43*b* | When one number modifies another, write one as a figure, the other as a word

■ 1 Writing large rounded numbers

Write large rounded numbers as a combination of figures and words.

43*d* num

The population of China today is **1.25 billion.**

Congress proposes to cut **$375 million** from the national parks budget.

■ 2 Writing back-to-back numbers

Write back-to-back numbers as a combination of figures and words.

Last year Maria taught a class with **34 ten-year-olds.**

The order requests **seventy-five 8 × 10 glossy prints.**

The **first 10** customers were given a potted plant.

43*c* Write related numbers alike, as words or figures

■ Related numbers that appear together in the same sentence or paragraph should be written alike, as words or figures. If, according to the guidelines in 43a, you write some numbers as figures, be consistent and write all the numbers in your series as figures.

10,000
Within two decades, the university has grown from ~~ten thousand~~ to
^

25,550 students.

43*d* Use roman numerals for outlines, persons in a series, and preliminary pages

■ 1 Outlines

Use capital roman numerals for the primary divisions of an outline: *I, II, III, IV, V,* and so forth. Use arabic numerals for all other subdivisions. (See 2c3.)

■ 2 Persons in a series

Use capital roman numerals for persons in a series: *Ramses II, Pope John XXIII, Henry VIII.*

■ 3 Preliminary pages

Use lower-case roman numerals (*i, ii, iii,* and so forth) to number the preliminary pages of research papers (abstract, outline, and so forth) and to cite book pages that are so numbered.

A note: Your instructor may require that you number the pages of your paper consecutively from the first page to last using arabic numerals.

The Hyphen

Type a hyphen as one keystroke, with no space before or after: *student-athlete.* Do not confuse a hyphen (-) with a dash (—). (See 39a.) To use hyphens correctly, note how your dictionary lists words:

- Use a hyphen to join words listed with a hyphen (*half-life*).

- If you must divide a multisyllable word listed with dots between syllables, use a hyphen. The word **har•mo•nize** may be divided *har-monize* or *harmo-nize.*

- Compounds listed as two words (*half note*) are written without hyphens.

44*a* Avoid word division at the end of a line

The Modern Language Association and American Psychological Association guidelines forbid word division at the end of a line, and this is good advice for most writing. If a whole word won't fit within the margin, leave the line a little short and begin on the next line. Most word-processing programs have automatic "word wrap" to do this for you. However, you may have to divide an already hyphenated word or personal name.

■ 1 Dividing already hyphenated words

Divide already hyphenated words only at the hyphen.

brother-
Downhill skiing became more frightening than exciting for me after my ~~bro-~~
in-law
~~ther-in-law~~ broke his leg in a bad fall.

■ 2 Dividing personal names

Divide personal names (1) between first and last names: Mary / Cassatt; (2) after the middle initial: Susan B. / Anthony; (3) if necessary, between initials and the last name: H. L. / Mencken. Never divide between initials.

44b Use a dictionary to hyphenate compounds

■ Compounds are formed of two or more words. They may be hyphenated (*cross-stitch, cross-reference, cross-examine*), written as separate words (*cross hair, cross section, cross matching*), or written as one word (*crossbow, crossroad, crossword*). Your dictionary will show you the correct forms. If you don't find a compound listed, write it as two words.

Last month in San Francisco I spent a whole afternoon riding the

cable/cars.

John reached into his pocket and discovered that his check book was

missing.

The lines at the check out counters stretched to the back of the store.

44c Hyphenate compound adjectives before a noun but not following the noun

■ Compare the following pairs of sentences.

I've written a **first-rate** essay. My essay is **first rate.**

Darrell uncorked a **seven-year-old** bottle of wine. Darrell uncorked a bottle of wine that was **seven years old.**

The film received **less-than-enthusiastic** reviews. The reviews were **less than enthusiastic.**

A note on an *-ly* adverb followed by an adjective: Do not hyphenate *-ly* adverbs and adjectives that follow.

Heavily/traveled mountain paths contribute to significant soil erosion.

A note on hyphenated adjectives in series: In a series of hyphenated adjectives, suspend the second word of each compound until the last: *We plan to rent a two-, three-, or four-bedroom cottage for our vacation.*

44d Hyphenate following the prefixes *all-*, *ex-*, *great-*, *self-* and before the suffix *-elect.*

all-American athlete	great-grandson	self-respect
ex-mayor	great-great-grandmother	senator-elect

44e Hyphenate spelled-out fractions, the numbers twenty-one to ninety-nine, and combinations of figures and words

one-half	forty-seven	100-yard dash
two-thirds	fifty-two	mid-1800s
seven-eighths	eighty-eight	pre-1960

44f Hyphenate to prevent misreading

Without hyphens, some words might be misread or confused with other words.

Until a fertilized ovum is implanted in the uterus, it exists in a
pre-embryonic
~~preembryonic~~ state.

[Without a hyphen, readers may pronounce one long *e* sound instead of a long *e* followed by a short *e*.]

re-sign
The lawyer asked her client to ~~resign~~ the agreement.

[Without a hyphen, *re-sign*, "to sign again," could be confused with *resign*, "to relinquish."]

45 Spelling

45a Use a word guide, electronic dictionary, or spell checker

As you edit your writing, look up any words not part of your everyday writing vocabulary. Use one of the following aids.

■ 1 Using word guides

Word guides such as *Webster's Instant Word Guide* are pocket-sized books that list words without definitions, pronunciations, or grammatical

How to . . .

How to Edit Spelling

With the help of a proofreader or spell checker, list your spelling errors, first as you've misspelled them, then as they are spelled correctly. Alphabetize your list and underline the errors. Use this list as you write and revise.

If you don't have a dictionary, spell checker, or spelling guide available, try these tricks to figure out the correct spelling of words.

1. Compare spellings. Write out alternate spellings to compare. Correctly spelled words often look and feel right.
2. Disassemble words. Divide them into syllables and sound them out. Try to see and hear the word as you've actually spelled it. Is it *tra-deg-y* or *tra-ged-y*? *lon-li-ness* or *lone-li-ness*? *nec-cess-ary* or *ne-cess-ary*? *di-satisfied* or *dis-satisfied*? *tom-morrow* or *to-morrow*?
3. Find related words to help you spell the unaccented vowels that often sound like *uh* no matter what their spelling.

comp ? tition + comPETE
  = competition

democr ? cy + demoCRATic
  = democracy

exhil ? rate + hiLARity
  = exhilarate

gramm ? r + gramMARian
  = grammar

infin ? te + fiNITE
  = infinite

mir ? cle + mirACulous
  = miracle

monot ? nous + monoTONE
  = monotonous

prev ? lent + VALue
  = prevalent

rel ? tive + reLATE
  = relative

sep ? rate + PARE
  = separate

4. Use memory aids. Make up phrases or sentences to associate with the correct spelling of words—the sillier the better. Everyone knows "The princiPAL is my PAL." How about "I get all *A*'s in grAmmAr" or "A secretAry never tAries"? You can think of others.

When you've finished revising, focus on spelling as you proofread. Read your writing backward, from the end to the beginning, to help you look at each word. Lay a straight edge beneath each line. To spot omitted or sound-alike words, point at each word with a pen or pencil.

information. Because they show only how words are spelled, they're quick and easy to use. If you're sometimes so unsure of a spelling that you can't look up the word, consider a word guide like *Webster's Bad Spellers Dictionary* that lists words spelled correctly and as frequently misspelled.

■ 2 Using electronic dictionaries

Pocket-sized electronic dictionaries such as the *Franklin Wordmaster* and the *American Heritage Dictionary* will confirm an accurate spelling, correct a misspelling, or provide alternatives for unrecognized words you've typed in. Look for one with a word list of at least 80,000 words. Test it by misspelling a hard or unfamiliar word like *subpoena*. If the dictionary doesn't recognize your error, try another model or brand.

■ 3 Using spell checkers

If you write with a computer, your word-processing program probably has a spell checker. Use it. Many writers who seem to be poor spellers are, in fact, poor typists who forget to run their spell checkers. But even if you use yours faithfully, proofread carefully when you finish to guard against the limitations of these software programs.

- Spell checkers do not distinguish between sound-alike words. If you type *their* when you mean *there,* your spell checker will not correct you.

- Spell checkers do not correct mistakes that produce correctly spelled words. If you mean to type *band* but type *hand* or *and,* your spell checker will not recognize your mistake.

45*b* Make a checklist of your spelling errors

■ Even poor spellers spell correctly most of the time, and when they do misspell, they misspell the same words over and over or repeat the same kind of error. Make your own personalized spelling checklist to help you avoid errors. Buy a small alphabetically arranged address book or a pocket notebook. Find out which words you misspell and list them there. If necessary, ask friends to proofread your writing. If they point out an error, write the word down, first as you misspelled it (to help you spot errors as you proofread) and then correctly spelled. To help you see the error, underline it.

WRONG	RIGHT
for̲f̲illing	*fulfilling*
gove̲r̲ment	*government*
gramme̲r̲	*grammar*
reco̲n̲ize	*recognize*
thie̲r̲	*their*
we̲r̲e	*where*

As you compile your checklist, look for patterns in your errors and ask questions to uncover the reasons for your misspelling.

- Do you hear all the letters or syllables? *boundry/boundary, logicly/ logically, studing/studying, suppose/supposed, reconize/recognize*

- Do you hear what you've actually written? *forfilling/fulfilling, lose/loose*

- Do you have trouble distinguishing sounds? *seperate/separate, angle/angel*

- Do you reverse letters? *thier/their*

- Do you know the rules? When to write *i* before *e*: *recieve/receive*? When to add or drop the silent *e*: *arguement/argument, changable/changeable*? When to change *y* to *i*: *studing/studying*? When to double consonants: *writting/writing, occurence/occurrence*?

45*c* Learn the most important spelling rules

■ 1 Putting *i* before *e*

Almost everyone knows the beginning of this rhyming rule: *i* before *e* except after *c*. Not many know the remainder.

> *i* before *e* except after *c*
> when pronounced long *e*;
> *e* before *i* when pronounced long *a*,
> as in *neighbor* or *weigh*.

- *i* before *e* when pronounced long *e* = *believe, chief, field, relief, siege, yield*

- *i* before *e* except after *c* = *ceiling, conceive, deceive, receive*

- *e* before *i* when pronounced long *a* = *eight, freight, neighbor, weigh, vein*

- *i* before *e* exceptions: *conscience, financier, science, species, sufficient*

- *e* before *i* exceptions: *counterfeit, either, foreign, forfeit, height, leisure, neither, seize, sheik, sovereign, weird*

■ 2 Adding silent *e* at the end of a word

English generally requires a silent *e* at the end of a word to keep a preceding vowel long in sound: *mat/mate, met/mete, kit/kite, hot/hotel, cut/cute*. To add a suffix to a silent *e* word, follow these rules.

- Drop the silent *e* when the suffix begins with a vowel: *cute/cutest, desire/desiring, fame/famous, imagine/imaginary, love/lovable, prime/primal, retrieve/retrieving*. An exception: *mileage*.

- Keep the silent *e* when a suffix begins with a consonant: *achieve/achievement, care/careful, live/lively, lone/lonely, sincere/sincerely.* Exceptions: *argument, judgment, awful, truly, duly, wholly.*

- Keep the silent *e* when a word ends in *-ce* or *-ge* and the suffix begins with *a* or *o*: *service/serviceable, change/changeable, courage/courageous.*

- Exceptions to avoid confusion or mispronunciation: *dying/dyeing, hoeing, toeing, shoeing, singing/singeing.*

■ 3 Changing *y* to *i*

- When a word ends consonant + *y*, change *y* to *i* and add the suffix: *busy/business, community/communities, embody/embodiment, lonely/loneliness, modify/modifier, penny/penniless.* Exceptions: *babyish, cityless, fairylike.*

- When the suffix is *-ing* or *-ist*, do not change the *y* to *i*: *copy + ing = copying, essay + ist = essayist, lobby + ing = lobbying, study + ing = studying.*

- When a word ends in a vowel + *y*, add the suffix: *boy/boyish, buy/buyer, obey/obeying, sway/swayed, valley/valleys.* Exceptions: *daily, gaily, laid, paid, said.*

■ 4 Doubling consonants

Double the consonant at the end of a word when the word meets all three of these tests:

- The word ends in a vowel + consonant: *begin, cut, fog, glad, occur, prefer, regret.*

- The suffix begins with a vowel: *-ed, -en, -ing, -y.*

- The word has one syllable or is accented on the final syllable: *begínning, cutting, foggy, gladden, occúrrence, preférring, regrétted* but: *bénefited, concealed, gláddened, láboring, préference*

■ 5 Adding the suffix *-ly*

- When a word ends with one *-l*, add *-ly*. Do not drop the *-l* at the end of the word: *casual/casually, formal/formally, real/really, usual/usually*

- When a word ends *-ll*, add only a *-y*: *chill/chilly, hill/hilly*

■ 6 Adding suffixes to words ending in *-ic*

- When a word ends in *-ic* and the suffix begins with *-e, -i,* or *-y*, add a *k*. *Traffic + ed =* add a *k: trafficked; picnic + ing =* add a *k: picnicking; panic + y =* add a *k: panicky.*

- Some words ending in *-ic* take the suffix *-ally*: *heroically, logically, tragically.*

▮ 7 Forming plurals

- To form the plural of most nouns, add *-s* to the singular: *boat + s = boats, glove + s = gloves, shoe + s = shoes, Johnson + s = Johnsons.*

- When a noun ends *-s, -sh, -ch, -x,* or *-z,* form the plural with *-es*: *Jones + es = Joneses, dish + es = dishes, church + es = churches, box + es = boxes, buzz + es = buzzes.*

- When a noun ends in a consonant + *o*, the plural varies:

ADD *-S* ONLY	ADD *-ES* ONLY	ADD *-S* OR *-ES*
autos	echoes	zeros, zeroes
memos	heroes	cargos, cargoes
pianos	tomatoes, potatoes	

- When a noun ends in *-f* or *-fe*, add *-s* to some words: *roofs, safes, chiefs.* To form the plural of others, change the *f* to *v* and add *-es*: *hoof/hooves, thief/thieves, wharf/wharves, wife/wives.*

- Some words have irregular plurals: *child/children, ox/oxen, goose/geese, mouse/mice.*

- Some words have the same form for singular and plural: *deer, jeans, glasses* (for the eyes), *pliers, rice, sheep, swine, trousers, wheat.*

- To form the plural of letters and numbers, add *-s*; use an apostrophe only to prevent confusion: *the three* R's, *BAs, 1990s, dot your* i's *and cross your* t's.

- To form the plural of most compounds, add *-s* to the last word unless the first is more important: *checkbooks, masterminds, student-athletes,* but *mothers-in-law, attorneys general, courts martial, editors-in-chief, passers-by.*

- To form the plural of most foreign words, use the original plural:

SINGULAR	PLURAL	SINGULAR	PLURAL
alumnus (men)	alumni	datum	data
alumna (women)	alumnae	a medium	media
antenna	antennae	a memorandum	memoranda
basis	bases	phenomenon	phenomena
chateau	chateaux	a psychosis	psychoses
criterion	criteria	a radius	radii
crisis	crises	a thesis	theses

■ 8 Identifying differences in American, British, and Canadian spelling

American spelling varies slightly from the British and Canadian in the use of *a/ae*, *e/oe*, *o/ou*, the silent *e*, *c/qu*, *ck/que*, *ct/x*, *l/ll*, *ter/tre*, and *z/s*. Consult your dictionary, and use American spelling in the United States.

AMERICAN SPELLING	BRITISH AND CANADIAN SPELLING	AMERICAN SPELLING	BRITISH AND CANADIAN SPELLING
anemia	anaemia	honor	honour
apologize	apologise	judgment	judgement
check	cheque	licorice	liquorice
connection	connexion	theater	theatre
fetus	foetus	traveled	travelled

Formatting Your Writing ■

46*a* Give your writing a professional, easy-to-read appearance

■ The idiosyncrasies of handwriting, stationery, and layout that add warmth to personal writing may only distract readers who don't know you well. To communicate effectively, your academic, business, and public writing must be neat, easy to read, appropriately formatted, and carefully edited. Two formats for academic writing, the Modern Language Association (MLA) and the American Psychological Association (APA), are described later in this chapter. (See 46c and d.) Other formats are described in the style manuals listed in 56. (For business formats, see Chapter 61.) To determine appropriate manuscript form, check with your instructor.

A note on saving copies: Save copies of written or typed work and back up all computer files. They provide insurance against loss and may be useful if you later revise.

■ 1 Writing with computers

- Paper. Use high-quality, white, 8½ × 11-inch computer paper. If you use continuous-form paper, remove the perforated edges, separate the pages, and put them in order.

- Printers. Ink jet or laser printers are always acceptable, but some readers object to dot-matrix printers. Find out before you begin. If you use a dot-matrix or print-wheel printer, be sure your ribbon is fresh and the paper properly aligned to produce correct margins. If necessary, set your printer to letter-quality or near letter-quality printing.

- Fonts. Use standard 10- or 12-point fonts: Times Roman, Courier, Geneva, or Helvetica. Avoid cursive and other fancy fonts.

- Formatting. Set automatic formatting commands in advance, including spacing, margins, line justification, automatic paging, word wrap, and headers (most word-processing programs do this for you). Use italics, underlining, and boldface sparingly (see 41), and avoid stylistic flourishes that may distract readers.

- Margins. Leave 1-inch margins on the top, bottom, and both sides of the page. If required to submit your paper in a binder, leave a 1½-inch left margin.

- Line justification. Print your margins justified (aligned) left, ragged right. Avoid right justification and proportional spacing.

- Punctuation. Never begin a line with a comma, colon, semicolon, hyphen, dash, end punctuation, or part of an ellipsis. Never end a line with opening quotation marks, parentheses, or brackets standing alone, disconnected from a word.

- Corrections. Proofread your final draft carefully. Run your spell checker, correct, and reprint. Give your paper a last check to be sure everything has printed correctly.

- Binding. Paperclip the pages of your writing. Do not use staples, pins, or braids.

■ 2 Writing with a typewriter

- Paper. Use high-quality, white, 20-pound, 8½ × 11-inch typing paper. Avoid erasable paper. If you wish to use erasable paper to make corrections easier, turn in a clean, dark photocopy of your final draft. Type on one side of the paper only.

- Ribbon. Use a fresh ribbon, and be sure the typeface is clean.

- Fonts. Use 10- or 12-point standard fonts, such as Times Roman, Courier, Geneva, or Helvetica. Avoid cursive fonts and the all-capitals format.

- Margins. Leave 1-inch margins on the top, bottom, and both sides of the page. If you are required to submit your paper in a binder, leave a 1½-inch left margin.

- Punctuation. Never begin a line with a comma, colon, semicolon, hyphen, dash, end punctuation, or part of an ellipsis. Never end a line with opening quotation marks, parentheses, or brackets standing alone, disconnected from a word.

- Corrections. Use correction fluid. Insert corrections by hand or typewriter. If you make numerous or lengthy corrections, retype the page. (For correction symbols, see 3c2.)

- Binding. Paperclip the pages of your writing. Do not use staples, pins, or braids.

3 Writing by hand

If possible, avoid handwritten work. Your school or local library probably has typewriters or computers for your use. See your Writing Center head or a librarian for information. If you must do an out-of-class paper by hand, check with your instructor first, then follow these guidelines:

- Paper. Use high-quality, wide-ruled, white theme paper, 8½ × 11 inches. Do not use spiral notebook paper. Write on one side of the paper only.

- Ink. Write in blue or black ink. Form your letters carefully. Don't run words into each other, and guard against smudges. If your handwriting is difficult to read, print, but do not use all-capital letters.

- Spacing and margins. Write on every other line to the right of the ruled vertical margin. Leave 1-inch right and bottom margins.

- Punctuation. Never begin a line with a comma, colon, semicolon, hyphen, dash, end punctuation, or part of an ellipsis. Never end a line with opening quotation marks, parentheses, or brackets standing alone, disconnected from a word.

- Corrections. Make corrections neatly, using correction fluid produced for pen and ink. (For a list of correction symbols, see 3c2.)

- Binding. Paperclip the pages of your writing. Do not use staples, pins, or braids.

46b Use headings, lists, tables, and graphics to clarify ideas

Computer word-processing programs have given writers powerful tools for enhancing ideas. Even if you don't have a computer, you can add headings, lists, tables, and graphics to your writing. But be aware that too many extra features will break your continuity and distract readers. To be effective, these visual aids should

- Add to rather than duplicate your text
- Convey essential information, not be merely decorative

- Be easy to understand
- Make your subject easier to understand

A note on format: Specific subject areas may have differing formats for visual aids. See your instructor.

■ 1 Formatting in-text headings

Many kinds of writing, especially essays, do not require headings. However, reports and other technical documents such as proposals and grant requests are divided by headings that identify topics and guide readers. If headings are appropriate for your writing, use the following format based on American Psychological Association (APA) guidelines:

- Heading levels. Use from one to five levels of heading, depending on the complexity of your writing. The following headings are arranged from most to least important.

CENTERED ALL-CAPITALS HEADING (e.g., OUTLINE)

Centered Upper- and Lower-Case Headings (e.g., Introduction)

Centered, Underlined, Upper- and Lower-Case Headings (e.g., <u>Background</u>)

Flush-Left, Underlined, Upper- and Lower-Case Headings (e.g., <u>Important</u>

<u>Definitions</u>)

    Run-in underlined paragraph headings ending with a period (e.g.,

<u>Functional literacy.</u>)

- Numbering. Headings are unnumbered except in scientific writing.

- Punctuation and capital letters. Do not end centered and flush-left headings with a period. For run-in heads at the beginning of a paragraph, capitalize the first letter of the first word, lowercase the remaining words, and end with a period. Underline as in the preceding examples.

- Spacing. Doublespace above and below headings; doublespace within multiline headings.

- Length and consistency. Keep your headings brief and be grammatically consistent. Headings at a particular level should have the same grammatical form: noun phrases, verb phrases, questions, and so forth.

- Grammar. Use the grammar of a heading to suggest the contents of the section. Use nouns or noun phrases to introduce information or explanation (e.g., *Exotic Species*); *-ing* verbs to introduce processes, actions, or events (e.g., *Preserving Native Species*); commands to introduce instructions (e.g., *Reintroduce Natural Predators*); questions to interest readers (e.g., *How May Endangered Songbirds Be Saved?*).

- Format. Do not begin a new page for each heading. But if a heading comes at the bottom of a page, move it to the next page unless it is followed by at least two lines of text.

■2 Formatting lists

Use lists to clarify steps in a process, materials, ingredients, parts, advice, or items to be covered. To make a list, follow these guidelines:

- Write an introduction followed by a colon, as in the preceding sentence.

- Precede each item in a list with a marker: a number or letter plus a period and two spaces, a dash, or a bullet (•) plus a space.

- Begin each item flush with the left margin. Indent runover lines one-half inch or five spaces to form a hanging paragraph. For greater emphasis, you may indent the first line of each item five spaces, runover lines 1 inch or ten spaces.

- Make items grammatically parallel: a phrase, sentence, or other grammatical form.

■3 Formatting tables

Tables present information in a systematic order, usually in columns. Use tables sparingly to eliminate complex, number-filled text, and place them near their related text. Here are the Modern Language Association (MLA) guidelines for tables.

- Place tables close to the text to which they relate. Briefly introduce each table, or in parentheses write *See Table 1, 2, 3,* and so forth.

- Label each as "Table" followed by an arabic numeral (e.g., Table 1), placed flush left. Doublespace throughout. Do not use all capitals.

- On a separate line two spaces below the table heading, provide a descriptive caption placed flush left; do not use all capitals. Doublespace this caption.

- Between ruled lines, write descriptive headings for each column.

- Arrange each column beneath its heading.

- Two spaces below the table make a ruled bottom line.

- Two spaces beneath the bottom line, following the word *Source* plus a colon and a space, give the source of the table, if necessary. Indent additional lines a quarter-inch or three spaces.

- Use raised lower-case letters (e.g., [a, b, c,] and so forth) to identify notes to the table.

Table 1

1992 Recreational Visits to Selected Areas Administered by the National
Park System

Classification	Recreational Visits
National Lakeshores	3,906,495
National Parks	58,729,193
National Parkways	30,652,974
National Recreation Areas	50,315,794
National Rivers	4,532,849
National Seashores	19,954,228
Wild and Scenic Rivers	895,945
Parks--Other[a]	15,346,962
National Total	211,906,380

Source: Adapted from U.S. Dept. of the Interior, National Park Service,

Statistical Abstract (Denver: U.S. Dept. of the Interior, 1992) 2.

[a]Parks without national designation include National Capital Park,

National Mall, and the White House.

An APA note: Underline the descriptive caption preceding the table
(e.g., 1992 Recreational Visits to Selected Areas Administered by the National Park System). After the table, in place of the word *Source,* use *Note*
underlined and followed by a period also underlined, and two spaces
(Note.). Give the source of the table using the appropriate APA citation
format. (See 54c.)

■ 4 Displaying graphics

Graphics include charts, drawings, maps, graphs, and photographs.
Draw them by hand, cut and paste reproductions, or use a computer
graphics program. Introduce each graphic and place it appropriately on
the page near related text. Give appropriate documentation following the
graphic. These are the Modern Language Association guidelines:

- Flush left and two spaces beneath your graphic, write the label *Figure*
  (abbreviated *Fig.*) and an arabic numeral followed by a period (Fig. 1.).

- On the same line, write a caption using upper- and lower-case letters,
  followed by a comma and the documentation of the source. Doublespace throughout.

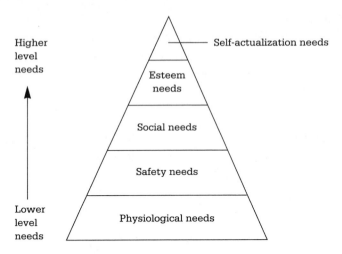

Fig. 1. Maslow's Needs Hierarchy, from Abraham H. Maslow, <u>Motivation and Personality</u>, 2nd ed. (New York: Harper, 1970).

An APA note: After the graphic, write and underline the word *Figure,* the numeral, and a period, followed by two spaces (<u>Figure 1.</u>   ). If necessary, document the source of the graphic using the appropriate APA citation format. (See 54c.)

46c Use the Modern Language Association format for writing in the humanities

■ The following format, based on the *MLA Handbook for Writers of Research Papers,* 4th ed. (New York: MLA, 1995), is appropriate for writing in English composition, literature, and foreign language courses; it is also used in the humanities, philosophy, religion, and history. To determine the appropriate format for your papers, check with your instructor.

A note: See 46a for general information on computerized writing, typing, and handwritten work.

■ **1** Formatting the identification heading and title

Most college writing does not require a title page. Use an identification heading instead: On your first page, 1 inch from the top and left margins, list your name, your instructor's name, course, section number, and date, doublespacing throughout. Doublespace to reach the title line; center your title. If your title runs more than one line, doublespace the lines; use a colon between a title and subtitle. Capitalize the first and last words and all words except articles, prepositions, conjunctions, and the *to* in infinitives (e.g., *to Write*). Do not use underlining, italics, and quotation marks unless your title contains another title or a direct quotation. Doublespace between your title and the first line of text. (See 4c, Chapter 53, and 59d for sample papers in the MLA format.)

■ 2 Formatting the title page

If a title page is required by your instructor, center your title one-third down the page. In the center of the page, write "by," doublespace, and give your name. Two-thirds down the page and centered, write the course name, your instructor's name, and the date, doublespacing between lines. On the first page of text, repeat your title, centered on the first line. Doublespace between the title and first line of text. (See the sample title page in Chapter 53.)

■ 3 Indenting

- Paragraphs. Indent the first word of a paragraph one-half inch or five spaces from the left margin. If you write by hand, indent one inch.

- Long quotations. If a prose quotation runs more than four typed lines, indent 1 inch or ten spaces from the left margin, none from the right. If indented quotations run longer than one paragraph, indent the first line of successive paragraphs an additional quarter-inch or three spaces. Indent more than three lines of poetry 1 inch or ten spaces from the left margin, or center the poetry to appear balanced on the page. (See 38c.)

■ 4 Spacing

Doublespace between all lines, including titles, headings, indented quotations, and outlines. Space once after a colon, twice after end punctuation (periods, question marks, and quotations). Leave no space between end punctuation and closing quotation marks, parentheses, and brackets. Space once after periods following initials or abbreviations, twice after periods within bibliographic citations.

■ 5 Paging

For papers without title pages, begin numbering on the first page. In the upper right corner, one-half inch from the top of the page, put your last name followed by a space and the page number (e.g., *Lopez 1*). Do not use the word *page*, the abbreviation *p.*, parentheses, dashes, or other punctuation. Number consecutively to the end of your paper, including notes and documentation. Doublespace beneath the page heading or position the first line of text 1 inch from the top of the page.

If your paper has a title page, use lower-case roman numerals for preliminary pages such as an outline. Count the title page, but do not begin numbering until the following page. In the upper right corner, one-half inch from the top, put your name followed by a space and a roman numeral (e.g., *Lopez ii*). On the first page of text, begin a new series of numbers; put your last name followed by a space and an arabic numeral (e.g., *Lopez 1*). Doublespace beneath the page heading or position the first line of text 1 inch from the top of the page.

A note on computerized paging: If you use a computer, you can probably create a page header to insert your name and page numbers automatically at the top of each page. If necessary, turn on consecutive page numbering.

■ 6 Headings

Identify the parts of your paper by appropriate section headings: Outline, your title on the first page of text, Notes, and Works Cited. Write the heading centered 1 inch from the top of the page and capitalized correctly. Doublespace to the first line of text. (See the sample research paper in Chapter 53.)

In-text topic headings that divide the body of a paper are seldom necessary for essays. However, they may be useful or required for complex technical writing such as reports. (See 46b1.)

■ 7 Order of pages

Arrange your paper in this order:

Title page, if required
Acknowledgments page, if required
Outline, if required
The body of your paper
Notes, if necessary
Works Cited, if necessary

46d | Use the American Psychological Association format for writing in the social sciences

■ The following format, based on guidelines for student writing in Appendix A to the *Publication Manual of the American Psychological Association*, 4th ed. (Washington, DC: APA, 1994), is appropriate for writing in the social sciences, education, business, linguistics, biology, and earth sciences. Note that the APA format for student papers differs slightly from that of papers to be published in APA journals. See your instructor for the appropriate format for your writing.

A note: See 46a for general information on computerized writing, typing, and handwritten work.

Research
—MLA
Documentation

part VI. Research—MLA Documentation

■ 1 Formatting the title page

Use a title page for your paper. (See the APA sample report in 54d.)

- Page head. In the top right corner, one-half inch from the top of the page, put a short form of your title (the page head) followed by one-half inch or five spaces and the page number (e.g., Standardized Testing   1). The page head will appear with the page number at the top of all pages of your paper. If you use a computer, you can probably insert the heading and page numbers automatically.

- Title. Center your complete title in the middle of the page. Capitalize the first and last words and all words of four letters or more. If your title runs more than one line, doublespace; use a colon between a title and subtitle.

- Identifying information. On separate, double-spaced lines beneath the title, put your name, the course and section number, your instructor's name, and the date.

■ 2 Formatting the preliminary pages

In addition to the title page, you may be required to include acknowledgments, a table of contents, a list of tables and figures, or an abstract. For each preliminary page, type your page header and page number at the top right. Type the heading for each page centered, in upper- and lower-case letters: Table of Contents, Abstract, and so forth. Doublespace beneath the heading.

■ 3 Formatting the abstract

An abstract is a brief, comprehensive summary (100–120 words) of your paper. Write the abstract after you have written the paper itself. Report rather than evaluate or comment. Do not use *I* or *we*. Define all terms and abbreviations; write all numbers as figures. Type the abstract in one double-spaced paragraph beginning two spaces beneath the heading (*Abstract*). Do not indent the first line. See the example in the sample APA report in 54d.)

■ 4 Indenting

- Paragraphs. Indent the first word of a paragraph one-half inch or five spaces from the left margin.

- Long quotations. If a quotation runs more than forty words, indent one-half inch or five spaces from the left margin, none from the right. If indented quotations run longer than one paragraph, indent the first line of successive paragraphs an additional one-half inch or five spaces. Do not use quotation marks unless they appear in the original.

■5 Spacing

Doublespace throughout, including titles, headings, quotations, tables, graphics captions, notes, and references. Space once after commas, semicolons, colons, and after punctuation at the end of a sentence. Leave no space between end punctuation (periods, question marks, and quotations) and closing quotation marks, parentheses, and brackets. Space once after periods following a person's initials and within reference citations.

A note: If your instructor permits, you may singlespace within titles, headings, and references to improve readability. You may triple- or quadruplespace before major in-text headings and before and after in-text tables.

■6 Placing tables and figures

Unless instructed otherwise, place tables and figures in the body of your paper, near the text they illustrate. (See also 46b3.)

■7 Paging

Unless instructed otherwise, number the pages of your paper consecutively, beginning with the title page and continuing to the end, including notes, references, and appendixes. Use arabic numerals (1, 2, 3, and so forth). At the right margin, one-half inch from the top of the page, put the page header of your paper followed by one-half inch or five spaces and the page number. Doublespace beneath the page number.

A note on preliminary pages: Your instructor may require that you use lower-case roman numerals (i, ii, iii, and so forth) for preliminary pages such as title pages and abstracts.

■8 Formatting in-text headings

APA-style papers frequently contain in-text section and topic headings. (See 46b1.)

■9 Arranging the order of parts

Arrange an APA paper in this order:

Title page
Acknowledgment page, if required
Table of Contents, if required
List of Tables and Figures, if required
Abstract, if required
The text of the paper
References
Appendixes, if required

The Research Project

Getting Started

The research project is such an efficient method for gathering and pre-senting reliable information that it is a frequent assignment in college and other environments where facts and ideas are important. The research papers you write will be similar to those written by professionals: reports, reviews of other researchers' findings (the "review of research"), thesis-support essays, and literary research papers. The following guidelines will help you meet the special challenges of these projects.

47a | Choose a "researchable" topic

In most respects, choosing a research paper topic is like choos-ing any topic. The topic you choose should interest you and stimulate your curiosity. (See the guidelines for choosing topics in 1b.) Research projects, however, follow an additional guideline: Your topic must be genuinely researchable, with reliable information and trustworthy opinions available to you. To identify appropriate topics:

- Ask the experts. If you don't already have a list of topics given to you as part of an assignment, ask your professor or other experts for recommendations.

- Check reference sources. Read about interesting topics in encyclopedias or other reference works. Look for problems, questions, or controversies that have stimulated the writing of scholars and others. A librarian will help you locate these sources.

- Check source lists. Skim bibliographies, indexes, and other source lists in your library. The titles of books and articles may suggest topics that have received the serious attention necessary for your research.

- Beware of "headline" topics. Current topics may attract attention, and newspapers and popular magazines may be filled with articles about them. But recent events, personalities, or trends may not yet have received the expert attention that usually leads to the most reliable information.

47*b* | Narrow and focus your topic

■ Professional researchers rarely investigate a whole topic in one project. They choose a part, a single issue, or a key question to investigate in depth in the time available. Do the same. Once you have a topic, narrow it and draw the line of inquiry you'll follow in your research.

- Writing baseline notes. Before you begin research, write brief notes exploring your current thinking about your topic and establishing a baseline for investigation. Write down what you feel, believe, and know. Remind yourself where your ideas have come from. Are your sources trustworthy? Your notes may raise research questions for you to answer. They may also reveal assumptions that influence your thinking. Knowing your biases will help you evaluate information more objectively.

- Reading background material. If you haven't already read encyclopedias or reference sources, do so now. Look for issues, questions, or problems having to do with your topic. Your librarian will help you locate these sources.

- Posing key questions or describing a problem. Pose questions to answer. They may combine the reporter's six questions: *who, what, when, where, why*, and *how*. Or briefly describe a problem for your research to solve. For example:

The exploding popularity of America's national parks is reducing the enjoyment of visitors and harming the environment. What can be done to protect park environments and at the same time increase the enjoyment of these beautiful attractions?

- Stating your purposes. Your purposes may change as you investigate a topic, perhaps transforming you from a reporter of information to an advocate for a position. But thinking about your purpose will reveal what you're looking for and why. Write a brief statement about why you're investigating your topic. For example:

My purposes are to investigate interpretations of Charlotte Perkins Gilman's "The Yellow Wall-Paper" to discover the symbolism of the wallpaper and the causes of the narrator's insanity.

- Writing a tentative thesis. What do you expect to discover by your research? If you know little about your subject, you'll have little to say here, but if your purposes are critical or argumentative, you may already have opinions. Research may lead you to revise your thesis, even disprove it, but stating it now will point the direction of your investigation. Write your thesis as a declarative sentence:

I expect to discover/prove/explain/demonstrate/show that __[make an assertion about your subject]__.

I expect to prove that the wallpaper in Charlotte Perkins Gilman's "The Yellow Wall-Paper" symbolizes the narrator's suffocating life and the causes of her deepening insanity.

How to Focus a Research Project

How to . . .

At the beginning of a research project, many things about your project will seem unclear—especially if you've not written many research papers. Help yourself focus your project by writing the following exercise. Complete as many items as possible.

1. My general subject area:
2. My specific research topic:
3. My key question:
4. My purposes (to report, explain, evaluate, or persuade):
5. My tentative thesis (if possible):
6. What words in my topic, question, or thesis are vague or unclear? What opposing opinions or questions could be offered in response to my thesis? Do my stated purposes fit the language of my questions or thesis?
7. The date this project is due:
   a. Number of days for researching:
   b. Number of days for organizing:
   c. Number of days for writing:
   d. Number of days for revising and preparing the final draft:

48 Finding Sources, Preparing a Bibliography

48a Choose a variety of sources appropriate to your topic

Good research projects use a variety of sources that provide different kinds of information and differing viewpoints. As you begin a search for sources, consider what will meet your needs.

1 Locating primary and secondary sources

Primary sources provide the raw materials of a subject, unfiltered and unexplained. Charlotte Perkins Gilman's story "The Yellow Wall-Paper," like all literary works, is a primary source. So are statistics about visits to America's national parks. So, too, are interviews, eyewitness accounts, personal papers, court records, news stories, and the results of surveys and experiments. Part of your work as a researcher is to give raw materials the evaluation and explanation that will make them meaningful.

Secondary sources explain, interpret, and support opinions. A scholar's essay interpreting "The Yellow Wall-Paper" is a secondary source, as is an essay proving the damage caused to national park environments by large numbers of park visitors. Secondary sources use primary source information to help fulfill their purposes.

In your research, you'll use both kinds of sources, perhaps secondary more than primary. But whenever possible, use primary sources to form your own opinions.

2 Locating balanced sources

If you've chosen a controversial topic, look for sources to represent all sides. The best correction for undue bias in one source—which you may not see if you read only one side of an issue—is a voice from the other side. Divide your research among competing opinions. Read those you disagree with as well as those you agree with. You'll end up with a fairer, clearer presentation of your topic and opinions.

3 Locating electronic sources

With the rapid development of computer technology, a vast number of sources are now available electronically. CD-ROM publications will, among other things, provide you with reference sources, indexes such as the *Academic Index,* and encyclopedias such as *Encarta.* Sources available through a computer network and modem include electronic books and periodicals, government documents and information services, scientific and meteorological databases, business documents, announcements by special-interest organizations, mailing lists, and personal communications. There are electronic sources for nearly every researcher.

■ 4 Using a checklist of sources

The following list indicates the range of sources available to you. Look it over now, at the beginning of your project, and check off appropriate sources. Come back to the list later, in the middle of your research when you know more about your topic, to identify other sources.

_____ Bibliographies, abstracts, and indexes. These references provide the publication information necessary to locate books, articles, and other sources on your topic. Examples: *MLA International Bibliography, Academic Abstracts, Social Science Index.* Available in print or electronically.

_____ Encyclopedias. General encyclopedias such as the *Encyclopedia Britannica* will provide background information on your topic. Specialized encyclopedias such as the *Encyclopedia of American History, Encyclopedia of Psychology,* and *Encyclopedia of Biological Sciences* provide more specific information. Available primarily in print.

_____ Other references. Similar to encyclopedias are biographical guides such as the *Dictionary of American Biography;* abstracts, almanacs, and yearbooks such as *Facts on File* or *World Almanac and Book of Facts;* atlases such as the *National Geographic Atlas of the World;* and dictionaries.

_____ Books. Indispensable for most academic research, books give the long and broad views of a subject. Classic literary works are increasingly available electronically.

_____ Essays in anthologies. Scholars frequently compile the best essays on a particular topic and publish them together in book form. These anthologies are frequently available on literary and controversial topics.

_____ Book reviews. Book reviews are available in the periodicals where first published, in electronic versions of these periodicals, and in summarized form in *Book Review Digest, Book Review Index,* or *Current Book Review Citations.* Check these sources to evaluate a book's quality.

_____ Articles. Periodical articles are often more current and focused than books. When possible, rely on scholarly articles in academic journals, written by experts for experts, instead of articles in popular

magazines, written for general audiences. Available in print and
electronically.

_____ Newspapers. Complete editions of major newspapers such as the
New York Times are available at your library in microfilm form.
Daily editions are available electronically. Individual news stories
from local newspapers are available through *Newsbank,* available
on CD-ROM.

_____ Government documents. Government sources contain legislative
and judicial information, scientific reports, statistics, cultural and
historical information, recreational and health information, and
practical how-to information. Available in print and electronically.

_____ Archival materials. Most libraries have special collections of letters,
diaries, rare books, and local historical materials.

_____ Audiovisual materials. Maps, charts, photos of visual art, films,
musical recordings, tapes, or recorded television and radio programs may be appropriate for your topic. Many are available both
in print and electronically.

_____ Special online sources. E-mail, computer bulletin boards, news
group subscription services, and discussion groups may provide
you with expert or personal sources of information. Use these
sources with care. (See 49a3.)

_____ Businesses, government agencies, and other organizations. Businesses and other special-interest organizations may provide you
with print or electronic sources of information related to your
topic, or experts to interview.

_____ Surveys and interviews. You may develop your own sources of information by conducting interviews or surveys.

48*b* To identify sources, follow a systematic search strategy

■ 1 Following general search guidelines

■ Consulting reference librarians. Whenever you have a research question you can't answer on your own, turn to reference librarians. They
are experts on the library and research.

■ Listing key words. List key words for your topic that you'll
use to search for sources. For example, key words for research
on Charlotte Perkins Gilman's "The Yellow Wall-Paper" might include her name and the title of the story, *mental illness* (one of the
topics of the story), *nineteenth-century medicine* (another topic), and
feminism (an intellectual movement that considers Gilman's work
important).

- Listing synonyms and related terms. As you list key words, think of synonyms to expand or narrow your search. Research on overcrowding in national parks might use such related terms as *government lands, federal lands, national forests, national monuments, wilderness, conservation,* or *environmentalism.*

- Using the *Library of Congress Guide to Subject Headings.* This multi-volume work, available in your library's reference section, identifies subject headings for the US Library of Congress classification system. Your reference librarian will show you how to use it to identify key search words.

- Expanding or narrowing a search. If key words are not leading to sources, expand your search with more general words, or narrow it with more restrictive ones. A researcher getting nowhere using "The Yellow Wall-Paper" as a search term might expand his search with the author's name. Another researcher, not finding what she wants using the term *national parks,* might narrow her search to specific parks like Grand Canyon or Yellowstone.

- Learning the abbreviations for search terms. Nearly every search tool, print or electronic, uses abbreviations in its description of sources. Learn what these stand for by checking introductory glossaries or Help screens.

- Special library services. Many libraries will reserve sources for you on request or order them through interlibrary loan. See your reference librarian early in your research process.

■ **2** Following special guidelines in electronic searches

- Finding help electronically. Most electronic search tools come with instructions for their use. Look for introductory screens, welcome messages, Help screens, or files with names like "?", "Readme," "About . . . ," "FAQ [frequently asked questions]," or "Formulating a search with . . . "

- Using word variations. In addition to key words and synonyms, try singular or plural word forms, different word combinations (*parks, national parks, government land,* and so forth), different disciplines (botany instead of biology, psychology instead of literature), and truncated words in which an asterisk (*) replaces part of a word (*environ** will help you search for sources containing key words such as *environment, environmental, environmentalist, environmentalism,* and *environmental movement*).

- Boolean searching. A **Boolean search** (named after George Boole, a nineteenth-century mathematician and logician) uses the terms *and, or,* and *not* to expand or restrict a search.

And. If you tell an electronic search tool to look for *national parks* alone and *pollution* alone, it will list all works having to do with either subject. But if you tell it to search for *national parks and pollution,* it will narrow your search to only those sources in which both terms appear.

Or. If you wish to expand a search, use *or.* Telling a search tool to look for *preservation or conservation* will lead to all sources that contain either term.

Not. Using *not* will narrow a search. Telling a search tool to look for *national parks not Yosemite* will lead to all sources about national parks except those mentioning Yosemite National Park.

- Checking accuracy. If you're not getting anywhere, check your typing for correct spelling and accurate search commands.

- Checking abstracts. Some search tools, especially on CD-ROM, include abstracts briefly summarizing sources. Check these to decide whether a source is worth reading.

- Accessing sources. Many electronic databases provide options for viewing all or part of a source, downloading it to your computer, or printing it out as hard copy.

48c
Use library catalogs to identify sources

■ 1 Using card catalogs and microfilm files

If your library uses cards in drawers or microfilm files to catalog its holdings, each source will be listed at least three times according to subject, author, and title. Look for a heading at the top of each card. If yours is a literary topic, look up the author's name to find information about the work you're studying. Microfilm catalogs may permit you to print publication information.

■ 2 Using computerized catalogs

If you use a computerized library catalog, you will be presented with a series of successively restricted screens, beginning with an initial search screen, then lists of subject categories, followed by lists of sources, and finally a screen containing detailed publication and availability information about a single source.

- Subject, author, and title searches. Search electronic catalogs for sources as you would a print catalog, according to subject, author, or title.

- Expanding or narrowing a search. To expand or narrow your search you may combine search terms and use the Boolean operators *and, or,* and *not.* (See 48b2.)

- Partial title or author names. You can search for sources even when you have only a partial title or name. Type in what you know, and the catalog will list all sources with titles or author names that contain what you've typed.

- Checking availability. After you've recorded or printed complete publication information for a likely source, use the computer to check for availability (whether it's on the shelf or checked out) and location (in the main stacks, on reserve, or at a branch library).

48*d* | Use CD-ROM or print indexes to identify sources

Some indexes, like *The Reader's Guide to Periodical Literature,* list only periodical articles; others include books, articles, and other sources. Some list sources on a broad range of topics; others are devoted to one subject area. Be sure the index you're searching lists the kinds of sources you want. For example, in the *Humanities Index* you would probably find few sources about overcrowding in national parks, but you might find some in the *Social Sciences Index.*

■ 1 Using CD-ROM indexes

Many indexes to books, periodicals, and other sources are now available on CD-ROM disks read by standard personal computers.

- Years of coverage. CD-ROM indexes usually cover several years of publication, making them more comprehensive than a single print volume of an index. If a CD-ROM index does not go back far enough for the sources you need (e.g., for literary or historical research), use the print versions of the index.

- Search strategy. Search for sources as you would in any electronic catalog, by key words, title, author, or combinations of these.

- Viewing and recording information. Generally, you can print publication information from CD-ROM indexes, and many will also permit you to view and print abstracts or complete copies of articles.

■ 2 Using print indexes

Print indexes, usually found in the reference section of a library, are issued annually, listing publications for a single year. To investigate what has been published over a number of years, you would have to search several volumes. Search for sources as you would in any index—by subject, author, or title.

48*e* | Use the Internet to identify sources

▮   If you use a computer for research, sooner or later you'll come to the **Internet,** an expanding global information network of more than 4 million computers. It contains many lists of sources and often the sources themselves, which you can read on screen or, perhaps, transfer to your own computer.

To search the Internet, rely on your reference librarian, computer lab personnel, the Help screens that accompany search tools, or one of the many books on Internet research, such as *Navigating the Internet* or *The Student's Guide to Doing Research on the Internet.*

■1   Using Internet resources

To do research on the Internet, use the following resources.

■ The World Wide Web. The **World Wide Web (WWW)** is, as its name suggests, a network of pathways through the Internet connecting "pages" of text, graphics, or sound—whatever can be sent electronically. Because of its size, ease of use, and the kinds of information it connects, the WWW is currently the most popular method for gaining access to and using the Internet. Web browsers such as Netscape, Mosaic, or Lynx will give you access to search tools (often called "search engines") such as Lycos, Web Crawler, Yahoo, EINet, and Galaxy. Because not all search tools lead to the same sources, you should use more than one. *Bookmarks* or *hot lists* (accompanying each search engine) will help you keep track of sources to which you want to return.

■ Gopher. Developed at the University of Minnesota and named after its mascot, **Gopher** enables you to "go for" Internet sources by burrowing through a series of hierarchically arranged menus leading more deeply into a topic. A search tool called Veronica will enable you to identify key words in Gopher menus. Another called Jughead will search local computer networks for you. And Archie will let you search for files you already know exist or look for key words in directories. Bookmarks will help you keep track of sources to which you want to return.

■ WAIS. Pronounced *ways* and standing for **Wide Area Information Service, WAIS** enables you to search for key words in the actual text of documents, thus increasing the likelihood that a document you've identified has information about your topic. You can use WAIS to search World Wide Web and Gopher documents.

- News groups. **News groups** are collections of people interested in a specific topic who share information electronically. You can communicate with them through a Listserv, an electronic mailing list for subscribers interested in specific subjects, or through Usenet, special-interest news groups open to the public. Because participants in news groups may range from experts to anyone with an opinion, the reliability of their information varies widely. (See 49a3.)

- E-mail. Using electronic mail, you can communicate electronically with specific persons. Senders and receivers must have e-mail addresses. Finder programs such as finger, Whois, Netfind, Knowbot Information Service (KIS), and the MIT address server will act like telephone books to help you find the person you're looking for.

■ 2 Using source locations and addresses

Sources on the Internet are sometimes difficult to locate, and their contents are often not permanent like that of printed books or articles. Therefore, you must keep detailed information about your Internet searches. Record this information for yourself and to enable others to reconstruct a search if they wish. (See 52b3 for Modern Language Association citation formats and 54c3 for American Psychological Association formats.)

- Bookmarks. Whenever possible, use **bookmarks** or **hot lists** to record electronic addresses automatically for you. Doing so reduces the possibility of error.

- Publication information. To document a source of information, record the author's name, if available, and publication information for both print and electronic versions.

- The URL, or computer address. To preserve the electronic pathway to a source, record its URL (Uniform Resource Locator), composed of letters, numbers, and punctuation marks that identify the source's address at a specific site. Here, for example, is a World Wide Web address for a national parks environmental group, Save the Grand Canyon:

  http://www.well.com/user/savegc

■ 3 Obtaining Internet sources using FTP

Once you identify and locate an online source, you can read it on screen. If the URL address identifies it as an FTP (file transfer protocol) source, and if your computer has FTP software, you can transfer the source from the host computer to yours to read now or to print and use later. Your reference librarian or computer lab personnel will help you learn how to make these transfers. (Also see Appendix.)

48_f_ | Compile a bibliography of sources

A **bibliography** is a systematic list of sources. You'll use this list to locate sources and, as you write your paper, to document borrowed information.

■ 1   Noting bibliographic information

As you identify a source on your topic, record publication and location information for it. At the beginning of your research, you may simply print this information from electronic catalogs and indexes. Later you'll turn it into bibliography notes written in a format appropriate to your discipline or subject area.

- Writing note cards. If you write out this information by hand, use cards instead of lists on sheets of paper. Individual cards, each with its own source, will be easier to use as you search for titles, add and drop sources, and arrange them for documentation. A shortcut: Divide sheets of notebook paper into quarters, write a citation in each quarter, and cut the sheets into individual slips when you begin searching for the sources themselves.

- Using a computer. If you write with a computer, you may compile bibliographic information in a file that you alphabetize, update, and correct as you go along. You won't need note cards. At the end of your project, you can rework this file to become the works cited or list of references accompanying the final draft of your paper.

- What to include. Note the author's name, title of the individual work, other relevant identifying information such as editor and edition, publication information, page numbers, and call numbers for locating a source in the library. If it is an electronic source, note the medium—for example, *CD-ROM* or *online;* the computer service; the date of your search; and the URL, or electronic address.

- Incomplete information. If a catalog or index does not provide complete information, leave blanks to be filled in later when you have the actual source.

- Documentation styles. As you write bibliography notes, follow the documentation style assigned by your instructor or preferred by the discipline in which you are writing. Use the Modern Language Association (MLA) style for papers in the humanities, including literature, history, religion, and the arts. (For sample MLA citations, see 52b.) Use the American Psychological Association (APA) style for writing in the social sciences. (For sample APA citations, see 54c. For a list of style manuals in other disciplines, see Chapter 56.)

48f dev

- Comparing publication information. When you actually locate a source, compare the publication information on its title page or in preliminary matter with the publication information in your notes. Correct or complete your citation.

The following are bibliography notes for a book and an article. The notes are written in the MLA documentation style.

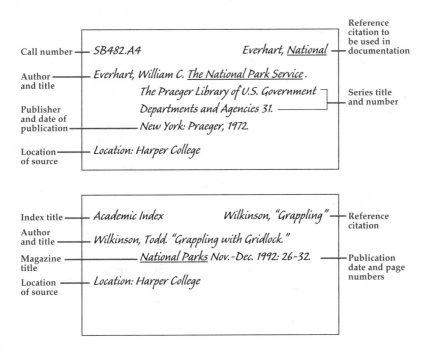

■2 Writing a working bibliography

At the beginning of your research, your instructor may ask you to prepare a **working bibliography** listing all the sources you plan to read. When you've finished your paper, you'll use an updated and corrected version to prepare the works cited or reference list accompanying your finished project.

To prepare a working bibliography, arrange your note cards in the order required by the documentation system you're using and copy your entries on a sheet of paper following the appropriate format. Or, if you've compiled a computerized bibliography file, format your citations appropriately and print them. See 52a for Modern Language Association guidelines and the sample MLA papers in Chapter 53 and 58d. See 54b for American Psychological Association reference list guidelines and 54d for a sample reference list.

49 Evaluating Sources, Writing Research Notes

49a | Evaluate your source

■ As you gather information from your sources, evaluate them for their appropriateness and quality. Not all will be of equal value. Some may not suit your purposes; others may be flawed or unreliable.

■1 Evaluating appropriateness

To decide whether a source suits your purposes, read introductions and abstracts, study chapter headings in tables of contents, look for key words in indexes, read book reviews. Then answer these questions:

- Does this source have the information I need? Does it suit my purposes (to report, explain, evaluate, or persuade)?

- Who is its audience? Experts or general readers? Is it written at a level appropriate for my knowledge and interests? Can I locate, read, and understand it in the time available?

- What are this source's main idea, thesis, and major supporting points? Do they suit my purposes? Will they lead me away from my topic?

■2 Evaluating quality

To evaluate the quality of a source, answer these questions:

- What are the author's credentials for writing about this topic? Is this person an expert or eyewitness? Is the publication source (e.g., a university press, scholarly journal, or major publisher) known for publishing reliable information?

- When was the source published? Is it up to date? Is it a first edition, reprint, or revision?

- Is this source complete? Are there important omissions of information or explanation? Where else should I go?

- Is this source biased? Bias itself is not bad—all arguments are biased. But is this source biased in a way that leads to distortions, flawed reasoning, omissions, or irrelevancies?

■ **3** Evaluating electronic sources

To evaluate electronic sources, answer the preceding questions as well as the following:

- Is this source portable or online? Portable sources, such as CD-ROM encyclopedias and databases, are like printed books and periodicals: their texts are more or less permanent, changing only with the release of new editions or issues. You can determine their value as you would a book. Online sources, however, such as an electronic journal, a news group, or a database, may be published anonymously. Also, they may be updated, revised, or deleted without notification. It is often difficult to determine their authority and reliability. Use online sources with care.

- Where does an online source come from? Clues to its quality may be found in its address, or URL (Uniform Resource Locator). The abbreviation *edu.* identifies an academic site; *sci.* identifies a special knowledge news group; *com.* identifies a commercial site.

49_b_ Follow effective strategies for gathering information

■ **1** Reading for research

As you read your sources, take notes on whatever seems relevant. If you're like most researchers, you'll end up taking more notes than you need, especially in the beginning. The deeper you dig into your subject, however, the more perceptive you'll become about what is right for you.

- What to look for. Look for facts, of course, but also explanations or interpretations, expert opinions, evaluations, and examples that illustrate ideas. A note on conflicts: Take note of any controversies involved with your topic. If you already have an opinion, pay attention to the other side. Use this opportunity to test the quality of your opinion or to make up your mind.

- Where to begin. Before you begin reading, arrange your sources according to difficulty. Read general or introductory sources first, as background for more specialized or technical sources.

- Reading by the paragraph. Finish reading a paragraph before taking a note about something you've found in it. In this way you'll see how the information that interests you fits into its context.

⬛ 2 Gathering information with surveys and interviews

- Conducting surveys. Plan survey questions carefully to avoid personal bias or charged language. Avoid asking "yes or no" questions whenever possible, because they are often not very informative. Guard against overly personal questions that may hinder respondents from answering truthfully. Ask one question at a time; don't combine two or more questions in one sentence.

- Interviewing. Make appointments with your sources and keep them promptly. Be clear about your purposes for the interview. Prepare your questions in advance using the preceding guidelines to surveys; ask clarifying or follow-up questions as necessary. As you listen, take careful notes; doublecheck quotations to be sure they're accurate. If necessary, ask your sources whether they're speaking "for the record" and may be cited by name. Tape-record sources only with their permission. Offer to send them a copy of your completed project.

49_c_ Take notes in an easy-to-use format

⬛ 1 Taking notes on cards

For brief papers involving only a few sources, you can gather information informally, photocopying or highlighting important information, jotting ideas marginally or on a sheet of paper. But if you have more than a few sources and if your paper is longer than a page or two, you'll have to take note cards to handle your information effectively.

- Size. Make note cards easy to sort by using one size for all. Avoid sizes too small for complete notes or so large you may write too much on one card. Buy a package of 4 × 6 inch cards, or make your own by dividing notebook sheets into four slips each. Cut the sheets into individual notes after you've finished your research. A computer note: Make a template for a "Notes" file by creating and saving properly sized columns or boxes. Adjust margins as necessary. Print and cut these computerized notes when you finish your research.

- Length. Generally speaking, the shorter the note the better. Put one piece of information on each card. More than one idea makes a note difficult to sort and organize. When in doubt, divide an idea in two and put each on a separate card. Never write notes on the backs of cards. If you have a long note that won't fit on one card, write _Note 1 of 2, Note 2 of 2,_ and so forth on the appropriate cards.

- Plagiarism. Use quotation marks around all word-for-word quotations. Compare summaries and paraphrases with the original to be sure you haven't quoted unintentionally. (See 50d.)

■ 2 Formatting note cards

Every note should contain the following information, which you'll use as you think about your topic, organize your paper, write it, and document your borrowing.

- A subject heading to identify the topic of the note.
- A reference citation for identifying the source of the note parenthetically in the text of your paper (the author and a short version of the title).
- A page number, if a print source.
- An introduction that provides a context for the note: *who, what, when, where, why,* or *how.*
- The note itself: quotation, summary, paraphrase, or a combination.
- Your comments on the note, if necessary, explaining it or telling how you intend to use it. Here is a sample note card for an environmental research paper based on Aldo Leopold's *A Sand County Almanac:*

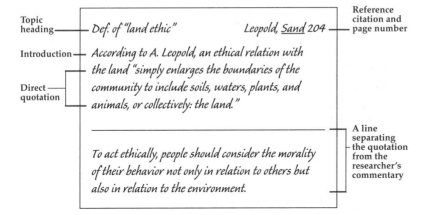

49*d* | Take notes by an appropriate method: quotation, summary, or paraphrase

■ 1 Notetaking by direct quotation

A direct quotation is a word-for-word reproduction of an original source. Quote often but briefly as you take notes. Remember that long quotations may be difficult to weave into a paper and difficult for readers to use. What to quote:

- Key points. Quote passages that sum up a key point in a condensed, emphatic way.

- Expert opinions. Quote sources when they offer an expert's opinion.

- Powerful passages. Quote dramatic, memorable, or well-known passages.

- Subtle ideas. Quote passages whose meaning may be lost in a summary.

- Concise passages. Quote passages whose meaning cannot be expressed in fewer words.

For a sample direct quotation note card, see 49c. To quote effectively, you'll need to know how to use quotation marks (see 38a–d), commas and colons to introduce quotations (see 34g and 36a), brackets to insert editorial comments within a quotation (see 39c), and the ellipsis to signal omitted words (see 39d).

■ 2 Notetaking by summary

A summary condenses an original in your own words, reducing a passage as short as a sentence or as long as a paragraph or a chapter to its central meaning and essential details. Summarize carefully. Your words should not distort the original or drift into direct quotation. Read a passage, look away to write your summary, then check your words against the original. If you quote words or phrases, use quotation marks. What to summarize:

- Background information.

- Commentaries, explanations, and evaluations.

- Arguments or a line of thinking.

- Facts.

- In literary works: description, events, episodes, and lengthy speeches or dialogue.

Here is an original passage about the impact of pollution on national parks and a note summarizing it.

> But scientists at Sequoia and other national parks are finding that forests, though enduring and resilient, are increasingly vulnerable to the influence of modern civilization. For example, plant and insect pests, often introduced by humans, have blighted and killed trees and forests in many parks, from conifers in California to palms in Biscayne Bay. Ozone, a common component of smog, is slowing tree growth at Virginia's Shenandoah National Park and along the Blue Ridge Parkway and threatens the health of conifers in Sequoia, Kings Canyon, and Yosemite National parks.
>
> (Steve Nash and Mike Spear, "Ghost Forest," p. 20)

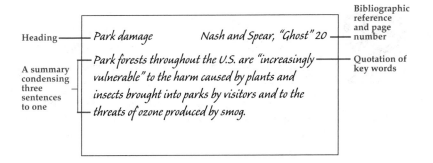

Heading —— Park damage   Nash and Spear, "Ghost" 20 —— Bibliographic reference and page number

A summary condensing three sentences to one

Park forests throughout the U.S. are "increasingly —— Quotation of key words
vulnerable" to the harm caused by plants and
insects brought into parks by visitors and to the
threats of ozone produced by smog.

■ 3 Notetaking by paraphrase

A **paraphrase** restates a passage in your own words and phrasing. Usually about as long as the original, it includes examples and explanations from the original. Paraphrase what readers might otherwise misunderstand. Avoid a word-for-word translation of the original into your words and phrases; that is plagiarism. (See 50d.) If you quote key words or phrases within a paraphrase, enclose them in quotation marks. Here is an original passage about the role the land plays in the natural life cycle and a note paraphrasing it.

> Land, then, is not merely soil; it is a fountain of energy flowing through a circuit of soils, plants, and animals. Food chains are the living channels which conduct energy upward; death and decay return it to the soil. The circuit is not closed; some energy is dissipated in decay, some is added by absorption from the air, some is stored in soils, peats, and long-lived forests; but it is a sustained circuit, like a slowly augmented revolving fund of life.
>
> (Aldo Leopold, *A Sand County Almanac,* p. 212)

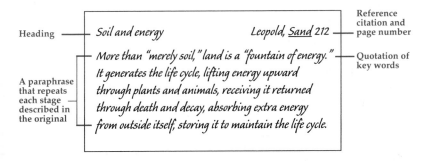

Heading —— Soil and energy   Leopold, <u>Sand</u> 212 —— Reference citation and page number

More than "merely soil," land is a "fountain of energy." —— Quotation of key words
It generates the life cycle, lifting energy upward

A paraphrase that repeats each stage described in the original

through plants and animals, receiving it returned
through death and decay, absorbing extra energy
from outside itself, storing it to maintain the life cycle.

Chapter **50**   Planning, Writing, Using Sources, and Revising

Planning and writing a research project are much like writing other kinds of papers. (See the guidelines to planning, writing, and revising in Chapters 2–4.) The following guidelines will give you tips for meeting the special challenges of research writing.

50*a*   As you finish your research, take stock of it

■ Making planning notes

As you do research, your initial thoughts about your topic and paper will change. That's natural. You should expect to change your mind as the result of new information. To keep your thoughts straight and keep track of changing plans for your paper, write them down in planning notes. What should you write down?

- New ideas. Keep track of your new thinking as the result of research.
- New versions of key questions or statements of your problem.
- New versions of your thesis. Rewrite your thesis until it fits your research. Avoid overgeneral or incomplete thesis statements. A report note: If you're writing a formal report, draw conclusions about the results of your research. (See 61d.)
- Organizing plans. Write lists of ideas or brief sketch outlines to help you organize your research.
- Good lines. Write brief passages you might use to begin your paper, introduce parts, or explain key ideas.

Your aim here is to write down as much as possible about your paper before you write it. The more you write now, the less you'll have to think of later as you write a draft.

50*b*   Plan a communications strategy

■ 1 Organizing

One of the biggest challenges of a research paper is organizing all your materials to support your thesis or, if you're writing a report, to lead logi-

How to Refocus Your Research Project

As you near the end of your research, write the following exercise to help you refocus your thinking and see your project more clearly.

1. I can now state my specific research topic as:
2. My key question or problem to be solved is now:
3. What I've discovered about my topic from my sources:
   a. What did I expect to find? What have I found instead?
   b. What are the controversies? Who agrees with whom?
   c. Which sources are the best? Why? What sources do I have left to check? (Reconsider the checklist in 48a4.)
4. My tentative thesis: "What I want to prove/explain/demonstrate/ show about [my topic] is that. . . . What I mean to say is that . . . " A report note: If you're writing a formal report, say: "My conclusion about [my topic] is that . . . "
5. I now have _____ days left to organize, write, and revise my paper.

cally to your conclusion. Avoid organizing source by source, one after another. Your paper is about the point you want to make, not about your sources. Its design should support that point and reflect the logic of your thought. Here are organizing patterns traditionally used by researchers. See whether one is right for you.

- Thesis support. State your thesis early and then support it systematically, point by point.

- Classical organizing patterns. Arrange your ideas by *order of importance, classification, part by part (analysis), cause/effect,* or *comparison/contrast.*

- Persuasion. If you aim to persuade readers to change their beliefs or behavior, see the organizing patterns in 58a3.

- Review of research. If you're writing a survey of research, classify your sources into groups, explain their differing views, and then evaluate them to determine the most informative, insightful, and useful.

- Problem/solution. First describe the problem in detail, then pose a solution for it, if necessary explaining how the solution might be implemented.

- Tracing an historical pattern. Give necessary background information and then trace the unfolding of an event from one episode to the next. Be sure to show how one relates or leads to the next. Conclude by describing the consequences of the event.

- Formal report. For guidelines to organizing a formal report see 61d2. If your report will use in-text subject headings, see 46b.

Note on outlining: for a paper as complex as a research project, outlining is usually essential to discover an effective pattern of organization. (See 2c for guidelines.)

■ 2 Planning for readers

Focusing intently on their research, researchers sometimes lose sight of their audience, what their readers need to know and what will interest them. (See 2b.)

- An introduction. Many kinds of introductions are appropriate for research projects. (See 6c1.) Be sure that your topic and purpose are clear from the outset; unless you have good reasons for doing otherwise, your opening should lead directly to your thesis, key question, or problem.

- Illustrations. Plan for examples and, if necessary, visual aids to explain or dramatize your ideas. (For more on visual aids, see 46b2–4.) Think of figurative language, especially analogies. (See 6b7 and 26c.)

- Conclusions. The following are appropriate ways to conclude research projects: warn about the need to act on your topic; pose solutions or make recommendations; show how your topic relates to some larger subject; identify a path that future researchers should take. (See 6c2 for other strategies.)

50*c* Integrate source materials into your project

■ Your paper should weave other people's words and ideas so smoothly into your own that readers feel they are following one unbroken thread as they read. The following tips, based on the Modern Language Association style, will help you achieve this effect. (For tips to the American Psychological Association style, see 54a.)

■ 1 Presenting borrowed material

Generally speaking, present borrowed materials in a four-step process. With practice you'll learn to vary it in artful, interesting ways.

- Step 1: Use a signal phrase. Whenever you quote, give another's opinions, or provide disputed information, write a **signal phrase** to introduce your borrowing. Give the author's name (full name for first references, last name for later references) and, if necessary, his or her credentials or the name of the work you're borrowing from. Use a variety of verbs to signal the original writer's purpose. (See also 13b1.)

acknowledges	admits	agrees	asserts	claims
adds	advises	argues	believes	comments

compares	describes	hopes	objects	responds
confirms	disputes	illustrates	observes	reveals
contends	emphasizes	implies	points out	suggests
declares	endorses	indicates	reasons	thinks
defines	grants	insists	refutes	urges
denies	hints	notes	reports	warns

Critic Mary Beth Pringle **points out that** . . .

Barry Herr, president of Bio-Systems International, **argues** . . .

Annette Kolodny **agrees**: . . .

. . . **observes** Aldo Leopold in *A Sand County Almanac.*

- Step 2: Present the quotation, summary, or paraphrase.

- Step 3: Document the borrowing. Provide enough information about the source to guide readers to complete publication information in the works cited or list of references at the end of your paper. (See the MLA style, 52a and b; the APA style, 54a and c; endnotes or footnotes, 55a; or the appropriate style manuals listed in 56.)

- Step 4: Explain the borrowing. If readers may not understand the meaning or purpose of your borrowing, explain it. Don't assume readers will see what you do or get your message without assistance.

For example:

Signal phrase	The problems created by the popularity of U.S. national parks
	begin with the numbers themselves. As the nineteenth-century
Direct quotation	naturalist and author George Perkins Marsh warned, "Man is
	everywhere a disturbing agent. Wherever he plants his foot, the
Parenthetical documentation	harmonies of nature are turned to discords" (qtd. in Stegner 38).
	Each park has its own "carrying capacity" and can accommodate
Explanation	only so many visitors before their pleasures and the environment
	are adversely affected.

■ 2 Taking credit for your ideas

Occasionally you'll have an idea about your topic and then find that a source has had a similar idea. To take credit for original thinking yet be fair to others, present your source's version of your idea, quoting if necessary, but also give your version, if necessary explaining how yours differs from theirs.

An idea that a writer shares with a source	Where overcrowding is most intense and harm to the environment greatest, officials should adopt the suggestion of former National Park Service director James M. Ridenour and adopt a

Citation of
the source

reservations system for regulating entry ("Crocodiles" 71). This

system need not be permanent or universal, nor operate throughout

The writer's
version of
the idea

the year. It would, however, permit the NPS to reduce the flow of

visitors to the "carrying capacity" of individual parks and give

harmed environments time to heal themselves.

■ 3 Working with several sources at once

Occasionally, you will present several sources together.

- Presenting one source at a time. The standard procedure is to present your sources one at a time, documenting each as you borrow from it, as in the preceding examples.

- Summarizing sources as a group. A second method, useful when sources agree, is to summarize all of them at once, without mentioning names. After the summary, document them in one citation. But be aware that lengthy citations can be distracting.

  Throughout America's national parks, environmental damage from

  automobile air pollution is severe and well documented (McMahon 26;

  Coates, "Threat" 1; Craig 42).

- Selecting a spokesperson. A third method is to select a spokesperson to speak for all your sources. Document the person you quote or summarize.

  As many recognize, the great popularity of our national parks threatens, in

  James Coates' words, "to hit delicate natural resources particularly hard"

  ("Threat" 16).

■ 4 Quoting briefly

Quote whenever you need a source's exact words. But be brief; use only the words you need. More may only mislead. Try to keep quotations to a sentence or less, punctuate them correctly, and connect them grammatically to your own words. (See 38b.) Here are two examples, the first quoting a phrase, the second a complete sentence.

  The cliff faces of many mountain parks are so covered by bolts drilled to

  make climbing routes that, according to Claire Martin, they are becoming the

  "equivalent of artificial climbing walls" (37).

  Most old growth forest has disappeared from the Northwest: "Less than one-

  fifth of the old growth that once covered the landscape of western Oregon

  and western Washington still stands" (Ervin 4).

■ 5 Setting off long quotations

If you must quote more than four typed lines of prose or more than three of poetry in an MLA paper, indent the quotation an inch (10 spaces) from the left margin. Do not indent the right margin or single space. (For more on long quotations, see 38c; for APA guidelines, see 46d4.) Introduce long quotations with a signal sentence, generally followed by a colon. Do not enclose them with quotation marks. Place the parenthetical reference two spaces after the final punctuation.

> Aldo Leopold, in <u>A Sand County Almanac</u>, explains that human beings will continue their harm to the environment until they create what he calls a "land ethic":
>
> > An ethic, ecologically, is a limitation on freedom of action in the struggle for existence. An ethic, philosophically, is a differentiation of social from anti-social conduct. These are two definitions of one thing. . . . A land ethic changes the role of <u>Homo sapiens</u> from conqueror of the land-community to plain member and citizen of it. It implies respect for his fellow-members, and also respect for the community as such. (202, 204)

■ 6 Using the ellipsis to signal omissions

Use an ellipsis (three evenly spaced periods) to signal that you have omitted words from a quotation. (See 39d.)

- An omission of less than a sentence. Use an ellipsis for omissions within a sentence or at the end. The remaining words must themselves be grammatically complete. Do not use an ellipsis before or after fragmentary quotations or for an omission at the beginning of a sentence.

  > Bruce Craig, a former park ranger, argues that "national parks . . . are not able to withstand the daily assaults of thousands upon thousands of visitors without experiencing change or degradation" (42).

  > [The writer has omitted the words *which preserve unique and delicate ecosystems and fragile historic treasures.* The remaining words make a grammatically complete statement.]

- An omission of more than a sentence. If you omit more than a full sentence, place a period before the ellipsis, as in the indented block quotation in 50c5.

■ 7 Using brackets for insertions

Use typed or hand-drawn brackets (not parentheses) to insert your words into a quotation to explain a reference or complete the grammar of the sentence. (See 39c.)

> Nature writer Wallace Stegner believes that "recreation could
>
> be as dangerous [to wilderness areas] as logging or extractive
>
> use" (43).

50*d* Avoid plagiarism

■   When you use a person's words or ideas, or facts that are not common knowledge, you must credit your sources, first by giving in-text documentation and then by listing your sources in a works cited or list of references at the end of your paper.

Failure to document your borrowing is **plagiarism,** a form of theft and a serious breach of the researcher's code of ethics. On the other hand, frequent, fair, and accurate documentation will give credibility and authority to your writing. (For the MLA style of documentation, see Chapters 51 and 52; for the APA style, see Chapter 54. For other styles, see Chapters 55 and 56.)

A note on recycled papers: Many instructors consider it unfair to resubmit a paper in one course which you previously submitted in another. Check with your instructor.

■ 1 Documenting common knowledge

You should always document the sources of direct quotations, opinions, explanations, and interpretations, but facts are sometimes difficult to handle. A fact is "common knowledge" if educated men and women would be expected to know it or when experts repeat a fact or idea from one source to the next without documentation.

That Christopher Columbus first sailed to the Western Hemisphere in 1492 is a fact that requires no documentation. But what should a researcher do with the fact that automobile emissions are damaging vegetation in many U.S. national parks and forests? If many sources cite this development without documentation, it is common knowledge and need not be documented. However, if only one source presents it, the fact is original information and must be documented. When in doubt, document your borrowing.

A note on quoting or paraphrasing common knowledge: If you quote or paraphrase a writer's statement of common knowledge, you must document that.

■ 2 Documenting quotations

You must enclose direct quotations with quotation marks and document your borrowing.

- An original source:

    In Maine's Acadia National Park, needle rot on eastern white pines may be the result of acid fog and ozone pollution moving up the Eastern seaboard from the megalopolis to the south.

    (Steve Nash and Mike Spear, "Ghost Forest,"
National Parks, March-April, 1991, p. 20)

- Plagiarism (emphasized):

    In Maine, white pines are being killed by *acid fog and ozone pollution moving up the Eastern seaboard from the megalopolis to the south* (Nash and Spear 20).

    [Even though this example is documented, the writer has quoted half of the original without using quotation marks. Take care to prevent summaries from drifting into quotations without quotation marks.]

- Fair use:

    Steve Nash and Mike Spear declare that "in Maine's Acadia National Park, needle rot on eastern white pines may be the result of acid fog and ozone pollution moving up the Eastern seaboard from the megalopolis to the south" (20).

■ 3 Documenting key words

Even if you take only one or two key words from a source, you must enclose them with quotation marks and document your borrowing.

- An original source:

    In short, a land ethic changes the role of *Homo sapiens* from conqueror of the land-community to plain member and citizen of it. It implies respect for his fellow-members, and also respect for the community as such.

    (Aldo Leopold, *A Sand County Almanac*, p. 204)

- Plagiarism (emphasized):

    Americans must enlarge their concept of morality to include *a "land ethic"* to guide their relationship with the natural world.

    [Even though the borrowed words are enclosed in quotation marks, the writer has not documented the source.]

- Fair use:

    Americans must enlarge their concept of morality to include what naturalist Aldo Leopold calls a "land ethic" to guide their relationship with the natural world (204).

■ 4 Documenting opinions

You must document an author's opinion or line of thinking. Writers have rights to their ideas as well as their words.

■ An original source:

At the heart of the issue is the fact that the welfare of the national parks is inextricably linked to the lands around them.

> (John Kenny, "Park Boundaries," *National Parks,* July-August, 1991, p. 22)

■ Plagiarism (emphasized):

Unfortunately for U.S. national parks, they do not exist like islands in a sea, separate from urban America and its ecological threats. Their fate is shaped by the lands that surround them.

[Although this passage is in the writer's own words and even imaginatively written, its ideas are based on those of the original source and must be documented.]

■ Fair use:

Unfortunately for U.S. national parks, they do not exist like islands in a sea, separate from urban America and its ecological threats. As John Kenny argues, their fate is shaped by the lands that surround them (22).

■ 5 Documenting a paraphrase

To paraphrase effectively, restate the author's words and phrasing in your words and phrasing. Avoid the mere substitution of synonyms for the author's original.

■ An original source:

In the East, to "waste" water is to consume it needlessly or excessively. In the West, to waste water is not to consume it—to let it flow unimpeded and undiverted down rivers.

> (Marc Reisner, *Cadillac Desert: The American West and Its Disappearing Water,* p. 16)

■ Plagiarism (emphasized):

Americans from the East say they "waste" their water when they consume it unnecessarily. In the West, however, water is wasted when it is not consumed but allowed to flow uninterrupted down rivers (Reisner 16).

[The writer has documented the source of the original but has merely substituted synonyms for the original words and retained the original sentence structure.]

■ Fair use:

Americans define the "waste" of water in contradictory ways. To those in the East, waste means using water unnecessarily, while to those in the West, waste means leaving water in rivers, unused (Reisner 16).

50*d* doc

How to Revise and Edit a Research Project

Use the following checklist to guide your revision and editing. Or ask peer editors to read your draft with these questions in mind and answer the most important. (For more on revision, see 3b and c.)

1. Does the paper's thesis appear somewhere in the introduction? Is it clear and complete? For a formal report: Does the introduction describe a problem or pose a key question?

2. Does the paper include all the information, explanation, and interpretation needed to support its thesis or, in a formal report, to justify its conclusion?

3. Does the paper introduce and explain borrowed materials? Is the documentation complete and appropriate to the discipline in which the paper is written? Are all direct quotations enclosed by quotation marks?

4. Do the paper's ideas make sense and fit together logically and smoothly? Does the paper follow its outline? If not, which is the more logically organized? Would another design improve the paper?

5. If the project uses subject headings, as in a report, are they correctly placed? Do headings clearly identify the sections they introduce? (See 46b1.)

6. Is the language appropriate to research writing: accurate, precise, objective, and appropriately formal? (See 27a and c.)

7. Does the paper include appropriately formatted drafts of a title page, outline page, acknowledgments, or abstract, if required? (See 46c, MLA format, or 46d, APA format.) Has the writer prepared a Works Cited or References list? (See 52a to prepare an MLA Works Cited list or 54b to prepare an APA References list.)

For a sample MLA research project with title and outline page, see Chapter 53.

MLA Documentation

Chapter 51 Writing MLA In-Text (Parenthetical) Citations

For papers written in the humanities, the preferred way to cite borrowed materials is the Modern Language Association (MLA) system of in-text citation. (For the American Psychological Association's author-date system, see Chapter 54. For footnotes or endnotes, see Chapter 55. For a list of style manuals used in various fields, see Chapter 56.)

51a Follow MLA citation guidelines

■ As you write a first draft, document your borrowing at the appropriate places in the text of your paper.

- Signal phrase. Name your source in an introductory signal phrase when you quote directly or borrow an explanation, opinion, interpretation, or disputed fact. Give the author's full name for first references and the last name thereafter. (See also 50c1.)

- Parenthetical citation. In parentheses following your borrowing, provide enough information to guide readers to full publication information in the Works Cited list at the end of your paper. Give page numbers for sources that have paging. Place the citation after the borrowing, following quotation marks, but before the period at the end of a sentence.
  A note on indented quotations: In block quotations, place the parenthetical reference two spaces after the last punctuation mark.

- The Works Cited. In a Works Cited list at the end of your paper, provide full publication or source information for each source you've used.

51b Follow parenthetical citation formats

■ The following guidelines will show you how to match signal phrases with the appropriate citation formats.

■ 1 Naming an author in a signal phrase

If you name an author in a signal phrase and use only one source by that author, cite the page number of your borrowing in parentheses.

Ann J. Lane suggests that "The Yellow Wall-Paper" is the "most directly, obviously, self-consciously autobiographical" of all of Charlotte Perkins Gilman's short stories (16).

■ 2 Naming a corporate author in a signal phrase

Cite a corporate author as you would a person.

> The Wilderness Preservation Society has proposed reservation systems to
>
> regulate access at fourteen national parks (32).

■ 3 Omitting an author name and a signal phrase

If you do not name the author in a signal phrase and use only one source by that author, cite the author's last name and the page number in parentheses. No punctuation separates the author's name and the page number.

> At the present time, vegetation at more than seventy national
>
> parks is severely affected by automobile air pollution (McMahon 26).

■ 4 Citing two or more sources by the same author

If your paper includes two or more sources by the same author, follow these guidelines to parenthetical citation.

- Author named in a signal phrase. If you name the author in a signal phrase, give a short form of the title and the page number in parentheses. Enclose article titles in quotation marks; underline book titles.

> Gene Rose has revealed that during 1991 the National Forest Service
>
> recorded a net loss from timber sales in sixty-nine of one hundred twenty
>
> forests ("Wood Cutting" 35).

- Author and title in a signal phrase. If a signal phrase includes the author's name and title of the source, give only the page number in parentheses.

> In A Sand County Almanac, Aldo Leopold explains the necessity of a "land
>
> ethic" to guide human relationships with the land (204).

- Author and title not named in a signal phrase. If you do not give the author or title in a signal phrase, include both in the parenthetical citation separated by a comma.

> In the Florida Everglades, picnickers have left behind the seeds of 221
>
> nonnative species that are now driving out native species (Coates,
>
> "Threat" 16).

■5 Citing more than one author of a source

■ Two or three authors. If a source has two or three authors, name them in the signal phrase or parenthetical citation.

Campers who show up at national parks to claim the daily campsites may

wait in line for hours (Adler and Glick 48).

■ Four or more authors. If a source has four or more authors, you may give only the first author's name followed by *et al.* ("and others") in the signal phrase or parenthetical citation.

Only recently have detailed proposals been made showing how to

preserve spotted owl habitats without costing loggers their jobs

(Peters et al. 48).

■6 Citing an unknown author

If an author's name is not given in the source, use the complete title in a signal phrase or the first key words in the parenthetical citation.

In Minnesota's Voyageurs National Park, snowmobilers have disturbed the

habitat of the endangered gray wolf ("Shattering" 140).

■7 Citing authors with the same last name

If your paper includes two or more authors with the same last name, include each author's first and last name in signal phrases, or in parenthetical documentation include each author's first initial (full first name if the initial is shared, too) and last name.

Handsome park lodges entice visitors to such national parks as Mt. Rainier,

Yellowstone, Bryce Canyon, and Grand Canyon (James Adams 19).

■8 Citing a multivolume source

If your paper uses more than one volume of a multivolume source, give the volume followed by a colon, a space, and the page number in the parenthetical citation.

Thoreau describes in his <u>Journals</u> how, in the natural world, humans "behave

like oxen in a flower garden" (8: 110).

9 Citing literary works

Provide enough information in the parenthetical citation to enable readers to locate your reference even if they use an edition different from yours.

- Undivided works. For undivided works such as short stories, include the page number in the parenthetical citation.

- Divided works such as a novel. For divided works, parenthetically cite the page number followed by a semicolon and the part, section, or chapter.

> In <u>Light in August</u>, novelist William Faulkner traces the complex
>
> process by which his protagonist's childhood memories are transformed
>
> into knowledge and then belief: "Memory believes before knowing
>
> remembers" (104; ch. 6).

- Poetry. For poetry that has been divided into books or numbered sections, cite the part and line numbers.

> Our birth is but a sleep and a forgetting:
>
> The Soul that rises with us, our life's Star,
>
>   Hath had elsewhere its setting,
>
> And cometh from afar. . . . (5.59-62)

- Plays. Cite modern plays as you would a book, including page numbers. Cite verse and classic plays by act, scene, and line. Use arabic numerals unless instructed otherwise.

> As Othello plots Desdemona's murder, he confesses her enduring power over
>
> him: "I'll not expostulate with her, lest her body and beauty unprovide my
>
> mind again" (4.1.200–201).

10 Citing an indirect source

If you quote a writer whose words appear in a source written by someone else, name the source you are quoting in a signal phrase. Begin the parenthetical citation with *qtd. in* ("quoted in") and identify the source where you found the quotation.

> As historian Kenneth Clark has observed, "Nothing except love is so
>
> universally appealing as a view" of beautiful scenery (qtd. in McMahon 26).

■ 11 Citing an entire source

To document an entire source, give the author's name and the title, if necessary, in a signal phrase or parenthetical citation.

Henry David Thoreau's <u>Walden</u> is the source of many of the attitudes

Americans hold about the value of wilderness.

■ 12 Citing two or more sources in one citation

To cite two or more sources in one citation, separate them with a semi-colon. Be aware, however, that multiple references may be distracting. For other ways to handle multiple sources, see 50c3.

Many who oppose restricting access to national parks profit economically

from that access (Coates, "Comfort" 14; Stapleton 34).

■ 13 Citing an interview

To document an interview, name the source in a signal phrase or par-enthetical citation.

Raymond Marks, an official at Rocky Mountain National Park, reports that

visitors' most frequent complaints have to do with overcrowding.

51c | Include content and bibliography notes when necessary

■ Use notes in a research paper only when you must provide ad-ditional information that cannot be worked into the text of your paper. Put raised numbers in your text to refer readers to a footnote at the bot-tom of the page or to a note on a page headed *Notes* immediately preced-ing the Works Cited. Number your notes consecutively throughout the paper. (For more on the use of notes, see Chapter 55.)

■ 1 Writing content notes

Content notes include definitions, formulas, explanations, and transla-tions that would interrupt the flow of ideas if placed in the text of your paper.

▪ Text:

In 1992, the 53 national parks received more than 58 million visitors, more

than half, 35 million, visiting the 11 most popular parks.[1]

■ Note:

> [1] The parks receiving the heaviest use were Great Smoky Mountains,
>
> 8.9 million; Grand Canyon, 4.1 million; Yosemite, 3.8 million; and
>
> Yellowstone, 3.1 million.

■ 2 Writing bibliography notes

Bibliography notes let you cite several sources at once without a lengthy parenthetical citation, make cross-references, or refer readers to sources relevant to a topic.

■ Text:

> Throughout America's national parks, environmental damage from
>
> automobile air pollution is severe and well documented.[3]

■ Note:

> [3] For examples of this damage, see McMahon 26; Coates, "Threat" 1;
>
> "Haze" 95; "Tools" 14; and Craig 42.

52 Preparing the MLA Works Cited List

52a | Following the MLA general guidelines

■ A list of Works Cited gives full publication information for all sources cited in a research paper. (See the example in Chapter 53.) However, your instructor may ask you to provide a Works Consulted list that includes all the works you've read, whether you cite them parenthetically or not.

■ 1 Placing the Works Cited

Place the Works Cited on a separate page at the end of your paper, after other concluding materials. (See 46c7 for the order of pages in an MLA paper.)

■ 2 Following the Works Cited format

- Title. Center the title Works Cited (without italics, underlining, or quotation marks) 1 inch from the top of the page. Continue page numbers from the text of your paper.

- Spacing. Doublespace before the first entry and throughout all entries.

- Indentation. Begin each entry flush with the left margin. Indent second and successive lines one-half inch (five spaces).

- Numbering. Do not number the entries.

- Alphabetical order. Arrange entries alphabetically according to the author's last name. Use square brackets to indicate parts of a name that are known but not given or to identify the true name when a pseudonym is given: _Eliot, T[homas] S[tearns], Mark Twain [Samuel Langhorne Clemens]._ If an entry has no author, alphabetize according to the first word of the title (except for _A, An,_ and _The_).

McMahon, Edward T. "The Point of a View." National Parks Mar.-Apr. 1992:

26-27.

National Park Service Information Office (Rocky Mountain National Park).

Telephone Interview. 15 July 1993.

"Parks Have Few Tools Against Air Pollution." National Parks July-Aug.

1992: 14-15.

■ 3 Formatting citations

See 52b for sample MLA citations.

- Two or more sources by the same author. To cite two or more sources by the same author, arrange them alphabetically by title. List the author's name for the first entry only. For the remaining entries, in place of the name type three hyphens followed by a period.

Lane, Ann J., ed. <u>The Charlotte Perkins Gilman Reader: "The Yellow Wall-</u>

<u>Paper" and Other Fiction</u>. New York: Pantheon, 1980.

---. Introduction. <u>Herland</u>. By Charlotte Perkins Gilman. New York:

Pantheon, 1979.

---. <u>To "Herland" and Beyond: The Life and Work of Charlotte Perkins</u>

<u>Gilman</u>. New York: Pantheon, 1990.

- Punctuation of entries. Place a period followed by two spaces after each part of a citation:

Author.   Title.   Publication information.

52*b* MLA

- Publication dates. For books, use the most recent publication date. For periodicals, abbreviate all months except May, June, and July.

- Page numbers. For the second of inclusive page numbers, give only the last two digits unless more are necessary, e.g., *1–21, 88–93, 95–121, 141–61, 1198–213.* When a periodical or newspaper article is not printed on consecutive pages, give the first page number and a plus sign, e.g., *36+.*

- Incomplete entries. If an entry is incomplete, use the following abbreviations in the appropriate places: *n.p.* = no publisher given; *n.p.* = no place of publication; *n.d.* = no date of publication; *n. pag.* = no page numbers.

52*b*

Sample citations

■ 1 Citing books

The basic citation for a book:

Author's last name, first name. Title and subtitle underlined or italicized.

Place of publication: publisher, date of publication.

If the place of publication is not well known or may be confused with another city, give the state, using postal code abbreviations. Separate the place of publication from the publisher with a colon: *Springfield, IL: Thomas, 1996.*

Shorten publisher names: Use the publisher's last name (e.g., *Knopf* for *Alfred Knopf*). Use the first last name if the publisher's name includes more than one person (e.g., *Farrar* for *Farrar, Straus and Giroux*). Or use the first key word (e.g., *Random* for *Random House*). Abbreviate *University Press* as *UP* (without periods).

- A book with one author:

Tuchman, Barbara. <u>A Distant Mirror</u>. New York: Knopf, 1978.

- Two or three authors. List authors in the order in which they appear on the title page; reverse the name of only the first author. Use commas to separate three authors' names.

Fogel, Robert William, and G. R. Elton. <u>Which Road to the Past: Two Views of</u>

<u>History</u>. New Haven: Yale UP, 1983.

- Four or more authors. Cite all authors in the order in which they appear on the title page, or cite only the first author, followed by *et al.* ("and others").

Frampton, Merle E., et al. <u>Forgotten Children</u>. Boston: Sargent, 1968.

■ Corporate or institutional publication. Give the name of the corporation or institution as the author, even when it is also the publisher.

American Friends Service Committee. <u>Who Shall Live?</u> New York: Hill, 1970.

■ A book title within a title. If a book title appears within the title of another book, do not underline or italicize the shorter title. If the shorter title is normally enclosed with quotation marks, retain the quotation marks and underline the complete longer title.

Ruland, Richard, ed. <u>Twentieth Century Interpretations of</u> Walden.

    Englewood Cliffs, NJ: Prentice, 1968.

Golden, Catherine, ed. <u>The Captive Imagination: A Casebook on "The Yellow</u>

    <u>Wall-Paper."</u> New York: Feminist, 1992.

■ An introduction, foreword, preface, or afterword. If you borrow from an introduction, foreword, preface, or afterword, begin with the author of the element being cited; then identify the element. Place the author of the book following the title.

Duncan, Jeffrey L. Introduction. <u>Thoreau: The Major Essays</u>. By Henry

    David Thoreau. New York: Dutton, 1972.

■ An author and an editor. Cite the author's name, the title, and then the editor. Use *Ed.* for one or more editors.

George Orwell. <u>1984</u>. Ed. Erich Fromm. New York: Harcourt, 1949.

■ An editor or editors. Give the editor(s), followed by *ed.* or *eds.*

Finch, Robert, and John Elder, eds. <u>The Norton Book of Nature Writing</u>. New

    York: Norton, 1990.

■ An edition other than the first. Include the number of the edition following the title and the name of the translator or editor, if any.

Holman, C. Hugh, and William Harmon. <u>A Handbook to Literature</u>. 5th ed.

    New York: Macmillan, 1986.

■ A republished edition. Give the original publication date before the place of publication.

Roberts, Elizabeth Madox. <u>The Time of Man</u>. 1926. Lexington: UP of

    Kentucky, 1982.

■ A book in a series. Following the title, include the name of the series and series number.

Howard, Lillie. <u>Zora Neale Hurston</u>. Twayne's United States Author Ser. 381.

    Boston: Twayne, 1980.

■ A translation. Following the title, write *Trans.* ("translated by") and the name of the translator.

Camus, Albert. <u>The Stranger</u>. Trans. Matthew Ward. New York:

Knopf, 1988.

■ A multivolume work. Give the number of volumes before the place of publication.

Blotner, Joseph. <u>Faulkner: A Biography</u>. 2 vols. New York: Random, 1976.

■ A volume in a series. If you borrow from only one volume of a multi-volume series, give its number and the series to which it belongs (following *of*) before the place of publication. Give the total number of volumes following the date of publication.

Durrell, Lawrence. <u>Mountolive</u>. New York: Dutton, 1959. Vol. 3 of <u>The</u>

<u>Alexandria Quartet</u>. 4 vols. 1957-1960.

■ A selection in an anthology. Give the author and title of the selection, followed by the title of the book, the editor's name, the edition if appropriate, and the publication information.

Tolstoy, Leo. "The Three Hermits." <u>Short Shorts: An Anthology of the</u>

<u>Shortest Stories</u>. Ed. Irving Howe and Ilana Wiener Howe. New York:

Bantam, 1983.

■ A selection reprinted in an anthology. If a selection in an anthology was originally published elsewhere, cite the original source first. Follow with *Rpt. in* ("reprinted in") and a citation for the anthology. Original sources are usually listed on acknowledgment pages at the beginning or end of a book or at the bottom of the first page of a selection.

Schorer, Mark. "With Grace under Pressure." <u>The New Republic</u>. 6 Oct.

1952: 19-20. Rpt. in <u>Ernest Hemingway: Critiques of Four Major Novels</u>.

Ed. Carlos Baker. New York: Scribner's, 1962. 132-34.

■ Cross-references to an anthology. If you cite more than one source from an anthology, provide full publication information for the anthology in its own citation. Cross-reference individual selections, giving author, title, editor's last name, and page numbers.

Bone, Robert. "Ralph Ellison and the Uses of Imagination." Cooke 45-63.

Cooke, G. C., ed. <u>Modern Black Novelists</u>. Englewood Cliffs, NJ:

Prentice-Hall, 1971.

Tibble, Anne. "Chinua Achebe." Cooke 122-32.

■ Anonymous or unknown author. Alphabetize the entry according to the first word of the title, except for an initial *A, An,* or *The.*

Sir Gawain and the Green Knight. Ed. J. A. Burrow. Baltimore:

Penguin, 1972.

■ Encyclopedia or dictionary. Give the author of the entry, if any, followed by the entry title, title of the encyclopedia or dictionary, edition number if any, and the date.

"Mexico." Encyclopedia Americana. 1985 ed.

■ Publisher's imprint. If a book was published by an imprint of a publishing company, give the name of the imprint followed by a hyphen and the publisher's name.

Selzer, Richard. Mortal Lessons. New York: Touchstone-Simon, 1976.

■ 2 Citing periodicals and newspapers

■ Article in a monthly magazine. Give the author's name, the title of the article enclosed by quotation marks, the name of the magazine underlined or italicized, the month and year of publication, and the page numbers on which the article appears. If the pages are not consecutive, cite the first page number followed by the plus sign (+).

McAuliffe, Kathleen. "The Undiscovered World of Thomas Edison." Atlantic

Monthly Dec. 1995: 80+.

■ Article in a weekly magazine. Cite the exact date of publication, not only the month.

Begley, Sharon. "The Puzzle of Genius." Newsweek 28 June 1993: 46-51.

■ Article in a journal paged by volume. For scholarly journals paged consecutively throughout the volume, give the volume number following the name of the periodical and then the date in parentheses.

Rout, Kathleen. "Dream a Little Dream of Me: Mrs. May and the Bull in

Flannery O'Connor's 'Greenleaf.'" Studies in Short Fiction 16 (1979):

233-34.

■ Article in a journal paged by issue. For scholarly journals paged separately by issue, give the issue number following the volume.

Kasmer, Lisa. "Charlotte Perkins Gilman's 'The Yellow Wall-Paper': A

Symptomatic Reading." Literature and Psychology 46.3 (1990): 1-15.

■ Signed newspaper article. Cite the author, title, name of the newspaper, and date of publication as you would a weekly magazine article. If an edition is given on the masthead of the paper, include it in your citation following the date. If each section of the paper is paged separately, include the section number preceding the page number.

Coates, James. "Crowds Pose Threat to U.S. Park System." <u>Chicago Tribune</u>

21 Apr. 1991, Chicagoland North, sec. 1: 1+.

■ Unsigned magazine or newspaper article. If no author is given for an article, begin the citation with the title.

■ Editorial. Identify the element by writing *Editorial* following the title.

"Turning Nature On and Off." Editorial. <u>Los Angeles Times</u> 6 Sept. 1988,

sec. 2: 6.

■ Letter to the editor. Write "Letter" following the author's name.

Stout, Michael. Letter. <u>Harper's</u> Feb. 1993: 5-6.

■ Review of a book, movie, or play. Following the author and title of the review, write *Rev. of* and then name the work reviewed. Give important information about the work reviewed such as the author (preceded with *by*) or the director (preceded with *dir.*).

Rafferty, Terrence. "Fidelity and Infidelity." Rev. of <u>Sense and Sensibility</u>, dir.

Ang Lee. <u>New Yorker</u> 18 Dec. 1995: 124-26.

■ 3 Citing CD-ROM, computer online, and other electronic sources

Electronic sources may be the same as or differ from print counterparts. Or they may have no print counterparts. Some, especially those available through computer networks, may be updated, revised, or deleted without notice. Take care that your citations of these sources are accurate and complete. If not all of the information required for a citation is available, cite as much as you can find. (See Appendix for more formats.)

■ Periodical sources published on CD-ROM and also available in print. Many electronic sources are published at regular intervals, as magazines are, and also have print counterparts. For these, give the name of the author, if available; publication information for the printed source; the title of the database underlined; the publication medium (*CD-ROM*); the name of the vendor or distributor, if any; and the electronic publication date.

Lacayo, Richard. "This Land Is Whose Land?" <u>Time</u> 23 Oct. 1995: 68-71.

<u>Academic ASAP</u>. CD-ROM. Infotrac. Dec. 1995.

- Nonperiodical sources published on CD-ROM, diskette, and tape. Some CD-ROM sources and those published on diskette or magnetic tape are issued only once, as books are. For these, give the author's name, if available; the title underlined or in quotation marks, as appropriate; the title of the product underlined; the edition, release, or version; the publication medium (*CD-ROM*); the city of publication; publisher; and date of publication.

  "Grand Canyon National Park." <u>The Random House Encyclopedia</u>. 1990 ed.

      CD-ROM. Pittsford, NY: Mycrolitics, 1991.

- Sources available through a computer service. Computer services such as America Online, Compuserve, Dialog, and Nexis make available a wide variety of sources to their customers. For these sources, give the author's name, if available, then the title of the source or information about its print counterpart, including publication date. Follow with the title of the database underlined, the publication medium (*Online*), the name of the computer service, and the date of your access.

  Jones, Jerry. "Congressional Investigations of the Waco Incident." <u>New York</u>

      <u>Times</u>. 8 May 1995, late ed.: B10. <u>New York Times Online</u>. Online.

      America Online. 8 May 1995.

- Journals, newsletters, and conferences available through a computer network. Computer networks such as the Internet provide access to sources available only electronically and also to those with print counterparts. To cite online sources, give the author's name, if available; the title of the article or document in quotation marks; the title of the journal, newsletter, or conference underlined; the volume, issue, or other identifying number; the date of publication in parentheses; the number of pages or paragraphs, if given, or *n. pag.* (no pagination); the publication medium (*Online*); the name of the computer network; the date of access; and, if required, the electronic address (*URL*) preceded by *Available*. A punctuation note: Although bibliographic citations usually end with a period, computer addresses have no period at the end.

  "Gilman Inducted into National Women's Hall of Fame." <u>Charlotte</u>

      <u>Perkins Gilman Newsletter</u> 5.1 (Spring 1995): n. pag. Online.

      Internet. 8 Dec. 1995. Available http://orchard.cortland.edu/

      PerkinsGilmanNews.html.

- Electronic bulletin board and newsgroup sources. To cite a reliable source from an electronic bulletin board or newsgroup, give the author's name, the title of the document, the date the source was posted, the description *Online posting*, the location of the posting, the name of the network, and the date of access.

MacDonald, James C. "Suggestions for Promoting Collaborative Writing in

College Composition." 10 Nov. 1994. Online posting. NCTE Forum,

Current Topics. America Online. 12 Mar. 1995.

■ Electronic mail. To cite electronic mail, give the sender's name, a description of the document that includes the recipient, and the date of the document.

Buss, Pauline. "Choosing a New Computer for Your Office." E-mail to

Joseph Sternberg. 18 Jan. 1996.

■ 4 Citing other sources

■ Pamphlet. Cite a pamphlet as you would a book.

Schubert, John. <u>The Tandem Scoop: An Insider's Guide to Tandem Cycling</u>.

Eugene, OR: Burley Design Coop., 1993.

■ Government publications. The formats for government publications are many and varied. The order of an entry is as follows:

Government body. Subsidiary body. <u>Title of Document</u>. Type and number of

document. Publication information.

If you know the author's name, place it at the beginning of an entry or after the title, following the word *By*.

President's Commission on the Assassination of President Kennedy.

<u>Hearings before the President's Commission on the Assassination of</u>

<u>President Kennedy</u>. 26 vols. Washington: GPO, 1964.

United States Cong. House. Subcommittee on Science, Research, and

Technology. <u>Genetic Engineering, Human Genetics and Cell Biology</u>.

96th Cong., 2nd sess. Washington: GPO, 1980.

■ Legal references. Do not italicize or underline the titles of laws, acts, or legal documents or enclose them with quotation marks; give the section and, if appropriate, the year. With cases, however, italicize or underline the name in the text of your paper but not in the Works Cited.

US Const. Art. 2, sec 2.

Brown v. Board of Ed. 347 US 483. US Sup. Ct. 1954.

■ Published dissertation. Give the author and title as you would a book, followed by the abbreviation *Diss.*, the university granting the degree, the date it was granted, the publisher, and date of publication. If the dissertation was published by University Microfilms, add the order number at the end of the citation.

Smith-Hawkins, Elaine Yvonne. <u>Ideals and Imagination in the Novels of Willa</u>

<u>Cather</u>. Diss. Stanford U, 1984. Ann Arbor: UMI, 1985. 8408359.

- A dissertation abstract. Give the author's name followed by the dissertation title in quotations, the abbreviation *Diss.*, the name of the university granting the degree, the date granted, the abbreviation *DA* or *DAI* (*Dissertation Abstracts* or *Dissertation Abstracts International*) as appropriate, the volume number, date of publication, and page number.

DiPierro, Marianne Elizabeth. "The Utopian Vision in the Works of

Wollstonecraft, Gilman, and Chopin." Diss. U of South Florida, 1994.

<u>DAI</u> 54 (1994): 3737A.

- Published proceedings of a conference. Cite a selection from the published proceedings of a conference as you would a book. After the title of the publication, give information about the conference. Then give the editor's name if available, followed by the publication information.

Peden, Margaret Sayers. "The Arduous Journey." <u>The Teller and the Tale:</u>

<u>Aspects of the Short Story</u>. Proceedings of the Thirteenth Comparative

Literature Symposium, Lubbock: Texas Tech U, 23-25 Jan., 1980. Ed.

Wendell M. Aycock. Lubbock: Texas Tech U, 1982. 63-86.

- Lecture or speech. Name the person making the speech, followed by its title in quotation marks, the name of the conference or sponsoring organization, the location, and date. If not all of this information is available, provide as much as possible.

Fleenor, Juliann E. "Illinois Women: Quilt-Making--History-Making." Illinois,

Beginning with Women . . . Histories and Cultures [Conference]. Urbana-

Champaign. 26 Mar. 1993.

- Interview. To cite an interview you have conducted, name the person interviewed followed by *Personal interview* or *Telephone interview* and the date. To cite a radio or television interview, name the person interviewed followed by *Interview* or *Interview with* and the name of the interviewer.

O'Connell, Edward J. Personal interview. 4 May 1993.

Oates, Joyce Carol. Interview with Terry Gross. <u>Fresh Air</u>. Natl. Public

Radio. WHYY, Philadelphia. 3 Aug. 1993.

Paz, Octavio. Interview. <u>Paris Review Interviews: Writers at Work</u>. Ed.

George Plimpton. 9th series. New York: Viking, 1992. 81-108.

■ **Personal letter.** Cite a letter addressed to you as follows.

Linville, Troy M. Letter to the author. 4 June 1993.

■ **Radio or television program.** When appropriate, identify those involved with the production preceded by the following abbreviations: *Narr.* (narrator), *Writ.* (writer), *Dir.* (director), *Perf.* (performer), *Introd.* (introducer), *Prod.* (producer).

"Hunger in America." CBS Reports. Narr. Charles Kuralt. Writ. Peter Davis.

Prod. Martin Carr. WBBM, Chicago, 21 May 1968.

■ **Play performance.** Give the title underlined, followed with *By* and the author's name, *Dir.* and the director's name, *Perf.* and the leading actor's name.

The Tempest. By William Shakespeare. Dir. George C. Wolfe. Perf. Patrick

Stewart. Broadhurst Theatre, New York. 24 Dec. 1995.

■ **Film or video recording.**

Shall We Dance. Dir. Edward Everett Horton. Perf. Fred Astaire and Ginger

Rogers. 1937. Videocassette. RKO Radio Pictures, 1987.

■ **Musical composition.**

Tchaikovsky, Peter. The Nutcracker Suite.

Mendelssohn, Felix. Symphony no. 4 in A Major, op. 90.

■ **Record, tape, or CD.**

Ellington, Edward Kennedy ["Duke"]. "Harlem Airshaft." The Duke Ellington

Carnegie Hall Concerts. Rec. 26 Dec. 1947. LP. Prestige, 1977.

■ **A work of art.**

Hopper, Edward. Railroad Sunset. Whitney Museum of American Art,

New York.

■ **Map or chart.**

Mt. Rainier NP, Washington. Map. Reston, VA: Dept. of the Interior, U. S.

Geological Survey, 1975.

■ **Cartoon.** Give the cartoonist's name, followed by the name of the cartoon or its caption if any, the label *Cartoon,* and appropriate publication information.

Ziegler, Jack. "The Artist Who Wakes Refreshed." Cartoon. New Yorker

25 Dec. 1995: 106.

chapter 53 MLA Research Project with Title and Outline Pages

The writer of the following project was instructed to include title and outline pages. The paper follows the guidelines for parenthetical in-text documentation and the MLA Works Cited given in Chapters 51 and 52. Marginal notes indicate important features of research projects and MLA documentation. For an MLA paper without title or outline page, see 4c.

Modern Language Association format, with title and outline pages added.

America's Crowded Parks

Center title one-third down the page

by

Eric Martin

Doublespace

English 102

Professor J. Lindsay

April 30, 19- -

Center course information two-thirds down the page

Martin ii

Use lower-case roman numerals for preliminary pages.

Outline

Center heading 1 inch from top of page

Thesis: At US national parks where overcrowding and harm to the environment are greatest, officials should adopt a reservation system to control park use and aid environmental recovery.

I. The popularity of US national parks is increasing.

II. Popularity has led to problems of overcrowding.

    A. Overcrowding causes problems for visitors.

        1. Visitors experience delays and inconveniences.

        2. Visitors are unable to enjoy the views.

    B. Overcrowding harms national park environments.

        1. Indirect harm: automobile air pollution damages vegetation.

Doublespace throughout.

        2. Direct harm: visitors cause erosion and pollution, deface natural sites, and disrupt ecosystems.

    C. Park Service budget cuts will increase the problems of overcrowding.

III. A reservation system is one obvious solution.

    A. A reservation system at the most threatened parks would reduce overcrowding.

    B. Opposing arguments are flawed.

        1. A reservation system is democratic, not elitist.

        2. Free access does not mean use without restrictions.

        3. Opponents make a faulty comparison of public lands and private property.

For guidelines to formal outlines, see 2c.

    C. A reservation system is an effective method to meet the threats to US national parks.

Martin 1

Title centered, double-spaced, if necessary, and typed 1 inch from top of page

America's Crowded National Parks

As historian Kenneth Clark has observed, "Nothing except love is so universally appealing as a view" (qtd. in McMahon 26). And the views Americans seem to love most are views of the forests, mountains, and waters of the US National Parks. In 1992, over 270 million people--a number equal to the total population of the United States--visited the more than 360 parks, monuments, and historic sites administered by the Park Service (National). More than 58 million visited the 53 national parks alone, more than half, 35 million, visiting the 11 most popular parks. Each year, the Great Smoky Mountains and Grand Canyon are visited by the combined population equivalents of New York, Los Angeles, and Chicago (United States 2).

Introduction: a dramatic quotation cited from an indirect source

Part I: Essential information about the topic

These figures have increased nearly every year during the more than seventy years of the National Park Service (NPS) and will only continue to increase. By the year 2010, annual park visits are projected to reach 90 million (National). If these nature lovers were religious pilgrims, their journeys would constitute one of the great pilgrimages in human history.

Double-spacing throughout

The problem of such devotion begins with the numbers themselves. As the nineteenth century naturalist and author George Perkins Marsh warned, "Man is everywhere a disturbing agent. Wherever he plants his foot, the harmonies of nature are turned to discords" (qtd. in Stegner 38). Each park has its own "carrying capacity" and can accommodate only so many visitors before their pleasure and the environment are adversely affected. Such is often the case at many of the most popular parks, which receive the most destructive use.

Part IIA: An expert source's warrant (see 57b2) introducing the first half of the thesis: the claim for an argument

For visitors to these parks, overcrowding means just that, crowds of people instead of nature views. At Yosemite, the roads

Martin 2

Writer's name and the page number typed one-half inch from top of each page

are filled with traffic. At Bryce Canyon, lines of sightseers along the canyon rim block other visitors' views. At Grand Canyon, 70,000 hikers annually trek down its steep sides, and its skies are filled with 400,000 who take airplane or helicopter overflights (Coates, "Creature" 1). In 1993, 90,000 mountain bikers rode the Slickrock Trail outside Moab, Utah, and in northern Minnesota's Boundary Waters canoe area, "the most popular lakes . . . resemble Walden Pond less than a summer camp in the Poconos, with a steady stream of paddlers never out of sight of one another." Those who show up at national parks to claim the daily campsites may wait in line for hours (Adler and Glick 48). Instead of what former park ranger Bruce Craig calls the "national park experience" (43), what too many visitors experience is more like rush-hour in a crowded city.

> An ellipsis signaling an omission of part of a sentence

> Citation of a source by two authors

> Signal phrase citing an author and his credentials

A more distressing problem is the harm such numbers of visitors cause to the natural environment. As nature writer, poet, and novelist Wallace Stegner speculates, "Recreation could be as dangerous [to natural areas] as logging or extractive use" (43). Bruce Craig agrees: "National parks, which preserve unique and delicate ecosystems and fragile historic treasures, are not able to withstand the daily assaults of thousands upon thousands of visitors without experiencing change or degradation" (42).

> Transition to Part IIB: Harm to the environment

> Brackets used to insert an explanation within a quotation

The greatest danger is air pollution, caused in large measure by the vehicles that bring visitors into the wilds. Nearly seventy national parks and wilderness areas are affected (McMahon 26). At Acadia National Park and in Yosemite, air quality is so poor that the parks receive the same pollution warnings as Denver and Los Angeles (Coates, "Crowds" 1). Visitors to Tennessee's Great Smoky Mountains

> Topic sentence

> Examples supporting the thesis

> An author named in the citation because he is not mentioned in the signal phrase

Martin 3

see smog instead of the views; visitors to many other parks
see the gray skeletons of trees killed by ozone ("Parks Have
Few Tools" 14).

A source by
an unnamed
author

Visitors also cause more direct harm. Hikers, horses, and
mountain bikers are eroding trails and causing endangered
species of raptors to abandon their nests (Martin 37). No matter
how far one hikes into the Rocky Mountain National Park back
country, rivers and streams are infested with giardiasis bacteria,
largely produced by human waste (National). In Florida, unskilled
divers destroy coral with their feet (Coates, "Buried" 8). The
cliff faces of many parks are so covered by bolts drilled to
make climbing routes that, according to Claire Martin, they are
becoming "the equivalent of artificial climbing walls." Climbers
have severely damaged park archeological sites in Texas, Arizona,
Colorado, and Utah (37). In Death Valley, off-road vehicles are
destroying the habitat of the endangered desert tortoise (Heacox
75). At high-altitude parks like Rocky Mountain, the feeding of no-
longer-wild animals has contributed to the destruction of delicate
Alpine vegetation, whose seeds are no longer spread by these
animals (Coates, "Threat" 16). In place of natural vegetation
grow noxious weeds and grasses, their seeds deposited in
the manure of passing horses (National). In Florida, visiting
picnickers have left behind the seeds of 221 nonnative species
that now grow in the park (Coates, "Threat" 16). And in
Minnesota's Voyageurs National Park, snowmobilers have
disrupted the habitat of the endangered gray wolf
("Shattering" 140).

Topic
sentence

Citation
of an
author who
provides
more than
one source
for this paper

Unfortunately, these conditions will only worsen. To
handle the growing numbers, NPS budgets have for some
time stressed visitor services over science, preservation, and

Part IIC:
Budget cuts

Martin 4

maintenance ("Report" 13). Currently, there is a 2.2 billion dollar backlog of maintenance needs; 477 million dollars is needed to prevent "serious and irreversible damage" ("Parks Hit" 8) that will be caused if 4,700 projects are not begun immediately ("Report" 13). At the same time, spending on the environment has declined from 3% of the federal budget in 1980 to 1.9% in 1988 and 1% currently (Craig 43). In 1993, Congress reduced the National Parks budget by $48 million; what remains is not enough to provide adequate services and programs ("Parks Hit" 8).

What should be done? The first nonnative American visitors journeyed to what would become our nation's natural monuments attracted by their wonders and beauties (Stegner 40). In 1916, the National Park Act set aside these "pleasuring grounds" for contemporary visitors and "to conserve the natural and historic subjects in such manner as will leave them unimpaired for the enjoyment of future generations." But many of America's national parks have been so severely damaged and the funds to repair the damage are so few that the promise of the National Parks Act is being broken. Many reforms are needed to rescue our parks from the excess of adoration they have received. But one would specifically meet the problem of overcrowding: Where overcrowding and harm to the environment are greatest, officials should adopt the suggestion of former NPS director James M. Ridenour and adopt a reservation system for regulating entry ("Crocodiles" 71). Such a system need not be permanent or universal, nor operate throughout the year. It would, however, allow officials to reduce the flow of visitors to the "carrying capacity" of individual parks and give harmed environments time to heal themselves.

Margin annotations:

Transition to Part III: The solution

A warrant (a federal law) that requires action to solve the problem

Part IIIA: The second half of the writer's thesis: a claim proposing action

Martin 5

Opponents argue that such a system is "elitist environmentalism" and that government lands belong to all tax-paying Americans. But such arguments spring from opponents like former Tucson mayor Don Hummel, a national park hotel operator, and others who benefit economically from unrestricted access to federal lands and their natural resources (Coates, "Comforts" 14). What they do not admit is that the environments providing them with profits are being destroyed by their actions, that a reservations system is the simplest method for preventing damage to the parks, and that it is a democratic system applying equally to all, first come, first served.

> Part IIIB: A rebuttal of opposing arguments: opponents' self-interest and the negative consequences of their actions

Freedom involves responsibilities. It is time for Americans to take what Aldo Leopold, one of the founders of the modern environmental movement, calls the next step in "ecological evolution," an "extension of ethics" into the human relationship with the natural world. As he explains in <u>A Sand County Almanac</u>, what is needed is a "land ethic":

> A second rebuttal of opposing arguments: an expert opinion

> An ethic, ecologically, is a limitation on freedom
> of action in the struggle for existence. An ethic,
> philosophically, is a differentiation of social from
> anti-social conduct. These are two definitions of
> one thing. . . . A land ethic changes the role of <u>Homo
> sapiens</u> from conqueror of the land-community to
> plain member and citizen of it. It implies respect
> for his fellow-members, and also respect for the
> community as such. (202-204)

> A block quotation stating a warrant

> A period and ellipsis signaling the omission of a sentence or more

> Documentation of a block quotation following the final punctuation

A national parks reservation system, limiting admission to environmentally threatened parks, pays respect to the land and to our membership in the community of nature. It is a gesture of cooperation and an ethical act that meets the

> An explanation showing how the quotation supports the thesis

Martin 6

"use without impairment" requirements of the National
Parks Act.

Opponents of a reservation system have fallen into the
fallacy of faulty analogy in a flawed comparison of national park
lands to private property. They reason that just as private land
owners pay property taxes and enjoy rights to their property,
paying federal taxes gives them the right to use government
lands as they wish. But the payment of property taxes does not
convey land rights or ownership to tax payers. And private land
owners are bound by zoning laws restricting the uses they make
of their property. Americans pay a portion of their taxes to
preserve and maintain parks, not as the purchase price of
ownership but as a duty of citizenship. A parks reservation
system is equivalent to a zoning regulation established for the
common good.

A third
rebuttal of
opposing
arguments:
explaining
an error in
reasoning

In a time of crisis, such as during World War II, Americans
have accepted rationing as a way to meet that crisis. Our
national parks are in crisis. If a reservation system--entry
rationing--were presented as a way to meet such a crisis,
park visitors would accept it, especially when they understood
the benefits they would receive from the reduced numbers
of visitors. Fairly applied to all users of the most severely
threatened parks, it would lighten the burdens on these parks,
maintain and preserve the environment, and ensure that the
pleasures of natural beauty that brought the first visitors long
ago would remain to be enjoyed by new visitors when it was
their time to visit.

Part IIIC:
Conclusion,
the benefits
of adopting
the writer's
proposal

Works Cited

Adler, Jerry, and Daniel Glick. "No Room, No Rest." <u>Newsweek</u> 1
    Aug. 1994: 46-51.

Coates, James. "Creature Comforts Taking Toll on Park
    Wilderness." <u>Chicago Tribune</u> 22 Apr. 1991, sec. 1: 1, 14.

- - -. "Crowds Pose Threat to U.S. Park System." <u>Chicago Tribune</u>
    21 Apr. 1991, sec. 1: 1, 16.

- - -. "Parks' Neighbors Buried Under Tourism 'Slop-Over.' "
    <u>Chicago Tribune</u> 23 Apr. 1991, sec. 1: 1, 8.

Craig, Bruce. "Diamonds and Rust." <u>National Parks</u> May-June
    1991: 41-44.

"Crocodiles vs. Condos: Can We Protect Our National Parks?"
    <u>Business Week</u> 20 Aug. 1990: 70-71.

Heacox, Kim. "A Poet, a Painter, and the Lonesome Triangle."
    <u>Audubon</u> May 1990: 66-78.

Leopold, Aldo. <u>A Sand County Almanac and Sketches Here and</u>
    <u>There</u>. 1949. New York: Oxford UP, 1987.

Martin, Claire. "Set in Stone." <u>National Parks</u> Nov.-Dec. 1990: 37-38.

McMahon, Edward T. "The Point of a View." <u>National Parks</u>
    Mar.-Apr. 1992: 26-27.

National Park Service Information Office (Rocky Mountain
    National Park). Telephone interview. 15 July 1993.

"Parks Have Few Tools Against Air Pollution." <u>National Parks</u>
    July-Aug. 1992: 14-15.

"Parks Hit Hard by Budget Cuts." <u>National Parks</u> Mar.-Apr. 1993: 8-9.

"Report Finds Serious Damage to Parks." <u>National Parks</u> Jan.-
    Feb. 1993: 13-14.

"Shattering the Snowy Silence." <u>Sierra</u> Jan.-Feb. 1991: 139-140.

Stegner, Wallace. "It All Began with Conservation." <u>Smithsonian</u>
    Apr. 1990: 34-43.

United States. Dept. of Interior. National Park Service Socio-
    Economic Studies Division. <u>National Park Service Statistical</u>
    <u>Abstract</u>. Denver: US Dept. of Interior, 1993.

Title centered 1 inch from top of page

A source with two authors

Three sources by the same author: alphabetical arrangement, double-spacing throughout

First lines flush left, second and successive lines idented one-half inch.

A source with no author given

A citation of a book

A citation of an interview

APA
and **Other**
Documentation
Styles

APA and Other
Documentation Styles

APA Documentation

Other Styles

APA Documentation

chapter 54 | Using the APA In-Text Citation Style

The American Psychological Association (APA) recommends an author-date style of documentation for papers written in the social sciences. This style is also used in anthropology, the biological sciences, business, economics, education, linguistics, and political science.

54a | Follow APA citation guidelines

■ 1 Citing a summary or paraphrase

To summarize or paraphrase a source, use a signal phrase containing the author's last name followed by the publication date in parentheses, or include the author's name and the date in parentheses at the end of the borrowed material, preceding the period.

- Author and date preceding the borrowing:

  Sanchez (1993) reported that students from small, often rural schools do not fare as well on standardized tests as students from urban areas with large economic bases.

- Author and date in parentheses following the borrowing. Use a comma between items in parentheses.

  Students from small, often rural schools do not fare as well on standardized tests as students from urban areas with large economic bases (Sanchez, 1993).

■ 2 Citing a quotation or specific reference

To quote directly or refer to a specific part of a source, include page numbers in the parenthetical citation, preceded by *p.* or *pp.* ("page" or "pages").

  In its statistical sense used in standardized testing, bias refers to "constant or systematic error as opposed to chance errors" (Anastasi, 1988, p. 194).

■ 3 Citing authors' names

- A source by one author. Follow the examples given in 54a1 and 2.

- A source by two authors. For a source by two authors, give both last names in all signal phrases and parenthetical citations. In parentheses, join the two authors' names with an ampersand (&).

  Aptitude tests have assisted "students who vary in significant respects from the traditionally academically successful students" (Tyler & Wolf, 1974, p. 47).

- A source by three to five authors. For a source with three to five authors, give all last names in the first signal phrase or parenthetical citation.

  Elder, Lopez, Smith, and Breen (1993) have systematically documented the social bias in standardized tests.

  In later citations, give the last name of the first author, followed by *et al.* ("and others").

  Elder et al. (1993) have proposed greater minority involvement in the design of standardized tests.

- A source by six or more authors. When a work has six or more authors, give the last name of the first author followed by *et al.* in signal phrases and parenthetical citations.

- Corporate authors. Spell out corporate names generally. Always spell out all corporate names in the reference list at the end of your paper. If corporations have well-known abbreviations, spell out the name in the first citation and abbreviate thereafter:

  First citation: (National Educational Association [NEA], 1982)

  Subsequent citations: (NEA, 1982)

- Unknown author. When a work has no author, use the complete title in a signal phrase or the first few words of the title in a parenthetical citation.

  Standardized testing puts students from rural, often poor areas at a great disadvantage ("Opportunity for All," 1995).

- Two or more sources in one parentheses. To cite two or more sources in one citation, put them in the order in which they appear in the references, separated by semicolons.

  (Anastasi, 1988; "Test Bias," 43; Tyler & Wolfe, 1974)

  If two or more sources are by the same author, give the author's last name once followed by the dates of publication in chronological order.

  (Anastasi, 1988, 1991)

- Authors with the same last name. When two or more authors have the same last name, include initials in all signal phrases and parenthetical citations:

(G. B. Dukes, 1991)

(L. K. Dukes, 1989)

- Personal communication. To cite personal communication such as a letter or e-mail, give the author's initial(s) and last name, followed by the words *personal communication* and the date.

  W. Hine (personal communication, October 8, 1995) has proposed three

  reforms for standardized tests.

Prepare the APA reference list

■ 1 Placement of the reference list

On a separate page at the end of your paper headed *References,* give full bibliographic information for your sources. See the sample citations in 54c and a complete reference list at the end of the sample research project in 54d.

■ 2 Reference list format

- Alphabetical order. Arrange entries in alphabetical order according to the last names of first authors or corporate names. If the author is not given, alphabetize by the first word of the title, except *A, An,* and *The.*

- Two or more works by one author. If you use two or more works by the same author, arrange them by date of publication, with the earliest first.

- Indentation. Do not indent the first line of an entry. Indent following lines up to one-half inch (three to five spaces). A note: In projects sent to APA journals for publication, first lines are indented and successive lines typed flush left. If you are uncertain which format to use, see your instructor.

- Spacing. Doublespace throughout, unless instructed to singlespace within an entry.

■ 3 Citation formats

- Author names. For all author names, write the last name first and then first name initials. With two or more authors, use the ampersand (&) instead of *and*; separate three or more names with commas. Write all authors' names; do not use *et al.*

- Date of publication. Put the date of publication in parentheses following the author's name.

- Punctuation. Space once after punctuation within an entry. Underline periods and commas following the titles of books, the names of periodicals, and volume numbers.

- Capitalization. Except for proper nouns, capitalize only the first word of article and book titles and the first word following a colon:

  Article: "Pollution damage in America's national forests"

  Book: National park environments: An ecological guide

  Capitalize the names of periodicals as you would ordinarily.

- Quotation marks and underlining. Do not enclose article titles in quotation marks. Underline book titles and the names of periodicals. Underline the volume number of periodicals.

- Abbreviations. Use standard bibliographic abbreviations when appropriate: *chap.* (chapter), *Ed.* (editor), *ed.* (edition), *n.d.* (no date), *p.* or *pp.* (page or pages), *Rev. ed.* (revised edition), *Trans.* (translator), *Vol.* (a single volume), *Vols.* (number of volumes), *No.* (number).

- Publisher names. You may shorten publisher names, so long as they are recognizable.

- Page numbers. Write out consecutive page numbers, not *341–44* but *341–344.*

54c Sample APA citations

■ 1 Books

- One author:

  Berman, J. (1985). The talking cure: Literary representations of

      psychoanalysis. New York: New York University Press.

- Two or more authors:

  Mack, K., & Skjei, E. (1979). Overcoming writer's block. Los Angeles: Tarcher.

- Corporate or institutional author:

  American Medical Association. (1990). The American Medical Association

      handbook of first aid & emergency care (Rev. ed.). New York: Random

      House.

- An unknown author:

  Justice: Alternative political perspectives (2nd ed.). (1992). Belmont, CA:

      Wadsworth.

- Edited book:

  Kamerman, S. B., & Hayes, C. D. (Eds.). (1982). Families that work.

      Washington, DC: National Academy Press.

- An edition other than the first:

  Strunk, W., Jr., & White, E. B. (1979). <u>The elements of style</u> (3rd ed.). New
  York: Macmillan.

- Source in an anthology or a chapter in an edited book:

  Hocket, C. F., & Ascher, R. (1968). The human evolution. In Y. A. Cohen (Ed.),
  <u>Man in adaptation: The biosocial background</u> (pp. 237-256). Chicago:
  Aldine.

- Translation:

  Fanon, F. (1963). <u>The wretched of the earth</u> (C. Farrington, Trans.). New York:
  Grove. (Original work published 1961)

- Multivolume work:

  Shepard, L. A. (Ed.). (1991). <u>Encyclopedia of occultism and parapsychology</u>
  (Vols. 1-2, 3rd ed.). Detroit: Gale Research.

■ 2 Periodicals and newspapers

- Journal article, one author, journal paged by issue:

  Kraft, R. J. (1992). Closed classrooms, high mountains and strange lands: An
  inquiry into culture and caring. <u>Journal of Experiential Education, 15</u> (3),
  8-15.

- Journal article, two authors, journal paged by volume:

  Gilula, M. F., & Daniels, D. N. (1969). Violence and man's struggle to adapt.
  <u>Science, 164,</u> 396-405.

- Journal article, three, four, or five authors:

  Nickle, M. N., Flynt, F. C., Poynter, S. D., & Rees, J. A., Jr. (1990). Does it
  make a difference if you change the structure? School-within-a-school.
  <u>Phi Delta Kappan, 72,</u> 148-152.

- Magazine article:

  Gagnon, P. (1995, December). What should children learn? <u>The Atlantic, 276,</u>
  65-78.

- Signed newspaper article, discontinuous pages. If an article appears on
  discontinuous pages, give all page numbers, separated by commas.

  Kilborn, P. T. (1990, December 23). Workers using computers find a supervisor
  inside. <u>New York Times,</u> pp. 1, 18.

■ Review:

> Kermode, F. (1996, January 29). Beat the devil [Review of the book <u>The death</u>
>> <u>of Satan: How Americans have lost the sense of evil</u>]. <u>The New Republic,</u>
>> 214, 36-39.

■ Letter to the editor:

> Levy, P. S. (1993, September 8). Abuse and illness [Letter to the editor].
>> <u>Chicago Tribune,</u> sec. 1, p. 18.

■ 3 Electronic sources

When writers use electronic sources such as those available on CD-ROM or from computer databases and networks, they have the same obligations as with other sources, to credit authors and enable readers to find the materials. For sources with print counterparts, cite the print publication and then the location of the electronic version. Do not put periods after online addresses or electronic pathways. (Also see Appendix.)

■ Abstract on CD-ROM:

> Rubin, D. (1992, May). Cultural bias undermines assessment [CD-ROM].
>> <u>Personnel Journal, 71</u> (5), 47-50. Abstract from: Infotrac File: Academic
>> ASAP Item: 12422735

■ Sources from online periodicals:

> Shimabukuru, J. (Ed.). (1995, February 5). Internet in ten years--essays [62
>> paragraphs]. <u>Electronic Journal on Virtual Culture</u> [On-line serial], <u>3</u>(1).
>> Available: FTP: 138.122.118.1

■ Electronic data file or database:

> National Council of Teachers of English. (1987). <u>On writing centers</u>
>> [Electronic data tape]. Urbana: ERIC Clearinghouse for Resolutions on
>> the Teaching of Composition, II. SilverPlatter [Producer].

■ Computer software:

> Herrmann, B. C., Pointer, R. A., & Vogler, D. E. (1992). PEAKS exambuilding
>> software (Version 2.01) [Computer software]. Eden Prairie, MN:
>> Instructional Performance Systems.

■ E-mail. Because e-mail is not easily recoverable, it is not cited in the reference list. Cite personal communications only in the text of your paper. (See 54a3.)

■ 4 Other sources

- Government reports:

    Chilman, C. (1966). <u>Growing up poor</u> (Welfare Administration Publication 13).

    Washington, DC: U.S. Department of Health, Education, and Welfare,

    U.S. Government Printing Office.

- Source from an information service such as NTIS or ERIC. To cite a
  source from the National Technical Information Service (NTIS) or Educational Resources Information Center (ERIC), include the name of
  the information service and the number assigned to the source at the
  end of the citation.

    U.S. Forest Service. (1992). <u>Leave no trace! An outdoor ethic: A Program to</u>

    <u>teach skills for protecting wilderness environment.</u> Washington, DC:

    U.S. Department of Agriculture. (ERIC Document Reproduction Service

    No. ED 354 112)

- Published proceedings of a conference or symposium. Present the
  regularly published proceedings of a conference as you would a
  periodical.

    Aguilar, A. (1984). Communication of emotion. <u>Proceedings of the 23rd</u>

    <u>International Congress of Psychology, 5,</u> 79-103.

- Dissertation abstract:

    Gilyard, R. K. (1985). Voicing myself: A study of sociolinguistic competence

    (Doctoral dissertation, New York University, 1985). <u>Dissertation</u>

    <u>Abstracts International, 46</u> (12), 3636A.

- Videotape:

    Peters, W. (Producer), & Peters, W. & Cobb, C. (Writers). (1985). <u>A class</u>

    <u>divided</u> [Videotape]. Washington, DC: Public Broadcasting Service

    Video.

54_d_ A sample APA research project

The following report has been written in the APA manuscript
format for student papers (see 46d), with APA in-text documentation and
a reference list. (For more on reports, see 61d. For more about the headings often used in reports, see 46b1.)

American Psychological Association (APA) Format

Page header and page number ½ inch from the top of the page

The Problems of Standardized Testing

Ashley Sheffer

English 201: Advanced Composition

William Rainey Harper College

October 13, 1992

Number pages consecutively from the title page to the end of the paper, including references

Center title, author, and other identifying information

Standardized Testing   2

Abstract

This report investigates social bias in standardized educational placement tests such as the SAT and ACT. According to the most recent sources, such tests are being required by a diminishing number of colleges and universities. Whether expert sources favored or opposed standardized testing for college admissions, they generally agreed that these tests are flawed. They measure only a narrow range of skills; they do not accurately predict student success; and they are biased against minorities, women, students of low socioeconomic status, and students from disadvantaged backgrounds. Recommendations include decreasing reliance on test scores for admission purposes, an expanded definition of academic preparedness, and reform of standardized tests to eliminate bias.

An abstract is a block paragraph of 100-150 words.

Standardized Testing 3

The Problems of Standardized Testing

Each year, out of the millions applying to college, many are
denied admission to the school of their choice because of poor
performance on entrance examinations like the SAT and ACT. Have
these students not done well because they are not as gifted as
those who are accepted? Or have disadvantaged or nontraditional
backgrounds failed to provide many with the skills necessary to do
well on admissions tests? What do these tests measure, exactly?
Are they fair? How well do they predict college success?

(1) Background

(2) History

(3) The Scholastic Aptitude Test (recently renamed the
Scholastic Assessment Test). Among the 127 million students
who take education achievement tests each year, the largest
number take the SAT. First used in 1926, it was developed by the
Educational Testing Service to measure "developed abilities"
(Anastasi, 1988, p. 330) in reading comprehension, vocabulary,
and math. Taken by 12th graders in one of several new forms
introduced each year, it is used for college admissions and
counseling (Dejnozka & Kapel, 1982, p. 456).

The American College Test. Founded in 1959, The American
College Testing Program (ACT) is currently the second largest
testing organization in the country. Overlapping traditional
aptitude and achievement tests (Anastasi, 1988), the ACT
Assessment Battery measures preparedness in English, math,
the social sciences, and natural sciences (Geisinger, Test
Critiques, 1985, p. 11).

Important Definitions

Achievement test. A standardized test measuring what
students have actually learned.

Margin annotations:

1-inch margins; page header one-half inch from top of page

An introduction that states a problem and poses a research question

Headings: (1) primary centered, (2) secondary flush left, (3) tertiary run-in

APA citation of a source not mentioned in a signal phrase

Citation of a source with two authors, names linked by ampersand

Page numbers to refer to a specific part of a source

Standardized Testing 4

Aptitude test. A standardized test measuring "the capacity or potentiality of an individual for a particular kind of behavior" (Nairn, 1980, p. 55).

A quotation identified by a specific page number

Bias. In the popular sense, a biased test favors some test takers and penalizes others. In its statistical sense, bias designates "constant or systematic error as opposed to chance errors" (Anastasi, 1988, p. 194).

Reliability. A test is reliable when the same test taker earns consistent scores on the same or equivalent versions of the test.

Standardization. Preparing a "standardized test" to make it a reliable and valid measure for all test takers. When a test has been "standardized," the value of an individual's score can be determined by comparing it to established norms (Anastasi, 1988, pp. 25-26).

Validity. "The extent to which a test does the job desired of it" (Lyman, 1971, p. 196), whether "a test actually measures what it purports to measure" (Anastasi, 1988, p. 26). If an aptitude or achievement test measures class membership or economic status instead of educational preparedness or achievement, it is invalid.

Results and Discussion

Reduced Reliance on Standardized Tests

Even though standardized tests continue to be popular college and university admissions tools, they are beginning to lose favor, even at highly selective institutions like Harvard and Princeton. College officials state that they are paying less attention to standardized tests and more to the personal qualities vital to academic performance (Elkind, 1991, p. 173). What are the reasons for these changing admissions standards?

Cause/effect organization of the body of the report: The writer examines why standardized tests are losing favor as a method for determining college admissions.

The Skills Measured by Standardized Tests

One reason standardized tests now receive failing grades is that they measure only a narrow range of skills, factual recall,

A topic sentence to introduce a paragraph

and theoretical knowledge (Willie, 1985, p. 627), not such qualities as judgment, motivation, academic commitment, honesty, and altruism. These are the qualities that, according to a survey of 300 teachers reported by Nairn, have most to do with college success (1980, p. 71). Ernest Boyer, president of the Carnegie Foundation for the Advancement of Teaching, indicated that "with few exceptions, standardized testing ends up evaluating what matters least" (Willie, 1985, p. 628).

A quotation integrated into the writer's sentence

Predictive Failures

Perhaps because standardized tests measure so few traits essential to academic success, they are not particularly accurate predictors of it. According to Persell, "considerable evidence refutes the predictive validity of . . . aptitude testing" (Willie, 1985, p. 626). Even the Educational Testing Service admitted that the correlations between some ETS tests and academic success are "near zero" (Nairn, 1980, p. 63). Anastasi noted that "high school grades can predict college grades as well as most tests or slightly better. When test scores are combined with high school grades, however, the prediction of college performance is slightly improved" (1988, p. 331).

An ellipsis to signal omission of part of a sentence

Author named in a signal phrase; verb in past tense (*noted*)

Bias

A third cause of the decline in popularity of standardized tests is their bias against test takers who might be considered "different." Nairn showed that among those taking the SAT, "the more money a person's family makes, the higher that person tends to score . . . ; people from white collar homes tend to score higher than people from blue collar homes" (1980, p. 200). The reason is that tests designed by members of a particular group tend to favor that group. Lyman explained that "because tests are usually developed by upper-middle-class people who have

A topic sentence that introduces a multipara- graph section

An ellipsis followed by a semicolon to complete a grammatical unit

Standardized Testing 6

upper-middle-class criteria in mind, the tests naturally are most likely to favor the upper- and upper-middle-class groups" (1971, p. 165).

Involved with this economic bias, both as symptom and result, are ethnic, gender, and geographic bias. Williams claimed that the culture in which a person lives may penalize him or her when it comes to achievement or aptitude tests (1970, p. 15), and the evidence seems to support him. Steelman and Powell discovered that "the composition by sex, the composition by race, and the average family income of the test-taking population . . . affected state averages" of scores (1985, p. 604). And Sanchez (1993) reported that students from small, often rural schools lacking economic and educational resources do not fare as well on standardized tests as students from urban areas with large funding bases and access to a wider variety of educational offerings. "Simply put, states that tend to spend more money on education generally have higher corrected average SAT scores" (Steelman & Powell, 1985, p. 606).

Conclusions

The narrow focus, predictive failures, and significant bias of standardized tests make them unreliable instruments for evaluating students. This fact is recognized by the more than 1,000 colleges and universities that no longer require the SAT or ACT as an admissions requirement. Because such tests contribute so little to our national goal of excellence in education, other schools should follow their lead. Instead of test scores, admissions officials should focus on the achievements and personal traits shown to predict success in college and afterward. As postsecondary education is increasingly required of greater and greater numbers, the emphasis should change from measuring

> The writer's conclusion, based on information and expert opinion in the Results and Discussion
>
> The writer's proposal of a solution to the problem uncovered by the report

students to fit a particular pattern to enlarging the pattern to
accommodate diverse student needs (Gordon, 1974, p. 59).

References

Anastasi, A. (1988). <u>Psychological testing</u> (6th ed.). New York: Macmillan.

Dejnozka, E. L., & Kapel, D. E. (1982). <u>American educators' encyclopedia.</u> Westport, CT: Greenwood.

Elkind, D. (1991, October). Applying to college. <u>Parents,</u> 173.

Geisinger, K. (1985). The ACT assessment. <u>Test Critiques,</u> 11-20.

Gordon, E. W. (1974). Toward a qualitative approach to assessment. In R. W. Tyler & R. M. Wolf (Eds.), <u>Crucial Issues in Testing</u> (pp. 58-62). Berkeley, CA: McCutchan.

Lyman, H. B. (1971). <u>Test scores and what they mean.</u> Englewood Cliffs, NJ: Prentice-Hall.

Nairn, A. (1980). <u>The reign of ETS: The corporation that makes up minds.</u> Washington, DC: Ralph Nader.

Sanchez, C. (1993, September 28). Bates College takes issue with SATs. <u>All Things Considered.</u> National Public Radio.

Steelman, L. C., & Powell, B. (1985, May). Appraising the implications of the SAT for educational policy. <u>Phi Delta Kappan, 66,</u> 603-606.

Tyler, R. W., & Wolf, R. M. (Eds.). (1974). <u>Crucial Issues in Testing.</u> Berkeley, CA: McCutchan.

Williams, R. I. (1970). Black pride, academic relevance, and individual achievement. In R. W. Tyler & R. M. Wolfe (Eds.), <u>Crucial Issues in Testing</u> (pp. 13-20). Berkeley, CA: McCutchan.

Willie, C. V. (1985, May). The problem of standardized testing in a free and pluralistic society. <u>Phi Delta Kappan, 66,</u> 626-628.

Reference list arranged alphabetically

APA guidelines for student papers: First lines of a citation typed flush left, second and successive lines indented one-half inch

A source from an edited book

A book with one author

A radio broadcast

A source with two authors

Other Styles

Using Endnotes
or Footnotes
(The Chicago Style)

Endnotes and footnotes, a system of documentation sometimes referred to as the Chicago style or CMS (after the University of Chicago's *Manual of Style*), are often used in business, the humanities, and the fine arts to cite the sources of borrowed materials. If you use endnotes or footnotes, you may not need a bibliography; check with your instructor. If a bibliography is required, see 55c.

Note: The preferred style for papers in the humanities is the in-text parenthetical system of documentation outlined by the Modern Language Association. (See Chapters 51 and 52.)

55*a*

Choose an endnote or footnote format

- Choosing endnotes or footnotes. Use endnotes unless you are instructed otherwise.

- Numbering. Number consecutively from beginning to end after each use of source material. Do not assign each source its own number. Use a new number for each citation even if several numbers refer to the same source. At the first break after a summary, paraphrase, or quotation, write a raised or superscript arabic numeral outside all punctuation except dashes.

  Charlotte Perkins Gilman described her nomadic childhood as "thick with railroad journeys."[14]

- Placing notes. Endnotes appear on a separate page headed *Notes* at the end of your paper, following the text and preceding the bibliography. Doublespace between and within endnotes. If you must use footnotes, place them at the bottom of the page, four spaces below the text. Singlespace footnotes; doublespace between them. If a note continues to the next page, type a solid line two spaces below the text on the new page, continue the note two spaces below the line and place new notes immediately after it.

- Indenting. Indent the first line the same number of spaces as other paragraphs in your paper, generally one-half inch (five spaces). Make second and succeeding lines flush with the left margin.

- Formatting the numbers preceding a note. The number preceding each note should be the same size as the text (not superscript), followed by a period and one space.

- Making the first reference to a source. When you cite a source for the first time, include complete publication information in the note. Begin each note with a capital and end with a period. Do not use internal periods. Give the author's name in normal word order. For books, enclose the place of publication, publisher, and date of publication in parentheses. Always give the exact page number(s) of a borrowing.

     1. Aldo Leopold, <u>A Sand County Almanac</u> (New York: Oxford University

     Press, 1987), 204.

- Making subsequent references to a source. For subsequent references to a source, give the author's last name or a short form of the title if no author's name is given, followed by the page numbers of the borrowing. This information will allow readers to locate complete information for a source in an earlier reference or in the bibliography.

     2. Leopold, 169.

     3. "Report," 14.

- Making subsequent references to an author of more than one source. If you use more than one source by an author, use the author's last name and a short form of the title in subsequent references to distinguish one source from another.

     23. Coates, "Crowds," 16.

     24. Coates, "Creature Comforts," 14.

- Making a reference to a source an immediately preceding note. Use *Ibid.* (an abbreviation of *ibidem*, "in the same place") to refer to a source cited in an immediately preceding note. Follow with a page number if different from that in the preceding note.

     24. Coates, "Creature Comforts," 14.

     25. Ibid., 15.

55b

Make a full first reference to a source

■ 1 Citing books

- Basic reference to a book. Cite two or more authors in the order given on the title page of the book. Use commas to separate the names of three or more authors. Use *and* before the second or final author's name. For a corporate publication, cite the corporation as the author.

Following a book title, include the translators or editor(s), if any; editions other than the first; and the name of the series, if any. Cite a pamphlet as you would a book. Note that the Chicago style uses complete publisher names (*Random House*) and old-style state abbreviations (Del., Fla., N.J.).

> 1. Barry Lopez, <u>Arctic Dreams: Imagination and Desire in a Northern Landscape</u> (New York: Scribner's, 1986), 104.

- An introduction, foreword, preface, or afterword:

> 2. Jeffrey L. Duncan, introduction to <u>Thoreau: The Major Essays,</u> by Henry David Thoreau (New York: Dutton, 1972), xi.

- One volume from a multivolume work. Place the volume number following the general title. If a particular volume is titled separately, include the individual title following the volume number.

> 3. Joseph Blotner, <u>Faulkner: A Biography,</u> vol. 2 (New York: Random House, 1976), 426.

- Part of a book:

> 4. Anne Tibble, "Chinua Achebe," in <u>Modern Black Novelists,</u> ed. G. C. Cooke (Englewood Cliffs, N.J.: Prentice-Hall, 1971), 128.

- An encyclopedia or dictionary. Begin with the name of the reference work followed by the edition, *s.v.* (an abbreviation of *sub verbo,* "under the word"), and the item cited, which is capitalized if a proper noun and otherwise written in lower case.

> 5. <u>Encyclopaedia Britannica,</u> 11th ed., s.v. "Mexico."

■ 2 Citing periodicals and newspapers

Write out the names of months in publication dates. Do not capitalize the names of seasons: (*fall 1996*).

- Article in a weekly or monthly magazine:

> 6. Sharon Begley, "The Puzzle of Genius," <u>Newsweek,</u> 28 June 1993, 50.

- Article in a scholarly journal. If the periodical is paged by issue, include the issue following the volume number of the journal.

> 7. Lisa Kasmer, "Charlotte Perkins Gilman's 'The Yellow Wall-Paper': A Symptomatic Reading," <u>Literature and Psychology</u> 46, no. 3 (1990): 14.

- Review of a book, movie, or play:

> 8. Terrence Rafferty, "Fidelity and Infidelity," review of <u>Sense and Sensibility</u> (movie), directed by Ang Lee, <u>New Yorker,</u> 18 December 1995, 124.

■ Signed newspaper article. To cite an unsigned newspaper article, begin with the title. When appropriate, include the edition, section number, and page number.

> 9. James Coates, "Crowds Pose Threat to U.S. Park System," <u>Chicago Tribune,</u> 21 April 1991, Chicagoland North edition, sec. 1, p. 1.

■ 3 Citing electronic sources

If a source has a print counterpart, give that information first, and then identify the electronic source. At the end of the entry, include the electronic address (URL) you used to access the source and the name of the network.

> 10. "Gilman Inducted into National Women's Hall of Fame." In <u>The Charlotte Perkins Gilman Newsletter</u> (vol. 5, no. 1) [electronic serial] Cortland, N.Y., 1995 [cited 8 December 1995]. Available from http://orchard.cortland.edu/PerkinsGilmanNews.html; INTERNET.

■ 4 Citing other sources

■ Government publications. The format for government publications follows this sequence: government body, subsidiary body, title of document, individual author if given, identifying numbers, publication information (in parentheses), page number(s).

> 11. House Subcommittee on Science, Research and Technology, <u>Genetic Engineering, Human Genetics and Cell Biology,</u> 96th Cong., 2nd sess. (Washington, D.C.: GPO, 1980), 47.

■ A dissertation. If you are citing a published dissertation, follow the title with *Ph.D. diss.*, the institution granting the degree, the date it was granted, publication information, and page number. If you are citing an abstract, follow the title with a reference to *Dissertation Abstracts* or *Dissertation Abstracts International.*

> 12. Marianne Elizabeth DiPierro, "The Utopian Vision in the Works of Wollstonecraft, Gilman, and Chopin" (Ph.D. diss., University of South Florida, 1994), abstract in <u>Dissertation Abstracts International</u> 54 (1994): 3737A.

■ A letter:

> 13. Troy M. Linville to author, 4 June 1993.

■ Lecture or speech:

> 14. Carl A. Battaglia, "Filmmaking and the Composing Process" (paper presented at the Forty-Seventh Annual Conference on College Composition and Communication, Milwaukee, Wis., 30 March 1996).

- Interview:

> 15. Joyce Carol Oates, interview by Terry Gross, <u>Fresh Air,</u> National Public Radio, WHYY, Philadelphia, 3 August 1993.

- Film or video recording:

> 16. <u>Shall We Dance,</u> prod. Pandro S. Berman, perf. Fred Astaire and Ginger Rogers, 116 min., RKO Radio Pictures, 1937, reissue, Fox Hills Video, Los Angeles, 1987, videocassette.

- Recording:

> 17. Edward Kennedy ["Duke"] Ellington, "Harlem Airshaft," on <u>The Duke Ellington Carnegie Hall Concerts,</u> Prestige 24075.

55c | Prepare a bibliography

■ If a bibliography is required to accompany your project, follow these guidelines.

- Placement. Place the bibliography on its own page immediately following the endnotes or, if you have used footnotes, following the text of the paper. Center the heading Bibliography one inch from the top of the page. Continue page numbering from the notes page or text of the paper.

- Spacing. Doublespace throughout.

- Indentation. Do not indent the first line of an entry. Indent following lines one-half inch (five spaces).

- Alphabetical order. Do not number the entries of a bibliography. Arrange them in alphabetical order according to the author's last name or the first word of the title, excluding *A, An,* and *The.*

> Lau, Beth. "Coleridge's Reflective Moonlight." <u>Studies in English Literature</u> 24 (autumn 1983): 533-48.
>
> Radley, Virginia. <u>Samuel Taylor Coleridge</u>. New York: Twayne, 1966.

- Punctuation. Separate the major parts of an entry with a period and one space.

- A titled part of a book. Cite the pages of the part immediately following the title and the editor.

> Tolstoy, Leo. "The Three Hermits." In <u>Short Shorts: An Anthology of the Shortest Stories,</u> edited by Irving Howe and Ilana Wiener Howe, 3-11. New York: Bantam, 1983.

A List of Style Manuals ■

Every scholarly field has a preferred manuscript form and system of documentation. This chapter presents a list of style manuals for a variety of fields.

- Biology. Council of Biology Editors. *Scientific Style and Format: The CBE Manual for Authors, Editors, and Publishers.* 6th ed. New York: Cambridge UP, 1994.

- Chemistry. American Chemical Society. *The ACS Style Guide: A Manual for Authors and Editors.* Washington: ACS, 1985.

- English and the humanities. Gibaldi, Joseph. *MLA Handbook for Writers of Research Papers.* 4th ed. New York: Modern Language Association, 1995.

- Engineering. Michaelson, Herbert B. *How to Write and Publish Engineering Papers and Reports.* 3rd ed. Phoenix: Oryx, 1990.

- Geology. United States Geological Survey. *Suggestions to Authors of the Reports of the United States Geological Survey.* 7th ed. Washington: GPO, 1991.

- Law. *The Bluebook: A Uniform System of Citation.* Comp. Editors of Columbia Law Review et al. 15th ed. Cambridge: Harvard Law Review, 1991.

- Linguistics. Linguistic Society of America. *LSA Bulletin,* Dec. issue, annually.

- Mathematics. American Mathematical Society. *A Manual for Authors of Mathematical Papers.* 8th Rev. ed. Providence: AMS, 1990.

- Medicine. Iverson, Cheryl, et al. *American Medical Association Manual of Style.* 8th ed. Baltimore: Williams, 1989.

- Music. Holoman, D. Kern, ed. *Writing about Music: A Style Sheet from the Editors of* 19th-Century Music. Berkeley: U of California P, 1988.

- Physics. American Institute of Physics. *AIP Style Manual.* 4th ed. New York: AIP, 1990.

- Psychology. American Psychological Association. *Publication Manual of the American Psychological Association.* 4th ed. Washington: APA, 1994.

- General. *The Chicago Manual of Style.* 14th ed. Chicago: U of Chicago P, 1993. United States. Government Printing Office. *Style Manual.* Rev. ed. Washington: GPO, 1984.

Other
Writing
Projects

VIII. Other Writing Projects

Argument and Persuasion

57 Creating Logical Arguments

In most people's minds, argument involves anger and other heated emotions. But here, and in most academic writing, it is nothing more—and nothing less—than a process of reasoning about an issue whose truth or plausibility is in doubt. In its simplest form, argument consists of an assertion supported by factual information and logic.

Consider, for example, two friends planning a vacation. One says, "If it's real wilderness you want, let's go to Capitol Reef National Park, in Utah. You'll see few tourists, fewer RVs and buses, and no souvenir stands cluttering the landscape. That's about as close to my definition of wilderness as we're going to get." What we have here is a capsule argument (and note that in its classic definition an argument requires only one participant):

- Assertion. "If it's real wilderness you want, let's go to Capitol Reef National Park, in Utah."

- Factual information. Capitol Reef has "few tourists, fewer RVs and buses, and no souvenir stands cluttering the landscape."

- Logic. A definition of wilderness shows that the factual information supports the assertion.

As you will see in this chapter, this process of reasoning in its more fully developed form is a feature of many kinds of writing you do, in school, on the job, in public. In essays, reports, business writing, and elsewhere, it provides a way to determine the truth, make sound judgments, and decide on the best course of action.

57a

Write arguable claims

■ 1 Identifying the point of an argument

An argument begins when someone makes an assertion—a claim—needing support before others will accept it. Like the thesis of an essay, a **claim** is the point of an argument, what it is all about. Just as the contents of an essay provide support for the thesis, the factual information and logic of an argument provide support for the claim. There are four kinds of claims. Knowing what they assert will help you see how to support them.

- Factual claims. A **factual claim** asserts that something about a subject is true or plausible. For example: _Standardized achievement tests are biased against racial minorities, the poor, and rural students._ The subject of this claim is _standardized tests._ The claim asserts that these tests are biased. To prove the truth of this claim, an argument would have to provide factual information about standardized test scores and logic showing that these scores reveal bias.

- Cause/effect claims. A **cause/effect claim** makes an assertion about the causes of an effect or, conversely, the effects resulting from a cause. For example: _Television advertising targeted to children raises unattainable expectations and promotes their unhappiness._ This claim asserts that a cause, television advertising, has two effects on children. An argument supporting it would have to show that young viewers of television advertising are affected in these ways.

- Value judgments. A **value judgment** is a claim that evaluates a subject for its usefulness, beauty, desirability, or rightness or wrongness. For example: _The Dynacomp Personal Computer has the internal memory, disk space, and speed to meet the needs of most college students._ An argument supporting this evaluation of a computer's usefulness would have to present information about the needs of college students and then show that the features of this computer meet those needs.

- Proposals. A **proposal** is a claim advocating a course of action or a policy. It may assert a need for action, the benefits of action, or both. For example: _To protect endangered park environments, the National Park Service should begin restricting admissions at parks most threatened by visitor overcrowding._ An argument supporting this proposal would have to show a need for action with information about the conditions of national parks, the benefits of reduced park use, and the practicality of restricting admission.

■2 Writing a tentative claim

When you have a project requiring an argument, begin by writing a tentative claim that you hope to support. Write it as you would a tentative thesis, using the formula _My point is that. . . ._ (See 1e.)

> My point is that bilingual education is the most effective and economical method for teaching English to nonnative speakers.

As you gather support for your claim, revise the claim to fit that support. Later, as you write the actual argument, remove the formula phrase. For example: _Bilingual education is the most effective and economical method for teaching English to nonnative speakers._

■ 3 Converting a tentative claim to an arguable assertion

As you write a claim, make it an arguable assertion, one whose truth or plausibility is in doubt but which can be supported by factual information and logic. Follow these guidelines.

- Avoid subjective assertions of personal preference. An arguable claim is more than an expression of personal preference or taste.

  Our   so overcrowded that visitor enjoyment and the environment are suffering.
  I think our national parks are too crowded.

  [The original claim may have meant only that the writer doesn't like all those others visiting national parks. The revision makes a value judgment claim that can be supported by factual information and logic.]

- Avoid easily verifiable statements of fact. Statements that are obviously true or easily shown to be true do not require argument.

  killing the forests of many national parks.
  The smog from auto pollution is as bad in many national parks as in

  downtown Los Angeles or Denver.

  [The original claim is an easily verifiable statement of fact. The revision is a cause/effect claim whose truth must be established by an argument showing that smog is killing the forests.]

- Use exact, specific language. You and your audience must know exactly what your words refer to.

  devote more funds to protect wildlife and restore historic monuments.
  The U.S. Park Service must act now to save the treasures of our national

  parks.

  [The meaning of the words *save* and *treasures* is imprecise and vague. The revision makes a proposal in which the subject of the argument is well focused and clear.]

57*b*

Gather two kinds of support for your claim

■ 1 Collecting evidence

Evidence consists of factual information presented to support a claim. (For methods of research to help you gather evidence, see Chapters 48 and 49.) You'll probably collect three kinds.

- Data. **Data** may be facts, statistics, experimental data, research findings, or reliable observation.

- Examples. **Examples** are specific instances or illustrations of the point being made.
- Expert opinion. You may use an expert's opinion based on an examination of the facts as evidence unless it is challenged. In that case, its truth must be established independently.

■2 Establishing warrants

A **warrant** makes a connection between evidence and a claim, showing how or why the two connect. For an argument to be effective, there must be a link, and it must be clear and logical. Consider: Two people are driving down a busy street, late for a concert. As they approach an intersection, the passenger says, "Here, turn right on Highland Avenue. There's less traffic, and it's shorter." In a diagram of this passenger's argument, the evidence is connected to the claim by the warrant, an assumption travelers make when choosing a route.

Evidence: Highland Avenue is the shorter route and has less traffic	**Unspoken implicit warrant:** The best route is the shortest one with the least traffic.	**Claim:** Turn right on Highland Avenue.

In simple arguments like this, the logic is so clear that the warrant need not be explicitly stated. In other arguments, however, the link between evidence and claim may not be clear or more than one warrant may be at work, and people who have trouble following the line of reasoning will say, "I don't see the connection." Consider another argument:

EVIDENCE	CLAIM
During the last fifty years, canals have been dug through the Florida Everglades and vast amounts of water have been diverted for human consumption. The result is that many species of animals, fish, and birds have disappeared, vegetation is dying, and the region is beginning to resemble a desert.	The National Park Service should allocate resources to repair damage to the Everglades and restore the park as much as possible to its original state.

Even if the claim is one you could agree with, it may not be clear why the evidence calls for the action the claim proposes, and so the link must be identified. Here is the way this argument looks written out, with several warrants connecting the evidence to the claim.

> [*Evidence*] During the last fifty years, canals have been dug through the Florida Everglades and vast amounts of water have been diverted for human consumption. The result is that many species of animals, fish, and birds have disappeared, vegetation is dying, and the region is beginning to resemble a desert. [*Partial claim*] Something must be done. [*Warrant 1: an ecological principle*] After all, if the Everglades is destroyed, the surrounding environments will also suffer. [*Warrant 2: the principle of self-interest*] Our way of life may be threatened. [*Warrant 3: an assumption*] Besides, the natural world is beautiful and valuable in itself, and deserves protection. [*Warrant 4: a law*] And there's no alternative, really, because the National Parks Act requires that parks should be preserved "unimpaired for future generations." [*Complete claim*] So the National Park Service should allocate resources to repair damage to the Everglades and restore the park as much as possible to its original state.

Singly and together, these warrants reveal the logic of the argument, showing how evidence and claim are related.

As this example shows, we take warrants from many sources: natural laws (like gravity or photosynthesis), scientific and mathematical formulas (πr^2), theories (evolution), human laws, institutional policies, standards of artistic taste, moral values, principles of human nature, rules of thumb, proverbs ("Waste not, want not"), basic assumptions ("All people are created equal"), and precedent (the assumption that past events may be a guide to future events).

■ 3 Building logic into your argument

As you construct an argument and look for warrants linking evidence to your claim, follow these guidelines.

- Writing a claim based on evidence. If you're unsure what to claim about a body of evidence, ask yourself what laws, policies, principles, assumptions, or procedures apply to that evidence. They will act as warrants leading you to a logical claim.

- Identifying the link between evidence and claim. If you already have a claim and evidence and need the link tying the two together, ask what laws, policies, principles, assumptions, or procedures explain the connection. These are your warrants.

- Stating warrants in an argument. As you design an argument for an audience, ask whether the connection between evidence and claim is clear and logical. If you have doubts, express your warrant or warrants directly in your argument. If you're certain the relationship is clear, they can remain unstated.

57c

Test your argument; modify it, if necessary

■ 1 Testing an argument

Throughout the process of building an argument, check its accuracy, logic, and strength by applying the following tests. Some will apply only to certain parts or to certain kinds of arguments. But the more tests your argument can pass, the more confident you can be that your reasoning is sound.

- The truth test. Is everything supporting your claim true or plausible? Facts must be facts, opinions must be accepted as true, and assumptions must be plausible. If your evidence and warrants are unreliable, you cannot be confident your claim is true.

- Relevance. Do your evidence and warrants actually apply to the case you're arguing? Your support must be relevant to your claim. Evidence about tourist overcrowding in the state parks of Virginia, for example, may not be relevant to an argument about overcrowding in national parks.

- Timeliness. Do your evidence and warrants represent the most recent or up-to-date information? Statistics about the number of visitors to Yosemite National Park in the 1950s are not very useful for an argument about overcrowded national parks in the 1990s.

- Sufficiency. Do you have enough support to make your claim convincing? Evidence for the destruction of forests in Acadia National Park is not sufficient to prove a threat to forests throughout the National Park system.

- Representativeness. Have you gathered your support from a variety of sources—more than just one or a few? Your support should broadly represent the facts of your case. One National Park Service official speaking about overcrowding in national parks will not be as convincing as three park officials, a U.S. Senator, and several park visitors just returned from vacations.

- Occam's razor. Named for a medieval theologian, *Occam's razor* is the principle that the simplest argument is usually the best. What is the simplest case you can make for your claim and still support it convincingly?

- Utility. Apply this test to proposal arguments. Is your proposal practical and workable? How confident can you be that it will achieve your aims?

■ 2 Modifying an argument

As you apply the preceding tests, you may find that an argument has fatal flaws of truth or logic. To be reasonable, you'll have to abandon it in favor of a better alternative. But you may find that although an argument is weak, it can be improved. The following modifications will help you clarify or strengthen your case.

- Citing sources. If your audience may not accept the truth of your evidence or warrants at face value, citing their sources may improve your credibility. In academic writing especially, cite your sources by name and document them appropriately. (For MLA citations, see Chapter 51; for APA citations, see Chapter 54.)

- Adding qualifiers. Qualifiers are words that indicate degrees of strength, confidence, or certainty: *may, must, certainly, probably, necessarily, it is unlikely, as far as the evidence goes, it seems, as nearly as I can tell,* and so forth. Rarely will you be able to argue with ironclad proof and reach absolute certainty. Add qualifiers to assertions to show the degree of confidence you have in their truth or logic.

       may be
Tourists ~~are~~ responsible for the loss of Alpine vegetation in Rocky
         ^

Mountain National Park.

[The original version expresses complete confidence in the truth of the assertion; the revision reflects incomplete or inconclusive evidence.]

- Identifying exceptions. Rarely will an argument apply to all situations, so explain where it applies and where it doesn't by stating the exceptions. An argument that appears to cover many situations when it really covers only a few will lack credibility.

To protect national park environments, the National Park Service

should begin regulating park admissions/ *at those parks most affected by*

overcrowding.

[The original seems to apply to all parks without exception. The revision limits the case to parks needing protection; others are exceptions to the claim.]

- Adding rebuttals. Most arguments have counterarguments that can be made against them. You will strengthen your case if you summarize opposing arguments and answer them with a rebuttal. Apply the tests in 57c1 to discover their weaknesses and describe what you find.

57d | Identify logical fallacies

■ You'll improve your ability to test an argument if you can recognize errors in reasoning, known as **logical fallacies.** The following are the most common.

- **Against the person** (*ad hominem*). Attacking a person instead of rebutting an argument, often through name calling, as in "those weak-kneed, do-good liberals." Attacking a person's character is justified only when self-interest or incapacity may affect that person's ability to argue truthfully or logically.

- **Appeal to the people** (*ad populum*). Appealing irrelevantly to the attitudes of an audience instead of convincing them with argument. "Reelect Representative Hamm! Born and raised here in Pleasantville, in the good old USA, he's a freedom-loving veteran who will oppose every attempt to pick your pocket with new taxes." Evidence should support a claim rather than play to an audience's personal sympathies.

- **Bandwagon.** Arguing that one should accept a claim because everyone else does. Consider: "You still don't have a Dynacomp 68040 Computer? Why, you're the only person in the dorm without one!" The value of a claim does not depend on how widely it is supported.

- **Begging the question.** Assuming the truth of a statement without proof, arguing in a circle. "State U. should drop its literature requirement. So much literature is bad for growing minds, filled as it is with sex and violence." This argument uses as evidence the unproven—"begged"—statement that literature containing sexual subjects and violence is bad for growing minds. Until a statement has been proven to be true or plausible, it cannot be used to support a claim.

- **Either/or.** Arguing that only two alternatives exist when there may be more and, often, rejecting one as inappropriate. "Either we provide weapons for the freedom fighters of Santa Costa, or we abandon them to dictatorship." In fact, there are many kinds of aid one country can give to another. The alternatives in argument are often more than two.

- **Faulty analogy or comparison.** Comparing two subjects that are not really similar in order to force a conclusion. "We must reform schools to make them more like businesses. In business, employees are held accountable for the products they produce. The same should be true of schools, whose product is educated youngsters." Students are more than raw materials to be shaped into products, and so the analogy is false.

- False cause *(post hoc)*. The post hoc fallacy (which comes from the Latin *post hoc ergo propter hoc*, "after this, therefore because of this") assumes that because one thing precedes another, the first caused the second. But sequence does not always signal a cause/effect relation. "Most people who succeed in business wear suits. If you want to succeed, you'll wear a suit, too." Events may be coincidental, or one may only be an insignificant cause of another.

- Hasty generalization. A generalization about a group is hasty when based on insufficient, unrepresentative, or irrelevant evidence. "Walking around campus, I see students with stereo headphones on, students reading comic books or playing computer games, students lying on the grass sunning themselves. Obviously, today's students are illiterates!" A generalization this broad must depend on more evidence than the casual observations of one person.

- Irrelevant emotional appeals. Appealing to emotion rather than reason. "Please don't give us a final exam, Professor Moore. It's been a long semester. We've worked so hard, and we're tired. Besides, you're such a hard grader." Irrelevant appeals to fear, pleasure, or pity (as in the "sob story") are used to coerce, seduce, or mislead rather than persuade.

- Irrelevant authorities (testimonial). Using an opinion that comes from outside that person's area of expertise. Consider political ads in which actors endorse politicians or other ads in which athletes sell motor oil or clothing. This fallacy of irrelevancy attempts to transfer prestige and authority from one area to another.

- *Non sequitur* ("it does not follow"). Making false assumptions based on signs or symptoms. "Fred loves to read. I see him in bookstores and the library all the time. With his thick glasses, he even looks like the studious type. He must get straight *A*'s." These traits do not necessarily signal a person's academic success. The support for an argument must lead logically to the claim.

- Red herring. Red herring refers to the practice of hunters long ago who dragged strong-smelling herring across the path of dogs to divert them from their prey. An arguer uses a red herring when he or she purposely introduces irrelevant issues to divert an audience from the real issues. "Sure, you support raising admission fees to U.S. national parks. You're wealthy, retired, your children all grown. You have no financial worries." The status of the audience has nothing to do with support for the claim. A red herring is a way of ducking issues.

Arguing Persuasively

If the audience for an argument were all like Mr. Spock, the thoroughly rational Vulcan of *Star Trek* fame, a logical argument would be persuasive by itself. But audiences naturally bring their own interests, understanding, and priorities to an issue, which means that they use more than reason alone to make up their minds. To win your audience's agreement involves adapting an argument to their priorities, building their trust in you, and rousing their desire to accept your position.

58a Adapt your argument to your audience's needs and interests

■ 1 Knowing your audience

Arguments often fail because people make cases that would persuade themselves but not necessarily their audiences. As you build an argument, think of your audience and what it will take to persuade them.

- Audience profile. Construct a profile of what you know about your audience. (See 1a3.)

- Audience knowledge. Decide what your audience knows or believes about your subject. Are they opponents or potential allies, skeptical or merely undecided?

- Interests and priorities. Identify your audience's interests and priorities. Where your subject is concerned, are your readers interested in fairness, justice, effectiveness, efficiency, health, safety, pleasure, or some other priority? Do they have a "hidden agenda" about your topic—fears or motives they may be reluctant to acknowledge?

■ 2 Building a persuasive argument

As much as possible, make a claim that respects your audience's interests, needs, and capacities. Be clear about what, exactly, you want from them. Avoid claims that may leave them asking, "So? What should be done? By whom? How?" An effective claim answers these questions.

How to Argue Persuasively

How to . . .

As you build your argument, construct an audience profile of those you want to persuade. (See 1a3.) Be sure to note their priorities or a "hidden agenda" influencing their response to your case.

Write a specific claim tailored to their interests and capacities for action. (See 57a.)

From the support for your claim, choose the evidence and warrants most persuasive for this particular audience. Don't distract or alienate them with irrelevant appeals. Arrange your argument for greatest clarity and power. (See 58a3.)

Decide what opposing arguments your audience may find appealing. Build a rebuttal of these positions, making concessions or proposing compromise where appropriate.

Plan an introduction that will earn your audience's trust. Present your credentials, establish common ground with your audience, create a persona they'll find easy to listen to, and demonstrate your fairness. (See also 6c1.)

Plan a conclusion that will rouse your audience's feelings in support of your claim. Consider an emotionally compelling story that proves your point, vivid description of something having to do with your subject, or a powerful quotation. (See also 6c2.)

Because visitor overcrowding
~~Overcrowding~~ threatens plant and animal life in our most popular

parks,
national ~~parks.~~ *environmentally minded tourists should take their vacations elsewhere.*

[The original claim does not involve the audience. The revision proposes their action in response to the environmental threat.]

As you build your argument, avoid issues that may distract your audience or work against you. For example, if you intended to persuade people concerned with fairness that visits to overcrowded national parks must be reduced, you would probably avoid a quota system as one solution. This audience may become resentful at the thought of being denied access to a park their tax dollars support.

■ 3 Organizing persuasively

Organize your argument for greatest clarity and logical impact on your readers. You can adapt or combine the following common patterns of argument.

- Thesis/support. Putting your claim first, followed by your support, is an effective strategy if your claim is especially strong.

- Emphatic order. Generally, the most emphatic arrangement of ideas from a reader's point of view is to place the most important last, the next most important in the beginning, the least important in the middle.

- Warrants first (deductive order). Begin with the warrants linking your evidence to your claim, follow with the evidence covered by them, and conclude with your claim. This design is effective when an audience may not understand how your evidence supports your claim or when they will accept your warrants without question. If they accept these warrants without question and if you can show that your evidence is covered by them, you've made your case.

- Evidence first (inductive order). Place your evidence before your claim. Use this pattern when your evidence is dramatic and leads clearly and logically to your claim, or when your audience might reject your claim if you put it first.

- The pro/con pattern. Begin by summarizing the arguments for and against a position, follow with a claim that chooses between the positions, and conclude by defending your claim as the best choice.

- The classical argument. Begin with a summary of the problem and at least a partial statement of the claim. Follow with an argument supporting the claim, a rebuttal answering opponents, and a conclusion that makes new appeals or summarizes your case.

- The needs/benefits and problem/solution patterns. First, show that change is necessary. Follow with a claim proposing change or a solution. To conclude, show the benefits of your proposal, explain why it is the best, and, if necessary, explain how to implement it. (See the sample essay in 58d for an illustration of this pattern.)

- The narrative pattern. An argument in story form is most effective when you are offering your own experiences as proof for your claim. But be sure your audience keeps sight of your claim, and remember that anecdotal evidence is the weakest, least convincing kind. If you can add evidence from other sources as you tell your story, you'll strengthen your case.

- Rogerian argument. This model of argument proposed by psychiatrist Carl Rogers aims at building understanding between opponents when no agreement is currently possible. Begin by summarizing your opponents' position fairly in words they can accept. Then summarize your position in words that won't alienate them while at the same time being fair to your beliefs.

Point out key differences dividing you and your opponents, what common ground (values, priorities, interests) you share. If possible, conclude by proposing interim activities to foster relations, maintain communication, and lead to eventual resolution.

58b In your introduction, present yourself as trustworthy

■ An argument may be entirely logical, but if an audience doesn't know or trust the person making it, it will not, by itself, be persuasive. For this reason most persuasions open with what the philosopher Aristotle called *ethos,* an introduction of the person making the case. If you present yourself in the beginning as someone your audience can trust, you'll have an easier time winning them to your position. Here are ways to build trust in your introduction.

- Presenting your credentials. Present your credentials for writing about your chosen subject. What knowledge, experience, or expertise qualifies you? How can you work these qualifications into your opening without seeming to brag?

- Establishing common ground. If yours is a "friendly persuasion," addressed to people with whom you share values and experiences and who are likely to become your allies, plan an introduction that establishes common ground with them. Identify common experiences or values creating a bond between you. Show that you speak their language; create a persona they will feel comfortable listening to. (See 1d.)

- Being fair. If you're addressing people with whom you have little in common, win their trust by showing fairness to all involved, concern for others instead of yourself, willingness to compromise, and respect for others' opinions.

- Building trust in academic audiences. Most academic writing does not require special efforts to build trust. Your knowledge of your subject, fairness, and documentation of your sources will build academic readers' trust. (For more on introductions, see 6c1.)

58c Conclude with suitable emotional appeals

■ Most academic writing has little room for emotion; objectivity is the required point of view. But when the occasion permits—in school or out—you can give an argument additional power by including relevant emotional appeals to audience feelings, which Aristotle called *pathos*. Persuasions often conclude with such appeals. Aim to make your position attractive or your opponents' position unattractive. How to rouse an audience's feelings? Use the following strategies.

- Anecdotes. Tell a moving story that illustrates your point.

- Description. Describe an emotionally charged scene that helps your audience see things as they were, are, or could be.

- Quotations. End with a dramatic quotation, especially a quotation by someone your audience finds sympathetic.

- Figurative language. End with a fresh, vivid metaphor or simile that expresses feeling and understanding. (See 26c.)

A note on irrelevant emotional appeals: Appealing irrelevantly to your readers' feelings, as in a "sob story" or name calling, is a logical fallacy. (See 58d.)

How to Revise and Edit Persuasive Writing

How to...

Use the following checklist to guide your revision and editing. Or ask peer editors to read your draft with these questions in mind and answer the most important. (For more on revision, see 3b and c.)

1. Does this paper have a clearly identifiable and arguable claim? What revisions would make it clearer or more arguable? (See 57a3.)

2. Does the paper support the claim with factual, relevant, timely, representative, and sufficient evidence? Does the paper supply warrants showing the connection between the evidence and claim? What changes will strengthen its argument? (See 57c.)

3. Who is the audience for this paper? Will its argument appeal to their interests and priorities? What changes would strengthen its appeal? (See 58a1.)

4. What has this paper done to earn readers' trust? Consider the writer's credentials, persona, establishment of common ground, and fairness. What changes would increase readers' trust? (See 58b.)

5. What has this paper done to make its case emotionally appealing? Look for moving stories, description, and figurative language. Are they relevant to the argument? What changes would improve the appeal of this case? (See 58c.)

58*d* | A sample persuasive essay

The student author of the following persuasive essay, Eric Martin, wrote his paper in a composition course focusing on argument and persuasion. He first conducted research into the issue of overcrowding in US national parks and wrote a research project. (See the paper in Chapter 53.) For his persuasive paper, he was assigned to use this research in an argument attractive to a clearly identifiable audience. In the earlier paper, Eric wrote objectively about the environmental threats to national parks and the need for a reservations system to regulate use. Here he writes more personally, addresses outdoor enthusiasts like himself, and tries to persuade them to change their vacation plans and, in so doing, reduce the problems of overcrowding in national parks. The general subjects of the two papers are similar, but the differing purposes and audiences have led to distinctly different projects. (See 46a for guidelines to the manuscript form for academic writing. See 46c for the Modern Language Association documentation format used in this paper and appropriate for college English classes. See 46d for the American Psychological Association documentation format.)

On Not Seeing the Forests for the People

An anecdote that dramatizes a problem and presents the writer as an eyewitness

What a disappointment! For months my friend Peter and I had been planning a trip to US national parks in Utah and Colorado. Our high point was to be Rocky Mountain National Park and Trail Ridge Road winding across the summit of the Rockies at over 12,000 feet. The air might be thin and the weather chill, but what views! Snowy peaks. Subalpine valleys. Forests and streams. Arctic tundra. Wildlife. What we didn't anticipate was how many others had the same plans.

Emotionally charged language to describe the effects of over-crowding

Trail Ridge Road was jammed bumper to bumper with cars and RVs. Medicine Bow Curve, the visitor center at Fall River Pass, and the Gore Range Overlook might as well have been New York City at rush hour. I could see the mountains, all right—through a forest of other people's heads, elbows, and camera straps. Peter and I ended up as two of the 2.9 million visitors who yearly stand where we stood and like us, probably, wondered whether there were more people than trees in these mountains. One of my keenest memories is of two park workers straining to lift a barrel of garbage into their truck as the wind sent candy wrappers and hamburger bags scudding in an ugly blizzard across the snow fields. This was the high point of my vacation? Next year I'm doing something different.

Ethos: the writer's values that establish common ground with the audience and establish a warrant

Now, I'm no hermit. People and the pace of city life suit me fine. But from time to time I want something underfoot besides concrete—I long for the wind in trees, wild flowers, colors that are not dyed, the feel of rock and leaf and moss, the sight of animals not tamed into pets. And, like most people these days, I consider myself an environmentalist and believe with Henry David Thoreau that "in wildness is the preservation of the world" (qtd. in Stegner 37).

So my disappointment at Rocky Mountain National Park comes from more than irritation that I wasn't first in line at the sightseeing overlook. Since my vacation I've done some reading, and what I've discovered is that my experience is not uncommon. Our fifty-three national parks, America's most popular nature preserves, are overcrowded and becoming more so each year. In 1992, 58 million people visited them (United States 2), more than two for each of the national park system's 24.6 million acres. This figure will swell to 90 million by 2010 (Coates, "Crowds" 16). Consider the consequences: Each park has what ecologists call a "carrying capacity." That is, each can accommodate only so many visitors before they and park environments begin to suffer. And that is what is happening at the most popular national parks, which are crowded beyond capacity. Increasingly, America's "pleasuring grounds," as Yellowstone National Park was once called, are no longer providing pleasure, and the environment is being devastated.

At Yosemite, as in Rocky Mountain National Park, the roads are filled with traffic ("Crocodiles" 70). During peak season at Denali, finding space on the shuttle bus that takes visitors through the park may require waiting as long as two days (Chadwick 80). At Bryce and Grand Canyon, streams of hikers along the canyon rims block other visitors from the views. In northern Minnesota's Boundary Waters canoe area, "the most popular lakes . . . resemble Walden Pond less than a summer camp in the Poconos, with a steady stream of paddlers never out of sight of one another" (Adler and Glick 48). According to a Park Service official at Rocky Mountain National Park, most visitors now feel that crowds are reducing the quality of their visits (NPS). They lose what former park ranger Bruce Craig calls "the national park experience" (43).

To meet the needs of these visitors, more and more of our national parks are being transformed into "destination resorts" like Disney World (Coates, "Creature" 14), no longer nature parks but "theme parks," filled with stores, hotels, and amusements. George Siehl, natural resources specialist at the Congressional Research Service, predicts that in the coming years visitors will "demand even more high-impact amenities," more "canyon flights, warm hotel rooms, groomed snowmobile trails, dirt bike race courses, and fast food" (qtd. in Coates, "Creature" 14). Even now, Park Service rangers increasingly report vacationers "more concerned with the amenities of the park than they [are] with the scenic and cultural wonders they [are] experiencing" (Coates, "Crowds" 16).

What many distracted visitors may not see are the environmental consequences of their increasing numbers and the "amenities" they demand. Former ranger Bruce Craig warns, "National parks,

---

MLA in-text citation of sources

The writer's credentials: research

Evidence: statistics

Warrant: a definition of "carrying capacity" used to link evidence to the claim

A factual claim

Factual evidence cited from sources: one consequence of national parks' popularity

Citation of authorities

Evidence: a second consequence of national parks' popularity (their transformation into "theme parks")

Evidence: a third consequence of national parks' popularity (environmental damage)

which preserve unique and delicate ecosystems and fragile hisoric treasures, are not able to withstand the daily assaults of thousands upon thousands of visitors without experiencing change or degradation" (42). Automobile air pollution from visitors' vehicles is destroying national forests (McMahon 26). Hikers, horses, and mountain bikes are causing national park trails to erode. The water in park streams and lakes is everywhere polluted. Climbers are destroying rock faces. Other visitors are destroying vegetation, disrupting habitats, and endangering wildlife (Martin 37). As the nineteenth-century naturalist and author George Perkins Marsh declared, "Man is everywhere a disturbing agent. Wherever he plants his foot, the harmonies of nature are turned to discords" (qtd. in Stegner 38).

Transition to the writer's second claim

Enough! America's national parks, "the best idea America ever had," according to Britain's Lord Bryce, deserve better. They need funds restored to National Park Service budgets so that preservation projects can continue. They need our votes for environmentally aware legislators who will change government funding priorities. And they need a rest from at least some of us nature lovers.

Claim: a proposal for action

The next time I plan a vacation, I'm going to leave national parks out of my plans—at least the most popular, most crowded ones during their most popular seasons. I urge you to do the same. Oh, I'll get there someday. But for now, I say, give the harried park staff, the trampled landscape, and the threatened wildlife a rest. With reduced pollution and use, the air will clear, the scars will heal themselves, the plants will regenerate, the animals return.

Explanation to enable readers to act on the claim

Where to go instead? Consider state parks, Bureau of Land Management lands, or National Forests. Any good map, atlas, or travel guide will identify them. Instead of the Great Smoky Mountains, there is the Joyce Kilmer Wilderness in North Carolina (Reed 64). In Alaska, instead of Denali National Park and Preserve, consider Denali State Park, 324,240 acres, with a "fine trail system, . . . abundant wildlife and spectacular views of the Alaska range" (Chadwick 64). There's the important point. Most alternative vacation spots offer their own attractive vistas and activities made more so without all those other vacationers to block the view or clog roads and trails. What will you find off the beaten track? Here's an example.

This summer, after nearly a week of weaving through crowds at Utah's Zion and Bryce Canyon National Parks, my friend Peter and I headed across Utah toward Arches National Park. Along the way, east of Escalante, we happened upon Dry Hollow, the tiny town of Boulder (population 65), and Boulder Mountain. Before we arrived, they were just names on a map, unremarked by us and most other vacationers. But surprise! This became the best part of our trip. Except for the welcoming residents of Boulder glad for two new faces, we were alone, away from the crowds, the enticements of *un-natural* "theme park" activities, and the souvenir stands packed with trinkets stamped out who knows where.

Over two days a wonderful experience opened to us. The cliffs
of the hollow were as sheer and deeply red as Zion or Bryce, the
textures of rock as sharp to the touch and the eye, the rush of
wind as constant, the road even steeper in its hairpin turns dropping to the canyon floor. On the floor of the hollow, not dry at all,
rippled a muscular ribbon of creek flowing into the Escalante
River. Everywhere were flowers: desert marigold, thornapple,
Sego lily, desert paintbrush, blue flax, Tahoka daisy, and wild
rose. Up on Boulder Mountain, aspens shimmered, streams sang,
snow glistened. And there was this: in purple dusk, in the middle
of Boulder, deer bounded in silent arcs from the playground of
the one-room school, across a meadow, over a fence, and into the
evening. Above them in the distance, like sentinels watching over
our two-days' travel, stood the Henry Mountains. To be in such a
place and have such experiences was, in the words of Chief
Luther Standing Bear of the Oglala Sioux, to live "surrounded
with the blessing of the Great Mystery" (qtd. in Stegner 35). The
pleasure of this mystery is there for you, too, out there somewhere along a road less traveled.

Emotional appeal: description to make the writer's proposal attractive to the audience

A concluding quotation from a sympathetic source to emphasize the value of accepting the writer's proposal

MLA documentation of the writer's sources

Works Cited

Adler, Jerry, and Daniel Glick. "No Room, No Rest." *Newsweek* 1
Aug. 1994: 46-51.

Chadwick, Douglas H. "Denali: Alaska's Wild Heart." *National
Geographic* Aug. 1992: 62+.

Coates, James. "Creature Comforts Taking Toll on Park Wilderness." *Chicago Tribune* 22 Apr. 1991, sec. 1: 1, 14.

—. "Crowds Pose Threat to U.S. Park System." *Chicago Tribune* 21
Apr. 1991, sec. 1: 1, 16.

Craig, Bruce. "Diamonds and Rust." *National Parks* May-June 1991:
41-44.

"Crocodiles vs. Condos: Can We Protect Our National Parks?"
Business Week 20 Aug. 1990: 70-71.

Martin, Claire. "Set in Stone." *National Parks* Nov.-Dec. 1990:
37-38.

McMahon, Edward T. "The Point of a View." *National Parks*
Mar.-Apr. 1992: 26-27.

National Park Service Information Office (Rocky Mountain
National Park). Telephone interview. 15 July 1993.

Reed, J. D. "Take a Number To Take a Hike." *Time* 23 July 1990: 64.

Stegner, Wallace. "It All Began with Conservation." *Smithsonian*
Apr. 1990: 34-43.

United States. Department of the Interior. National Park Service
Socio-Economic Studies Division. *National Park Service Statistical Abstract*. Denver: U.S. Dept. of the Interior, 1993.

—Eric Martin (student)

Writing about Literature

Writing about Literature

You're reading literature in college for the same reasons you might read while relaxing at home, for the pleasures of escape, vicarious experience, suspense, and surprise. But you're also reading for the deeper pleasures that come from an enlarged understanding of yourself and the world. The writing you do in response to your reading may be notebook or journal entries, in-class writing, essays, reviews, research projects, or creative assignments. Their form will depend on your focus, whether on the work itself, on your responses, or on the context (historical or biographical) in which the work was written. In any case, you are writing to enlarge your understanding, explore your feelings, develop your creative powers, and share your responses with others.

59a
Read literature, using these guidelines

■ 1 Reading for pleasure and insight

The following guidelines will help you increase your pleasure in reading and add to your insights.

- Reading and rereading. Most literature that you read in college will need rereading before you are able to absorb all that it contains. Don't worry if you don't understand everything on a first reading; you'll have other opportunities. One of the pleasures of rereading is discovering what you didn't see the first time.

- Marking your reading. Using the following symbols, mark your reading to record your responses and stimulate reflection. (If necessary, add a marginal word or two explaining them.) If your response is complex, you may make more than one mark next to a passage. In the beginning, until marking becomes a habit, you'll have to urge yourself to respond. But you'll find this exercise well worth your effort.

✦ for positive feelings, thoughts, memories, or associations.

— for negative feelings, thoughts, memories, or associations.

= where you agree with something (an idea, a quotation, or value), ≠ where you disagree.

∿ where you feel tension or conflict.

? where you have a question.

/ where the writer has written something important.

z where your attention drifts or you lose interest. (Ask yourself why.)

⬭ words you don't know. (Look them up as you read or when you finish.)

- Reading aloud. Read poetry and complex passages aloud. Listen to the rhythms; try to capture the personalities or tones of the characters you're quoting. If you're reading poetry, don't stop at the end of a line unless the punctuation or word order signals a stop.

- Reading yourself. Pay attention to your responses as you read. Your understanding of literature depends on your individual experiences, outlook, and knowledge. Because readers bring so much of their own lives to their reading, there is usually no single "right interpretation" of a work of literature. Note, however, that many wrong interpretations result from misreading, misunderstanding, or inattention. And one "right interpretation" may be more insightful than another. To begin forming an interpretation, be sensitive to your own feelings, memories, and associations. Ask yourself what you're responding to, how, and why.

■ 2 Reading the elements of literature

As you read, look for the literary elements writers use to create their art. These elements open a doorway to response and understanding.

- Characters. Greet literary characters as you do real people you're meeting for the first time—with healthy skepticism. Don't believe everything they say. What do they know, exactly? Are they reliable observers? Compare words to deeds and to other characters' remarks.

- The narrator. Every work of fiction and poetry has a narrator, a person who tells the story or presents the poem, even if there is no *I* in the work. Narrators do not necessarily speak for their author. Unless they earn your trust, treat narrators with the same healthy skepticism you would any other character in the work.

- Stylistic devices. Look for the stylistic devices writers use to dramatize their message: irony (discrepancies between words and deeds, between your expectation and what actually happens, between what a character says and what you know to be true), symbols (things, places, or people that have meaning beyond themselves), and figurative language (metaphor and simile). (See 26c.)

- Mood. As you read, be sensitive to the feeling expressed in the work toward the subject (serious, humorous, mocking, amused, and so forth). Mood is expressed by the narrator's point of view, details of characterization, the course of events, and the way events and setting are described.

- The title. Decide what the title suggests about the mood, subject, or message of the work.

- Key passages. Look for key passages in which the narrator or another character seems to step back and comment on the subject or action.

- Layout and staging. Use white space inserted between passages and stanza forms as clues to structure or meaning. A drama note: Use stage directions and descriptions of set design to help you imagine setting, events, and the personality of the characters. Note the instructions for characters' actions or speeches that suggest personality, motivation, and conflict.

59*b* Choose your options for writing about literature: analysis and interpretation

■ Analysis and interpretation are methods readers use to understand a work, their response, or the historical context. **Analysis** is the systematic description of literary elements (character, setting, plot, imagery, and so forth) and the way they work together to form your opinions as you read. **Interpretation** focuses on elements in a work that are not immediately apparent (for example, the hidden causes of an event or the reasons for two characters' conflict) and then, using evidence and logic, tries to clarify these elements.

■ 1 Selecting literary elements to analyze and interpret

Adapt the questions after each of the following elements to your chosen literary work. Your answers will provide materials for your writing.

- Character. Explain your opinion of a character by answering one or more of these questions: What kind of person is this? Consider appearance, dress, speech, action, thoughts, feelings, flaws, relationships, and motives. Does this character change? If so, how? What is the secret of the relationship between this character and another? Why do these characters engage in conflict? How are conflicts resolved? What is this character's role in the work: main character (protagonist), antagonist, confidant(e), or foil (a minor character whose personality sheds light on a main character's personality)?

- Setting. Describe the setting of the work—natural, social, political, or cultural. What does setting contribute to the mood, your understanding, or your evaluation? What force does it exert on the characters?

- Plot and structure. Describe the change taking place in the course of the narrative. What are the causes and consequences of this change? What mood or message is expressed by the arrangement of events? Consider the use of flashback. What patterns of imagery, language, dialogue, or poetic form do you see? What does each contribute to mood or message?

- Symbols. Identify and explain literary symbols. What characters or details of setting seem to be symbolic? What ideas, values, or conditions do they symbolize?

- Mood. Explain the overall feeling or attitude expressed in the work about its subject. What do the characters, setting, plot, imagery, and style contribute to this mood?

- Style. Describe the style of a work and the contributions of this style to the work's mood or theme. Consider formal or informal word choice (see 27a), metaphor and simile (see 26c), and complex or simple sentence structure (see 10c).

- Point of view. **Point of view** is the narrator's vantage point for presenting the action of a literary work. Who is the narrator, an actual character in the work (an *I* telling his or her story or someone else's) or a disembodied voice writing in the third person (*he* or *she*)? What does the narrator know or not know? Do you trust this narrator? Why? How do the narrator's knowledge, values, and relationships with other characters affect the structure, mood, and message of the work?

- A key passage. Explain how a brief key passage sums up the mood or message of a work.

■2 Defending a theme

In a broad sense, a **theme** is the message of a work but more than simply a moral. A moral says "Do this; don't do that." A theme says, "Life is like that." Theme is a message or judgment a work dramatizes about its subject. Present the theme of a work and show how it is embodied by the characters, plot, imagery, mood, and style. Follow these guidelines for theme statements:

- A formula for writing theme statements. Use this formula to write a tentative theme statement: "The message of _____(the name of the work)_____ is that . . . "

- A generalization. A theme is a generalization about life; therefore, it does not identify characters by name but makes statements about people in general or certain types of people.

- A complete sentence. A theme is a complete declarative sentence, not a fragment or question.

- A stated or implied theme. A theme may sometimes be located in an actual statement in a work. Or it may only be implied, and you'll express it in your own words.

- An insightful statement. A theme statement for a serious work of literature will always be more insightful than pronouncements on "the moral of the story" or a trite saying ("Love conquers all").

- A unifying statement. As a unifying statement, a theme should not be contradicted by any major details of a work.*

For example: *Eudora Welty's short story "Death of a Travelling Salesman" portrays materialistic human beings prevented by fear, mistrust, and materialism from fulfilling their desire for human companionship.*

59c | Choose your options for writing about literature: the review

■ Analysis and interpretation *explain* a literary work or some part of it. A **review,** on the other hand, *evaluates* a work or some part of it. But a review does more than present one reviewer's personal preferences. Skillful reviewers rely on widely shared standards of value and recognized points of comparison to decide the value of their subjects.

■ 1 Applying standards of value

There are three kinds of standards for evaluating literature.

- Technical and aesthetic. Reviewers apply technical and aesthetic standards to judge how well a work achieves its intended effects. Is a humorous story humorous; is a tragedy tragic? What explains a work's success or failure in achieving its aims: point of view, structure, plot, characterization, or style? How well constructed is it in comparison with others of its type?

- Psychological and social standards. Reviewers use psychological and social standards of personality and behavior to evaluate the plausibility of characters and their world. How "real" are these characters? Or how well do they express the conventions of their literary type?

---

*For these guidelines to theme statements, I am grateful to Laurence Perrine's *Literature,* 5th ed. (New York: Harcourt, 1988).

- Ethical standards. Reviewers use ethical standards to evaluate the morality of a work and its contents. What values does this work seem to endorse? Do you share them?

■ 2 Writing a review

The thesis for a review will be your dominant impression, an overall judgment of the work or the feature you've chosen to evaluate. You may focus your review in two places, drawing from the standards in 59c1 to make your judgment.

- Evaluate a literary work or some feature of it. How effectively has the writer handled characters, setting, plot, structure, or style? Is the work believable, consistent, appropriate to its type, or well constructed?

- Evaluate the ideas or values expressed in a literary work. What does the work dramatize as useful, valuable, desirable, or virtuous? What does the work suggest about the way things should be? Consider description, dialogue, and the narrator's comments. Do you agree with what the work seems to favor? Why or why not?

59*d* | Choose your options for writing about literature: the personal or creative response

■ 1 Writing a personal response

- The responsive essay. Write an essay in which you explain your responses to a literary work. Answer these questions: What in the literary work prompted your responses? What were your feelings, memories, or associations as you read? What personal experiences, observations, or beliefs explain these responses?

- The relation between art and life. Explore the relationship between art and life by writing a comparison. Use your experiences to help you explain something in a literary work: character, setting, plot, or theme. Or use something from the work to help make sense of something in your own life.

- Then and now. Responses and opinions change as readers re-read and discuss a literary work. Trace the evolution in your thinking by answering these questions: What did I originally think or feel and why? What made me change? What do I now think and feel?

■ 2 Writing a creative response

Use literary techniques to dramatize your feelings or opinions about a work or some part of it: Imagine a revealing scene that the author has not presented. Or dramatize the thoughts of a character in a soliloquy (a monologue in which a character expresses thoughts or feelings that would otherwise be unspoken). Or narrate events that might have occurred "off-stage." Or present an episode in a character's life from before or after the events described in the literary work. Whichever strategy you choose, try to remain faithful to the characters, plot, mood, theme, and style as the original author expressed them.

59*e* Choose your options for writing about literature: the research project

■ Many literature classes require some form of research paper. (For guidelines, see Chapters 47–50.)

- Writing a review of research. Your project may expand on one of the preceding options, using scholars' interpretations to enrich your own. With whom do you agree? Why? How has your research changed your thinking?

- Writing a biographical project. Investigate a writer and his or her work. How does this writer's work reflect his or her life? How did he or she come to write this work? What is the history of the work's reputation?

- Writing about historical context. Investigate the historical context of a work or some part of it. What does this work reveal about the culture and period in which it was written? How accurately does it present historical figures, conditions, or events?

59*f* Write a literary paper, using these guidelines

■ 1 Preparing to write

- Focusing. Write a key question about your topic or a tentative thesis to provide focus as you reread your chosen work and gather ideas for your paper. (See 1c and e.)

- Taking notes. To support your thesis, take notes as you reread. Provide a context for each note: Who's speaking to whom? What's happening where and when? (See 49c and d.)

- Refocusing your thesis. When you've finished rereading and taking notes, reconsider your thesis to see whether it fits what you've discovered. (See 2a.) Beware of "So?" statements, incomplete assertions.

Revise to make assertions about the causes, consequences, or importance of your topic.

Laura Sheridan, of Katherine Mansfield's short story "The Garden

Party," lives in a dream world/ *until her visit to the grieving Scott family, when she*

awakens from her dream and discovers what it means to be fully alive.

[The original is a "So?" thesis: So what's the point about Laura and her dream world? The revision answers the question.]

- Organizing to support your thesis. In an important sense, your paper is not about your chosen literary work. It's about your thesis. Organize so that everything in your paper follows from or leads to your thesis.

■ 2 Writing and revising

- Identifying author and title. Identify the author and title of your literary work early in your essay, even in the first sentence. Use quotation marks around the titles of poems and short stories ("The Garden Party"). Italicize or underline the titles of novels, plays, and films (*Hamlet* or <u>Hamlet</u>). (For quotation marks, see 38e; for italics or underlining, see 41a.)

- Avoiding an all-summary paper. Unless instructed otherwise, the audience for your paper is your instructor and the other members of your class. They've probably read your chosen work and won't want to read a book report–style summary. But they may not understand the work as you do or remember the small details you have in mind. Summarize briefly to present evidence supporting your opinions.

- Using the present tense for summaries. Use the present tense to write about an author's work and to summarize action in the work. The original may read: *As Laura walked up to the workmen, she blushed and tried to look severe.* But you would write: *As Laura **walks** up to the workmen, she **blushes** and **tries** to look severe.* Events occurring before the opening of a work should be summarized in the past tense. (See 13b1.)

- Using quotations. Quote often but briefly to explain and illustrate. (See 38a and b.) Indent long quotations of more than four typed lines. (See 38c.) Use an ellipsis to signal omissions from quotations (see 39d) and brackets to insert clarifications (see 39c).

- Following the proper format. Format the final draft of your paper according to Modern Language Association guidelines for writing in the humanities. (See 46c.)

How to . . .

How to Revise and Edit a Literary Essay

Use the following checklist to guide your revision and editing. Or ask peer editors to read your draft with these questions in mind and answer the most important. (For more on revision, see 3b and c.)

1. A question for peer reviewers: Describe the thoughts and feelings you had as you read this paper. Do your responses to the literary work agree with the writer's? If not, where do you differ? Can you explain the differences?

2. Identify this paper's purpose: analysis, interpretation, evaluation, or personal response. Point out any passages that may not fit this purpose.

3. Point out or summarize the thesis of this paper: Does it seem to be a "So?" thesis? Does the paper include another version at the end? Is that statement clearer? Does it better fit the evidence of the paper? (See 3b4.)

4. Does the paper present enough evidence (quotation, summary, and explanation) to support the thesis? Point out places where more support is needed.

5. Can readers follow this essay from beginning to end? Does its design follow the order of events in the original literary work (summary order) or the order of ideas in the thesis (logical order)? What design is clearest and most appropriate?

6. Does this paper follow the format for literary essays? (See 59f.)

59g A sample literary essay

The following essay was written by student-author Leslie Kelly in an introduction to literature course. Her assignment was to write a character study of the narrator of William Stafford's poem "Traveling Through the Dark." To make her interpretation, she considers the narrator's personality and the poem's setting, imagery, and style. She concludes by explaining how the narrator embodies the poem's theme. (For guidelines to the format of a literary essay, see 59f2.)

"Traveling Through the Dark" by William Stafford

Traveling through the dark, I found a deer
dead on the edge of the Wilson River road.
It is usually best to roll them into the canyon:
that road is narrow; to swerve might make more dead.

By glow of the tail-light I stumbled back of the car
and stood by the heap, a doe, a recent killing;
she had stiffened already, almost cold.
I dragged her off; she was large in the belly.

My fingers touching her side brought me the reason—
her side was warm; her fawn lay there waiting,
alive, still, never to be born.
Beside that mountain road I hesitated.

The car aimed ahead its lowered parking lights;
under the hood purred the steady engine.
I stood in the glare of the warm exhaust turning red;
around our group I could hear the wilderness listen.

I thought hard for us all—my only swerving—
then pushed her over the edge into the river.

Dark Necessity

An opening that identifies the author and title of the literary work

A general statement of the thesis

On a first reading of William Stafford's "Traveling Through the Dark," the narrator of the poem appears admirable, a hero, even. He is a good Samaritan, sensitive but in control of his feelings, thoughtful, and capable of decisive action. Who wouldn't trust him to be the driver on a journey down a dark, dangerous, lonely road? And yet a careful rereading reveals that there is more to this man and his actions than first appears.

Topic sentence introducing the first part of the essay

The use of brackets to insert a clarification into a quotation

Make no mistake. He is a good man doing the right thing for the right reasons. From the first stanza, as soon as he sees the dead deer, he shows his concern for others and their safety. You or I might whiz by, unseeing, indifferent, or pressed for time. But he sees that if he does not act, because the "road is narrow; to swerve might make more dead." Other travelers might swerve to avoid the carcass and turn into the path of oncoming traffic or over the edge into the river. Three times he acts. He "dragged her [the dead doe] off the road." He "thought hard for" "our group" about what should be done after he discovers that the dead doe's unborn fawn is alive. Then, deciding what must be done, he "pushed her over the edge into the river."

Quotations from the poem woven into the text of the essay to support the writer's interpretation

He acts decisively, in part, because he thinks so clearly. Nearly every stanza reveals his logic. In the first, he reasons about what he has discovered—the dead deer, the narrow road, and the potential consequences of a swerve. In stanzas 2 and 3 he reasons inductively. Already stiffened, "almost cold," the deer was a "recent killing." But "large in the belly," "her side [still] warm," "her fawn lay there waiting," He knows from common sense that there is no saving this fawn. Reasoning by analogy, he knows that to pause in pity is a "swerving" as dangerous as the actual swerve of a car.

A topic sentence to introduce another trait of the narrator's personality

An interpretation of poetic language

Throughout, however, his logic is tempered by sensitivity. "Her fawn lay there waiting, alive, still, never to be born." The word "still" seems to mean both "yet," as in "yet alive," and "quiet" or "unmoving," as one might expect of an animal connected by umbilical cord to its dead mother. There is paradox and enormous awareness in these lines. As he thinks of what to do, he personifies the silence of the wilderness into listening attention. In these connections between life and death, self and wilderness, he understands the importance of his decision. How often do we think and act so decisively but with such understanding and awareness?

A transition to the second part of the essay

And yet . . . even if the narrator is as admirable as these details make him appear, there are other details to be accounted for. Consider the title. The narrator is not driving through the dark; he's "traveling." This word suggests more than a drive in the country, not the fact of a journey so much as its condition. He may be driving his car, but to no near destination.

An interpretation of a key word from the title

An interpretation of the setting that reveals a contrast between the narrator's civilized world and the natural world

Here is a man whose condition is being in the dark. In such darkness, some things are difficult to see. One is the world of the poem. It is a pair of parallel universes existing simultaneously in the same space. There is, first of all, the natural world of night, mountain, river, canyon, dead doe, and dying fawn. The other world penetrates, dominates, and finally destroys the former. Its features are the human name for the river, the road, the man, the darkness of the poem's title that refers to more than night, and, most vivid of all, the narrator's car. In contrast to doe and fawn, it lives in images of "the steady engine" that "purred" "under the hood," in the breath of "warm exhaust turning red," in its readiness for purposeful action as it "aimed ahead its lowered parking lights." Given these powerful differences, the human, technological world must displace the natural as it does in the narrator's last, symbolic act, when, with an energy not called for in the first stanza, he does not "roll" the [deer] into the canyon, he "*pushed* [emphasis added] her over the edge into the river."

The narrator's behavior explained in terms of the values of his world

He pushes despite his feelings for the fawn because he stands apart from the natural world. His first response, in stanza 1, is to the social code covering such encounters with the natural world: "It is usually best to roll them into the canyon." The deer is a "*heap*" *before* it is a "doe" ("the heap, a doe"), the descriptive word suggesting debris more than a "recent killing." He does not perceive the presence of the fawn directly. Instead, "my fingers touching her side brought me the reason," as if his fingers were intermediaries between the natural world and human world of reason and technology. Throughout, of course, he thinks and acts "by the glow of the tail-light." The only sound the wilderness can hear as he thinks and it listens is the purr of the car, the sound of the life that directs his life and decides his choice.

A conclusion that states the theme of the poem as the writer of the essay understands it.

Given his character and the nature of his world, what other choice does he have? He may think hard, but his concern for the fawn is only a "swerving"—a dangerous reflex from a civilized point of view. Viewed in the dim taillights of the car, "roll" comes naturally to "push," and "shove" is not far behind. "Traveling Through the Dark" dramatizes the force of civilized life in the natural world. However much human pity may give it pause, its effects are inevitably disregarding, brutal, destructive. For travel through the dark must continue.

—Leslie Kelly (student)

Essay Examinations

Essay Examinations

Essay exams will usually ask you to demonstrate three skills:

- Recall. You'll show your grasp of the facts by recalling information.

- Clarification. You'll demonstrate your understanding of facts (their meaning, causes, consequences, sequences, relationships, points of comparison, and priorities) by clarifying and organizing information.

- Argument. You'll apply your knowledge to new situations by constructing arguments that use factual information to prove a point. (See Chapter 57.)

A note on instructors as examination readers: Your instructors may know what you do about the subject of the examination. But don't take their knowledge for granted and leave out information because you assume they know it. Treat them as intelligent, curious readers interested in your subject. Provide them with what they need to understand you.

60a Deciding what a question calls for

When you receive an essay exam, study each question carefully before you begin writing.

- Topical terms. Look for **topical terms** identifying the subjects you'll cover in your answer. Frequently nouns, they identify people, events, issues, and concepts.

  List the most prominent abolitionists of the pre-Civil War era. Discuss their contributions to the abolitionist movement.

  [Topical terms here are *abolitionists, Pre-Civil War era, contributions,* and *abolitionist movement.*]

- Operators. Locate **operators** to decide what skills the question calls for. Frequently verbs, these terms will tell you what to do with your information: inform, clarify, or argue. In the sample question earlier, students are asked to *list* (recall) and *discuss* (recall and clarify)—in other words, to describe what each abolitionist did, identify influence, and evaluate achievement or importance. Here is a list of operators that appear frequently on essay exams. Note the accompanying definitions and synonyms.

Analyze: divide into parts, explain features, describe the structure or operations.

Argue: make a point and prove it with evidence.

Classify: divide into groups based on shared characteristics.

Comment: describe, analyze, or explain.

Compare: show similarities.

Contrast: show differences.

Criticize: evaluate positively or negatively, giving your reasons.

Defend: support a statement with facts, statistics, authorities, and logic.

Define: tell what something is, how it works.

Describe: present features, parts, or details about a subject.

Develop: explain, analyze, or present details involved with the subject.

Discuss: explain, trace, analyze, or make a subject clear.

Enumerate: list.

Evaluate: present and defend a judgment about a subject.

Exemplify: present examples that illustrate or explain a subject.

Explain: make clear by description, definition, or enumerating.

Identify: describe, list, explain, or offer examples.

Illustrate: present examples.

Interpret: analyze, explain, or present and defend your opinion.

Judge: evaluate.

Justify: explain, prove, or defend.

List: recall.

Outline: give steps or stages; identify major points or topics.

Persuade: argue; support a statement with evidence and reasoning.

Prove: argue.

Provide information: give facts and figures.

Rebut: oppose a statement with evidence and reasoning.

Refute: oppose.

Review: summarize, explain, or provide information.

Show: explain, illustrate, or prove.

Summarize: give the main points of your reading, observation, or study.

Trace: identify the steps or stages in a process; describe causes or effects.

- Modifiers. Look for **modifiers** indicating how to organize or focus your answer. Usually these will be adjectives or adverbs: *most important, primary, briefly, thoroughly,* and so forth. In the sample question earlier, *most prominent* indicates that students must decide who were the most important abolitionists and focus on their *contributions.*

- Sample questions. Here are other essay questions. Before you read the accompanying analysis of each question, try to identify their topical terms, operators, and modifiers.

Describe the operation of the adrenal glands.

[This recall question asks students to define the adrenal glands before describing their operation.]

Briefly define and illustrate the concept of determinism.

[This question's first word, *briefly,* provides a clue that this is primarily a test of re-call and understanding. Students are being asked to state the meaning of a key term—presented in class discussion or a textbook—and summarize examples that illustrate the way determinism works.]

Analyze the characters of the Duke and Duchess of Ferrara in Robert Browning's poem "My Last Duchess." Trace the Duke's growing disenchantment with his wife; evaluate his reasons for his actions.

[To answer this question successfully, students would have to do more than sum-marize the poem. To *analyze,* they must describe the personalities of the Duke and Duchess and then support their opinions with details from the poem. To *trace,* they must describe a process. To *evaluate,* they must judge the quality of a character's reasoning.]

60*b* | Planning and writing your answer

■   If scratch paper is available, use it. Even if you're well prepared, the answer to a complex question may not spring to mind fully formed.

- Brainstorming and freewriting. Make lists, jot down ideas, freewrite.

- Noting your main idea or thesis. Write out the main idea or thesis of your essay. Be sure that this most important part of your essay in-cludes key topical terms from the question to keep you on course as you write. Consider the thesis:

  Determinism is the philosophical doctrine that every event, human or natural, can be explained as the result of earlier events. Everything is caused; there is no such thing as free will; no event is purely accidental.

  [This thesis gives the definition called for by the question. The following explana-tory sentence clarifies the definition by telling what *determinism* is not and lists the areas from which the writer will draw the examples called for by the question: ex-amples of causality, the absence of free will, and the absence of chance.]

- Writing a sketch outline. To complete your plans, sketch an outline of your answer. Think of your answer as a pyramid with the thesis or main idea at the top and your facts and explanations spreading out beneath, following a line of reasoning and providing support.

- Manuscript form. If permitted, write in pencil so that you can erase. Write on every other line, allowing generous margins. A note on writ-ing with computers: Check with your instructor before bringing a lap-top computer to the exam.

- Organization. Don't waste time with introductions. Get to the point. Follow your outline.

- Rereading. If you have time, read your answer twice. Once to make sure you've actually answered the question, a second time to check grammar, punctuation, spelling, and legibility.

Business Writing

61 Business and Professional Writing

61a
Write effective business letters

■ 1 Following the conventions for writing business letters

- Paper. Use good-quality, heavy, white bond paper. Letterhead paper makes the best impression.

- Typescript. Type your letters or use a computer. Use a black ribbon and standard typeface. If you use a computer, note that many readers object to dot matrix printers. (See 46a.)

- Length. When possible, limit letters to one page. If you write a longer letter, put second and successive pages on plain white paper. One inch from the top, type a heading: the addressee's name flush left, the page number centered, and the date flush right.

- Balance. Make your letter look easy to read by centering it on the page. Keep paragraphs relatively brief; doublespace between them. Provide ample white space surrounding your text. To help readers keep track of important information, use indented lists, bullets, or enumeration. (See 46b2.)

- Format. Among letter formats, one of the most common and attractive is the modified block, illustrated by the sample letter that follows. Near the right margin, place the return address (unless you're using letterhead stationery), the date, complimentary close, and signature section. All other parts begin at the left margin.

- Nonsexist address. Use nonsexist forms of address. Address readers by name or specific title: *Dear Mr., Ms., Mrs., Dr., Professor,* and so forth. Call ahead to find out your readers' names. When you do not know their names, address them by title alone: *Dear Editor, Service Manager, Director of Admissions,* and so forth. Do not use first names unless you know your reader personally. (See 27e.)

- Envelopes. Mail business letters in standard business-size envelopes, 4 × 9½ inches.

■ **2** **Conveying your personality to readers**

Whatever your reasons for writing, your readers will usually be reading as part of their jobs. They'll appreciate anything in your letter that makes their work easier, including layout, detailed information, and style. Be businesslike. You shouldn't sound stuffy, but you should be as serious as the occasion requires. Avoid the features of an informal style: slang, most contractions, sentence fragments, and inappropriately charged language. (For more on persona, see 1d and 27a.)

Whenever possible, adopt what business writers call a "you" attitude. Try to see things from your readers' point of view, keeping their interests, needs, and benefits uppermost in mind. Most public letters are, after all, persuasive. You'll be persuasive if your readers know you're thinking of them as you write. (See 58b.)

■ **3** **Organizing business letters**

Make your letters easy to follow by adopting the standard three-part design: In your opening paragraph, identify your subject and purpose and provide necessary background. In your middle paragraphs, provide information, explanation, and reasons. Close with a brief paragraph describing the action you want your audience to take. If you have bad news, save it until you've presented all the information and reasons explaining it.

■ **4** **Using electronic communication**

- Faxes. Because faxes are easily lost, advise the recipient that one is coming. Include a cover sheet that gives the recipient's name, company, fax number, date, time, subject, your name, fax number, and the total number of pages, including the cover sheet.

- E-mail. E-mail messages are less formal than business letters or even memos; sometimes they seem closer to speech than writing. But as you write, keep your readers in mind: their knowledge, their positions, and your relationship with them. Be courteous—say "please" and "thank you"—and take the time to be sure your language is accurate and that your message will be clear to its reader. Headings for e-mail depend on the network you're using, but you can still address your reader by name and sign off with your name. Finally, remember that e-mail is not confidential.

61b Write effective résumés

■ The résumé presents important information about your background, education, experiences, achievements, and references. It is the proof of your qualifications.

1201 W. Chase Avenue, Apt. 2C
East Lansing, MI 48824
April 14, 199-

Maria L. Garcia
Director of Student Services
Harley Williams School
Institute of Child Psychiatry
709 W. Greenleaf Avenue
Chicago, IL 60626

Dear Ms. Garcia:

Professor Gerald Ashby, Chair of the Psychology Department at Michigan State University, has informed me that you have three openings for Child Care Worker-Summer Interns. I wish to apply for one of these positions.

As my enclosed résumé indicates, I am now a college sophomore studying for a degree in child psychology. I plan a career as a child psychologist working with institutionalized children. Most of my work so far has been with children.

For two years I worked as a summer counselor at a camp for children with developmental disabilities. My responsibilities were to provide tutoring, physical therapy, and recreational supervision.

For one year I worked as a Boys Club Recreation Supervisor. Besides my supervisory and coaching duties, I was assigned to five boys to act as their "big brother."

My current position as a hospital orderly not only helps me pay for tuition, books, room, and board but also provides a valuable introduction to institutional work.

I believe I am qualified by education and work experience to be a Child Care Worker-Summer Intern at Harley Williams School. I can be available for an interview at your convenience; if you wish, I will have my references and academic records sent to you. I can be reached by mail at the above address or at (517) 555-1541 weekdays from 9 to 11 a.m. I look forward to hearing from you.

Sincerely,

Matthew Leigh

Matthew Leigh

Enclosure: Résumé

Margin annotations:

Modified block business letter format

Heading (return address omitted with letterhead stationery) and date

Inside address

Salutation followed by a colon

Itemized information

Block paragraphs

Complimentary close

Reference area: enclosures, typist's initials, copies, and so forth

■1 Preparing a résumé

As you prepare a résumé, be brief but complete. If possible, limit it to one page. Use clipped phrases rather than complete sentences: *Career Objective: To become a child psychologist working with autistic children in an institutional setting.* Group related information to make it easy to locate, and make headings grammatically parallel, such as all nouns or noun phrases: *Education, Experience, References,* and so forth. (See Chapter 19.) A note: Never send a résumé without a cover letter.

■2 Formatting a résumé

The formats for résumés are varied; make yours look professional and easy to read. If you have important achievements, list them first. Follow a chronological order, most recent job first, or describe the functions of your job, most important first. If you're a recent graduate or still in school, place your education first, beginning with your most recent schooling. See the sample résumé on page 404.

61*c* | Write effective memos

A memo is a written document sent within an organization to specific persons or departments. Its purposes are to inform, summarize, record, or call for action. Successful memos are usually sensitive to writer-reader relations. (See 1a3 for questions about audience; see 1d for guidelines to creating a persona.) Often customized to suit the needs of a particular organization, memos vary widely in their formats. The sample memo on page 405 illustrates standard memo parts and a common pattern of organization.

61*d* | Choose your options for writing an effective report

A report is a systematic presentation of information to a specific audience for a specific purpose. The reports you'll write in college and on the job may take several forms: informal memo or letter reports, technical field or lab reports, informative reports, problem/solution reports, progress reports, proposals, and case studies.

■1 Preliminary activities

Your preliminary preparations will be similar to those for other investigative writing: surveying the situation (see 1a), posing key questions or describing the problem, and identifying your purpose (see 47b). You will gather the information for your report from appropriate sources: interviews, minutes, letters, questionnaires, surveys, experimentation, direct

MATTHEW R. LEIGH
1201 W. Chase Avenue,
East Lansing, MI 48824
(517) 555-1541

Position Desired: Child Care Worker-Summer Intern

Career Objective: To become a child psychologist working
with autistic children in an institutional
setting

Education:

199- to present: Michigan State University
Major: Child Psychology
Minor: English
Grade Point Average: 3.75 (Possible 4.0)
Honors: Dean's List, 199- to 199-
Leonard E. Frank Scholarship

199- to 199-:   William Rainey Harper College
Phi Theta Kappa Honor Society
Editor, The Harbinger, Campus
Newspaper
Basketball and Track Teams,
199- and 199-

Experience:

199- to present: Orderly, Weldon Memorial Hospital,
East Lansing, MI
199- and 199-:   Camp Counsellor, Camp Onewata,
Schroon Lake, NY
Tutored and supervised recreation at
this camp for developmentally disabled
children, ages 8-14

199- to 199-:   East Lansing Boys Club, East Lansing, MI
Supervised group recreation

References: References and credentials available on
request from the Placement Office,
Michigan State University,
East Lansing, MI 48824

Side annotations:

Academic history to highlight training

Honors listed

Experience listed in reverse chronological order

Relevant activities or accomplishments

TO:	Laura Chin, Selection Committee, State College Student Anthology	Block format memo
FROM:	Beth Logan, Editor *BL*	Writer's initials
DATE:	December 10, 199-	
SUBJECT:	Reading this year's submissions to the student literary anthology	Begin the body of the memo three spaces beneath the subject line.

Enclosed are the submissions to be evaluated for the next issue of the anthology. Read them in the usual way:

1) Award each entry from 1 to 5 points (1 low, 5 high).

2) If you discover incomplete or misassembled entries, let me know, and I'll try to get you good copies.

3) Record your votes beneath your initials on the enclosed alphabetized list.

(margin note: Do not indent memo paragraphs. Singlespace within paragraphs, doublespace between.)*

(margin note: Whenever possible, use lists for clarity and emphasis)*

We'll meet to discuss our evaluations at the end of January. Thanks for all your efforts on last year's issue. It was first rate. I know we can make this year's even better.

Enclosures: Anthology submissions
Author list

(margin note: Reference area)*

observation, published reports, and other documents. (For guidelines to research, see Chapters 47–49.) When you finish your investigation, write out your **conclusion,** the point of your report supported by your information.

■2 Organizing a report

Prepare an informal report as you would a letter, memo, or essay, with an appropriate beginning, middle, and end. Formal reports generally consist of (1) prefatory parts such as a cover, title page, letters of authorization or acceptance, acknowledgments, a table of contents, an abstract, and an executive summary; (2) the text of the report, including an introduction, body, and conclusion; (3) supplementary parts such as an appendix, bibliography, or index. Include all parts relevant to your report and required by your readers. Follow these guidelines to organize the text of your report:

- Introduction. The introduction includes all elements necessary to orient your readers and help them understand your information: a statement of the problem or key questions, a description of materials and methods, background or history, definitions, a review of relevant published research, or an overview of the presentation to follow.

- Body. The body of a report is often labeled *Results, Data, Findings,* or *Discussion.* The results and discussion may be separated or combined, depending upon their relationship, the length of the report, and your readers' needs. Organize the body of a report according to topics, chronology, importance, or other logical patterns. (See 6b.)

- Conclusion. A conclusion summarizes information, makes generalizations about it (comparisons, causes and effects, classifications, estimations, predictions), poses solutions to problems, makes evaluations and recommendations, or proposes action.

- Inductive vs. deductive organization. For readers who need detailed explanation or who may resist your recommendations without a full presentation of the case, organize the text of your report in an *inductive* or "conclusion-last" order: introduction, body, conclusion. For busy readers who may not read the entire report, who will agree with you, or who want your opinion promptly, use a *deductive* or "conclusion-first" order: introduction, conclusion, body.

■ 3 Formatting and style

- Headings. Informal reports are usually written as continuous documents, undivided except for paragraphing. The text of formal reports is usually divided by headings into clearly labeled parts: *Introduction, Background, Discussion, Conclusion,* and so forth. (For guidelines to effective headings, see 46b1.)

- Visual aids. Use lists, tables, and graphics to illustrate and group information as well as to help your readers understand it. (See 46b2–4.)

- Style. Generally write in the present tense unless you have a good reason for using the past tense: *This report recommends. . . .* (See 13b1.) Choose concrete, specific words as specialized as the subject requires and reader understanding will allow. (See 26a and b.) Except in conclusions, avoid generalities. Also avoid emotionally charged words that may make your report sound biased. (See 25b.)

- Documentation. Cite the sources of borrowed information in an appropriate format. (For Modern Language Association guidelines, see Chapters 51 and 52; for American Psychological Association guidelines, see 54a–c; for other formats, see the style manuals listed in 56.)

■ 4 A sample formal report

For a sample formal report written in the American Psychological Association style, see 54d.

Index

Using the
Internet
for
Research

Using the Internet for Research

Internet Research

The information in this Appendix is designed to supplement material in Parts VI and VII of the Handbook, which discuss strategies for finding, evaluating, and documenting both print and electronic sources. The detailed discussions and practical advice in this Appendix relate specifically to conducting research on the Internet (see 48e).

Using the World Wide Web for Research

As you learned in section 48e, the World Wide Web got its name because each site usually contains *links* to other sites the publisher thinks are related. Since each site has links to other sites, a kind of web is formed. This is the great power of the Web. Once you find a site that contains information you find useful, you can follow the links to other sites you think may be interesting, then continue with your research. This is like using the bibliography of one book to find other books, only much faster.

Structure of the Web: Making order out of chaos

Unfortunately, there's no overall organization for Web sites—no classification system or central catalog. Anyone can publish information on the Web. The result can be compared to a library without a book numbering system or card catalog. You must roam around until you happen to find what you are looking for.

The best strategies for finding information on the Web are to keep a short of list of sites that specialize in cataloging information from other Web sites, keep your own personal list of favorite Web sites, and learn to use at least one of the many *search engines* that will scan the Internet looking for Web sites that contain keywords or phrases that you specify.

Navigating the Web

Navigating the Web requires a program called a *browser.* The browser keeps track of where you are on the Web and displays the information sent to your computer by the Web site. Using the Web is an interactive process. Information is sent to you as you request it.

Information on the Web is independent of the type of computer you are using. It doesn't matter if you are using a Macintosh or a PC. To view information on any site, all you need is a browser for your specific computer.

There are several browsers on the market, but the two most popular are Netscape Navigator and Microsoft Internet Explorer. All browsers offer similar basic functions. The basic functions are:

- Site Name Selection: Go to a specific Web site

- HyperText Link: Move to a new site when an on-screen link is selected

- **Back** button: Back up to the previous site

- **Forward** button: Move forward to return to the site you just moved back from

- **Home** button: Go to your home or starting page

- **Print** button: Print the current page

- **Refresh** button: Refresh the current display

Uniform Resource Locators (URLs)

Web addresses, or *URLs*, always start with "http://", which tells the Web browser that the address you are about to give is for a Web site. Next comes the name of the site itself. Most, but not all, Web sites use the letters "www" as the first part of their address.

You can often guess the Web site address for large companies by typing "http://www.*name*.com", putting the company name or abbreviation in place of *name*.

The toolbar at the top of your browser window contains a place for you to type the address of the Web site you want to see. In Netscape Navigator it's labeled "Go to:" and in Microsoft Internet Explorer it's labeled "Address:". Both programs expect you to type the URL in exactly the same format. The URL for the site and page you are currently viewing will be displayed in this area as you navigate your way around the Web.

When you start your browser it will always take you to the same starting point or *home page*. The home page will usually contain links to other sites and so enables you to begin your Web exploration from a known point.

HyperText

When you look at a page in the browser window you'll see some highlighted words and phrases. The highlighted text is usually a different color than the main text; often it is underlined. Highlighted phrases are the *links* to other pages on the Web. Click your mouse on a highlighted phrase and the browser will jump you to the appropriate location. This type of text with embedded links to related details is called *HyperText*.

Some links are to programs or data files that can be downloaded to your computer. When you click on one of these links you will see a box asking for permission to download the file. Choose the "Save File" button on the dialog and the file will be sent to your computer.

Using bookmarks and history files

All browsers allow you to set electronic bookmarks, which enable you to return to a Web page without going through other links. This is useful when you find a site you think would be interesting to explore when you have more time, or when you finally find what you're looking for after following dozens of links.

Netscape Navigator files bookmarks under the **Bookmark** menu, while Microsoft Internet Explorer files them in the **Favorites** menu, but they work the same way. When you reach a site you want to bookmark:

1. Select the **Add Bookmark** option from the **Bookmark** menu in Navigator, or the **Add to Favorites** option from the **Favorites** menu in Internet Explorer.
2. Navigator immediately adds the site name to the **Bookmark** menu. Internet Explorer pops up a window that allows you to edit the name of the site and to organize your bookmarked favorites in folders.

To return to a bookmarked site, pull down the **Bookmark** menu in Navigator or the **Favorites** menu in Internet Explorer and click on the name of the bookmark.

Your browser is also recording the name of every Web site you visit as you surf around the Net. This is called a *history file* and lets you return to any site you have visited recently. Netscape Navigator gives you access to the history file from the **History** option in the **Window** menu. Microsoft Internet Explorer shows the history file via the **Open History Folder** option in the **Go** menu.

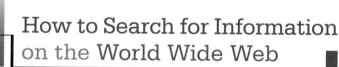

How to Search for Information on the World Wide Web

When you start on a research project, it's sometimes hard to know where to look for information. With so many diverse sites on the Web it would be impossible to visit them yourself looking for information. In section 48e, you learned that a whole new breed of programs called *search engines* will do the looking for you. You can use these search engines by performing the same kind of keyword searches you use for online sources (see 48b). This section provides more details about using search engines.

A search engine looks through a giant index of Web pages which is created by robot programs that roam the Web collecting and indexing information. The index on the largest of the search sites, AltaVista (http://altavista.digital.com), contains information from 31 million pages on 476,000 Web sites. The search engine will look through this massive index for key words and phrases in a fraction of a second! AltaVista displays a link for any page that contains the words you specify anywhere on the page.

Another popular search engine is maintained by *Yahoo!* (http://www.yahoo.com), a company that maintains an index of Web sites. The *Yahoo!* search engine is based on categories and shows links to Web sites that cover topics you specify.

Simple searches

It pays to spend some time experimenting with searches and learning advanced search techniques. It's just as bad finding too much information as too little. Here's an experiment you can try with AltaVista:

1. Start your browser and point it to URL **http://altavista.digital.com.** (You should also set a bookmark for AltaVista so you can come back here without remembering this URL.)
2. To research a well-known movie, type **The Net** in the search box and click the **Submit** button. AltaVista will search its index for all Web pages that have the words "The" and "Net." The results of your search will be returned to you in a few seconds.
3. You'll see that "Net" was found more than 1,700,000 times and "The" occurred so frequently that it was ignored. Clearly this search is not usable.
4. Now type **"The Net"** as the search string and click **Submit.** The quotation marks are very important. They tie the words together so that now AltaVista will only find sites that contain the entire phrase "The Net." This time the search engine will return about 30,000 sites. That's still too many to be of any value. Very few of the pages containing the phrase "The Net," a very common phrase, actually refer to the movie of that name. You need to refine your phrase by narrowing it.
5. Type **movie "The Net"** and click **Submit.** The search will actually return more sites (about 100,000 this time), but this time AltaVista will organize them so the sites that have the most matching words appear first on the list. Chances are that if you were doing research on the movie you would find what you are looking for within the first few pages of links, or, if you had a specific aspect of the movie in mind, you could refine the search even further by adding more keywords.

The moral here is to be as specific as possible when using a massive index search engine; try to trim down the number of sites returned. Search engines try to sort the sites they find based on the relevance of the words you specify. Each search engine uses a complicated, proprietary formula to try to bring the sites that are most likely to be of interest to the top of the list. As you scroll down the list, the links will be farther and farther off-topic, and there's no need to continue looking. You're better off submitting another search with a slightly different set of words and phrases to get the information you want.

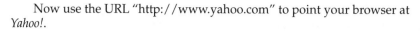
Now use the URL "http://www.yahoo.com" to point your browser at *Yahoo!*.

1. Type **"The Net"** into the search box and click the **Search** option. *Yahoo!*'s classification scheme will find 21 categories that have these words and 3,000 sites that have "The Net" in the title.
2. Type **"The Net" movie** and click **Search.** *Yahoo!* will find 1 category and 169 sites with these words in the title.

See what a difference the indexing technique makes? *Yahoo!* finds only a couple of sites that have relevant information because it's only looking at Web page titles. Because it searches entire documents, AltaVista is more likely to find what you're looking for than will *Yahoo!*. But AltaVista can also quickly lead to information overload.

Try searches in both sites and see which you like best. You can also try other search engines listed at the end of this Appendix.

Avoiding information overload: Advanced search techniques

■   Some of the search engines offer an *advanced* or *custom* search mode, which enables you to use special commands to narrow or widen a search. The most common special commands are included here.

AND

Use AND to narrow a search. This command causes the search engine to find Web pages that include all of the keywords you specify. For example, the search **"Chicago Hope" AND ER** will find Web pages that include the names of both TV shows. A page that contains only one of these names will not be found by the search. The AND command is a great tool when you know exactly what you're looking for.

NEAR

The NEAR command is used to find any Web pages on which two words are "close" to each other. For example, **Shakespeare NEAR sonnet** will find Web pages that include phrases such as "Shakespeare's sonnets" and "the sonnets of William Shakespeare." Different search engines have different tolerances for "closeness," but the words you specify must usually be between 6 or 8 words of each other to be found by a NEAR search.

OR

OR is used to widen a search when you're not sure how to find what you're looking for. This command will locate all Web pages that include any of the keywords you specify. For example, **"Chicago Hope" OR ER** will find any Web page that mentions either or both of these shows. The OR command greatly increases the number of links returned by a search, so it's most often useful when you are starting a research project and want to get an idea of what's available.

NOT

Careful use of NOT can trim a search down when you know that certain keywords should be eliminated. A search like **"endangered species" NOT plant** will find any Web page with the phrase "endangered species" on it as long as the word "plant" is not on the same page.

These commands can also be combined. If you are going use the Web for research, it's a good investment of time to learn about these advanced search commands. Click the **Help** link in the search engine you like best to read about the various advanced searching features it offers.

How to Evaluate Internet Sources

In many ways the problem of knowing what to do with the information you gather from the World Wide Web or other Internet sources is as knotty a problem as finding the information in the first place. You already have some experience with evaluating print media to draw on, however, so you simply need to be more vigilant in applying your criteria. Keep in mind that no one—no publisher, editor, review board of knowledgeable people in the field—is doing your evaluating and selecting for you. But the principles of critical thinking—whether applied to print media or visual media such as television or computer media—remain the same.

Develop a critical mindset

Critical thinking is, more than anything else, a habit of mind, a particular action you take almost reflexively when confronted with information. When using the Internet, it's crucial to question your information, to be a professional and committed Doubting Thomas. Assume, at the beginning, that anything you read is not true. Demand evidence or support from your sources. In the more interactive parts of the Internet—Usenet and listservs especially—you have the opportunity to question in person. In material you find that's not "live" and offers no interactivity, you must question your sources thoroughly, silently, and often alone.

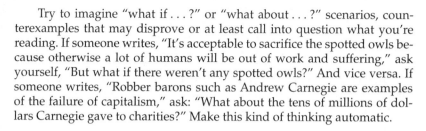

Try to imagine "what if . . . ?" or "what about . . . ?" scenarios, counterexamples that may disprove or at least call into question what you're reading. If someone writes, "It's acceptable to sacrifice the spotted owls because otherwise a lot of humans will be out of work and suffering," ask yourself, "But what if there weren't any spotted owls?" And vice versa. If someone writes, "Robber barons such as Andrew Carnegie are examples of the failure of capitalism," ask: "What about the tens of millions of dollars Carnegie gave to charities?" Make this kind of thinking automatic.

Specificity

One of the marks of a believable source is specificity—actual content, facts, figures, statistics, and research conducted or cited. If someone writes, "Most of the people who use the Internet are men," you may or may not be inclined to believe it, but you probably won't be swayed. But if someone writes, "Recent studies of Internet usage show that 78% are male, 90% are white, and 77% make over $60,000 per year," it sounds more convincing and can probably be verified by finding the "recent studies" referred to. But don't drop your critical guard—statistics can be misused, exaggerated, and even fabricated entirely (as those listed above are).

Audience

As in any writing project, you must know your audience well. You must consider what those who will be reading your research paper will accept as proof and authoritative commentary. If your audience will expect of you lots of facts and figures, then find facts and figures. If your audience disagrees strongly with you, you need strong and irrefutable evidence. If your audience is already on your side, you need more entertaining and enlightening data. If your audience consists of novices in the field about which you're writing, you need more accessible, easily visualized, and striking information. If your audience consists of other experts in the field, you need more precise and specialized information to make your case.

Knowledge of speaker

How much do you know about the speaker/writer? Particularly in listservs and Usenet newsgroups, it's possible to follow along for a few weeks and note who the frequent posters (a message sent to the list or newsgroup is called a "post") are and, more importantly, how authoritative they seem. Do they consistently know what they're talking about? Do other posters on the list recognize them as knowledgeable? Or does the poster have a history of flaming, of irrational and unjustifiable statements?

In Internet modes other than listservs and Usenet, it's more difficult to evaluate a source. Sometimes you can search in one of the engines for an author's or an organization's name and track down other works. This will allow you to get a fuller picture of the author, what she stands for, and what kind of biases or prejudices she seems to exhibit.

Verifiability

Much of what you read on the Internet will be unverifiable in the scientific sense of the word. You won't be able to reproduce experiments, find the ultimate source of information, or check out material presented as fact. In some instances, however, you will. Some information on the Net resembles pure academic discourse, complete with footnotes and a bibliography. Much material on the Net ranges from flaming to carefully considered opinion.

Other points of view

A critical thinker seeks other points of view like humans breathe oxygen. You need other viewpoints to help develop your own thinking, to learn by necessity how other people think and why they say what they say.

Fortunately, discourse on the Internet usually represents a multiplicity of views. If you seem to be receiving only one side of a story, it's a simple matter to find opposing points of view.

In the narrowly focused Usenet groups, you often won't find opposing viewpoints represented. The nature and purpose of newsgroups is to let people focus on a particular topic and discuss it. Usenet and listserv postings follow "threads"—sequences of postings on the same topic, each one responding to the previous message or perhaps introducing a new perspective. If you follow a thread over a period of a week or so (most don't last much longer than a week, burning out as participants move on to new discussions), you will be tossed to and fro intellectually as each new posting brings a new idea, a new perspective, a new "what if . . . ?" or "have you considered . . . ?" The thread represents a chain of critical thinking, as each contributor evaluates what has been posted and then either amplifies or counters those ideas.

In the less interactive modes of the Net (i.e., repositories of more or less unchanging information on FTP, Gopher, and Web sites), opposing points of view don't automatically appear. But you can search for them. You just need to remember to do so. Most Web search engines provide brief summaries of the contents of sites found while searching, so it's easy to tell at a glance when you've found conflicting information.

Evaluating Usenet postings

Usenet postings present the greatest challenge to your critical evaluation skills because of the amount of "noise" you have to filter through to get information. Usually, Usenet posters are just average people expressing their opinions—informed, misinformed; rational, biased; thoughtful, off-the-cuff. Occasionally there will be a posting by experts in a particular field who have substantial information to offer, but this is not common. Ultimately, recognizing misleading, inaccurate, or useless postings is a matter of skill, experience, and taste (different people will place more or less trust in the posting of an enthusiastic Rush Limbaugh supporter, for example), but here are some guidelines that may help as you gain experience in the Usenet world:

1. Consider your first impulse if the posting you're reading appears to contradict what you believe, what you've seen and heard firsthand, or what most other posters in the group are saying. Start with your gut feeling.
2. What are the motivations, biases, and outright prejudices of the poster?
3. This is the hardest part: If you agree with the poster, or most other authorities you've read appear to agree, put yourself in the position of someone who disagrees with you. How would that person react to this particular posting? For example, if you're prochoice and the poster makes an obviously prochoice statement, how would a prolife supporter respond (honestly!)? Recognize and critically examine the party line of *both* parties.
4. Try to verify with a second source any information you get from Usenet. How much of what a poster writes is verifiable fact, how much is well-considered opinion, and how much is just mindless ranting and raving?
5. Does the poster use inflammatory or blatantly prejudiced language? You know you wouldn't trust anyone, say, who refers to Italians as "wops"; how about someone who uses terms like "FemiNazis" or "tree-huggers" or "Luddites"?
6. Who is the poster? What do you know about him or her? A poster who signs himself as an employee of the Environmental Protection Agency has at least a head start on authority and believability compared with one who signs herself as a member of "Free Americans to Eliminate Government."

How to Use
FTP Sites

FTP stands for **F**ile **T**ransfer **P**rotocol and is the means by which you copy files from someone's computer to yours over the Internet (see 48e3). Knowing how to use FTP enables you to exchange and distribute lengthy documents for collaborative projects. It also permits you to store Internet files on your own computer so you can access them more easily as you write. There are many ways of transferring files, but the easiest one is to use your Web browser.

Both Netscape Navigator and Microsoft Internet Explorer utilize FTP in two ways. The first is by downloading a file when you click a link on a Web page. Links can be set up not only to take you from one page to

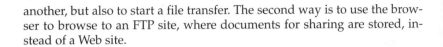

another, but also to start a file transfer. The second way is to use the browser to browse to an FTP site, where documents for sharing are stored, instead of a Web site.

Retrieving files from Web pages

When you are looking at a Web page, it's not possible to distinguish browsing links from file links, except by context. Click on an FTP link to activate it. The browser will display a message box asking if you would like to save the file on your computer's disk drive or open the file.

You normally choose to save the file. (If you choose to open the file instead, it will not be saved on your computer.) Choose the *Save* option and confirm the file name. After you confirm the file name a status indicator will appear on the screen.

Retrieving files from FTP sites

The URL for a Web site always starts with the letters "http://". For an FTP site the URL always starts with "ftp://". We're going to use Allyn & Bacon's FTP site as an example. The FTP address for Allyn & Bacon is "ftp://ftp.abacon.com". Type this address in your browser's **Go To:** or **Address:** window and press the **Enter** key. The contents of the FTP site will appear in the browser window.

Netscape Navigator

Netscape Navigator shows the structure of the FTP site by indicating files with an icon that looks like a sheet of paper with a bent corner and directories with an icon that looks like a folder. To download a file or see what's in a directory, click the highlighted link beside the icon. You will be asked if you want to save or open the file. Choose the *Save* option and the file will be sent to your computer.

Microsoft Internet Explorer

Microsoft Internet Explorer shows the structure of the FTP site by putting the size next to files and the word "DIRECTORY" next to directories. To download a file or see what's in a directory, click the highlighted link. Choose the *Save* option when prompted, then confirm the file name and start the download.

The status indicator will show the progress of the download. If you are connecting to the Internet using a phone line and modem, a download may take a long time—possibly hours, especially if the file is more than a

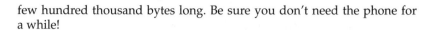

few hundred thousand bytes long. Be sure you don't need the phone for a while!

Posting Files

You can make files available to other people by placing them on an FTP site. Each site has its own procedure for making files available. Ask your Internet Service Provider how you can "upload" files to an FTP site so they will be available for other people.

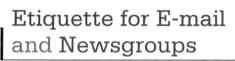

Etiquette for E-mail and Newsgroups

E-mail

When you exchange Internet messages to gather information, your goal is to make the interaction pleasant, orderly, and productive. If you want to get the most from the exchange, then you should learn to observe a set of etiquette rules, or "netiquette."

Don't use all upper case

Using upper case letters to emphasize words in your messages is the e-mail equivalent of shouting. It's considered very bad manners to write messages in upper case.

Use emoticons and acronyms

The person reading your messages does not have the benefit of seeing your facial expressions and body language as with a face-to-face encounter. This is a very important limitation of e-mail, and you must always consider how your words might be interpreted. It's very hard for someone to know if you are kidding or are being very serious. *Emoticons* and acronyms have been developed over the years as a way of showing facial expressions or conveying feelings in the text of a message.

An emoticon is a set of characters that represent an emotion or facial expression. Common emoticons you may see in messages are:

:-)	smile
;-)	wink
:-(	frown
\<g\>	grin
\<vbg\>	very big grin

An acronym is a form of shorthand. The letters of the acronym stand for an expression. Common acronyms in messages are:

AFAIK	as far as I know
IMO	in my opinion
IMHO	in my humble opinion
BTW	by the way
OTOH	on the other hand
CU	see you

Use emoticons and acronyms in your messages to help convey the subtle (or not-so-subtle) meanings behind your words. It may make a world of difference whether you write "Idiot!<g>" or "Idiot!" to the person reading your message.

Be polite

Somewhere a researcher is studying the curious phenomenon that people will write things in an e-mail message that they would never say to someone's face. On the Internet, being intentionally rude and insulting is called *flaming* and has become a kind of sport for some people. You can unwittingly become the target of a flame attack by simply making a breach of netiquette in a public forum. If someone sends you an e-mail message calling you a "clueless newbie," you've been flamed.

Many people enjoy flaming newcomers to the Net. They will try to insult you because of your lack of experience using the Net or the incorrect use of Internet terminology. Resist the temptation to reply to a flame attack. A flaming reply to a flame starts what is called a *flame war*, a kind of pointless Internet shouting match that can go on and on forever until one of the participants finally gives in at which point the opponent has "won" the war.

If you feel compelled to point out a mistake in someone's message, do it in a polite way and back up your point with facts. A critical response should be more like a debate than a brawl.

You can't take it back

While no one has the time (and very few people have the inclination) to go snooping into other people's e-mail, you should remember that the Internet is not a secure medium. Don't write anything—even in a private e-mail—that you wouldn't want posted on a bulletin board in your student union. Messages can be intercepted and read. Your school or ISP archives all e-mail sent through its system and can produce it by court order; you will regret angry or mean-spirited messages in the morning. Think before you hit the "send" button. Once you've sent it, you can't take it back.

Newsgroups

All the etiquette rules that apply to e-mail apply to newsgroups as well. Since messages in newsgroups may be read by thousands of people, however, there are a few additional rules you should keep in mind.

Keep it short

Keep your messages to newsgroups short and to the point. Many people have to pay for access to the Internet and the extra time needed to download long or off-topic messages costs them money.

Expect offensive messages

There's no control over what's posted in most newsgroups, so you're likely to find all types of information. Some of it is profane and inflammatory. If you are easily offended, you should be careful which newsgroups you read. If you have children, you may want to restrict their access to newsgroups. Many contain language and content that's not appropriate for children.

Be tolerant

Newsgroups are read by people all over the world, many of whom do not use English as their native language. Never flame or correct anyone's spelling or grammar, and be very tolerant of misused phrases or "broken English."

Don't send spam

Easy access to the Internet has spawned a new breed of junk mail known as *spam.* Spam is a message promising a new way to lose weight, get rich quick, or something similar. Some of these messages are chain letters; others are outright scams and hoaxes. A spam message is never about the topic of the newsgroup to which it has been posted. Don't respond to spam messages, and do not post off-topic messages like that yourself.

Additional Formats for Documenting Internet Sources

The guidelines for citing Internet sources are in flux, as new media constantly appear. Chapters 52 and 54 contain general citation guidelines for online sources as well as specific formats for many particular media. This section expands on the information offered in 52b and 54c.

MLA formats for Internet sources

These MLA formats were first designed by Janice Walker (http://www.cas.usf.edu/english/walker/mla.html), and later adapted into the *MLA Handbook,* 4th edition. In general, they apply the principles used by MLA to the special cases of online sources. Note that in-text citations remain the same as they are for regular print sources, i.e., author's last name in parentheses following the cited material.

- WWW sites (World Wide Web). Author's name (reversed), the full title of the work in quotation marks, the title of the complete work if applicable in italics, the full http address, and the date of visit.

  U.S. Fish and Wildlife Service. "Program Overview." <u>Endangered Species Home</u>

  <u>Page</u>. http://www.fws.gov/~r9endspp/programs.html (15 July 1996).

- FTP sites. Author's name (reversed), the title (which is not necessarily the same as the file name) of the paper (in quotation marks), and the full URL of the paper, i.e., address of the FTP site along with the full path to follow to find the file, and the date of access.

  Deutsch, Peter. "archie-An Electronic Directory Service for the Internet"

  ftp://ftp.sura.net/pub/archie/docs/whatis.archie (15 July 1996).

- Gopher sites. Author's name, the title of the paper in quotation marks, any print publication information, the Gopher URL, and the date of access.

  Massachusetts Higher Education Coordinating Council. "Using Coordination

  and Collaboration to Address Change." gopher://gopher.mass.edu:170/00

  gopher_root%3A%5B_hecc %5D_plan (15 July 1996).

- Telnet sites. Author's name (if applicable), the title of the work in quotation marks, the title of the full work if applicable in italics, the complete URL, and the date of visit. Include other additional directions to access the particular file as necessary.

  "Hubble Space Telescope Daily Report #1712." STINFO Bulletin Board

  (9 June 1996). telnet stinfo.hq.eso.org; login as "stinfo" (21 Sept. 1996).

- Listserv and Usenet citations. Author's name, (if known), the subject in quotation marks, the address of the listserv or newsgroup, and the date of the posting.

  Liberty Northwest. "Who funds the greenies." alt.politics.libertarian (15 July

  1996).

■ MOOs, MUDs, IRC, etc. The name of the speaker(s) and type of communication (i.e., Personal Interview or MOO posting), the address if applicable, and the date in parentheses.

Guest. Personal Interview. telnet du.edu 8888 (18 August 1996).

APA Formats for Internet Sources

■ These APA formats are based on the *Publication Manual of the American Psychological Association* (4th ed.), with modifications proposed by Russ Dewey (http://www.gasou.edu/psychweb/tipsheet/apacrib.htm). It's important to remember that, unlike the MLA, the APA does not include temporary or transient sources (e.g., letters, phone calls, etc.) in its "References" page, preferring to handle them in in-text citations exclusively. This rule holds for electronic sources as well: e-mail, MOOs/MUDs, listserv postings, etc., are not included in the "References" page, merely cited in text. However, many listservs and Usenet groups and MOOs actually archive their correspondences, so that there is a permanent site (usually a Gopher or FTP server) where those documents reside. In that case, you would want to find the archive and cite it as an unchanging source. Strictly speaking, according to the APA manual, a file from an FTP site should be referenced as follows:

Deutsch, P. (1991). "archie--An electronic directory service for the Internet"

[On-line]. Available FTP: ftp.sura.net Directory: pub/archie/docs File:

whatis.archie.

However, the increasing familiarity of Net users with the convention of a URL makes the prose description of how to find a file ("Available FTP: ftp.sura.net Directory: pub/archie/docs File: whatis.archie") unnecessary. Simply specifying the URL should be enough.

So, with such a modification of the APA format, citations from the standard Internet sources would appear as follows:

■ FTP site.

Deutsch, P. (1991) "Archie--An electronic directory service for the Internet."

[On-line]. Available: ftp://ftp.sura.net/pub/archie/docs/whatis.archie.

■ Gopher site.

Massachusetts Higher Education Coordinating Council. (1994) [On-line].

Using coordination and collaboration to address change. Available:

gopher://gopher.mass.edu:170/00gopher_root%3A%5B_hecc%5D_plan.

■ World Wide Web Page.

U.S. Fish and Wildlife Service. (1996) Program overview. [On-line]. Available:

http://www.fws.gov/~r9endspp/programs.html.

Useful URLs
for Writers

Search Engines

- AltaVista. Allows both simple and advanced searches of WWW and Usenet; fast and powerful.

  <http://altavista.digital.com/>

- Archie. Searches anonymous FTP sites; latest version has added Web searching capability.

  <http://archie.bunyip.com/archie.html>

- DejaNews. Searches Usenet newsgroups.

  <http://www.dejanews.com>

- Excite. An extensive multipurpose finder of information; includes a Web search engine, a directory, and other lookups; now allied with America Online.

  <http://www.excite.com/>

- Galaxy. "Professional" Web search engine, along with Gopher and telnet searches and a directory.

  <http://galaxy.tradewave.com/>

- HotBot. Powerful and customizable Web and Usenet search engine.

  <http://www.hotbot.com/>

- Infoseek. Allows searches of WWW, e-mail addresses, Usenet, and newswires. Also includes a directory.

  <http://www.infoseek.com/>

- Lycos. Web search engine and more: directory, graphics, PeopleFind, StockFind, Maps, etc.

  <http://www.lycos.com/>

- Magellan. A large collection of prereviewed sites (special "Green Light" database excludes all sites with adult content), along with a directory.

  <http://www.mckinley.com/>

- Open Text. WWW searches; in Power Search mode, provides menus for Boolean search operators; simple to use.

  <http://index.opentext.net/>

- Veronica. Searches Gopher sites; full set of Boolean and logical operators.

  <gopher://gopher.tc.umn.edu:70/11/Other Gopher and Information

     Servers/Veronica>

- W3 Search Engines. A single page with access to most major search engines.

  <http://cuiwww.unige.ch/meta-index.html>

- WebCrawler. A quick and simple-to-use Web search engine and directory; now owned by Excite Inc.

  <http://www.webcrawler.com/>

- Yahoo. Both a full-fledged WWW search engine and the most famous directory for browsing.

  <http://www.yahoo.com/>

General Directories

- Berkeley Digital Library. The online collection at the University of California; searchable.

  <http://sunsite.berkeley.edu/cgi-bin/welcome.pl/>

- Complete Reference to Usenet Newsgroups. A searchable listing of Usenet groups.

  <http://www.tile.net/tile/news/index.html>

- ERIC Clearinghouse on Information and Technology. The WWW starting point for the Educational Resources Clearinghouse.

  <http://ericir.syr.edu/>

- Gopher Jewels. An extremely thorough directory of Gopher sites, arranged hierarchically.

  <gopher://cwis.usc.edu:70/11/Other_Gophers_and_Information_Resources/

     Gopher-Jewels>

- Info Junkies Anonymous. A site for lovers of hard information, more pointed and less commercial than *Yahoo!*

  <http://www.globaldialog.com/~morse/ija.htm>

- Internet Public Library. A directory of Web information arranged like a public library.

  <http://www.ipl.org>

- InfoSurf: E-Journals and E-Zines. A categorically arranged list of magazines and journals available electronically.

  <http://www.library.ucsb.edu/mags/mags.html>

- LIBCAT. Comprehensive guide to libraries (U.S. and worldwide) that have Internet presence.

  <http://www.metronet.lib.mn.us/lc/lc1.html>

- Libweb: Library Servers via WWW. Directory of online libraries in 62 countries; searchable by location or affiliation.

  http://sunsite.Berkeley.EDU/Libweb/

- LISTSERV Lists Search. A searchable listing of e-mail discussion groups (listservs).

  <http://tile.net/listserv/>

- News and Information Services. A directory of hard news sources available on the Web.

  <http://escher.cs.ucdavis.edu:1024/newsandinfo.html>

- Social Science Information Gateway. A comprehensive listing of social science information sources available electronically worldwide.

  <http://sosig.esrc.bris.ac.uk>

- Supreme Court Decisions. A searchable database of recent Supreme Court decisions.

  <http://www.law.cornell.edu/supct/>

- Voice of the Shuttle: Web Page for Humanities Research. An amazingly comprehensive directory of humanities-oriented Web pages.

  <http://humanitas.ucsb.edu/>

- Webliography: A Guide to Internet Resources. A large, categorically arranged directory of Web sites, compiled by the Louisiana State University library.

  <http://www.lib.lsu.edu/weblio.html>

- WWW Virtual Library. One of the first directories of Web sites, and still one of the most comprehensive.

  <http://www.w3.org/pub/DataSources/bySubject/Overview.html>

Desktop References

- Acronym and Abbreviation List. Searchable list of acronyms; also reversible to search for acronym from a keyword.

  <http://www.ucc.ie/info/net/acronyms/>

- The Alternative Dictionaries. Dictionary of slang and expressions you most likely won't find in a normal dictionary; all entries are submitted by users.

  <http://www.notam.uio.no/~hcholm/altlang/>

- CIA World Factbook. Every hard fact about every country in the world.

  <http://www.odci.gov/cia/publications/nsolo/wfb-all.htm>

- Computing Dictionary. Dictionary of computing terms; often technical.

  <http://wombat.doc.ic.ac.uk/>

- Hypertext Webster Interface. A searchable dictionary.

  <http://c.gp.cs.cmu.edu:5103/prog/webster>

- The King James Bible. In addition to a searchable KJV, this site provides a side-by-side comparison of the King James and the Revised Standard versions.

  <http://etext.virginia.edu/kjv.browse.html>

- The Holy Qur'an. Searchable and downloadable English translation.

  <http://www.utexas.edu/students/amso/quran_html/>

- Quotations Page. Search for that quotation by keyword.

  <http://www.starlingtech.com/quotes/>

- Roget's Thesaurus. An online searchable version of the venerable book of synonyms.

  <http://humanities.uchicago.edu/forms_unrest/ROGET.html>

- Scholes Library Electronic Reference Desk. An index of "ready reference" sources.

  <http://scholes.alfred.edu/Ref.html>

- Shakespeare Glossary. Alphabetically arranged text file of words from Shakespeare; not a concordance.

  <http://english-server.hss.cmu.edu/langs/shakespeare-glossary.txt>

Writing Help

- Allyn and Bacon's CompSite. An interactive meeting place for teachers and students to share resources and work on projects.

  <http://www.abacon.com/compsite/>

- Anti-Pedantry Page: Singular "Their" in Jane Austen and Elsewhere. A compilation of famous writers who've ignored the singular "their" rule.

  <http://uts.cc.utexas.edu/~churchh/austheir.html>

- Capitalization. According to NASA's Handbook.

  <http://sti.larc.nasa.gov/html/Chapt4/Chapt4_TOC.html>

- Critique Partner Connections. A place to find a writing partner for help by e-mail.

  <http://www.geocities.com/TheTropics/8977/>

- Dakota State University Online Writing Lab (OWL). An online writing lab that provides writing help via e-mail.

  <http://www.dsu.edu/departments/liberal/cola/OWL/>

- DeVry Online Writing Support Center. Resources for integrating the Internet into your college composition classes.

  <http://www.devry-phx.edu/lrnresrc/dowsc/>

- An Elementary Grammar. Twenty-two sections of moderately technical discussions of grammatical topics from The English Institute.

  <http://www.hiway.co.uk/~ei/intro.html>

- Elements of Style. Will Strunk's 1918 classic.

  <http://www.cc.columbia.edu/acis/bartleby/strunk/>

- English Grammar FAQ As Posted to alt.usage.english. Answers to common grammar questions from linguist John Lawler.

  <http://www.lsa.umich.edu/ling/jlawler/aue/>

- A Glossary of Rhetorical Terms with Examples. Forty-five rhetorical terms (Alliteration to Zeugma) with links to classical text for examples.

  <http://www.uky.edu/ArtsSciences/Classics/rhetoric.html>

- Grammar and Style Notes. Alphabetically arranged guide to topics in grammar and style.

  <http://www.english.upenn.edu:80/~jlynch/grammar.html>

- A Handbook of Terms for Discussing Poetry. Compiled by students at Emory University.

  <http://www.cc.emory.edu/ENGLISH/classes/Handbook/Handbook.html>

- HyperGrammar. Hypertext grammar course/handbook from the University of Ottawa.

  <http://www.uottawa.ca/academic/arts/writcent/hypergrammar/intro.html>

- Inklings. A biweekly newsletter for writers on the Net.

  <http://192.41.39.106/inklings/>

- The Internet Writer's Guideline Listing. Guidelines on submitting to online publications.

  <http://wane5.scri.fsu.edu/~jtillman/DEV/ZDMS/index.html>

- The "It's" vs. "Its" page. The difference between the two homophones.

  <http://www.rain.org/~gshapiro/its.html>

- The King's English. Full text of H. W. Fowler's 1908 classic on English, Victorian style.

  <http://www.columbia.edu/acis/bartleby/fowler/>

- Nebraska Center for Writers. Online resource for writers of poetry, fiction, and creative nonfiction.

  <http://acm-www.creighton.edu/NCW/>

- Online English Grammar. Especially suited for nonnative speakers of English; includes some sound files.

  <http://www.edunet.com/english/grammar/>

- Online Writery. "The conversation zone for writers"; tutors and writers meet online and discuss writing.

  <http://www.missouri.edu/~wleric/writery.html>

- Paradigm: Online Writing Assistant. Almost a complete writing textbook online.

  <http://www.idbsu.edu/english/cguilfor/paradigm/>

- PEN Home. The home page of PEN, the professional association of writers and editors.

  <http://www.pen.org/>

- Poets and Writers Inc. Home Page. Support for professional writers and those who would be professional writers.

  <http://www.pw.org/>

- Politics and the English Language. Full text of George Orwell's plea for clarity in writing and thinking.

  <gopher://dept.english.upenn.edu/00/Courses/Lynch3/orwell>

- Punctuation. According to NASA.

  <http://sti.larc.nasa.gov/html/Chapt3/Chapt3-TOC.html>

- The Rhetoric Page at SDSM&T. Links to writing resources appropriate for both students and faculty.

  <http://www.sdsmt.edu/www/rhetoric/rhetoric.html>

- University of Michigan OWL. Receive advice about your writing via e-mail, link to other writing resources, or, if you're in Ann Arbor, make an appointment for a face-to-face tutoring session.

  <http://www.lsa.umich.edu/ecb/OWL/owl.html>

- The Word Detective. Online version of the newspaper column answering questions about words.

  <http://www.word-detective.com/>

- Rensselaer Writing Center Handouts. A collection of handouts on writing topics from "abstracts" to "writing with gender-fair language."

  <http://www.rpi.edu/dept/llc/writecenter/web/handouts.html>

- Undergraduate Writing Center. Services restricted to University of Texas students and staff; links to resources for writers.

  <http://www.utexas.edu/depts/uwc/public_html/>

- The University of Victoria's Hypertext Writer's Guide. Hypertext guides to writing and literature.

  <http://webserver.maclab.comp.uvic.ca/writersguide/welcome.html>

- LEO: Literacy Education Online. Help with "what's bothering you about your writing."

  <http://leo.stcloud.msus.edu/>

- BGSU Online Writing Lab. A Gopher site with downloadable grammar and writing tips.

  <gopher://gopher.bgsu.edu/11/Departments/write/>

- English as a Second Language. Bills itself as the starting point for learning English as a second language online. Includes visual and auditory resources, as well as a 24-hour help center.

  <http://www.lang.uiuc.edu/r-115/esl/>

- Main Writing Guide. Three complete online handbooks for writing.

  <http://www.english.uiuc.edu/cws/wworkshop/mainmenu.html>

- Non-Sexist Language. Tips for avoiding sexist language, based on National Council of Teachers of English guidelines.

  <http://mickey.la.psu.edu/~chayton/eng202b/nonsex.htm>

- Purdue Online Writing Lab. An extensive source of online help for writers, including professional help to specific questions by e-mail.

  <http://owl.english.purdue.edu/>

- Researchpaper.com. An impressive compendium of research paper help, including live chat rooms.

  <http://www.researchpaper.com/>

- Scrivenery: Articles and Essays on Prose Style. An individual essay, plus links to resources of interest to writers.

  <http://www.lit-arts.com/scriven/essays.htm>

- Tips and Resources for Writers. Materials for professional writers that are appropriate for beginners as well.

  <http://www.olywa.net/peregrine/index.html>

- Word Wizard. A page devoted to the fascination with words; requires registration (free).

  <http://www.columbia.edu/acis/bartleby/fowler/>

- Writer's Center Home Page. Resources for the creation and distribution of contemporary writing.

  <http://www.writers.org>

- The Writer's Depot. For a fee, professional writers and editors will critique your work.

  <http://members.aol.com/WritersD/index.htm>

- Writer's Resources. Grammar, research, and general writing help.

  <http://www.vmedia.com/shannon/writing.html>

- Writers' Workshop: Online Resources for Writers. A directory of online writing help at the University of Illinois at Urbana-Champaign.

  <http://www.english.uiuc.edu/cws/wworkshop/writer.html>

- Writing Centers Online. A directory of writing centers nationwide who have online presences.

  <http://www2.colgate.edu/diw/NWCAOWLS.html>

- WWWScribe: Web Resources for Writers. Writing for the WWW, along with using the Internet as a research and communication tool.

  <http://www.wwwscribe.com/>

Evaluating Information on the Internet

- Checklist for Evaluating Web Sites. Tips from the Canisius College Library.

  <http://www.canisius.edu/canhp/canlib/webcrit.htm>

- Criteria for Evaluation of Internet Information Resources. From an online Internet resources course from Victoria University, New Zealand.

  <http://www.vuw.ac.nz/dlis/courses/847/m2resevl.html>

- Critically Analyzing Information. Not specifically devoted to Internet information sources.

  <http://www.library.cornell.edu/okuref/research/skill26.htm>

- Evaluating Internet Information. Specific guidance from Johns Hopkins University.

  <http://milton.mse.jhu.edu:8001/research/education/net.html>

- Evaluating Internet Research Sources. A comprehensive essay, not just a checklist.

  <http://www.sccu.edu/faculty/R_Harris/evalu8it.htm>

- Evaluating Internet Resources. A worksheet from Illinois State University.

  <http://www.mlb.ilstu.edu/subject/intrnt/evaluate.htm>

- Evaluating Internet Resources. A checklist, links to more resources, and a bibliography.

  <http://www.snymor.edu/~drewwe/workshop/evalint.htm>

- Evaluating Quality on the Net. An excellent and continually evolving paper from Hope Tillman, Babson College.

  <http://www.tiac.net/users/hope/findqual.html>

- Internet Navigator—Evaluating Internet Information. From Salt Lake Community College's online Internet resources course.

  <http://sol.slcc.edu/lr/navigator/discovery/eval.html>

- Internet Tutorial: Evaluating Internet Resources. A short document from Long Island University.

  <http://www.liunet.edu/cwis/cwp/library/internet/evaluate.htm>

- Thinking Critically about World Wide Web Resources. A concise outline, from UCLA.

  <http://www.library.ucla.edu/libraries/college/instruct/critical.htm>

- Web Site Analysis. Focused on the issue of quality Web sites in general, not specifically on analysis of information.

  <http://www.ccsn.nevada.edu/English/siteanal.html>

Specialized Web Sites

- Abortion and Reproductive Rights Internet Resources. An extensive set of links to information both prochoice and prolife.

  <http://www.caral.org/abortion.html>

- Alex: A Catalog of Electronic Texts on the Internet. A listing of full-length texts available on the Internet.

  <http://www.lib.ncsu.edu/staff/morgan/alex/alex-index.ht ml>

- African Americana. A moderately extensive directory of Web sites (and more) dealing with the African-American experience.

  <http://www.lib.lsu.edu/hum/african.html>

- American Poetry Hyper-bibliography. A Web-based guide to American poetry, searchable on author or title.

  <http://www.hti.umich.edu/english/amverse/hyperbib.html>

- American Studies Web. A good jumping-off point for studies in Americana.

  <http://www.georgetown.edu/crossroads/asw/>

- AstroWeb: Astronomy/Astrophysics on the Internet. An extensive directory of links and a searchable database of topics in astronomy.

  <http://www.cv.nrao.edu/fits/www/astronomy.html>

- The Business Communication World Wide Web Resource Center. A guide for business writing, with links to other online resources.

  <http://idt.net/~reach/Lance/lance-cohen.html>

- Digests of Education Statistics. Department of Education Gopher site containing statistics on education in the U.S.

  <gopher://gopher.ed.gov:10000/11/publications/majorpub/digest/>

- Essays in History—University of Virginia. Full text of the journal *Essays in History* since 1990.

  <http://www.lib.virginia.edu/journals/EH/EH.html>

- FAQ: How to Find People's E-mail Addresses. A guide to the often frustrating process of finding an e-mail address.

  <http://www.cis.ohio-state.edu/hypertext/faq/usenet/finding-addresses/

  faq.html>

- Fedworld Information Network. The searchable gateway to the huge information resources of the federal government.

  <http://www.fedworld.gov/>

- Feminist Activist Resources on the Net. A compilation of useful links to feminist resources.

  <http://www.igc.org/women/feminist.html>

- GPO Access Databases. Another guide to government publications, online and print versions (with instructions for ordering print documents).

  <http://www.access.gpo.gov/su_docs/aces/aaces002.html>

- The Human-Languages Page. A huge compendium of links to resources in language.

  <http://www.june29.com/HLP/>

- Internet Movie Database. A keyword-searchable database of everything you ever wanted to know about movies.

  <http://us.imdb.com/>

- Journals. Alphabetical listing (with links) to hundreds of journals, both print-based and electronic, that have a Web presence; from Carnegie-Mellon's Humanities Server.

  <http://english-server.hss.cmu.edu/journals/>

- Library of Congress. The jumping-off point for the Library's online resources; not the whole Library itself, however.

  <http://lcweb.loc.gov/>

- Liszt. A searchable and browsable guide to listservs (e-mail discussion lists).

  <http://www.liszt.com>

- Media History Project. A gateway to information on communications and media studies; searchable.

  <http://www.mediahistory.com/>

- NASA Spacelink. NASA's fulfillment of its obligation to disseminate all the information it gathers through space exploration.

  <http://spacelink.msfc.nasa.gov>

- National Center for Health Statistics. The repository of the Centers for Disease Control's data.

  <http://www.cdc.gov/nchswww/nchshome.htm>

- The National Center on Addiction and Substance Abuse. The Web page of the think tank, devoted to providing resources on understanding the abuse of illegal substances.

  <http://www.casacolumbia.org/>

- National Organization for Women. A collection of on-site information and links to other Web sites for women's issues.

  <http://now.org/now/home.html>

- Nijenrode Business Webserver. Searchable guide to online business resources, focused on the needs of students, faculty, and researchers.

  <http://www.nijenrode.nl/nbr/index.html>

- Online Literary Resources. A searchable, categorized directory of academic sources of information in English and American literature; extensive.

  <http://www.english.upenn.edu/~jlynch/Lit/>

- Postmodern Culture. Current issue of the online journal of postmodernism.

  <http://jefferson.village.virginia.edu/pmc/contents.all. html>

- Project Gutenberg. The continuing project to make text versions of public domain classic literature available online; currently nearing 1,000 titles.

  <http://www.promo.net/pg/>

- Religion. A starting point for studies in world religions.

  <http://sunfly.ub.uni-freiburg.de/religion/>

- Resources for Diversity. A compilation of links to resources in issues of diversity.

  <http://www.nova.edu/Inter-Links/diversity.html>

- Rhetoric and Composition. An extensive guide to rhetoric, from the ancients to modern composition theory.

  <http://english-server.hss.cmu.edu/rhetoric/>

- Science Hypermedia, Inc. Focuses on chemistry, including an index of hundreds of full-text articles in the field.

  <http://www.scimedia.com/>

- Suicide Information & Education Center (SIEC). On-site resources, information, and links to more sites on issues of suicide prevention.

  <http://www.siec.ca/>

- Thomas. A searchable database of all bills before the most recent sessions of the House of Representatives.

  <http://Thomas.loc.gov/>

- U.S. Civil War Center. An index of over 1,700 Civil War related Internet sites.

  <http://www.cwc.lsu.edu/civlink.htm>

- U.S. Senate. A guide to business of the U.S. Senate.

  <http://www.senate.gov/>

- United States Census Bureau Home Page. A gold mine of statistics about the U.S. population

  <http://www.census.gov>

- University of Virginia Electronic Text Library. Provides access to the University of Virginia's extensive collection of digitized texts and images.

  <http://etext.lib.virginia.edu/uvaonline.html>

- Voice of the Shuttle: Web Page for Humanities Research. An amazingly comprehensive directory of humanities-oriented Web pages.

  <http://humanitas.ucsb.edu/>

- Welfare and Families. The Electronic Policy Network's electronic journal, archives, and links.

  <http://epn.org/idea/welfare.html>

- White House. The starting point for executive branch information.

  <http://www.whitehouse.gov/WH/Welcome.html>

- World Intellectual Property Organization (WIPO). A guide to resources on copyrights and patents in the electronic age.

  <http://www.wipo.org/eng/index.htm>

Current Events

- CNN. Multimedia, up-to-the-minute online news source; not adequately archived for searches.

  <http://www.cnn.com/>

- Electronic Newsstand. An extensive listing of thousands of magazines; searchable, though most articles are not available online.

  <http://www.enews.com/>

- *Forbes.* Online version of *Forbes* magazine; searchable archives.

  <http://www.forbes.com/>

- Fox News. News, business, health, sports, and technology.

  <http://www.foxnews.com/>

- The *New York Times* on the Web. The *New York Times* on the Web. Requires registration, but free.

  <http://www.nytimes.com/>

- The *New York Times* on the Web: Books. Web-based book section of the *Times.*

  <http://www.nytimes.com/books/>

- Newsstand. Links to over 4,200 Web sites of print publications—newspapers, magazines, computer publications. Searchable by publication name.

  <http://www.ecola.com/news/>

- *San Francisco Chronicle.* Online version; searchable.

  <http://www.sfgate.com/cgi-bin/chronicle/list-sections.cgi>

- *Time* Magazine. An online version of *Time* magazine; search feature searches *Time* and many others; also provides access to bulletin boards and chats.

  <http://pathfinder.com/time/>

- TotalNEWS. According to itself, "Information is the oxygen of the modern age. TotalNEWS is a directory of news sites designed to increase your access to information."

  <http://totalnews.com/>

- *USA Today.* Online version of the national newspaper.

  <http://www.usatoday.com/>

- *Washington Post.* Online version of the *Washington Post;* searchable for past week.

  <http://www.washingtonpost.com/>

Bibliographic Citation Guides

- American Psychological Association (APA) Guide to Style. Online version of the APA guide; abridged.

  <http://www.wilpaterson.edu/wpcpages/library/apa.htm>

- APA Publication Manual Crib Sheet. An intuitive and useful companion to the APA guide; may be more useful than the actual guide.

  <http://www.gasou.edu/psychweb/tipsheet/apacrib.htm>

- Citing Electronic Materials with the New MLA Guidelines. Modified MLA guidelines to apply to electronic sources.

  <http://www-dept.usm.edu/~engdept/mla/rules.html>

- Format for Citing Online Sources. Janice Walker's page takes up where the MLA guide leaves off: online sources.

  <http://www.cas.usf.edu/english/walker/mla.html>

- Modern Language Association (MLA) Guide to Style. Online version of the MLA guide; abridged.

  <http://www.wilpaterson.edu/wpcpages/library/mla.htm>

- Web Extension to American Psychological Association Style. One proposal for extending the APA's guidelines to online sources; also includes a full set of links to the major issues involved in establishing the new standards.

  <http://www.beadsland.com/weapas/>

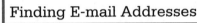

- World Wide Arts Resources. A searchable gateway to the arts online, plus a directory of Web sites, chats, and bulletin boards.

  <http://wwar.world-arts-resources.com/>

Finding E-mail Addresses

- Bigfoot. Supposedly the Internet's largest collection of e-mail addresses.

  <http://www.bigfoot.com>

- Four11. An extensive, searchable e-mail address directory, plus "yellow pages," a phone book, and government and celebrity addresses.

  <http://www.four11.com/>

- Internet Address Finder. Claims to be the fastest e-mail search engine, with nearly six million addresses in its database.

  <http://www.iaf.net/>

- Lycos EmailFind. Associated with the Lycos Web search engine.

  <http://www.lycos.com/emailfind.html>

- Phonebooke [sic]. Searches *Yahoo!*, Usenet, and its own e-mail address database.

  <http://www.phonebooke.com/>

- Switchboard. One of the most popular "people-finders" on the Internet; good for addresses and phone numbers, thin on e-mail addresses.

  <http://www.switchboard.com/>

- Usenet Addresses Database. A list of the e-mail addresses of posters to Usenet (actually a huge number, when you think about it).

  <http://usenet-addresses.mit.edu/>

- WhoWhere. One of the first, and still one of the most used, people-finders: e-mail addresses, phone numbers, home pages, business and government Web and e-mail addresses, 800 numbers, yellow pages, and more.

  <http://www.whowhere.com/>

- World E-mail Directory. Spreads itself thin, but your best chance at finding a non-U.S. address.

  <http://www.worldemail.com/>